Windows® Forensics

Windows® Forensics

The Field Guide for Conducting Corporate Computer Investigations

Chad Steel

Wiley Publishing, Inc.

Windows® Forensics: The Field Guide for Conducting Corporate Computer Investigations

Published by
Wiley Publishing, Inc.
10475 Crosspoint Boulevard
Indianapolis, IN 46256
www.wiley.com

Published by Wiley Publishing, Inc., Indianapolis, Indiana

Published simultaneously in Canada

ISBN-13: 978-0-470-03862-8
ISBN-10: 0-470-03862-4

Manufactured in the United States of America

10 9 8 7 6 5 4 3 2 1

1MA/SQ/QU/QW/IN

For general information on our other products and services or to obtain technical support, please contact our Customer Care Department within the U.S. at (800) 762-2974, outside the U.S. at (317) 572-3993 or fax (317) 572-4002.

Library of Congress Cataloging-in-Publication Data

Steel, Chad, 1975–
  Windows forensics : the field guide for conducting corporate computer investigations / Chad Steel.
    p. cm.
  Includes index.
  ISBN-13: 978-0-470-03862-8 (pbk.)
  ISBN-10: 0-470-03862-4 (pbk.)
  1. Computer crimes—Investigation—United States—Methodology. 2. Microsoft Windows (Computer file)—Security measures. 3. Computer networks—Security measures. 4. Internet—Security measures. 5. Computer security. I. Title.
  HV8079.C65S84 2006
  363.25'968—dc22

                    2006005530

To Laura. My search is over; love was right before my eyes.

About the Author

Chad Steel is a seasoned veteran with experience investigating more than 300 computer security incidents. Chad developed and taught the Computer Forensics graduate course in Penn State's engineering program as a member of the adjunct faculty and has taught both federal and local law enforcement, commercial clients, and graduate students in forensic analysis. He was the Head of IT Investigations for a Global 100 corporation and the Chief Security Officer and Managing Director, Systems Integration and Security Services, for a Fortune 100 consulting group.

Chad holds B.S. and M.S. degrees in Computer Engineering and is currently pursuing a Ph.D. at Virginia Tech. He can be reached at `csteel@yahoo.com`.

Credits

Executive Editor
Carol Long

Development Editor
Kelly D. Henthorne

Editorial Manager
Mary Beth Wakefield

Production Manager
Tim Tate

Vice President and Executive Group Publisher
Richard Swadley

Vice President and Executive Publisher
Joseph B. Wikert

Project Coordinator
Michael Kruzil

Graphics and Production Specialists
Jennifer Click
Carrie A. Foster
Brooke Graczyk
Stephanie D. Jumper
Barbara Moore
Lynsey Osborn

Quality Control Technicians
David Faust
Jessica Kramer
Brian H. Walls

Proofreading and Indexing
Techbooks

Contents

Acknowledgments

Getting a book from concept through to publication is a long road, and I would not have been able to complete the journey without the help of many folks along the way. I have some individual acknowledgments below but would like also to thank everyone who provided a tool, tip, or story that allowed me to complete this endeavor.

First, I would like to thank my wife, Laura, for her love and support in writing and editing this book. Without her, none of what I've accomplished would have been possible—the book is just a small part of that.

There is a quantum leap between writing a book and actually getting it published. To that end, I'd like to thank my agent, William Brown of the Waterside Agency, for making the quickest sale for a first-time author (at least one who hasn't been featured on the evening news) in history.

One thing authors have going for them that other artists don't is an editor (no one "touches up" the works of a painter). I'd like to thank Kelly Henthorne for making me look like a better writer than I am. I'd also like to thank Carol Long and all of the staff at Wiley for giving me this opportunity.

Isaac Newton was quoted as saying, "If I have seen further it is by standing on the shoulders of Giants," which was itself borrowed as a phrase from earlier writers. For tools, I've made heavy use in this book of the excellent array of free software made available by Mark Russinovich and the folks at www .sysinternals.com. Likewise, the knowledge base that is Sourceforge.net and the community of people who support it helped to fill in gaps on some of the more technical areas of the book.

Finally, I'd like to thank my dogs, Foxxy and Charlie, for providing support in return for biscuits during the process. If you look closely, you can see that one of them made it into the book!

Windows® Forensics

Windows Forensics

**fo·ren·sics (P) Pronunciation Key (f-rnsks, -zks)
n. (used with a sing. verb)
The use of science and technology to investigate
and establish facts in criminal or civil courts of law**

Forensics is a topic that has captured recent public interest. From DNA evidence in the O.J. Simpson trial to bullet fragment analysis in the Washington, D.C., sniper trials, the basic concepts of forensics have become more familiar to the American people now more than ever.

Fictional television programs such as *CSI: Crime Scene Investigation* and *Cold Case* showcase forensic science, and docudramas such as *New Detectives* and *Forensic Files* focus on cases in which forensic evidence has lead to or supported a prosecution. Both types of shows highlight the glamorous side of forensics, the discovery of the proverbial smoking gun, which ultimately leads to a successful arrest and prosecution. They do not do justice to the weeks and months of effort that go into the identification, acquisition, and analysis of the evidence by a team of dedicated, highly trained analysts. It makes for good television to show the comparison of two hair follicles under a microscope; the audience is much less interested in the days spent combing through a vehicle inch-by-inch to find and catalog those follicles. Similarly, in the world of computer investigation, it makes for better drama to show a graphical *phone trace* tracking a dial-up user located around the globe than to show the days spent acquiring and hashing a hard drive and the meticulous preparation of the evidence report.

Computer forensics applies the same scientific principles as other forensics fields to the identification, acquisition, and analysis of digital evidence. With the advent of the Internet, both network and system forensics are becoming increasingly interrelated. The digital evidence sought by an analyst might reside on any number of devices, including personal digital assistants (PDAs), USB pen drives, digital cameras, and cell phones. Additionally, all modern operating systems are network capable, and it is rare to find standalone PCs with no external connections, providing further evidence on routers, servers, firewalls, and proxys. The field of computer forensics encompasses both system forensics and network forensics, and an understanding of both is required to conduct a thorough investigation.

The Corporate Computer Forensic Analyst

Unlike most analysts in the field of criminal forensics, practitioners of computer forensics are not always working for or with law enforcement agencies. The demand for skilled computer forensic analysts in the corporate world exceeds the supply, and experienced analysts are highly sought-after. In addition to supporting law enforcement, a computer forensic analyst might be called upon to:

- Recover files intentionally deleted by a disgruntled employee.
- Determine the root cause of a computer compromise.
- Track down the author of a threatening email.
- Investigate unauthorized copying and intellectual property theft.
- Obtain evidence an employee viewed inappropriate material.
- Refute or support claims of overtime hours worked.

The end goal of an analyst working in a corporation might vary greatly from that of an individual working for or with a law enforcement agency. In the corporate world, the ultimate goal is to protect the company's interests, not to prosecute all potential offenders. For example, if an isolated brochureware website in a remote subsidiary is defaced and no sensitive information is involved, the corporate goals are likely as follows:

1. Identify the cause of the defacement.
2. Restore the site as quickly as possible.
3. Prevent future occurrences.

For most companies, it makes no fiscal sense to track down and prosecute the offender if there is no appreciable loss and reoccurrence can be prevented. If, however, an insider is found transmitting intellectual property to a competitor, the company may very well be interested in both civil and criminal proceedings.

Regardless of the final outcome of an individual investigation, the computer forensic analyst might not know whether his work will be presented in court for weeks, months, or even years after the initial incident. Therefore, he must take the same precautions as law enforcement officials in safeguarding the integrity of the investigation and must always work under the assumption that the results of the analysis will be presented in a court of law at some point. At the same time, the corporate analyst has an array of specialized tools at her disposal and is able to use them to her advantage in investigations. Although the typical computer incident response team (CIRT) in a company does not generally carry Luminol or fingerprint-gathering equipment in their response kits, a corporate CIRT may already have administrative rights (or the ability to obtain them) on corporate assets as well as the ability to search and seize company-owned equipment without the need for a warrant.

> **NOTE** Although computer data stored on a corporate asset and created using corporate systems is generally considered company property in the United States, it is not considered such in many other countries. The French Supreme Court ruled in the case of *Nikon France v. Frederic Onos* that a company was explicitly prohibited from viewing the personal emails or files of an employee, even if created with and stored on company-owned equipment.

Not everyone is cut out for the world of computer forensics. The work requires detail-oriented individuals who are willing to document everything they do. At the same time, analysts must think creatively and respond quickly and effectively to the unique situations that they face in the field. A typical CIRT includes executive management, public relations, corporate security, legal, and IT subject matter experts. For this reason, the analyst must communicate effectively both orally and in writing. In addition to being able to perform the technical tasks associated with the job, the analyst must successfully explain evidence to a variety of audiences, each with vastly different backgrounds.

One question that must be asked when hiring and training analysts is this: "Would I be comfortable with this person testifying on the company's behalf in court?" Individuals who are new to the field must be mentored and supervised appropriately, and a clean criminal history is a necessity. Convicted hackers need not apply.

Windows Forensics

To date, much of the literature and tools have focused on Unix/Linux-based forensic analysis. The Unix/Linux (*nix) environment provides many capabilities not natively present on the Windows platform, including the ability to mount drives as read-only, perform complex regular expression queries on content, and obtain easy hardware-level drive access (as opposed to partition-level). No good forensic analyst discounts the value of the tools available on a platform such as Linux, and all would do well to become familiar with these tools; indeed, this book directly references several Windows ports of decades-old *nix tools as well as Cygwin-based tools. Any complete forensics lab has at least one Linux environment either native or running through a virtual machine product such as VMWare. Additionally, a large number of today's top analysts are specialists in these environments, and they will continue to be critical to forensic analysis.

> **TIP** Cygwin is a Linux-like environment for Windows operating systems. Many commands useful in forensic analysis like `strings` and `grep` are included in the distribution. VMWare Workstation from EMC and Virtual PC 2004 from Microsoft are essential forensics tools for the loading of disk images as well as the analysis of forensic information.

Despite the historical grounding of computer forensics in the *nix world, the Windows environment is ubiquitous in many organizations today. Depending on whom you ask, Windows penetration ranges from 85 percent to 97 percent of all computer-based operating system installations in the United States. Even the low-end figures illustrate that Windows remains the dominant operating system by a large margin and the one that analysts are most likely to encounter in a corporate setting. As Windows usage has grown, so has the support for Windows-based forensic tools and techniques. Companies such as Guidance Software and NewTechInfosystems (NTI) produce Windows-based forensic suites, and Sysinternals produces support tools that are invaluable assets in any toolbox. Also, capabilities not generally present in the *nix world such as remote drive acquisition (at the hardware level) are being introduced and changing the dynamics of forensic response.

> **NOTE** Onestat quotes Windows penetration in the United States as 97.5 percent (www.onestat.com/html/aboutus_pressbox10.html). IDC shows Windows as having 85 percent of client sales in 2004 (news.com.com/ 2100-1001-243527.html?legacy=cnet)—amplified by the fact than many Linux clients aren't purchased. *LinuxWorld* disputes the numbers (www.linuxworld.com/ story/32648.htm) and moves by companies like IBM to Linux may change the statistics as well.

At the same time, new challenges are being presented to the forensic analyst. Encrypted File System (EFS), SYSKEY, and products like Microsoft Passport assist in providing increased security for the Windows environment, but they can make the job of the forensic analyst more difficult. The specifics of these technologies as well as everything from Windows file systems to Internet Explorer history files are currently relevant to most corporate investigators, but no comprehensive single source for this information is currently available. For the corporate investigator, this means having to cobble together information from numerous sources and apply *nix techniques to the Windows environment.

By providing a Windows-focused guide in terms of the target machines as well as the analysis tools, this book endeavors to provide *nix experts with the detailed workings of the Windows operating systems that pertain to forensic analysis. It also aims to provide solid grounding for Windows experts looking to break into the exciting and challenging world of computer forensics.

Not all investigations return the expected results. Investigating anomalous behavior can lead to unexpected findings (possibly the best example being

CASE STUDY: THE MYSTERY TYPIST

One afternoon my security team received an email message from our IT help desk. Attached was the re-created transcript of a user conversation and an unusual Microsoft Word document. The transcript was along the lines of the following:

> *User:* Someone broke into my computer and is typing odd messages to me when I use Microsoft Word.

> *Help Desk:* What type of messages, sir?

> *User:* Meaningless phrases, but I think he has a camera trained on me.

> *Help Desk:* Why do you think he has a camera trained on you, sir?

> *User:* He only types the messages when I'm in Word, and sometimes he types things related to phone conversations I'm having.

> *Help Desk:* Is it happening right now?

> *User:* Yes. He's typing things about our conversation right now. Should I hang up the phone?

> *Help Desk:* Save the document and send us a copy. We'll call security and have them come by.

When we opened the attached document, it appeared to be a standard memo with random phrases inserted, including pieces of the user's side from the previous conversation. An investigator was sent down to talk with the user and analyze the machine.

Faced with a likely lack of stored evidence (the user had saved only the one document we already had), the investigator tried to see whether she could reproduce the problem. She opened several documents, typed miscellaneous messages, recorded all incoming and outgoing network traffic, and found nothing unusual. A secondary search of running processes and an anti-virus and anti-spyware check likewise turned up nothing.

(continued)

CASE STUDY: THE MYSTERY TYPIST *(continued)*

After spending several hours analyzing and monitoring the user's laptop, the investigator called the user in to attempt to duplicate more precisely his actions. The user began typing in Microsoft Word, and no extraneous words appeared. After a few moments, the user began to get frustrated and used several expletives, which did appear on the screen. At that point, the investigator realized it was not actually a security breach; the user had accidentally turned on Windows voice recognition and every time he made a phone call, the mystery typist re-appeared!

Cliff Stoll's *Cuckoo's Egg*). One unusual-sounding referral from our help desk illustrates this and highlights a potential pitfall for investigators.

People, Processes, and Tools

In order to build a competent computer forensic capability within an organization, the initial focus must be on people, followed by process and tools. Many organizations looking to build competency in the computer forensics space reverse these priorities, spending large sums of money on enterprise-class software and lab hardware. When the hardware is in place, existing staff begin to develop processes around using their newly purchased tools. The tail wags the dog! Finally, companies begin to search for individuals who are certified in or experienced with the tool suite purchased to round out their capabilities.

The more effective way to build forensic capability is to start with people. The first step should be hiring an experienced examiner to mentor existing staff, bring in supplementary staff, and develop sound forensic procedures. To find a qualified individual, one must do the following:

- Go to a trusted source in information security and ask for recommendations on good people.

- Look to reputable organizations, including Infragard and the High Technology Crime Investigation Association (HTCIA) for pools of knowledgeable individuals as these groups have performed background/reference validation on members.

- Hire individuals with direct investigative experience.

- Evaluate certifications such as CISSP, CISA, SANS, and EnCase carefully.

- Approach candidates as if they were taking the witness stand in court, asking yourself whether they will hold up to judicial scrutiny as experts.

When the successful candidate is empowered in the role of running a CSIRT, the first order of business is to develop an investigative policy and associated procedures. At a minimum, the policy should address the following:

- Who is empowered to investigate and under what circumstances?
- What oversight is needed to approve investigations?
- How is the investigation run cross-functionally?
- What scenarios and circumstances warrant an investigation?
- How are the results of investigations processed, and how are disciplinary procedures carried out?

Policy dictates the operational structure, roles and responsibilities of the team, and the scope of its investigations. Procedures can then be developed for the individual aspects of an investigation, dictating who performs specific investigative actions, what steps must be taken for common procedures, and how these steps are validated. Common procedures involve the following:

- Evidence handling and chain of custody
- Forensic acquisition or duplication
- Communication of incidents
- Common analysis activities (mailfile, file system, logfiles, and so on)
- Terms of engagement for bringing in other parties
- Retention procedures for evidence

Many good sources can be shamelessly plundered for their expertise, including NIST and CERT. After the procedures have been adopted and tested, tools can then be purchased or acquired to fill the gaps or enhance the procedures.

The tools mentioned throughout this book vary greatly in cost, and the capabilities do not always merit the price tag. Since I am talking about Windows forensics, analysts need solid laptops and desktops for performing analysis — nothing fancy, but a decent amount of memory and the latest processor will pay for themselves in time savings when they are most needed, during an actual investigation. Secondly, a good tape backup unit, DVD-R drive, and lots of disk space are needed. One may begin using freely available tools, replacing them as necessary with more expensive toolsets. At a minimum, you will need:

- An acquisition tool to perform forensic duplications
- An analysis tool to search hard drives
- Basic text search and manipulations tools
- A data integrity verification tool

TIP Depending on your organization's specific policies, machines confiscated during investigations can become future lab machines.

For a barebones starter kit, free versions of dd can be used for the duplication of files (with netcat for remote duplication and data transfer). WinHex makes an excellent, inexpensive general-purpose drive analysis tool, and Windows ports of common *nix string manipulation utilities (grep, strings, cat, less, and so on) can be used for more complex file search and manipulation operations. Finally, the md5sum program provides data integrity verification. Placed in capable hands, these basic tools will yield a much better cost/benefit ratio than a full implementation of EnCase Enterprise, custom-built forensic computers, and single-purpose specialty tools in the hands of partially trained individuals.

Computer Forensics: Today and Tomorrow

The field of computer forensics is quickly maturing. Certification programs from organizations like SANS and Guidance train individuals in computer forensic analysis. Forensic-specific software packages are no longer restricted to the ad-hoc task-specific software built by enthusiasts. Complete packages such as EnCase, the NTI suite, and The Coroners Toolkit (TCT) offer support and court-proven solutions for the computer forensic analyst. Organizations such as the Infragard partnership between industry and the Federal Bureau of Investigation (FBI) and HTCIA consist of computer security professionals sharing knowledge and practical experience in the field. Research into computer forensics is being performed and taught at universities, including Carnegie-Mellon, the University of California at Berkeley, and Penn State. Literature on most aspects of computer forensics is widely available, including influential texts such as Eoghan Casey's *Digital Evidence and Computer Crime* and Kruse & Heiser's *Computer Forensics: Incident Response Essentials*.

Many of the tools, techniques, and practices in the field of computer forensics are still emerging, and the exponential growth of digital information ensures that the field will remain new and interesting for the foreseeable future. Although much effort goes into performing computer forensic investigations, the moment that you uncover a file that a user thought he had deleted or find evidence confirming that a suspect sent harassing messages is incredibly rewarding and fulfilling.

Additional Resources

Refer to the following list for additional resources:

Access Data — Forensic Toolkit
www.accessdata.com/Product04_Overview.htm?ProductNum=04

Computer Emergency Response Team (CERT)
www.cert.org

Cygwin Linux-like Environment
www.cygwin.org

Guidance Software (makers of EnCase)
www.encase.com

Infragard
www.infragard.net

High Tech Crime Investigation Association
www.htcia.org

Microsoft Virtual PC
www.microsoft.com/windows/virtualpc/default.mspx

NTI (makers of SafeBack)
www.forensics-intl.com

NIST Computer Security Division
csrc.nist.gov

SANS
www.sans.org

SysInternals
www.sysinternals.com

VMWare
www.vmware.com

WinHex
www.winhex.com

Processing the Digital Crime Scene

The digital crime scene consists of any location, logical or physical, where evidence of the crime in question may be present. Locations where digital evidence may be found include the following:

- The suspect's machine
- In the case of a hacking incident, the target machine
- Switches, routers, firewalls, and other network devices
- Log servers (proxy logs, DHCP logs, and Windows event logs)
- Media (floppy disks, CD-Rs, CompactFlash cards)
- Other electronic devices (PDAs, cell phones, digital cameras)

NOTE The term *crime scene* is used loosely throughout this book to indicate the scene of an incident. In the case of corporate investigations, the crime scene might not be the scene of an actual criminal act but the scene of corporate misconduct.

The computer investigator is responsible for the acquisition and subsequent processing of any digital forensic evidence. This is similar to the role of a traditional forensic analyst within the physical science fields in that the basic steps are the same, with the addition of digital evidence collection:

1. **Identify the scene.** Determine the location or locations where digital evidence of the crime may be resident. These might be physical locations (for example, Server Room 3, 2nd floor) or logical locations (for example, Syslog server sysloga.company.com).

2. **Perform remote research.** Gather as much information as possible from both open and private sources before taking any actions. Zero-touch analysis (network sniffing) and light-touch analysis (OS fingerprinting) might be performed at this stage as well.

3. **Secure the scene.** Secure the physical and logical crime scenes. Physical crime scenes require physical securing, including locks, tape, and guards. Logical crime scenes can be logically secured (for example, by locking out users and disconnecting their systems from the network) or physically secured (for example, by disconnecting a server and locking it in a safe).

4. **Document the scene.** When secured, the crime scene should be documented. Any evidence found as well as its location and condition need to be noted in the forensic logbook.

5. **Process the scene for physical evidence.** Prior to processing for digital evidence, the crime scene should be processed for DNA, fingerprints, and other physical evidence. This should be done by a trained physical forensic analyst.

6. **Process the scene for digital evidence.** After physical processing is complete, the scene can be processed for digital evidence. Acquiring drives, securing media, and live analysis all occur at this stage.

Ideally the computer investigator will work as a part of a team of trained specialists to fully process an investigation. Certain investigations will require the computer investigator to take the lead (for example, computer intrusions), and other investigations will require him to take a supporting role (for example, fraud investigations).

Where possible, the best-trained individual should perform the investigatory steps. If a crime scene photographer is available, use her. If physical security specialists are present, allow them to secure the scene. Just as computer investigators command a degree of respect for specialized knowledge and experience, they need to recognize and be respectful of the knowledge and experience that others on the response team bring to the table.

Identify the Scene

The computer investigator's crime scene is potentially broader than that of the traditional investigator. Identifying the crime scene may not be easy, and detailed research might be required just to know where to look. The remote nature of computing and evidence distribution present additional challenges to the investigator, including the following:

■ The scene might be distributed and consist of multiple server rooms, offices, and communications closets. The investigator must determine which evidence locations are true physical scenes that need to be physically secured (for example, a suspect's office) versus which locations harbor logical evidence and can be analyzed and secured logically (for example, a router in a remote, locked communications closet).

■ The scene may not be easily accessible. The physical crime scene may be located at another organization, within a private residence, or even in another country, which may or may not have similar computer crime laws. This might require court orders, visas, and cooperation before physical or logical access can be obtained to conduct a successful investigation.

■ A specific physical crime scene might not exist. With the advent of wireless technology, there may be no individual physical location to check. Similarly, a corporate user with a laptop might be performing actions at home and at work with the same machine, and the location where an action was taken may determine its corporate permissibility.

When identifying the crime scene(s), the investigator may want to ask a few questions to determine potential locations for evidence:

■ What machine was the target of the attack?

■ Where was the suspected source of the attack or wrongdoing?

■ Where did the data accessed reside?

■ What routers/firewalls/switches did the suspect traverse?

■ What printers does the subject use?

■ What file servers (shares) does the subject use?

■ What FTP servers does the subject use?

■ Does the subject have more than one machine? Where are they located?

■ Does the subject use a proxy server?

■ Does the subject use a DHCP server?

■ Are there any peripherals the subject owns (PDAs, cell phones, digital cameras, or USB drives)?

The potential locations for evidence will change over the course of the investigation. For example, when analyzing the subject's computer, an investigator might find FTP connections to a corporate server. An examination of that server's logs may show additional connections from the same suspect on a completely different system.

The most likely location for a physical crime scene is the actual location where the suspect initiated a digital connection. This might be an office, a residence, or even a vehicle and is the best candidate for establishing and securing a physical scene.

Targeted machines, log servers, and network devices may require handling as a logical scene. In order to make the determination about whether to treat the scene as physical or logical, an analyst must ask two questions:

1. Is there likely to be physical evidence present in addition to digital evidence?

2. Will not treating the scene as a physical scene result in the loss, corruption, or destruction of digital evidence?

If the answer to either question is yes, treat the scene as a physical crime scene.

CASE STUDY: UNAUTHORIZED NETWORK DEVICE

An external router was discovered bridging a switch on the corporate network of one of our clients directly to the Internet. Some initial analysis by the client's team determined that the router was connected to an internal switch but was placed on a different subnet and logically inaccessible from direct internal connections. It was likely that a member of the company's networking team made the connection to have a local port to plug in directly for unmonitored Internet access.

The location of the router and switch was an access-controlled server room. The server room itself was initially treated as a crime scene. The router was secured and removed for remote analysis, and card reader access logs to the room were obtained. Likewise, an intrusion detection system (IDS) sensor on the same switch was treated as a logical part of the scene, and forensic copies were made of its logs. Because the room housed other operational servers, it was not feasible to secure the entire room.

The IDS sensor logged the IP address assignments and subsequent connections made to two devices on the external subnet and their respective MAC addresses. As expected, one of the MAC addresses matched the router. After researching the organization associated with the second address, analysts determined that it was a built-in laptop card.

The badge reader logs from the site security team presented a few possible suspects, several of which regularly ran network sniffers as part of their normal course of business, thereby making remote probing difficult. Additionally, because the network team was potentially implicated, it was impossible to connect to the other switches at that location to sniff passively for the MAC address or to review network logs.

The MAC addresses of the machines assigned to each of the suspects were remotely queried using nbmac from an anonymous workstation, making a simple NetBIOS call unlikely to arouse suspicion. One of the suspects' MAC addresses matched the address found in the IDS logs, allowing analysts to identify a single suspect and laptop to continue to investigation.

Perform Remote Research

After initial identification of the possible locations where evidence may reside, the computer investigator performs remote research to gather more information and determine the best course of action for the investigation.

Remote research can be very useful to the investigator and consists of any information gathering and analysis actions that can be performed without the subject's direct knowledge. The action taken will depend on the potential suspect's wariness and technical savvy. A novice computer user sending harassing email messages might not notice a port scan of her system, but a network engineer might.

TIP The first six numbers (hexadecimal) of a MAC address are assigned to a unique organization, maintained by the Institute of Electrical and Electronics Engineers (IEEE). By contacting the organization and researching the remaining numbers, the type of Ethernet card (and possibly the batch and location) can be determined.

Remote research may involve probing specific systems and might require preparatory work based on other information gathered. If the model number of the PC to be acquired is known ahead of time from physical surveillance, an asset management database, or corporate standards, it helps to download the technical guide from the manufacturer before arriving. Likewise, if an obscure operating system is present, a refresher search on Google might be warranted. Any information that will shorten the on-scene and acquisition times and can be gathered without setting off alarms should be done.

A typical approach to remote research is to acquire the log files of any machines that the suspect would be unaware of or would have no access to and analyze them ahead of time. Likewise, a quick profile of the suspect's systems through physical surveillance or light network probing (that is, traceroutes and pings) may reveal details about the locations, configurations, and types of systems in question. If permitted by law, individuals can use a nontraceable machine connected with a nontraceable connection.

TIP DSL lines work well here for external connections. For internal corporate connections, try the accounting team's subnet instead of the standard one used by the security team.

If the suspect is known to be unsophisticated, more invasive techniques may be employed such as port scans, remote connections, and the mapping of drives and connections to the registry — with great care. For a full view of the suspect's actions and the most in-depth remote information gathering, the Enterprise version of EnCase provides a full system snapshot and drive search capability using a small servlet that can be deployed by an administrator or through social engineering.

TIP Because the MAC address cannot be determined using arp outside of the local subnet, the utility nbmac was developed for resolution on the Windows environment using a feature of the NetBIOS protocol.

CASE STUDY: REMOTE CORRUPTION

My forensics team was called in on an investigation of corporate corruption by a Global 500 company with a geographically dispersed footprint. Because of the unique nature of their business, they had corporate locations in countries to which there were strict travel restrictions for American citizens.

The allegations of corruption were in one such country located in the Middle East, and the company was sending a physical security team from another country there in two days time to collect evidence and conduct interviews. Our computer forensics team could not obtain travel visas quickly enough, and the physical security team needed a preliminary analysis of remote systems to which we did not have access (they were locally administered, and the corporate IT team did not have accounts.) The local IT team was implicated in the wrongdoing and could not be ruled out as suspects at the time, precluding any support from local staff. Further complicating matters, the connectivity to the remote location was over a 128Kb/s leased line, making a full remote acquisition of the multiple terabytes of potential evidence impossible.

We handled the distributed scene issue with a two-pronged approach. First, we used EnCase Enterprise with a bit of social engineering to perform a remote triage. EnCase relies on a servlet deployed on the remote system and a centralized analysis platform. The servlet was sent to the local IT team as part of a phony virus alert, requesting they install the patch attached to all critical systems within 24 hours. When the patch was installed, we were able to remotely preview numerous machines to better target the on-site investigation.

Then we engaged a local team to perform forensic imaging and provide us with the raw drive images. The hard drives of key individuals' laptops and servers were secured, imaged, and sent back to the United States for analysis. The actual drives were left with the local management to ensure continuing operations of the business.

By combining a remote preview and the use of on-site first responders to perform basic imaging, we were able to conduct an effective investigation in a foreign country with limited remote and no physical access directly available to our analysis team.

After all of the remote research that can be performed is completed, an investigative plan is put in place to acquire the remote equipment. This may include putting a response team together (including physical security, IT security, human resources, and legal), planning the actual acquisition times and locations (for example, at night without the suspect knowing or during the day while interviewing the suspect), and getting together any special adapters or devices needed on-scene.

WARNING The discussion in this section assumes a corporate response within the corporation's network. Depending on local laws, even a port scan might be too intrusive against another entity and require legal support. The analyst must check with his local legal team before taking any of the actions noted beyond simple Internet research. This is a good moment to bring in law enforcement as well if one has not already done so.

Secure the Crime Scene

Securing the crime scene requires that the analyst ensure the physical and logical security of components present. Physical security is essential in preserving evidence, reducing potential contamination, and safeguarding the data necessary for a case. For physical scenes, the area surrounding the suspect devices should be secured. Ideally, the physical security specialists on a team will be specifically trained at securing the physical scene, but there might be occasions when the computer investigator is the first to arrive or the only individual present. If so, the following actions should be taken:

- At a minimum, the office, cubicle, or room in which the equipment resides should be cordoned off with security tape.
- If possible, the area in question should be locked.
- Individuals who are not part of the response team should be denied access to the area.
- Response team members should sign in to the logbook before entering the area.
- Any items leaving the area must be signed out in the logbook before being removed from the area.
- No extraneous items should be brought into the area (for example, coffee and pastries).

The physical security of the scene is paramount to avoiding evidence contamination during an investigation, but for the computer analyst, ensuring the physical security of any electronic equipment is only half of the task. Logical security of the data on the equipment must likewise be ensured. The best way to ensure logical security of the data is to make a forensic copy. The acquisition of hard drives and other media will be covered in later chapters, but duplicates of log files that may be overwritten or volatile information including current network connections may need to be performed immediately to ensure that the logical information is safeguarded. Securing the logical scene will be highly dependent on the specific environment, but here are a few items to consider:

- **Remove all unnecessary network connections.** Unless one is monitoring current activity as part of the investigation physically or logically, disconnect any segments that are not necessary for the examination. Do not forget about phone lines.

- **Copy volatile data quickly.** Volatile data is information that may be altered before more detailed analysis can occur. This can include cell phone received call logs (another call can come in and drop the last item), event logs (which can be set to overwrite based on size), cached information (address resolution protocol caches of MAC<->IP translations are notoriously short), and active application information (what is currently on the screen). The copying can be accomplished using a pen and paper, digital camera, or electronic media.

- **Power down associated devices by removing the power source** if malicious destruction is suspected, but do not use the Power Off button. If one encounters a computer where programs are being actively deleted, shutting down the system might prevent further destruction.

- **Ensure appropriate power for dynamic memory-based electronic devices.** Not all devices have permanent storage or backup batteries (which may lose charge) and, thus, rely on a constant power source to retain information. These may include fax machines, PDAs, and network devices.

Document the Scene

The most important aspect in the entire field of computer forensics is documentation. In addition to documenting one's own activities, the entire scene must be documented before processing of the scene can take place. All scene documentation is best done with a team of two individuals: one individual to perform any processing of the scene and a second individual solely responsible for documenting the evidence found. The documentation can be in a general computer forensics logbook, or in the case of larger investigations, a logbook dedicated to that specific investigation.

In addition to cataloging to provide a written record of all potential items of evidence, the scene itself should be photographed prior to any actions. If a forensic photographer is available, allow her to photograph the entire scene. If one is not available, the analyst may need to use a time-stamped camera, either digital or film. Start with a few shots of the entire scene for overall layout. Follow with close-ups of each piece of evidence. Note cards bent in half make nice, inexpensive labels for purposes of photographing evidence locations.

Even if a professional forensic photographer is available, the analyst might have to assist her in identifying what to photograph from a digital perspective. Items that require special attention in a computer investigation include:

- **Computer screens.** Photograph the current screen with a still camera with a high enough resolution to read text if necessary.

- **Network connections.** Any network or phone cables going to or from the computer should have close-up shots taken of them. Both ends of every cable should be photographed in the event that the analyst has to prove that a computer was connected to a specific network or phone line when he arrived.

- **Peripheral connections.** Connections to peripherals should likewise be shot in close-up for later reassembly and proof of connection.

TIP Do not use a video camera to photograph a computer screen. Because of differences in the sampling rate of the camera and the refresh rate of the screen, images may not be properly viewable.

When in doubt, take additional pictures. It is impossible to go back and do so later. After all, even the location of the mouse can prove significant; it may help to show that a left-handed person was the last user.

Process the Scene for Physical Evidence

The processing of the scene for physical evidence is best left to those individuals who have been specifically trained to process it. The processing of the physical evidence should always take place prior to any processing of digital evidence unless there is reason to believe a delay in processing the digital evidence will result in its destruction or loss.

In addition to the digital evidence they may hold, electronic devices are frequent repositories of physical evidence. Anyone who has ever turned over a keyboard and examined the detritus that can be shaken out is aware of potential biological evidence. Likewise, anyone who has touched a computer screen has left his own mark for later examination. Indeed, computer screens and mice are excellent locations for fingerprints, frequently better than those on the textured keys of a keyboard.

The computer investigator can suggest items of interest in the digital investigation, which may be processed as part of the physical investigation. These include:

- **Post-it notes or scraps of paper on, around, or under desks and computer equipment.** Check under the keyboard. Post-its are an office favorite for writing down passwords.

- **Papers with passwords, user names, or URLs.** Any papers with information about the individual's computer system or potential usage should be collected.

- **Keys to laptops or locked drives.** They can be taped under desks or hidden in plants.

- **Media.** Any floppy disks, CD-Rs, CDs, or other removable media should be collected for analysis. Additionally, application CDs might be necessary to load an individual application in the lab environment for analysis.

- **Computer manuals, reference guides, and other electronic equipment documentation.** These guides may be useful in taking apart a system, figuring out what command accesses CMOS setup, and understanding an application.

EVIDENCE COLLECTION KIT

The collection of physical evidence at a crime scene requires the appropriate equipment for handling and processing. A fingerprint analyst without a dusting kit, a DNA collection expert without swabs, and a forensic entomologist without sample cases would be severely limited in their abilities to process a scene. Similarly, without the basic kit, the computer forensic analyst is like a carpenter without a saw.

Not all digital evidence processing kits are alike. Some analysts prefer to have a complete mobile lab available to them for on-site analysis. Companies such as DigitalForensics provide special purpose equipment for these scenarios. Other analysts work on a first responder model whereby evidence is collected by remote first responders and then shipped to a central location for analysis. The sophistication of the evidence collection toolkit depends on the response model used, but at a minimum the following items should be included in any forensic response toolkit:

◆ *Latex gloves.* Not only do they prevent one from leaving fingerprints everywhere, but thicker latex gloves are also good protection against jagged edges when pulling apart computers.

◆ *Security tape.* The computer forensic analyst in a corporate setting may be acting alone and may need to cordon off an area as part of a physical crime scene. Basic yellow "Do Not Cross" tape can be purchased at local hardware stores. It is sufficient for non-law enforcement use.

◆ *Evidence tags and labels.* Tags specifically designed for evidence collection can be purchased cheaply from any major supplier of law enforcement goods. They should be tamper-resistant and may have two parts: one that stays with the evidence and a second that remains in the custody of the analyst.

◆ *Cable ties.* Securing a label to a piece of evidence via adhesion may not always be possible. A few inexpensive plastic cable ties do the trick nicely.

◆ *Bolt cutters.* Many laptop locks can be bypassed with a pair of scissors and a paper clip. Key locks require a little practice, and number locks require a lot of time. If time is of the essence, a set of bolt cutters or cable cutters will make quick work of inexpensive cable locks.

◆ *Sharpies.* When writing on a CD-R, evidence tag, or any other surface, a Sharpie is unbeatable. Make sure that the pen has a felt-tip, preferably a fine point or better for those tight spaces.

◆ *Anti-static bags and evidence bags.* Anti-static bags are generally silver in color and protect computer equipment for static electricity both in the environment and generated by the analyst. Evidence bags are tamper-resistant and have a detachable evidence label. Buy several different sizes of each, ranging from floppy-disk size to laptop-size.

◆ *Digital camera.* Any digital camera with a time and date stamp will suffice. Look for a built-in macro lens for close-ups of network connections, components, and cables. Anything above three megapixels is sufficient. Do not attempt to compete with Ansel Adams.

◆ *Forensic notebook.* Any book with numbered pages that cannot be removed is good for this one. Lab notebooks and general bound logbooks tend to be cheaper and just as good as those sold specifically for the purpose.

◆ *PC toolkit.* This is one place not to skimp. Buy the larger-size PC toolkit (one hundred pieces or better) to get everything needed to take a machine apart on-site. Ensure that TORX bits are included.

◆ *Forensic laptop, hard disk, and adapters.* It is always nice to be able to do some analysis on-site. A basic laptop with external USB 2.0 or FireWire hard disk along with a hardware write-blocker helps here.

TIP Before destroying a laptop lock, try looking around the office for a hidden key, either taped under the desk or in an office plant. Some locks can even be picked with a Bic pen (see www.wired.com/news/culture/0,1284,64987,00.html for details).

Basic combinations on a number lock are worth a try also; the phone extension of the particular desk is a favorite one. Combinations can be brute-forced in a fairly short period. Four-digit locks have 10,000 combinations that can be tested in roughly an hour and a half.

Process the Scene for Electronic Evidence

The processing of digital evidence at the crime scene is the responsibility of the computer investigator. After the physical processing of all IT equipment, the computer investigator takes over and is responsible for the packaging and handling of any electronic components.

CASE STUDY: ELECTRONIC DEVICE MISUSE

An employee of one of our clients was suspected of misusing company funds and colluding with an outside party. The company believed that there was information stored on both the employee's cell phone and PDA. The Human Resources team obtained the phone and PDA and placed the employee on administrative leave during the investigation. Both devices were secured by the individual who received them and then shipped them to us after a few weeks.

When the equipment arrived more than a month later, however, we had a difficult time analyzing the evidence. The cell phone battery had expired; luckily, we had a compatible charger available in our lab and were able to recharge it. Unfortunately, the suspect's phone had continued to receive phone calls while locked up with HR. As a result, the received phone call log was overwritten. We were able to get the data through the phone company records given that it was a company phone.

The PDA faired worse. The battery had expired, as had the backup battery. When we recharged the device, we saw that the volatile memory had been wiped out with the battery failure, leaving us with a *clean* system.

Before disconnecting anything, every cable on the computer or electronic device should be labeled. A simple Brother P-Touch labeler is a cost-effective way to identify a specific cable and where it plugs in on both ends. The cable connections can then be noted in the logbook for later reference when reassembling. After all cables have been labeled, the power cable can be removed to shut down the computer (see the sidebar "Shutdown, Unplug, or Analyze Live" for details on powering down). On Windows systems, the power cable should be removed from the connection on the PC itself instead of the wall jack. Pulling out the wrong power cable can be embarrassing and lead to data loss (for example, if there is a UPS that communicates with the PC present). For laptops, the battery should be removed and then the laptop unplugged. If the laptop is unplugged first, the machine may switch powersave modes, which will also potentially alter data. The Shutdown function of Windows should not be used, nor should the power switch on the box.

TIP On older systems, the power switch was actually a relay on the power supply and using it caused all power to the system to be disconnected. Recent machines use a software switch, which causes a motherboard interrupt to be generated, resulting in a Windows-friendly system shutdown.

After powering down, each cable should be individually removed from the computer and placed in an evidence bag. After the cables have been removed, all components containing digital logic or that are sensitive to static charge should be placed in anti-static bags. The anti-static bags may then be placed into evidence bags and sealed. Peripherals, media, and other electronics such as floppy disks, CD-ROMs, USB Flash drives, PDAs, and cell phones should likewise be placed in anti-static bags prior to being placed in evidence bags.

SHUTDOWN, UNPLUG, OR ANALYZE LIVE

The decision to shut down, unplug, or analyze the system as live is case specific and critical in a Windows investigation.

Shutting down a Windows system using the Shutdown button will have tremendous impact upon a forensic investigation. From a forensic standpoint, shutdown will do the following:

- ◆ Overwrite sections of the hard disk free space as information in memory is written to disk.

- ◆ Remove the swap file (pagefile.sys) that stores cached memory, depending on the operating system version and system settings.

- ◆ Terminate any running processes or applications, some of which may prompt for the saving of data, rendering the information unrecoverable in certain cases.

(continued)

SHUTDOWN, UNPLUG, OR ANALYZE LIVE *(continued)*

- ◆ Alter date- and timestamps on numerous files.
- ◆ Delete temporary files.
- ◆ Add entries to the event log.

Although other operating systems may be damaged by an improper shutdown, Windows systems are generally better off being powered down by unplugging. The application data for currently open applications may or may not be written to disk, depending on the specific application. The contents of the memory are lost either way, and the hard disk structure is altered less by unplugging.

Although using the built-in shutdown feature is rarely the best approach, performing a live analysis may be valuable. The degree to which a live analysis is performed depends on the case and could consist of anything from a remote port scan to a full examination of the current operating conditions. Live Windows system analysis is covered in detail in Chapter 8, but the decision to do a live analysis can be evaluated by considering several questions:

- ◆ Is an incident actively occurring on the machine?
  - ■ Will capturing data about the incident as it is occurring be potentially useful? If so, keystroke monitoring, network sniffing, and other techniques may be appropriate.
  - ■ Is the active incident destroying data, attacking other systems, or performing another destructive act that will be stopped by unplugging?
  - ■ Will unplugging the system tip off the suspects?
- ◆ Are there currently open applications whose contents will be useful in the case?
- ◆ Are there suspected processes in memory that may be useful in the case?
- ◆ Is information stored in memory likely to be a key component in the case?
  - ■ Is that information likely more valuable than the information on the hard disk?

There are additional options between pulling the plug and performing an in-person, live analysis as well. They are as follows:

- ◆ Documenting the open applications before pulling the plug
- ◆ Evaluating the system remotely
- ◆ Performing a remote forensic duplication (using EnCase Enterprise) and then performing a live analysis
- ◆ Doing the critical pieces of a live analysis and then pulling the plug

When making the decision to pull the plug, the key to success is understanding the implications, applying them to the specific case, and fully documenting the reasons behind the decision.

NOTE Windows 95 sets the file size of the pagefile to 0 at shutdown. Later operating systems rely on the value of HKEY_LOCAL_MACHINE\SYSTEM\ CurrentControlSet\Control\Session Manager\Memory Management\ ClearPageFileAtShutdown to decide whether or not to shut down the system (1 indicates it should be cleared).

Chain of Custody

Chain of custody refers to maintaining a documented record of the location and possessor of each piece of evidence at all times from its initial collection through potential court use and subsequent storage. For a piece of evidence to be used effectively in court, chain of custody must be maintained.

Chain of custody begins with the securing of the evidence. The initial individual who secures and catalogs the evidence becomes the first custodian in the chain of custody. This person is responsible for ensuring that the evidence remains secured and intact until it can be brought back to the evidence room. This means that the evidence is in the possession of the custodian at all times or is locked in a location accessible only to the custodian.

TIP When transporting electronic media in a vehicle, do not place it in the glove box. Summer temperatures in hot climates of up to 140°F have been recorded in the glove box, well outside the recommended operating temperature of most electronics.

The evidence room should be access-controlled and have direct access by no more than two individuals. Upon arrival, all evidence should be signed in to the evidence room by filling out a chain of custody form. (See Appendix A for an example chain of custody form.) It is then turned over to the evidence room custodian. The evidence must then be logged as present in the evidence room. When the evidence is ready for analysis, the computer investigator requests signs the evidence out of the evidence room and takes custody for a period of time. After the evidence has been analyzed, it should be returned to the evidence room for proper storage.

Retention of evidence in the storage room will depend on space constraints, volume of evidence, and local statutes of limitations on the type of case. The retention policy should be documented and strictly enforced. Many companies use a 10-year rule for evidence of potentially illegal activity or evidence involved in civil litigation. When presented at court, the chain of custody form for a piece of evidence and any supplementary documentation may need to be presented to prove validity. The documentation should adequately show the following:

- The evidence collected is the same as that presented in court.
- The location of the evidence was known at all points in time.
- An evidence custodian was assigned at all points in time.
- No individuals outside of those listed on the chain of custody form had access to the evidence.
- The evidence was not intentionally or inadvertently modified as part of the investigative process.

Best Evidence

Computer evidence has special considerations when presented in a court of law. For non-electronic evidence, the Federal Rules of Evidence define "best evidence" as the original writing, recording, or photograph as opposed to a copy. Duplicates of the original data are not admissible unless the original is destroyed, unavailable, or unobtainable for specific reasons.

The typing of information and copying of data from an outside source now qualifies as an original writing, recording, or photograph in its electronic form. To handle computer evidence, an exception was made to the best evidence rule permitting paper copies that represented the electronic form to be admitted as documentary evidence in court. Written records of system contents could then be used in lieu of the actual equipment, eliminating the need for a mainframe and terminals to demonstrate that a particular file was present. This permits the investigator to submit printouts of actual activity where applicable, although a visual demonstration may be of great value in getting a point across.

A second clarification to the best evidence rule regarding electronic evidence concerns the definition of a duplicate. The original copy of a hard disk may be unavailable. Or the act of booting the disk in its original environment will alter it, making the original no longer valid. For this reason, full forensic duplicates are now permitted for electronic evidence. Duplicates are bitstream, sector-by-sector images of electronic equipment. As the electronic items and a visual representation of them are the actual evidence, there is no specific requirement that the disk itself be presented. Current case law permits the use of forensic duplicates as fully qualified substitutions as long as:

1. They are from the indicated source.
2. They were acquired using proven tools and techniques.
3. They have not been altered since the time of acquisition.

TIP Tools such as dd, SafeBack, and EnCase, when used according to proper procedures, have all been court tested.

EVIDENCE STORAGE

Two common questions are what specific evidence to store in an investigation and how to store it. There are three main ways to store electronic evidence as used in an investigation:

◆ Store the entire computer system itself.

◆ Store the hard disk or other drives from the computer system.

◆ Store a bitstream copy of the hard disk on write-protected media.

Making the determination of what to store is a question of policy, storage space, and operational impact. An organization should have a policy that specifies what specifically should be stored and for how long. This should also include how the data is stored, where it is stored, who has access to it, and ultimately how it is disposed of. Policy may be altered by the circumstances and outcome of the particular incident. For example, cases involving potential civil or criminal litigation may require more stringent or longer storage than cases with a "no findings" outcome. Given the current best evidence thinking, there is little legal reason to store the actual computer or hard disk itself provided that an authenticated bitstream copy is available with the appropriate procedural documentation on the acquisition.

Storage space is likewise a consideration. The acquisition of a dozen or more computers in a large case is not unheard of, and the machines may be large servers. Most companies are unwilling to lease an evidence warehouse specifically for this purpose, however. In many cases, an evidence safe in a locked room may be the only viable option. This precludes the storage of large amounts of equipment. Yet there is at least one valid reason to make space for entire systems: the potential unavailability of the hardware in the future. If there will be a need to reconstruct the hardware one day (for example, if the hardware used a proprietary storage device that was not acquired to another media), this warrants serious consideration.

Operational impact is always a concern when performing an investigation. The operational impact of removing a computer system or hard drive for an extended period, be it minutes or years, might outweigh any storage benefits of having the original media.

Barring the concerns noted previously, storing a bitstream copy of all evidence as a base copy is the best approach. The media should be write-protected to ensure that it cannot be altered. It must be of archival quality as some media, notably early CDs and DVDs, have longevity issues, as do many magnetic tapes. It must be a long-lasting format as well, for if the format is proprietary and the reading hardware dies, all of the evidence may be rendered unusable.

Working with Law Enforcement

In the past, corporate executives believed that reporting criminal activity associated with IT security meant creating bad press for their organizations. As a result, corporations often suffered unreported losses. Statistics on corporate IT security breaches were frequently inaccurate, and criminals were able to repeatedly and unabashedly perpetrate the same actions against different organizations.

Today, however, attitudes have changed. Thanks to increased pressure from federal legislation like Sarbanes-Oxley and state legislation in locations like California, many IT security incidents are required to be reported. Simultaneously, law enforcement outreach initiatives like the FBI's Infragard program foster industry partnerships to protect the national infrastructure. This allows individuals who work in corporate security to form all-important relationships with federal, state, and local law-enforcement agencies. They can then receive warnings of new threats and assistance with existing threats and give and obtain support in investigating incidents.

TIP Information security professionals should look to joining their local Infragard chapter. The contacts with professional colleagues as well as law enforcement officials are invaluable, and there is a negligible cost to join (free for some chapters). More information on this organization can be found at www.infragard.net.

The best time to engage law enforcement is before an incident occurs. If the investigator makes contacts with local, state, and federal officials ahead of time, she will find it much more efficient to work with them after the proverbial excrement hits the fan. Law enforcement agents bring skills and capabilities not generally accessible in the corporate world to the table. They are able to track incidents across borders (both corporate and geographic), pursue criminal actions against attackers, and provide expertise in the technical, legal, and logistical areas of an investigation.

At the same time, the corporate security investigator may be able to provide agents with information and expertise that they do not necessarily possess. The investigator may assist law enforcement by:

- **Acting as a liaison to internal staff.** By coordinating with corporate staff, the computer investigator frees law enforcement from the difficulties of navigating a complex organizational structure.

- **Acquiring and preserving evidence.** Not all evidence can wait for law enforcement to be engaged, and some evidence (especially evidence that is transitory in nature) may be easier for a corporate investigator to acquire based on existing laws (for example, keystroke monitoring of an employee). This information should be collected and preserved in a forensically sound manner for later law enforcement involvement.

- **Analyzing evidence.** Specifics regarding both one's business model and IT infrastructure may be useful to law enforcement. From the operations of proprietary IT systems to the analysis of the organization's supply chain, the computer investigator may have invaluable domain expertise.

- **Providing loss figures.** Many federal crime statutes require a loss to be shown in order to prosecute to the fullest. By calculating the dollar loss of an incident appropriately, the computer investigator can improve the chance of a successful prosecution.

Additional Resources

Refer to the following list for additional resources:

California Personal Information Disclosure Law
    `info.sen.ca.gov/pub/01-02/bill/sen/sb_1351-1400/`
    `sb_1386_bill_20020926_chaptered.html`

Federal Rules of Evidence
    `judiciary.house.gov/media/pdfs/printers/108th/`
    `evid2004.pdf`

Forensic Computers
    `www.forensic-computers.com`

nbmac
    `www.kostis.net/freeware/nbmac-e.htm`

MAC Address Organizations
    `standards.ieee.org/regauth/oui/oui.txt`

Remote Operating System Detection (by Fyodor)
    `www.insecure.org/nmap/nmap-fingerprinting-article.html`

Sarbanes-Oxley Act
    `thomas.loc.gov/cgi-bin/query/z?c107:H.R.3763.ENR:%20`

Windows Forensics Basics

Since the transition from the MS-DOS, command prompt–based platform, Microsoft Windows has been the predominant client operating system in both home and corporate environments. Today, Windows is by far the most prevalent operating system present in the corporate world. There are very few large organizations that do not have some Windows machines, and in most organizations, Windows machines make up the bulk of the environment. Since early 2000, Microsoft has taken over the corporate server marketplace in terms of the number of individual servers shipped annually.

There are numerous challenges for the computer investigator, given the pervasiveness of Windows. The existence of exploitable security flaws in Windows-based systems is a particular challenge. Because of the enormous installed base of systems, a single flaw can affect a significant amount of infrastructure in a typical company. It becomes impossible or at the very least impractical to trace the origins of a worm such as Slammer, and when an active infection occurs, the crisis can make a more directed attack difficult to detect.

Similarly, the perceived insecurity of Windows systems is changing the courtroom landscape. Recent claims that insecure operating systems or malicious software are responsible for user actions have already been put forth successfully as arguments in British court systems, and it is only a matter of time until American courts are faced with similar arguments. At the same time, the increasing complexity of Windows has actually added some benefits for the forensic world. Increased amounts of slack space, the use of paging files, and the inclusion of user-friendly features such as autofill forms using Intelliforms have increased the number of places a computer investigator can hope to find information.

Windows will continue to evolve, and the computer investigator will need to maintain familiarity with new versions to continue to perform effective analyses. The remainder of this book will focus on the most prevalent versions of Windows currently available — 98, 2000, XP, and Server 2003 — with notes of significance for older versions.

History and Versions

Microsoft Windows traces its history back to a prior command line–based operating system, MS-DOS. Founded in 1975, Microsoft Corporation built several BASIC language interpreters for personal computer kits available at the time. After gaining some prominence in the PC marketplace, Microsoft purchased the rights to an operating system that became MS-DOS in 1981.

MS-DOS

MS-DOS provided a small footprint operating system that became the *de-facto* standard for IBM-compatible personal computers. Offered as part of the original IBM PC, the MS-DOS operating system became the baseline for business applications and home applications. MS-DOS was non-graphical and used the FAT file system exclusively. Mice were not part of a standard PC offered at the time, and the original versions did not support hard disks. As a result, forensics was a bit easier, although the tools were not as robust; the entire contents of an evidence floppy, all 360K of it, could be printed out and reviewed manually.

A few third-party Graphical User Interfaces (GUIs) were made available for MS-DOS, but they were released with limited success, largely because color monitors with capable graphics card were not broadly available, and mice were just beginning to appear on standard PCs. In 1985, Microsoft released a graphical shell for MS-DOS titled Windows 1.0.

Windows 1.x, 2.x, and 3.x

The initial public and corporate reaction to both Windows 1.0 and its successors, Windows 2.0 (released in 1987) and Windows 3.0 (released in 1991), was lukewarm at best. By the end of 1991, MS-DOS was still the predominate client operating system, and both Unix and Netware servers had a dominant place in the newly emerging corporate microcomputer server market.

In an effort to improve previous versions and broaden its appeal, Microsoft released two products in the 1992–1993 timeframe. They were tremendously successful. In the home market, Windows 3.1 sold millions of copies and included hundreds of enhancements in graphics, usability, and functionality. Sales were likewise increased by the release of Microsoft Office and Microsoft Works products for home users, and the new, easy-to-use Microsoft Visual Basic programming environment expanded the number of developers exponentially almost overnight.

NOTE Visual Basic built upon the BASIC language, the predominant language taught in schools at the time. As a result, Microsoft released its development tools to a pre-trained audience. The easy-to-use integrated development environment (IDE) likewise made Visual Basic more accessible to non-programmers and new programmers, creating a plethora of new programs available and a resulting synergy in popularity.

In the business world, the counterpart to Windows 3.1 was Windows for Workgroups 3.11 (WFW 3.11). Enabling remote access, networking, and collaboration, WFW 3.11 became an instant hit in the corporate workplace. At the same time, the introduction of a new Microsoft mouse and the incorporation of the product into most of the major OEM vendors to corporations ensured its continued success.

Windows 3.1 and WFW 3.11 are the oldest Windows products a forensic examiner is likely to encounter. Both products are now well beyond their support expiration, but a few point machines running legacy software still exist with each of these installed. From a forensic examination standpoint, Windows 3.x systems are MS-DOS systems with a GUI on top of them. File system support was for FAT, and any of the analyses mentioned later that are related to FAT drives are applicable. The introduction of virtual memory is also of note. Windows 3.x used a hidden file called 386SPART.PAR, which was an early virtual memory file. This file should be analyzed the same way as the swap files listed for later versions of Windows.

Following the success of Windows 3.x, Microsoft branched off its operating systems in two separate directions. The corporate environment had a new operating system built from the ground up given the moniker Windows NT (for New Technology) that would compete for both the server and workstation markets. The home environment had its own new release, Windows 95, which remained backward compatible with the older versions on Windows and DOS but had a substantially new look and feel built on an updated architecture.

Windows NT and 2000

Windows NT 3.51 and 4.0 proved to be more stable and secure than previous versions of Windows. Both made strong headway into the corporate environment, frequently replacing Netware and other systems on the server with its ease-of-use, and replacing WFW 3.11 on the desktop with increased stability, performance, and security. For the computer investigator, Windows NT introduced the new file system, which has since become the most prevalent: NTFS. A major improvement on the FAT file system, NTFS lessened the amount of slack space available on large drives but increased the ability to recover damaged drives through the use of file systems mirroring. Additions to NTFS such as Alternate Data Streams, file compression, and the new Recycling Bin formats required additional effort in a forensic analysis. For the examiner, negligible differences exist in the architectures of the server and workstations products, although analysis might differ greatly based on the type of investigation. Support for Windows NT 4.0 is now terminated with the exception of those with custom support contracts, but many corporate environments still have a large installed base of NT machines.

Following the success of Windows NT, the corporate line of products was renamed Windows 2000 and released as the upgrade path for Windows NT 4.0 in both the server and workstation markets. Windows 2000 provided even more stability and better performance on both the desktop and server environments, offering support for larger server deployments as well as a robust management of users through Active Directory, Microsoft's LDAP effort.

Windows 2000 introduced the Encrypting File System (EFS), presenting a new challenge for the computer investigator. Now entire drives could be encrypted with a few mouse clicks, and key escrow became an important consideration in corporate forensics. At the time of this writing, Windows 2000 is the predominant Windows server in operation but has been surpassed by Windows XP in popularity on the desktop.

At the same time Windows NT and 2000 were released for the corporate market, Windows 95, 95 OSR2, 98, 98SE, and ME were released for the home market. Starting with Windows 95, Microsoft revamped the Windows 3.x look and feel as well as the underlying architecture. Because backward compatibility remained a major consideration, remnants of the legacy DOS architecture existed on the home environment for a longer period than in the corporate space.

Windows 95, 98, and ME

Windows 95 was replaced in popularity by Windows 98, a cosmetic and functionality-based update. Interim OSR2 (for Windows 95) and SE (for Windows 98) editions offered mid-stream updates to networking functionality, security, and feature sets. Windows ME (Millennium Edition) introduced several enhancements to user-friendliness but never supplanted previous versions in market share.

Windows 9x never integrated full support for the NTFS file system. As a result, permissions, compression, encryption, and other options were primarily limited to third-party products. Long file names and other additions to the original FAT specifications were included as part of FAT32, as were file recovery (Recycling Bin), networking, and registry features.

Although Windows 98 does exist in some corporate environments, it is still a predominantly personal-use operating system. The popularity of Windows 9x has been diminishing with the increased push for security and stability in the home environment. There is still a reasonable likelihood of encountering Windows 9x machines in a forensic investigation, although their usage will continue to decline rapidly as support wanes and users transition to newer operating systems.

Windows XP and 2003

In an effort to improve the security and stability of its home market while offering a competitive update for corporate users, Microsoft released Windows XP as its new client operating system. XP brought the previous features present in the Windows NT/2000 operating systems and the associated NTFS file system to the home market and introduced new usability features to the corporate market.

Windows XP SP2, the second service pack for the product, introduced further enhancements to the XP environment on security. The addition of an improved client firewall and integrated security management center increased the security of home machines and presented new challenges for the computer investigator (for example, the use of servlets and other remote analysis tools).

NOTE Although Microsoft dominates the personal computer market, embedded operating systems present on Programmable Logic Controllers (PLCs) and cell phones have more overall installations.

Windows XP is the predominant operating system in use globally (see Figure 3-1 for prevalence information). It has the largest market share of any personal computer operating system. With the next Windows version not expected until late 2006 (Windows Vista, formerly named Longhorn), XP will remain the most important system for the forensic examiner in the near future. Likewise, given its stability and functionality, XP is the best candidate for a Windows analysis system as well. Unless otherwise noted, the commands and tools listed in this book will all run under the XP operating system.

NOTE It is debatable whether *nix-based operating systems make better analysis environments when examining Windows machines. Any respectable examiner will have both environments available for analysis.

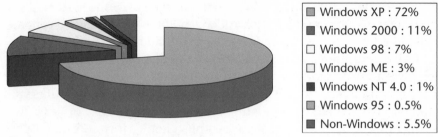

Figure 3-1: Windows client operating system usage

Replacing Windows 2000 on the server side is Windows 2003. Windows 2003 is achieving growth in market share but many corporations continue to use Windows 2000 as their core server platform. Usage of 2003 is expected to increase slowly, and familiarity with the environment is of current and future value to the computer investigator.

THE WORM DID IT!

A new strategy computer investigators have to consider is the computer-equivalent of the SODDI defense, "Some Other Dude Did It." The defense has been tried successfully by three individuals in the United Kingdom, twice in child pornography cases and once in a denial-of-service attack. The basic defense comes in one of two forms:

1. "Some malicious code on my machine automatically downloaded the content without my being aware of it."

2. "A Trojan horse on my computer allowed another individual the ability to access my machine and they actually committed the crime."

The computer investigator may be called upon to prove or disprove claims such as the ones given previously. It is easier to prove them rather than disprove them, and this can be done by illustrating the following:

- ◆ Malicious code that exhibits the behavior in question is known to exist.

- ◆ The machine in question was not adequately protected against said code through anti-virus, spyware detection, a host firewall, or other tools.

- ◆ The malicious code in question or remnants of it were found on the machine.

It is technically impossible to prove that malicious code was not responsible for a given action. The code may have been installed, ran, and then removed all reasonably obtainable traces of itself. Fortunately, the computer investigator does not need to prove beyond any doubt, only beyond a reasonable doubt. After all, aliens could have used a superior technology to magically plant the evidence, or a random re-alignment of the hard drive could have resulted in the creation of the images! In order to raise a reasonable doubt, the computer investigator should attempt to answer the following questions:

◆ Is there existing malicious code that mimics the behavior claimed by the suspect?

- Are the major anti-virus and spyware companies aware of similar code?

- Do any of the locations visited by the suspect recently have the code present?

◆ Was the subject's machine susceptible to the malicious code?

- Is it the right operating system and version to be infected?

- Was the machine patched at the time to the appropriate level?

- Was antivirus or anti-spyware software installed and up to date?

◆ Is the machine currently infected? If not, what did the suspect do to re-move the code?

- Does turning on the machine and mimicking the suspect's claimed actions duplicate the downloads?

- Is there evidence of automatically running services or applications running on startup (for example, Run, RunOnce, or RunOnceEx in the registry)?

- Does running the latest version of anti-virus software and anti-spyware software on the machine show this or other infections?

- Did the suspect take any actions to remove the infection?

◆ Is the behavior consistent with automated code or with human interaction?

- Does it occur only at the times when the user is active, or does it occur at other times when the user is not present?

- Is there consistent spacing between requests?

- In the case of downloads, were the files opened after downloading (for example, were they present in the Recent Docs lists of individual applications)?

- Are there spelling or typographical errors in requests?

- Is the activity corroborated by other electronic information (for example, typed emails, the TypedURL's registry key, and search engine queries)?

The SODDI defense strategy will likely be used again in court, and the computer investigator will need to work with legal and traditional investigators to take the possibility of malicious code into consideration. In a controlled, corporate environment, this may be easier to disprove, but in a home environment with multiple users on a computer, poor configurations, and open network connections, it becomes more difficult.

Non-Volatile Storage

Storage media are at the heart of most computer forensics cases. In many cases, data in-transit cannot be obtained, or historical data (for example, a suspect's email messages sent last June) is needed as part of the investigation. The majority of a computer investigator's analysis time is likely to be spent imaging, analyzing, and reporting information uncovered from storage devices.

The present-day storage landscape is complex. Information can be stored in many forms, on many different devices. Traditional storage media can be grouped into two categories: removable media and non-removable media. Removable media includes floppy disks, CD-ROMs, DVDs, Zip disks, and magnetic tapes. Non-removable media primarily refers to hard disks.

Traditional media (both removal and non-removable) use one of two primary technologies: optical data storage or magnetic data storage. Optical data storage devices use a laser to change read *pits* on a platter. Depending on the reflection/non-reflection of the light, each pit or lack thereof is read as a one or a zero by the computer. Writing to the media used by these devices generally occurs with a separate device used to press the pits in place or with a dye that changes properties (such as that used in CD-Rs) when a different wavelength or intensity of light is applied. Magnetic storage devices use an electromagnetic read/write head. The head is a sensor that either reads the charge present at a given location or changes the charge present at a given location.

In recent years, non-traditional storage media have made an appearance and are becoming more prevalent. USB-based flash drives, digital cameras with memory cards, and solid-state MP3 players all use different storage media. These devices can be used for their intended purpose or for general storage, and they will likely play a greater role in the future of computer investigations.

For a computer investigator, a basic understanding of each underlying storage technology is essential. When a sector-by-sector copy is made, the investigator should have a good understanding of what a sector is, how it relates to a cluster, and what is really being copied (and not copied) when this occurs. The next sections introduce the basics behind the major storage technologies as they relate to a forensic examination.

Floppy Disks

The 1.44MB DS/HD 3.5-inch floppy disk remains one of the primary mechanisms for the transportation of data, despite its age, slow access speeds, and storage limitations. The floppy disk (of which the 3.5 inch is just the latest manifestation) is a platter-based magnetic-media storage technology encased in plastic. There were later versions of the 3.5-inch floppy, such as the 2.88MB and 120MB, and even 200MB attempts, but none became widely adopted.

WRITE BLOCKING

When performing a forensic acquisition of media, it is critical to ensure that no intentional or unintentional alteration of the data on that media occurs. When Windows mounts a device, it can actually write a signature to that device, thereby altering the contents slightly. Although not an insurmountable legal issue (the specific changes Windows makes can be replicated and demonstrated), any alteration is likely to create a hassle down to road. To prevent this, write blocking is used.

Write blocking ensures there can be no accidental writing on a given piece of media. Some media, such as the pressed and write-once formats of CD and DVD, are write-protected by design. After data is written, it cannot be overwritten or altered. Other media types like backup tapes, floppy disks, and USB flash drives may have a switch, tab, or window that allows write protection. This can and should be used when acquiring information from these media to ensure alteration does not occur.

Some media, including most hard disks, do not have built-in write protection. For the forensic examiner, this requires the use of software or hardware write blockers to ensure that the media is not altered.

Software-based write blockers trace their history to the DOS days, when they were able to intercept interrupts on drive access and prevent writing. Beyond Windows 95, these devices lost their effectiveness and are being replaced by new versions of software write blockers such as the forthcoming Fastbloc SE from Guidance Software. Software-based write blocking has been shown to be effective in lab environments but has not been broadly tested in the courts and has been conceptually questioned in academic literature. The promise of a technology-independent way to provide write blocking is enticing, but the computer investigator should evaluate any new software-based write blockers carefully before using them in a forensically sensitive case.

Hardware-based write blockers are more commonplace and sit between the device to be acquired and the analysis system. They use physical protection (for example, not connecting the write wires) to ensure that accidental writing does not occur and come with interfaces for most major media types, including SATA, IDE, and SCSI hard disks as well as flash-based media formats. The hardware write blockers then connect back to the analysis PC through the use of USB 2.0 or FireWire connections for quick transfers. The Ultrablock line from Digital Intelligence and the Fastbloc line from Guidance provide an array of write blockers that are broadly used, court tested, and proven effective. Every computer analysis lab should have one of these products (or its equivalent) to ensure that acquisitions are free of alterations.

NOTE DS/HD refers to double sided (both sides of the disk are used for reading and writing) and high density (there are more bits per inch available). Older 3.5-inch 720KB disks were DS/DD (double sided/double density), with reduced storage available on each side. Their predecessors, 5.25-inch disks, were originally SS/SD (single sided/single density) and stored 180KB per side. Some original PC drives allowed that amount to be doubled by physically flipping over the floppy disk in the drive.

The standard floppy disk consists of four major components:

- **Plastic casing.** The plastic casing protects the floppy disk from dust and scratches and provides a rigid structure that can be placed inside a drive.

- **Metal slide window.** The spring-loaded metal on the bottom of the floppy disk protects the platter when not in use. It retracts when placed in the floppy drive to allow the read/write head access to the underlying platter.

- **Cleaning-strip.** Inside the plastic housing on most floppy disks is a cloth cleaning strip. The strip has light contact with the platter and permits the platter to be cleaned every rotation.

- **Platter.** The platter is the heart of the floppy disk. It is a two-sided, coated disk that maintains a charge when applied by the read/write head. The platter is spun by a motor in the drive itself to store or retrieve information.

The floppy disk itself is placed into a floppy disk drive, which contains the digital logic circuitry, the drive motor, and the read/write head. To use the disk, the floppy drive spins the platter at around 300 revolutions per minute. The read/write head moves back and forth across the platter and operates on individual sectors of data within a rotational track as noted in Figure 3-2.

NOTE In reality, the sectors are not the same size. Smaller sectors are present on the inner areas and larger sectors on the outer to account for the increased space as well as the difference in speed as the head traverses them.

Standard 3.5-inch floppy disks contain 80 tracks, with 18 sectors per track on each side of the platter. Each sector contains 512 bytes of usable information in addition to a basic preamble used by the read/write head for alignment and an error-correcting code to detect single and multi-bit errors on the disk. The only data directly accessible above the hardware layer is the sector data. A sector is likewise the smallest piece of information that can be read from or written to.

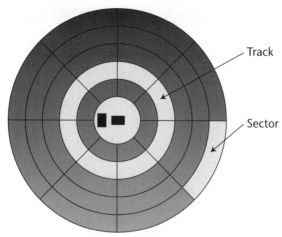

Track

Sector

Figure 3-2: Disk platter layout

TIP The computer investigator might still encounter legacy 5.25-inch floppy disks. If they are encountered, legacy 5.25-inch 1.2MB drives can still be purchased online, or the suspect's drive may be acquired for the explicit purpose of reading them.

Microsoft-formatted floppy disks use the FAT12 partition type, described later in the chapter, with a cluster size of 512 bytes. The cluster size is the smallest addressable space the operating system can read and write to and is made up of one or more sectors (one in the case of FAT12 floppy disks). Like all magnetic media, floppy disks degrade over time. Additionally, frequently used floppy disks can suffer from friction degradation. Unlike hard disks, the read/write head in a floppy drive actually rests on the platter. Over time, frequently used tracks might actually "burn-in" (visible as a white line around the disk) or individual sectors might become unreadable. When this occurs, standard operating system software may be unable to read the disk. Anadisk, specific to floppies and available from NTI, provides an easy-to-use mechanism to recover the remaining data on a disk with bad sectors for further analysis. This is one reason for slow transfer times on floppy disks. Higher rotational speeds would generate increased heat and degrade disks more quickly.

FLOPPY DISK REPAIR

Damaged floppy disks are not an uncommon thing for a computer investigator to encounter. In general, damage to any part of the disk (with the possible exception of gross damage to the platter) is something that can be recovered. Since floppy drives themselves are inexpensive, it is recommended that the investigator keep several drives laying around for "questionable" disks to prevent damage to one's regular floppy drive. Some possible situations of floppy damage and their solutions (short of using a Scanning Tunneling Microscope) are as follows:

◆ *Bent metal/non-retracting slide cover.* If the metal becomes bent on a floppy disk, it might not fit in the drive, get stuck, or not retract to allow reading. The metal is just an added layer of protection, and the disk will function without it. To remove the metal slider, gently pull on the part of the metal closest to the center of the disk, bending it away from the plastic. Eventually, the metal will separate from the plastic, and the spring mechanism will disengage. This disk can now be placed in a drive (and immediately imaged) without the metal attached.

◆ *Damaged plastic.* Damage to the plastic of a disk may make it impede the proper rotation of the platter or make it impossible to insert into a floppy drive. The plastic housing itself can actually be replaced with the housing from a good disk. To begin, remove the metal slider as noted from both disks. Most floppy disks are made by joining two pieces of plastic together on either side of the platter. Using a box-opener, pry open the seam on all four sides of the disk, cutting where necessary. The platter then can be removed from the defective disk and placed into the good disk. Wear gloves and do not touch the surface of the disk itself. When inside, the plastic halves can be put back together with super glue. Make sure that none gets on the platter. After the glue has dried, the new disk can be used in the drive.

◆ *Contaminated disk.* Like keyboards, floppy disks tend to be magnets for coffee spills and other workplace hazards. If a disk is contaminated with a liquid (even if it has dried), it still might be recoverable. To recover the disk, remove the platter as noted. Soak the platter in hot water (no soap) until the liquid is removed or contamination loosed. If necessary, gently remove any remaining contamination from the disk with a dry, lint-free cloth. Eyeglass cleaning cloths work well. Remove any excess water with a clean cloth as noted and allow the disk to dry for 24 hours. When dry, place the disk in a new plastic housing as described previously.

◆ *Physically damaged platter.* **Physical damage to the platter of a floppy disk is the worst possible scenario. A pencil through the disk, part of the platter cut off, and other such calamities are very difficult to undo. Do not try to repair these disks as more damage can be done to both the disk and drive. The leader in the field in this type of recovery is Kroll On-Track (www.krollontrack.com). Although expensive, Kroll OnTrack's lab environment is the last hope for damaged platter recovery. The missing portion will never be recovered, but Kroll OnTrack may be able to provide the raw data from the remaining pieces.**

Tapes

Magnetic tapes contain large amounts of data and are frequently used for backups. Like floppy disks, magnetic tapes contain a coated surface on a tape, which can be read from and written to. The tape itself generally sits between two spools within a plastic cartridge, with a coated and uncoated side present. Unlike floppy disks, tapes are sequential access devices, not random access devices. To read a particular portion of the tape, it must be rewound or fast-forwarded to the correct spot on the tape. When the correct location is found, the reading and writing can be done fairly quickly. The seek times, however, might be fairly large.

TIP **Always ask to see the backup strategy and inquire about off-site storage locations when dealing with tapes. Sometimes an old backup may contain data that was deleted on the production systems, and off-site facilities may have secured copies of tapes that "went missing" locally.**

The computer investigator is most likely to encounter backup tapes in server rooms. Although personal tape drives have been present, most individual PCs do not make use of discrete tape drives. Additionally, requests for old logfiles and previous copies of documents may require a tape analysis.

TIP **Keep in mind that not everything is backed up to tape, even if regular backups are performed. A file created and deleted between backup cycles will not be present. Likewise, a file that was open when the tape backup software was running may not be present, depending on the software used and its settings.**

Tapes present three problem areas for a computer investigator: hardware, software, and capacity. The predominant tape hardware technologies are DLT, LTO, Exabyte, AIT, DAT, and QIC. Additionally, each of these technologies comes in a variety of sizes. A given drive may or may not be able to read older or newer versions of the same technology. As a result, it is of critical importance that the tape hardware (including any controller cards) be acquired along with the tapes.

Typical tape hardware consists of a plastic cartridge containing two or more spools, around which is wound one-sided magnetic tape. The tapes generally have an optical signature block at the beginning and end of the tape to signal to the drive the starting and stopping positions of the tape. The tape cartridge is placed in the tape drive, which consists of digital circuitry, a motor to drive the spools, and a read/write head. The drive itself may be standalone or part of a tape library system and frequently has a dedicated controller card to use.

Software is a second issue with the analysis of backup tapes for forensic purposes. Microsoft backup programs use a format called MTF (Microsoft Tape Format), and this is the most likely format to be encountered on Windows systems. The Microsoft Backup utility includes support for Microsoft-formatted tapes, as well as Seagate/Veritas, which use the MTF format.

NOTE Despite its name, Microsoft Tape Format can be used to back up to other media as well, including hard disks and optical media.

Because of the varying block formatting options, redundancy setups, and write formatting, effective tape recovery might require the original software to effectively recover information. In these cases, it is important to recover the media and licenses for any relevant backup software present to have an effective recovery.

In terms of storage, tape backup units can hold hundreds of gigabytes of compressed data. This is normally a positive aspect of using backup tapes — storing multiple drives/systems on a single tape. For the forensic examiner, however, this may represent another challenge. Direct restoration of the tape byte-for-byte may not be possible due to storage limitations unless a multi-drive RAID array or similar storage mechanism is available.

Unlike disks, tape backups generally work on logical files; that is, they do not generally have slack space or store unallocated disk clusters unless the tape backup is an actual drive image. Because of this, a full, byte-by-byte image copy is not necessary to meet the best evidence standards. From an examination standpoint, this allows the forensic examiner to search for and recover only those files necessary for the examination if they are known ahead of time. By doing so, only enough space for the recovered files is required.

TAPE BACKUP METHODS

The computer investigator is likely to encounter multiple backup strategies for tape rotation and reuse. For forensic restoration, it helps to have an understanding of the three primary types of backup: full, differential, and incremental.

- ◆ *Full.* A full backup writes all files selected for backup to the tape or set of tapes in their current state. To restore from a full backup, one only needs the latest dataset or the relevant dataset, if the latest does not have what the investigator is trying to restore.

- ◆ *Incremental.* Incremental backups rely on an initial, full backup set. When the full backup is done, the following backups only store changes since the last backup. If a file has changed multiple times since the last full backup, it may reside on multiple incremental backup sets. The upside of incremental backups in forensics is that one may have multiple versions of files present, allowing for a timeline to be displayed. The downside is that to restore a given file to its present state, the analyst needs all of the incremental between the last full backup and the day desired.

- ◆ *Differential.* Unlike the Incremental backup, the differential backup stores all of the changes to a file since the last full backup. To restore any individual file in a differential backup set, only the full backup and the latest differential backup are required. Like incremental backups, multiple versions of a file may be present, but with differentials only the original, full backup and the desired differential need to be present for a restoration. Differential backups were not supported prior to Windows 2000 in the Microsoft Backup utility but are now available.

Tapes can degrade with age like all magnetic media and may have bad sectors. Most tape backup and restoration software can recover from these or skip effected files, and smaller bit-level errors may be handled automatically through redundancy checks and writing of duplicate data. Physical damage to a tape is a more difficult issue. It generally takes the form of a tape breaking under tension. Restoring a broken tape is a difficult task, and success is highly dependent on both tape format and the location of the break. Any damage to the lead-in sector or the beginning or end of the tape might be unrecoverable if that is the location of the tape catalog, where the contents of the tape and their location are written. A byte-by-byte read of the entire contents may still be an option, although one must reverse engineer the format. Damage in other tape locations might be salvageable, but the effected area will not be recoverable. Take the following steps:

- Using a box opener (or better yet a splicing tool) cut the damaged area of the tape away at a 45-degree angle on both sides such that the ends fit together with no overlap.

- Purchase a video tape repair kit (Radio Shack sells one) and remove the repair tape.

- Carefully align the edges of the tape to be repaired (a splicing kit will help here also).

- Place a piece of the repair tape on the dull side of the backup tape and smooth it over.

Depending on formats and the drive, the tape might still be readable up until the break at a minimum and with luck after the break. The tape break risks damage to the drive head, which spins significantly more quickly than that of a VCR. Do not go beyond it if at all possible.

CDs and DVDs

Optical media are presently the most likely to be found in an investigation. Although other optical technologies have existed over the years, the two most prevalent optical media found are CDs and DVDs in their various forms.

CDs and DVDs come in one of three write formats: commercially pressed, write-once, and re-writeable (with different flavors of each in the DVD space). The commercially pressed media use a master die, which is used to imprint pits and lands into the polycarbonate substrate on the media. This allows for mass production based on the creation of a single die for use in the pressing of multiple discs. Almost all commercially delivered discs are created with this method.

WARNING In general, these discs are designed to last decades, but manufacturing problems with a few runs led to rotting prematurely. Rotting is a corrosion of the aluminum layer of the disc due to poor construction. Either the plastic substrate separates and the aluminum is exposed to air, or chemicals from the label corrode the aluminum, making a disk unreadable. Since this does not affect write-once and rewritable disks, the computer investigator is unlikely to encounter evidence files on these but may need commercial software installs from them.

CD-Rs and DVD-Rs share a common technology with rewritable versions of the same media. Both use a dye layer in which pits are burned into the media, exposing the underlying reflective layer to store data by a hardware recorder. The write-once versions actually burn the die itself from the areas that are being written. The rewritable versions change the properties of the die, which can then be returned to its original state through annealing with a lower pow-ered laser beam to create the same effect. Restoration of erased rewritable media is not feasible with commonly available tools. Reading all formats of CD and DVD media can generally be accomplished with a basic DVD-ROM drive. Ensure the drive used supports –R, +R, –RW, and +RW to ensure the broadest media compatibility.

Microsoft uses a separate file system from the standard FAT and NTFS file systems for storage on optical media. CD File System (CDFS) is a version of the ISO 9660 standard for optical storage. Limitations in structure naming with this file system meant directories deeper than eight levels were not supported. Likewise, file system limitations prevented long file names (more than 32 char-acters), so file names may have been truncated when copying. The Joliet exten-sions to ISO 9660 included Unicode support as well as longer file name support, removing truncation as an issue for later CDs. Because of the trunca-tion, file names may not match, so a hash analysis or file search may need to be performed in order to identify specific content.

> **NOTE** Another file system, Hierarchical File System (HFS), may be present in hybrid discs. HFS was developed for Macintosh systems, and although rare, combination CDFS/HFS discs do exist.

To further extend the capabilities of optical media specifically for DVD sup-port, the Universal Disk Format (UDF) standard was adopted. UDF provides support for both long file names and Unicode characters, in addition to other enhancements allowing for rewritable disks as well as non-PC applications. UDF support has been present in Microsoft products since Windows 98 and is now broadly supported. Two directories, VIDEO_TS and AUDIO_TS, are spe-cial in the UDF file system and are used for playing video and audio DVDs, respectively, indicating that the disk may have additional audio/video content in addition to the data. A backward-compatible version called UDF-Bridge, which allowed ISO 9660 compatibility, was popular for a time but is no longer frequently used.

CD/DVD REPAIR

The most common problem with a forensic analysis of optical media is scratches on the surface of the disk. There are two basic ways to address scratches: Try different readers or repair the media. The first step is to try different players. Some players are better with vertical or horizontal scratches based on laser/sensor quality and placement than others. If possible, try multiple drives before attempting a repair.

(continued)

CD/DVD REPAIR *(continued)*

If, after trying multiple drives, an optical disc still is not readable, the first step in repair should be to clean the disc, making sure that physical evidence folks get that fingerprint before the disk is cleaned. To clean the disc, rub lightly with a dry lens cleaning cloth or other soft, lint-free cloth from the center of the disc to the outside in straight lines. If persistent dirt is present, liquid soap and water can be used. Avoid using other cleaning products, as they may damage the disc surface.

After a thorough cleaning, repeat the attempts to read the disc. If the disc still is not readable, the scratches themselves will have to be repaired. Scratches that breach the layer below the plastic likely cannot be repaired. Any scratches in the plastic itself may be buffed out with the proper abrasive. Commercial abrasives are available to repair the scratches, but plain white toothpaste works well also.

To repair the disc, use a clean, dry cloth and apply a small amount of abrasive to the worst scratch present. Rub in a straight line from the center of the disc until the scratch has lessened. Clean the disc as noted previously and retry. Repeated attempts at reducing the impact of a single scratch may be necessary, in addition to the repair of other scratches to get the disc to be readable.

Use of the motorized disc cleaners is not advisable. They generally work by spinning the disc, increasing the risk of introducing rotational scratches to the surface. It may be time consuming to repair the disc by hand, but it is safer as well.

NOTE Optical media starts at the center of the disc and reads outward in a spiral fashion; scratches that are parallel to the outer circumference are generally worse than one perpendicular to it. Cleaning across the spirals reduces the risk of introducing the more damaging type of scratch.

USB Flash Drives

Flash memory–based thumb drives that plug in to the Universal Serial Bus (USB) ports of a computer are now almost ubiquitous. Flash drives in the form of key chains, Swiss Army knives, and watches, which store upward of four gigabytes of data in a solid-state format, can all be purchased. Searching a suspect for the presence of these devices is now likely to bear fruit on a computer investigation.

Flash memory is a specific type of electrically erasable, programmable read-only memory (EEPROM). The EEPROM contains billions of transistors, each of which is capable of storing a charge through the use of a thin oxide plate which represents either a zero or a one. The charge itself remains present even after the electrical source is removed, differentiating the removal storage devices from other types of EEPROMS like CMOS RAM, used for storing BIOS in most computers.

Compared with hard disks, flash memory is faster, lighter, and has a greater bit density. Additionally, because flash devices have no moving parts, mechanical wear is not generally an issue, and their reliability predictions are much higher than those of hard disks. Unfortunately, the cost per gigabyte for flash memory is several hundred times that of comparable hard disks. Although they are continuing to grow in popularity and bit density, flash memory devices must drop in price exponentially before they can be considered as direct replacements for hard disks.

CASE STUDY: MISSING USB KEY

During the course of a forensic investigation into the theft of confidential information, we began to suspect an individual had been using a USB flash drive to remove information from the company's premises. The suspect of the investigation, a marketing manager, had given two weeks notice, and her manager found out from co-workers the suspect was going to work for a competitor.

The suspect's laptop was acquired and analyzed for any suspicious Internet activity (for example, the sending of files) with no success. An analysis of the mount points in the suspect's registry (HKEY_Local_Machine\System\MountedDevices) showed additional drive letters beyond what was on the system currently. The extraneous drive letter (F:) shown as a mount point had the words "STORAGE" and "Removable Media" in the value of the key.

A quick search of the hard drive turned up numerous .lnk files pointing to documents with suspicious file names on the F: drive. The suspect's purchasing card transactions were reviewed, and a Lexar Jumpdrive USB Flash Drive had been purchased several months earlier. The Jumpdrive was not found in the suspect's office and was considered company property, as it had been purchased with corporate funds.

The company requested the Jumpdrive and noted they would hold the employee's last paycheck until it was returned. The drive was shipped back, received a few days later, and turned over to the analysis team. Using EnCase, the flash drive was analyzed and found to have had a recent mass deletion of information relating to the company's new product launch campaign. The company considered this information to be very sensitive, and the loss to a competitor would be potentially damaging.

The company elected not to engage law enforcement (which, in the country in question, was not likely to be interested in intellectual property theft) but revised the product's marketing strategy based on the suspected disclosure. The new launch campaign differed significantly from the previously designed campaign, reducing the overall value of the leaked information to the competitor.

WARNING It is illegal to withhold a final paycheck in the United States, even if one suspects that a former employee still has company equipment. This particular employee was in an Asian country with less strict employee protection laws.

Flash memory is used under numerous brand names and is included in many non-computer devices such as digital cameras, MP3 players, and watches. Different forms of flash memory exist, including CompactFlash, Smart Media, and Memory Sticks. Through the integration of USB functionality, flash devices can be directly attached to a computer's USB port and in Windows 98 and later recognized as a hard disk for purposes of reading and writing.

USB flash drives are generally used for portable file storage and can even contain bootable operating systems. Some organizations have banned USB flash devices for just this reason. Individuals who want to acquire company secrets can copy gigabytes of information at a time and walk out with it on a key chain.

Forensic analysis of flash devices depends on the operating system present. Most flash devices come with a FAT32 partition, but many can be formatted with NTFS, EXT2, and other partition types as well. If one encounters a USB flash device that Windows does not recognize, it may have been formatted with a file system that Windows cannot read. In this case, the investigator must obtain a driver for that file system or try loading it on another platform.

TIP If the device is viewed with a hex editor such as WinHex, the partition table on the USB drive can be examined to determine the type of partition present. A list of partition types is included as an appendix.

USB flash drives might have a write-protect switch. If they do, this switch should be set to write protect the device before plugging in to a Windows system. For non-USB flash devices, the computer investigator may need to use a third-party card reader. USB-based combination readers for Smartmedia, Compact Flash, and Memory Sticks are available and should be part of any analysis lab. Embedded flash devices may have other interfaces such as FireWire. These may be directly connected to an analysis machine as necessary.

The forensic analysis of a USB flash drive is the same as the analysis of a hard disk. The major factor in analysis is the underlying partition type. Flash memory works on blocks instead of sectors, but from an examiner's perspective, the differences are minimal.

One item of note: Many USB flash drives are now being shipped with password protection capabilities. For most of these devices, the password protection is software- or hardware-based and does not encrypt the flash drive itself, but the partition itself may be inaccessible without the password. Although device-specific password crackers exist, for many of the systems a brute-force password guesser and a dictionary may be required to obtain access. This is where password re-use comes in handy; the individual may have used the same password in a more accessible area.

Hard Disks

Hard disks are the primary source of forensic information in most of today's computer investigations. The disks themselves span a number of technologies that define the logic used by the controller. They share similar underlying structures. Hard disk acquisitions may range in size from 10MB for the original PC hard disks (although the likelihood of finding one that is still physically sound is minimal) to multi-terabyte arrays.

The underlying principles of a hard disk are the same as those of a floppy. A charge is read from or written to a rotating platter using a movable head. The disk platter itself is broken up into sectors and tracks and holds logical data in partitions. There are a few significant differences between floppy disk storage and hard disk storage from an investigative standpoint:

- **Hard disks can use multiple platters.** Each hard disk may have two, three, or more platters present to increase the amount of data that can be stored on the drive. Each platter is two-sided, and multiple read/write heads are present (one per platter side). The introduction of multiple platters also introduces the concept of a cylinder. A cylinder is a logical structure that represents the same track on all of the platters in a drive.

- **Read/write heads do not make physical contact with the platters**. The read/write heads on a hard disk do not make physical contact with the drive surface, but instead float on an air cushion caused by a higher rotational speed (7,200 or 10,000 RPMs for the current models). Because the read/write heads are not in direct contact with platters, the track wear-out experienced by floppy disks is not as common. If the read/write head makes contact with the platter at the higher rotational speed, it is generally fatal for the drive.

- **Data densities of hard disk platters are higher.** With higher data densities, the storage capacity of hard drives is much greater. Likewise, the ability to view each individual sector in an analysis becomes impractical, focusing most efforts on automated analysis or logical file-system level analysis. Additionally, higher data densities mean physical issues with a platter (for example, the presence of dust) have a much greater impact on the overall amount of data affected.

- **Hard disk interfaces are diverse.** Between the numerous variations of SCSI and ATA hard disks, a computer investigator might need to have a large number of interface cards and connectors to support investigations. If interface cards or connectors are not available, the original computer may be needed to perform an acquisition of data on the drive.

NOTE A hard disk crash used to mean that the heads literally crashed into the platter, destroying both the head and the platter itself. Now crash is used to denote less fatal failures as well, such as damage to a small number of sectors or even data corruption.

The smallest amount of data a hard disk can write to is a sector, generally consisting of 512 bytes of data plus additional byte inaccessible beyond the drive logic itself. The location and number of sectors on a disk are determined and written permanently with a *low-level format* at the factory.

A typical sector layout for a hard disk is shown in Figure 3-3. The Intersector Gap refers to the area between sectors on the disk. The Prefix contains the sector and track number to allow the read/write head to determine location as well as a damaged bit to mark a sector as unusable if it becomes unreadable. The Sync field is an alternating pattern used by the drive for synchronizations. The Error Correcting Code (ECC) field is added by the drive hardware to detect bit-level errors in the data.

Since a sector is the smallest amount of space that can be written or read by drive hardware, any writes of less than 512 bytes (or which have a remainder after being broken into 512-byte chunks) will have additional sector slack written. For earlier versions of Windows (except Windows NT 4, 2000/2003, and XP), Microsoft products wrote the next bits from memory to this slack space, and it could be mined for fragments of data (because of this it is sometimes called RAM slack). Recent versions of Windows pad the extra sector space with repeating characters to prevent the inadvertent writing of this information. Tools such as EnCase from Guidance and GetSlack from NTI allow for the forensic gathering and analysis of this space.

Internal hard disks are based on two primary interface technology trees: SCSI and ATA. Within these trees multiple interfaces as well as generations of technology exist, but the basic operations of the drives remain the same, and backward compatibility (logic-wise if not connector-wise) is generally supported.

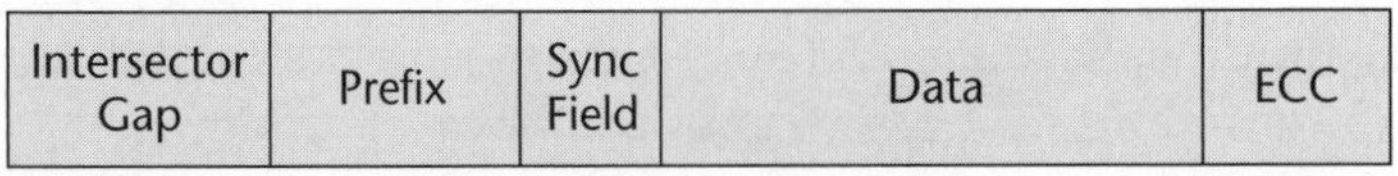

Intersector Gap	Prefix	Sync Field	Data	ECC

Figure 3-3: Hard Disk Sector Layout

HARD DISK PASSWORDS

The ATA-3 standard, released in 1997 as an update to the previous ATA-2 disk standard used by the majority of personal computers, provided an optional new security feature: the hard disk password. This password is separate and distinct from any BIOS passwords that might protect the computer at power-on in that it protects any operations to or from the protected disk. Although it applies to both laptop and desktop drives, it is most frequently used on laptop (2.5-inch) disks, most notably with the IBM Travelstar drives.

The hard disk password is of particular concern to the computer investigator in that it protects the drive itself and is actually written to the disk platter. The ATA-3 specification does not require that it be written to the disk platter, but in practice, the major manufacturers do so. Unlike BIOS passwords, which can be bypassed by removing the drive and placing it into an analysis machine, the hard disk password is part of the drive itself, and any operations to the drive are prevented by the on-drive logic without the password. The data on the drive platters is not encrypted, but access to the raw data is prevented without the password.

There are actually two hard disk passwords: a User password and a Master password. The User password can be set by the user to be anything up to 32 bytes in size. The Master password is generally set by the system vendor but can be reset by the user or the organization if it is known.

Upon bootup, any computer the hard disk is placed in will require the user to enter a password to allow any read/write operations to that drive. Standard duplication hardware and write-blockers will not bypass this control as it resides on the drive itself. The User password unlocks the drive. The Master password either unlocks the drive (in the High security setting) or only allows the Erase operation on the drive (in the Maximum security setting).

If the User password is unavailable to the investigator, the Master password may be available from the drive manufacturer, computer manufacturer, or the institution that manages the machine. It is a common practice for corporations to set the security on drives to High and use a common Master password as the escrow strategy. If the security level is set to Maximum, the User password will still be needed to read the drive.

There is no software solution for recovering hard drive passwords as the control resides in the actual drive controller. There is no way to bypass the password by removing platters as the digital logic is model-specific, and the password is on the platter itself. This leaves the investigator with three options, aside from analyzing the platters directly with an STM:

◆ Attempt to guess the password. The disk will lock after three invalid attempts, but a power reset will allow for an unlimited number of overall attempts.

◆ Send the disk to a third party, which will read the platters directly or overwrite the password on the disk using custom drive logic.

◆ Purchase custom hardware to force the password.

(continued)

HARD DISK PASSWORDS *(continued)*

Depending on the circumstances, the password may be guessable (for example, it may be a commonly used password or the same as a more easily crackable password from that user) or otherwise obtainable (for example, through social engineering). Otherwise, if there are a limited number of these encountered, the second option given previously to outsource the recovery is fairly inexpensive and a reasonable solution. If these are frequently encountered or the drives contain data that cannot be sent outside (for example, classified or higher information and corporate secrets), purchasing the custom hardware may be the best alternative.

Small Computer Systems Interface (SCSI) is a generic, high-speed interface technology first developed in the 1980s that allowed for the transmission of data in a parallel fashion. SCSI allows for multiple devices to be chained together on the same cable and was originally used on the Macintosh platform and later in servers because of performance advantages when multi-tasking. Versions of the SCSI interface are now the most frequently used interface on Windows servers, with a smaller percentage of desktops and laptops using SCSI-based hard drives.

NOTE Although there are serial and even network-based versions of SCSI, the original specification and most hard disk connections that utilize SCSI use a parallel interface.

SCSI disks represent a challenge for the computer investigator in that each generation has introduced at least one new connection standard, some with multiple connection standards. For example, SCSI-2 introduced Fast, Wide, and Fast-Wide variations with differing size 50 and 68 pin connectors. Low and High Voltage Differential (LVD and HVD) signaling standards likewise complicate things, and the need for terminators at the end of a SCSI chain requires even more equipment.

To best address SCSI disks, acquisition should be done whenever possible using the original host system's hardware. For standalone SCSI disks found during an investigation, the examiner will need to review the drive label or contact the manufacturer to determine what SCSI standard it uses (SCSI-1, SCSI-2, or SCSI-3), which variant it supports of that standard (for example, Ultra160), what signaling it uses (anything beyond Ultra2 SCSI should use LVD), and what connector size and gender is required. A compatible controller card and any required cables/adapters can then be obtained to acquire the drive. A good forensics lab has 50 and 68-pin gender changers, a host of adapters, and a few different controller cards available.

AT-Attachment, or ATA drives (sometimes called IDE, EIDE, or UltraDMA) are more frequently encountered on Windows workstations. There are multiple backward-compatible ATA standards, ATA-1,2, and 3 as well as ATA/ATAPI-4, 5, and 6. An ATA/ATAPI-6 controller will be able to connect to drives from all three generations. Enhancements between generations include hard disk passwords (see sidebar), increased throughput, and monitoring capabilities.

WARNING IDE, EIDE, and UltraDMA are all incorrect references for ATA drives. IDE refers to Integrated Drive Electronics, having digital logic present with the drive itself, which all modern disks, including SCSI, USB, and FireWire disks, use. EIDE was introduced by Western Digital in the early 1990s as a marketing term for proprietary extensions to ATA. UltraDMA is a performance enhancement to the ATA standard allowing for fast direct memory access for transfers.

ATA drives allow up to four devices on two channels (two devices per channel) to be connected to a system, including non-hard disk drives like CD and DVD-ROMs. Older versions contained jumper settings designating one drive to be a Master and the second a Slave on each channel. Newer drives use a Cable Select jumper feature to eliminate the need to designate these beforehand, although jumpers may need to be changed on older drives to get an analysis system to recognize them. Similarly, all drives manufactured in the last decade or so will automatically have their sizes and configurations in sectors, tracks, and cylinders recognized by BIOS, but older systems might require this information to be manually entered by the investigator.

There are three relevant connections for ATA drives, and all should be available to the computer investigator. 44-pin laptop connectors, 40-pin desktop connectors, and new Serial-ATA connectors can all be read by a Serial-ATA controller card with 40- and 44- pin converters.

Lately, external hard disks have been making inroads into the market. External hard drives are based on one of two technologies, USB and FireWire, with multiple speeds of each available. Both drive technologies have the same underlying drive structures as ATA and SCSI, but the interfaces were designed for external system use.

Universal Serial Bus (USB) was designed as a replacement for the myriad of differing serial and parallel connections to external peripherals. Early USB specifications for USB 1 and 1.1 were too slow for general-purpose external hard drives, but USB 2.0 connections permit speeds approaching that of internal drives. USB drives can be connected to a USB 2.0 port on an analysis machine and acquired the same as any other drive. There are two different USB connection sizes, type A and type B. Cables with each size (or an adapter) are a necessity for both hard disks and other USB device connections. Ideally, the analysis machine will also have a USB 2.0 hub for connecting additional USB 2.0 devices as necessary.

FireWire (IEEE 1394) was originally designed specifically for fast transfer rates to external devices. Initially popular on the Macintosh platform as well as in consumer electronics (especially camcorders), FireWire is now common on Windows machines. Like USB, an analysis machine should have at least one FireWire port available for acquisition. Likewise, both 4- and 6-pin connection cables (or an adapter) are a required in a forensic lab.

Physical damage to a hard disk is generally not recoverable outside of a laboratory environment. Logic board damage, head damage, or platter damage may be repairable using a clean room and replacement circuitry, but this is generally beyond the capabilities of a corporate or local law enforcement forensic lab. If physical damage to a drive is suspected, it is best not to allow the drive to spin-up and to transfer it intact in its present state to a clean room lab with reconstruction capabilities, such as those offered by Kroll Ontrack.

RAID ARRAYS

To provide fault tolerance, many server-based hard disk systems are arranged into groupings of disks called RAID (Redundant Array of Inexpensive Disks) arrays. The drives in these arrays contain all or a portion of the total data available in addition to error correcting code, depending on the RAID version used. RAID arrays can be configured through hardware (with a RAID controller card) or through software (Microsoft Windows NT, 2000, and 2003 server products). Most RAID subsystems use SCSI disks, although ATA-based RAID arrays are now being used on inexpensive servers and workstations.

RAID comes in four primary configurations a forensic examiner is likely to encounter: RAID 0, RAID 1, RAID 5, and RAID 0+1 (RAID 10).

◆ **RAID 0.** Two or more disks have the data striped (broken into chunks with each chunk residing on a different disks) between all of the disks in the array. RAID 0 configurations are occasionally used on workstations for performance (or to maximize usable storage space in one drive) but have poor reliability (the reliability of the array is actually $1/n$ that of a single drive, in which n is the number of drives in the array). RAID 0 arrays are best examined in place using the host system's controller or software. Missing disks from a RAID 0 array are a problem for examiners. They cannot be reconstructed, and the data on them is lost. Depending on the stripe size, whole files may be lost or large pieces of existing files may be missing. If the Master File Table is missing or partially missing, names of the lost files may not even be recoverable.

◆ **RAID 1.** Frequently called mirroring, RAID 1 uses two drives with identical information written to both. Write performance can be affected with mirrored disks, and half of the usable drive space is dedicated to redundancy, effectively doubling the reliability over a single disk drive itself.

For a computer investigator, a missing or corrupt drive from a mirrored configuration is not an issue. The remaining drive contains a duplicate of all of the information. Only a single drive from a mirrored array needs to be acquired for analysis in most situations. There are two exceptions. Drives that had previously been in other systems may have legacy data that differs in unused sectors. Similarly, if the drives are of a different size, which they can be with some controllers, part of the large drive will be unused by the array and may contain legacy information. If a duplicate is needed of the drive, either one of the pair can be taken for analysis or another drive placed in the broken array to allow the data to be reconstructed.

◆ RAID 5. Most common on server disk systems, RAID 5 provides increased fault tolerance with a minimal amount of storage lost to redundancy through the use of striping with distributed parity information. A RAID 5 array requires a minimum of three disks, with $1/n$ of the total disk space lost to parity information, where n is the number of drives in the array. RAID 5 arrays are most frequently acquired using the controller hardware on the host system. The loss of a single disk in a RAID 5 array can be easily recovered. Replacing the disk with a blank in the host system will automatically regenerate the missing information using the parity bits. Loss of multiple disks will result in lost data, with fragments recoverable from the remaining drives.

◆ RAID 0+1 and RAID 10. Combining the positive and negative qualities of mirrors and striping, theses versions of RAID represent mirrored stripes and striped mirrors, respectively. Each utilizes two banks of two disks in a mirrored configuration of two stripe sets or as a stripe across two mirrored sets. (More than two disks can be used as long as the number is divisible by two. These are less commonly found, however, because this technique is popular with ATA-based workstations that have four channels for drives.) In each case, half of the storage space is lost to redundancy. For the investigator, these systems are best acquired using the host system. If a single drive is missing, the mirrored set may be used. If two drives are missing, recovery may still be possible if two drives with complementary striping are remaining. Loss of more than two drives presents the same issues noted with RAID 0 previously.

A final configuration is occasionally encountered that is not a RAID configuration: JBOD or Just a Bunch of Disks. JBOD arrays aggregate disk space at the cost of reliability (all disks used for storage with no redundancy). Each disk in a JBOD array can be analyzed independently for content and is likely to contain whole chunks of information, but the drive containing the MFT is needed for full reconstruction. The data on a missing disk from a JBOD array is lost, although the MFT may still have references to what data was present.

Additional Resources

Refer to the following list for additional resources:

AnaDisk (from NTI)
  `www.forensics-intl.com/anadisk.html`

FastBloc Write Blocker From Guidance Software
  `www.guidancesoftware.com/products/FastBloc/index.shtm`

GetSlack (from NTI)
  `www.forensics-intl.com/getslack.html`

ISO9660 Details
  `alumnus.caltech.edu/~pje/iso9660.html?the_id=34`

Kroll OnTrack
  `www.krollontrack.com`

Microsoft Windows History
  `www.microsoft.com/windows/WinHistoryDesktop.mspx`

MTF Tape Format
  `http://www.layton-graphics.com/mtf/MTF_100a.PDF`

Nortek Hard Disk Password Recovery
  `www.nortek.on.ca/`

Slammer Worm Analysis
  `www.computer.org/security/v1n4/j4wea.htm`

Ultrablock Write Blocker From Digital Intelligence
  `www.digitalintel.com/ultrablock.htm`

Vogon International Hard Disk Password Recovery
  `www.vogon-international.com`

Partitions and File Systems

Windows systems operate off the concept of logical areas of a disk being appropriated for individual file systems. These logical areas are called partitions, and they might contain different operating systems or file systems. Additionally, available space on a disk might not be partitioned at all and be classified as unpartitioned space. This space is inaccessible to the logical structures of an operating system but can hold both current (if intentionally hidden) as well as legacy data.

Master Boot Record

Disk space is apportioned into partitions through the use of the master boot record (MBR). The MBR determines how partitions are allocated space, what type those partitions are, and which partition is the active partition. The MBR is always located in sector zero, track zero of the disk drive so ROM BIOS knows where to look for executable code.

WINDOWS BOOT PROCESS

Understanding the hardware boot process used by Windows allows the computer investigator to contextualize the partitioning schemes used on a hard disk. The boot process itself takes place as a transition from hardware to software, and the details of booting can provide insight into the use of an investigation of multi-partition and multiple operating system cases.

The boot process starts with the powering on of the computer. Pressing the power button no longer controls a relay but instead makes a contact that allows the PS_ON signal to be sent to the power supply, turning on the power to the motherboard itself. There is always a low-power, 5V supply to the motherboard in ATX-style cases whether the power switch is turned on or not. Some power supply units still provide a second, relay-based switch on the supply itself, which actually does disable the main AC power source in addition to the power button.

After power is applied, the CPU performs a basic initialization and then reads the system's ROM BIOS for the location of the first instructions to run. The first instructions, which perform a Power-On Self Test (POST), are then executed. The POST validates that the hardware and CMOS RAM are intact and functioning and then turns control back to the ROM BIOS to search for a boot device.

The boot device location is read from CMOS RAM and can be a floppy disk, hard disk, CD-ROM, network, or other device. In the case of the hard disk, the ROM BIOS reads the first sector of the disk, the MBR, always located at sector zero, track zero for information on the partitions present. After determining the boot partition, a JMP instruction in the boot sector of that partition is loaded and directs the CPU to the location of the first OS code to execute.

In the case of Windows NT/2000/XP, the first instructions to run are the bootstrap code located in the NTLDR. NTLDR provides for the capability to address all of the RAM on the system as well as the ability to read from and write to the file system. The boot.ini file is read from the root directory to determine the location of the operating system to be loaded. For dual boot machines, a menu is provided to select the operating system. If the operating system to be loaded is Windows NT/2000/XP, the NTDetect.exe program is run from the root directory to determine what hardware is present.

The Ntoskrnl.exe and Hal.dll kernel files are then loaded by NTLDR to provide for the raw operating system kernel's booting. These files are located in %SystemRoot%/System32 and provide the basis for later systems operations. After loading these files, the Windows Registry is read, and the associated hardware profile information loaded (or the specific profile selected by the user if multiple profiles are present). Additionally, any necessary device drivers are loaded at this point.

Execute control is transferred to the Ntoskrnl.exe file, which completes the boot sequence. The Smss.exe Session Manager code is executed as are any registry programs set to load on startup. Winlogon.exe is executed to begin the login process, and the Local Security Administration subsystem (lsass.exe) program is executed, culminating in the login prompt for the user.

> For Windows 9x, the IO.SYS and MSDOS.SYS files are loaded in place of the NTLDR. The config.sys and autoexec.bat files are executed to provide any basic configuration information, and then control is transferred over to the actual Windows kernel (win386.exe). Until the point win386.exe takes over, the system is functioning under the limitations of the older DOS operating system.
>
> The win386.exe file reads the registry and loads the necessary device drivers for the basic system hardware. The system fonts are loaded, as is the basic display system. Any specific display drivers are loaded, and finally the desktop and any associated startup programs are executed.

Each drive may be allocated up to four primary partitions, defined in the MBR. Each partition is described in the partition table with a 16-byte entry as shown in Table 4-1.

Table 4-1   Master Boot Record Partition Definition

LOCATION	# OF BYTES	IDENTIFIER	NOTES
00h	1	Active flag	Set to either 00h or 80h (active), this flag represents status of the partition.
01h	1	Start head	The starting head of the partition
02h	1 (10 bits)	Start sector	The starting sector of the partition
02h	1 (6 bits)	Start cylinder	The starting cylinder of the partition
04h	1	File system type	A designator representing the file system present on the partition. See Appendix D for details on the individual operating system types.
05h	1	End head	The ending head of the partition
06h	1 (10 bits)	End sector	The ending sector of the partition
06h	1 (6 bits)	End cylinder	The ending cylinder of the partition
08h	4	Offset sectors	The number of sectors from the beginning of the partition table to the start of the partition
0Bh	4	Total length	The total length of the partition, in sectors

Only one partition may be designated as active at any time (through the assignment of the value 80h). The boot sector of this partition is provided control of the system upon initial boot, although it might contain a boot loader allowing the transfer of control to other partitions. Windows refers to the active partition as the boot partition. The MBR may be viewed directly using a hex editor and viewing Sector zero, Track zero of a drive. The first two Partition Table entries and part of the bootstrap code are shown in Figure 4-1 using WinHex, which provides a template to view the hex information present.

WARNING The boot partition should not be confused with the system partition. In Windows, the boot partition contains the jump instruction to the location of the boot loader, but the system partition, which contains the operating system, may be different.

In addition to primary partitions, there can be other partitions present called *extended partitions*. An extended partition contains an entry in the MBR but instead of pointing to a bootable file system (extended partitions are not generally bootable), the entry points to a virtual MBR located in the place of that partitions boot sector. Under that extended partition entry, additional logical partitions may be added, increasing the total number of partitions permitted on a disk.

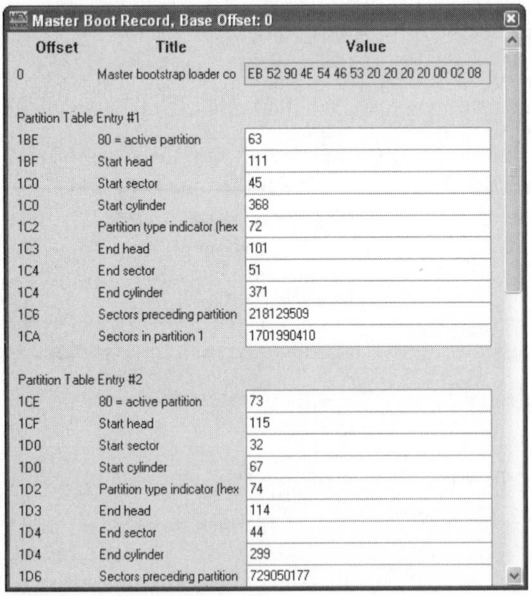

Offset	Title	Value
	Master Boot Record, Base Offset: 0	
0	Master bootstrap loader co	EB 52 90 4E 54 46 53 20 20 20 20 00 02 08
	Partition Table Entry #1	
1BE	80 = active partition	63
1BF	Start head	111
1C0	Start sector	45
1C0	Start cylinder	368
1C2	Partition type indicator (hex	72
1C3	End head	101
1C4	End sector	51
1C4	End cylinder	371
1C6	Sectors preceding partition	218129509
1CA	Sectors in partition 1	1701990410
	Partition Table Entry #2	
1CE	80 = active partition	73
1CF	Start head	115
1D0	Start sector	32
1D0	Start cylinder	67
1D2	Partition type indicator (hex	74
1D3	End head	114
1D4	End sector	44
1D4	End cylinder	299
1D6	Sectors preceding partition	729050177

Figure 4-1: Hard disk master boot record

TIP Command line tools to display partition information are available for all versions of Windows. For Windows 9*x* and NT, the `fdisk` command allows for the viewing of partition information. Likewise, for the Windows 2000/XP/2003 family, the `diskpart` command allows for the same information to be viewed.

If when analyzing the MBR you find additional partitions that do not appear in Windows, you will want to look at the File System Type field to determine what file system the partition is based on. That said, this can even be altered if the suspect really wants to disguise the system type, in which case an analysis of the boot sector of that partition is necessary to determine the file system present. If non-Windows file systems are present, an analysis tool capable of analyzing those file systems must be used (such as EnCase) or the appropriate Installable File System (IFS) module for Windows loaded.

Any discrepancy in the size of the disk and the total size allocated to partitions might indicate the presence of unallocated space. Unallocated space is not assigned to any particular partition and may represent a deleted partition, an area of the drive intentionally used to hide information from the operating system, or space that was never assigned to a partition.

FIXING THE MBR

Because the MBR controls the boot process itself, it is a popular target for virus infection (although most antivirus programs now protect the MBR to some degree). When a virus or other mechanism corrupts the MBR, the computer investigator might need to repair it to boot a given disk. Repairing an MBR can be fairly straightforward or a major challenge, depending upon the corruption type and the number/types of partitions present.

For Windows 9*x* and NT, the `fdisk` command is used to view, create, delete, and alter partitions. One less-known switch of `fdisk` is the `/mbr` switch, which reconstructs the MBR. To repair an MBR on a Windows 9*x* or NT machine, do the following:

♦ Reboot the machine using a bootable DOS disk that contains the fdisk.exe program.

♦ Type `fdisk /mbr` at the DOS prompt. Wait for the program to finish reconstructing the MBR.

♦ Remove the floppy disk and reboot.

The fdisk program will not function properly with Windows 2000/XP/2003. In Windows 2000/XP/2003, the Microsoft Recovery Console provides the tools necessary to automatically repair or reconstruct the MBR. To use the Recovery Console, do the following:

◆ Insert a bootable Windows CD for the relevant version of the operating system into the drive and ensure the CD is the first boot device.

◆ At the Welcome screen, type R to enter the Recovery Console.

◆ Enter the Administrator password.

◆ At the command prompt, type `fixboot` to repair the Windows boot sector.

◆ After repairing the boot sector, type `fixmbr` to repair the MBR.

◆ Remove the CD and reboot.

Both toolsets only repair the bootstrap code on the MBR. They do not actually repair the partition tables. To repair the partition tables, the investigator needs to know where each partition begins and ends as well as the type of partition. To gather the data to enter into the partition table:

◆ Search the drive using WinHex for the values 55 AAh, which indicate the end of a boot sector. This value will be offset by 01 FEh from the start of the boot sector for Windows machines.

◆ Note the start head, sector, and cylinder from WinHex of the location.

◆ Note the partition type name. It should be in readable ASCII right after the 3-byte-JMP instruction at the start of the sector. Look up the appropriate partition type for that name in the appendix.

◆ Repeat the search to find the next unique boot sector start. Compare the values to the previously found values. Copies of a boot sector might be present on the same partition.

◆ Find the start of that boot sector and note the head, sector, and cylinder of the byte immediately preceding it.

◆ Calculate the number of sectors as (end - start)/512.

◆ Calculate the offset by subtracting that MBR partition table start location from the start location of the boot sector.

◆ Repeat to find any other partitions present.

◆ Enter the information found directly into the MBR partition table at the appropriate locations.

When an intact, deleted partition is present (for example, the MBR has less than four records and the sectors of the unallocated space can be determined), the examiner will want to use a hex editor to view the boot sector of the suspected deleted partition. Unless a secure wiping utility is used, when a partition is deleted, only the MBR entry for that partition is erased. By reconstructing that MBR entry (use a tool such as WinHex to find the start and stop locations of the partition and partition type then add the appropriate

MBR hex values), the partition can be made accessible to forensic analysis. Even if inaccessible, a hex editor can be used to search the unallocated space for text fragments and other data remnants.

> **TIP** WinHex is a forensic Hex Editor, providing both traditional hex editing capabilities in addition to support for forensic searches and slack analysis. WinHex is produced by X-Ways Trace and can be found online at www.winhex.com.

Windows File Systems

Microsoft Windows comprises two main file systems of interest to the forensic examiner: FAT and NTFS. The original Windows files system was based on the FAT 16 file system. Later versions of Windows, starting with NT 3.1, were built on the enhanced file system, NTFS. Both file systems have characteristics that make them valuable for an examiner, and this section examines both the strengths and weaknesses of the file systems and how they are used. Future versions of Windows might use WinFS, a database-driven file system currently under development and slated for release after the Vista version of Windows. Table 4-2 provides an overview of the file system compatibility of different Windows versions.

File systems are created by formatting a specific partition on a hard disk. Formatting writes the partition boot record (also called the partition boot sector, or boot sector) for the file system chosen to the starting sector of that partition, in addition to updating the partition table to reflect the new partition type. Microsoft provides both visual and command line formatting tools.

Table 4-2 File System Compatibility

VERSION	NTFS	FAT16	FAT32
Windows 95	✗	✓	✗
Windows 95 OSR2	✗	✓	✓
Windows 98	✗	✓	✓
Windows ME	✗	✓	✓
Windows NT 4	✓	✓	✗
Windows 2000	✓	✓	✓
Windows XP	✓	✓	✓
Windows 2003	✓	✓	✓

When reformatting an existing drive, Microsoft leaves the existing data in place. The partition boot sector is replaced as is the file system type in the MBR, if necessary. The actual contents of the files present prior to formatting are still there and can be searched and recovered using the tools mentioned in Chapter 10. Quick formatting and standard formatting perform similarly in Windows. The difference is that the standard format performs a disk integrity check sector-by-sector to identify any areas with read errors.

Windows allows for the addressing of individual partitions, which have been formatted using drive letters. A drive letter designates the logical name (for example, C:) assigned to a partition. By convention, the A: and B: drives are reserved for floppy disks, the C: drive is assigned to the operating system drive, and the D: through Z: drives are assigned to other partitions, network drives, and removable media.

FAT

The File Allocation Table (FAT) file system traces its history back to the days of Microsoft DOS (MS-DOS) with FAT12. The "12" in FAT12 refers to the number of clusters that the operating system could handle.

NOTE It actually goes back to a predecessor operating system of DOS, CP/M. The first version of QDOS, which became MS-DOS, in 1980 supported FAT12.

The original FAT file system was capable of addressing 2^{12} clusters of a 512-byte fixed size. This allowed the file system to address 2,220,032 bytes of memory (512×2^{12}) or approximately 2MB of file space. This was adequate addressing for the available 360KB floppy drives available at the time but quickly grew dated as floppy drive capacity increased and hard drives were introduced in the PC marketplace. FAT12 is still used as the file system of choice for many floppy disks (including standard 1.44MB floppies).

NOTE A cluster is the smallest area a file system can directly address.

As hard disks became available in the mid-1980s, the need for a larger file system was addressed with the introduction of FAT16. Capable of addressing up to 2^{16} clusters, the FAT16 file system additionally allowed cluster sizes of 2K to 32K bytes. This permitted the addressing of drives up to 2,147,483,648, or 2GB in size ($2^{16} \times 32,768$). FAT16 was the original file system in Windows 95 and is still used for defining smaller partitions (for example, BIOS tool partitions) in current drives.

In the mid-1990s, drive capacity grew beyond 2GB and the need to address drives larger than that permitted by FAT16 led to the development of FAT32 with Windows 95 OSR2 and later Windows 98. FAT32 supports up to 2^{32} clusters,

SECURE DATA WIPING

Recent media stories and journal articles have highlighted problems with standard format commands not deleting data. Indeed, the Microsoft format command itself does not actually alter any drive data, just the metadata on the drive. From a forensic perspective, this is a good thing when recovering files but a bad thing when protecting data from one's own investigations.

Both before and after any investigation, the destination analysis disk should be wiped clean using secure wipe utilities before partitioning and formatting. Wiping involves the writing over of every byte in every sector of the disk with a pattern. Although there are proponents for multi-pass wiping, with the latest hard disks, the recovery possibilities using STM technologies are minimal for anything but top secret-level information. A search of the media shows no commercial endeavors ever having their data recovered maliciously after a single-pass wipe.

For forensic drives, a zero pattern tends to be well received because a disk-level analysis quickly shows that the drive has been adequately wiped. Likewise, any data written to the disk will write over the zero pattern, preventing the possibility of slack data previously existing on the drive being read as part of the investigation. To zero-out a drive, there are several good utilities available. Darik's Boot and Nuke, a floppy-disk and/or CD-based solution, is free and readily available online. Likewise, for those who have Cygwin installed or a Linux box available, using `dd if=/dev/zero of=/dev/hda` accomplishes the same thing from the Linux command line. Finally, those who use EnCase have a built-in disk wiping utility available. This is great for USB and FireWire drives that cannot be directly accessed without special drivers from a bootable floppy disk.

When disposing of disks permanently, the preceding utilities work as well and are recommended for any disks being retired or repurposed. Degaussing of hard disks does not work effectively. The logic circuits would fail if a field strength great enough to completely wipe the platters without residuals were present. Because the voltage requirement for a degausser strong enough to wipe hard disks is fairly high, the secure wipe is a cheaper and safer option.

For those ultra-paranoid about their data being recovered, the best mechanism available is still physical destruction of the disk platters. Shredding and then incinerating appears to be the Department of Defense method of choice. It is difficult to recover data from a solid hunk of metal.

For a definitive look at sanitization, see Garfinkel and Shelat, "A Remembrance of Data Passed: A Study of Disk Sanitization Practices," IEEE Security and Privacy, 2003.

with cluster sizes ranging from 4K to 32K. FAT32 theoretically supports larger cluster sizes and up to 2TB of total addressable storage, but realistically, the upper limit is 64GB per partition for performance reasons.

The original versions of FAT permitted the use of file names of up to 11 characters. (Hence the 8.3 DOS legacy naming convention still in use: eight characters for the file name and three for the extension.) To allow for larger file names (up to 255 characters), Windows introduced VFAT. VFAT is not a new version of FAT, but an extension to FAT16 and FAT32 to allow for long file names to be stored.

FAT clusters have a fixed number of physically addressable sectors per cluster, defined in the boot record. A cluster is the smallest area of space logically addressable by the file system. The file system does not directly reference sector-level information. This leads to an anomaly in disk storage: slack space. This is perhaps best illustrated with an example:

- A FAT16 disk with a cluster size of 32KB needs to store a file containing 1KB of data.

- Because the file system can access only an individual cluster (and not a sector), it must use a full 32KB entry to store the 1KB of data.

- When the 1KB of data is stored, the file system only overwrites the first 1KB of the 32KB cluster, leaving 31KB of old data in place and untouchable until the cluster is reclaimed. This is called slack space.

When conducting a forensic investigation, the slack space noted previously is useful when searching for content from removed files. The searching of slack space in an investigation is detailed in Chapter 5.

The FAT file system retains its name from the File Allocation Table, which identifies the status of individual clusters within a partition. On a FAT partition, the file allocation table is present immediately after the partition boot record. The overall layout of a FAT partition is shown in Figure 4-2.

The boot sector contains the specific information on the layout of the partition and is referenced by the MBR detailed in Chapter 3. The Boot Sector itself contains the meta-information on the structure of the hard disk and is useful to the forensic analyst in determining the starting locations of both the file allocation tables and the data itself. The boot sector on a FAT32 volume is composed of the key entries useful in forensic analysis shown in Table 4-3. (For the full layout, refer to Appendix D.)

Figure 4-2:   FAT partition layout

Table 4-3 FAT32 Boot Sector

OFFSET LOCATION	# OF BYTES	IDENTIFIER	NOTES
03h	8	OEM name	The name of the OS that formatted the partition. Can be used to determine legacy OS presence in the case of reformatted drives.
0Dh	2	# of reserved sectors	The number of sectors reserved for the boot record. This number indicates the beginning of the actual file allocation table.
15h	1	Media type	F0 for a floppy drive, F8 for a hard drive. If the media type is changed, the device might not be recognized properly (although it may still contain valid data).
28h	2	Flags	Reserved for determining FAT mirroring status. Allows for the use of the backup FAT as the primary on FAT32 systems. If the backup FAT is being used, this may be of importance and indicate data hiding.
40h	1	Drive Id	00 for a Floppy Disk, 80 for a Hard Disk
43h	4	Volume serial number	A unique number assigned to a partition at format time. Both Quick and Full formats reassign a serial number. This can be used to uniquely identify a partition on a given drive.
47h	11	Volume/ partition name	An 11 character name assigned to the volume by the person formatting the drive.

Immediately following the boot sector is a copy of the file allocation table itself. The file allocation table indicates the status of individual clusters on the partition and consists of the header and the cluster map.

The header for the file allocation table includes two entries (each two bytes) immediately following the boot sector: media type and partition state. The media type should match the media type identified at offset 15h. If it does not, this is an indication of potential drive corruption (accidental or intentional.) The partition state is used by Windows to indicate whether a proper shutdown has occurred. When Windows starts, this value is set to FF F7, indicating that the partition is actively in use. When Windows shuts down and when the partition is initially formatted, the state is set to FF FF. If Windows detects the partition state as FF F7, it knows that the operating system was not shut down properly and runs scandisk to verify file system integrity. If a system was shut down by pulling the plug, a hex editor should show the partition state as FF F7. This can provide independent verification of shut-down procedures.

Following the FAT header is the cluster map itself. The cluster map contains an entry for every cluster on the drive. For FAT12 and FAT16 file systems, each cluster is represented by two bytes. For FAT32, each cluster is represented by four bytes. The FAT entry contains one of a number of data entries:

- 0F FF FF F7 indicates a cluster is bad and should not be used by the operating system. Forensic tools such as hex editors will still allow the viewing of these clusters, which may contain intentionally hidden data (if the cluster is marked as *bad* by the user) or unintentionally hidden data (data left over in the cluster if the disk reports a single bad sector within it).

- 00 00 00 00 indicates that a cluster is available for storage of data. When a file is deleted, this cluster map is updated to indicate all clusters associated with that file are available. When this happens, the cluster map will contain 00 00 for any files previously in that cluster. Until another file is written to the disk and needs those clusters, the data in them is still present and may be recovered.

- 0F FF FF F8–0F FF FF FF indicates the cluster is the end of a file entry.

- 00 00 00 02–0F FF FF F6 indicate user data is stored in that cluster. The information contains the ordinal number of the cluster in a particular file. If the file is fragmented, that is if the clusters of a file are not contiguous, the cluster map will indicate the position on the drive of the next cluster in the file.

Fragmentation is normal on a disk drive and occurs with usage. Consider the cluster map scenario shown in Figure 4-3:

- A drive contains four files (File 1, File 2, File 3, and File 4), each three clusters in length.

- File 1 and File 3 are deleted. Their clusters are marked as available.

- File 5, which requires five clusters of space, is written to the disk. Because there are no contiguous groups of available clusters large enough, it is split between two groups of clusters. This is called *fragmentation*.

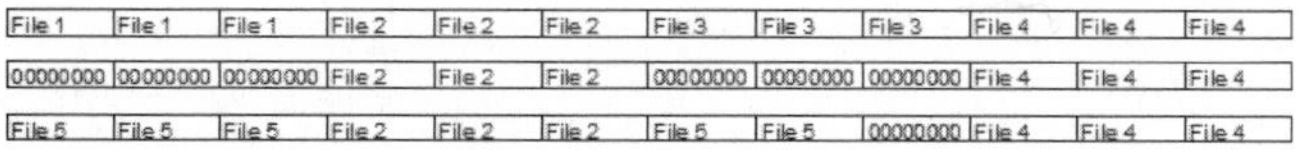

Figure 4-3: Drive fragmentation

Defragmentation is the process of consolidating the data so that the majority of clusters for a given file are contiguous. This optimizes drive speeds and simplifies the cluster map. Defragmentation can be both a boon and a bane to the forensic analyst. Any clusters at the beginning of a drive are likely to be wiped mostly clean and the information from other clusters stored there. An advantage to the analyst, however, is the fact that those clusters in the upper sectors of the disk now contain copies of information that may not be overwritten for a long time, even if the original files are securely wiped from their new locations.

Following the file allocation table and its backup is the root directory entry for the drive. Entries in FAT32 directories are 32 bits (four bytes) long, and contain the name and information on files that is used by the operating system. The root directory is the first directory on the drive, of which all other directories are subdirectories.

Within the root directory entry are the items shown in Table 4-4.

Table 4-4 Root Directory Entry

OFFSET LOCATION	# OF BYTES	IDENTIFIER	NOTES
00h	8	File name	The eight character short file name.
08h	3	File extension	The three-letter extension used to map the file to an executable.
0Bh	1	File attributes	Set to 1 if a given attribute is true. Attribute bits are as follows: 0 = Read Only 1 = Hidden 2 = System 3 = Volume Label 4 = Directory 5 = Archive 6,7 = Reserved
0Ch	1	Reserved	Reserved for future NT use.
0Dh	1	Reserved	Reserved for future NT use.

(continued)

Table 4-4   *(continued)*

OFFSET LOCATION	# OF BYTES	IDENTIFIER	NOTES
0Eh	2	File creation time	Time the file was last created.
10h	2	File creation date	Date the file was last created.
12h	2	Last accessed date	Date the file was last accessed.
14h	2	High half of start cluster	The high word of the starting cluster of the entry referred to.
16h	2	Time of last write	Time the file was last written to.
18h	2	Date of last write	Date the file was last written to.
1Ah	2	Low half of start cluster	The low word of the starting cluster of the entry referred to.
1Ch	4	File size	The size of the file. This is all zeros, if this is a subdirectory and not a file.

TIP   For general Windows date and time decoding during forensics, try the Decode tool available for free at www.digital-detective.co.uk/freetools/decode.asp.

Each and every file has an entry as shown in Table 4-4. Subdirectories have entries similar to files, and each subdirectory has two additional entries:

1. . (pronounced dot)—refers to the directory itself.
2. .. (pronounced dot-dot)—refers back to the parent directory.

When conducting a forensic analysis, the times and dates of file creation, access, and write are important. Although they can be intentionally altered through the use of a program or by changing the system time, they are still critical to an investigation. The creation time indicates the time at which an entry was first written into the directory for the file. The last accessed time indicates the last time an application referenced that particular file. Note that all applications do not necessarily update this date properly. A backup program, for example, reads these files without updating the access time.

Table 4-5 shows the date format used in FAT entries.

Table 4-5 FAT Date Format

NAME	# OF BITS	VALUE
Year (elapsed since 1980)	7	0–128
Month	4	1–12
Day	5	1–31
Hour (24-hour)	5	0–23
Minute	6	0–59
Seconds	5	0–29

NOTE As a result of space limitations, FAT permits the storing of even seconds only, so the seconds value is actually multiplied by 2 for display.

VFAT

Virtual FAT (VFAT) was introduced with Windows 95 to enable the use of long file names (up to 255 characters). In order to remain backward-compatible with existing operating systems (for example, DOS), the long file name (LFN) extensions are added as new directory entries, the same as existing directory entries. For older programs to ignore the entries (which, if they are designed to accept 8.3 filenames they cannot process), the directory entries containing the LFN have the Volume Label attribute set (the Read Only, System, and Hidden attributes are also set). Older programs will see these entries as being Volume Labels and not files and will ignore them.

The VFAT LFN entries are placed in the directory entry immediately preceding the existing FAT32 entry for a file, in reverse order, so the entries would be as follows:

- LFN n
- LFN n–1
- LFN n–2
- . . .
- LFN 1
- Legacy FAT entry

In addition to supporting up to 255 characters, VFAT supports the use of Unicode to enable support for multiple languages with more characters than ASCII can handle (for example, Mandarin Chinese and other *double byte* languages). As a result, every character in a LFN entry takes two bytes instead of one (as required for ASCII entries). For characters not requiring the use of Unicode, the first byte is the ASCII character value and the second byte set to 00. Each directory entry can store up to 13 LFN characters ($13 \times 2 = 26$ bytes; the other six bytes are for sequence number, checksum, and legacy support).

The format of the LFN entry is shown in Table 4-6.

Table 4-6 LFN Entry Format

OFFSET LOCATION	# OF BYTES	IDENTIFIER	NOTES
00h	1	Sequence number	Refers to which LFN entry this is. The last entry always has bit 6 set.
01h	10	File name(1)	First five Unicode characters of file name.
0Bh	1	File attributes	Set to 0F for LFN entries.
0Ch	1	Reserved	Reserved for future NT use.
0Dh	1	Checksum	Value to validate LFN entry, calculated as follows: Checksum is calculated on the short file name (not the long file name) as follows: 1. Start with the value of the first character. 2. Bitwise rotate right (ROR) the sum. 3. Add the value of the next character to the sum. 4. Repeat steps 2 and 3 for all 11 characters.
0Eh	12	File name(2)	Second six Unicode characters of file name.
1Ah	2	Start of cluster	This is in place to support legacy applications looking for a standard FAT entry. Set to 00 00 for LFN entries.
1Ch	4	File name (3)	Third two Unicode characters

The short name is stored as an abbreviated version of the long name. The short name takes the format NNNNNN~#.XXX, where NNNNNN are the first six characters of the LFN with spaces removed (and translated to uppercase), # is an ordinal number defined by Windows (in case there are multiple entries with matching NNNNN values), and XXX is the file extension. A LFN of "Long File Name.doc" would be stored as "LONGFI~1.DOC." These can be viewed from the command prompt by typing `dir /x` on Windows systems.

> **NOTE** If there are more than four files with the first six characters the same, VFAT short entries take the form NN####~1.XXX, where #### is a unique four digit number.

NTFS

To address the limitations of the FAT32 file system and add POSIX compliance, Microsoft began work on a new operating system in the early 1990s. At the time, Microsoft had a partnership with IBM to develop the next generation operating system: OS/2. As part of this development effort, Microsoft and IBM jointly developed the High Performance File System (HPFS).

> **NOTE** POSIX stands for Portable Operating System Interface and is a standard that allows interoperability between different operating systems.

Partway through the OS/2 project, the relationship between Microsoft and IBM dissolved, and they parted ways. Microsoft began development of its own operating system, Windows NT. The NT File System (NTFS) used many of the features present in the HPFS system used by OS/2 and greatly improved on the existing FAT16 file system. FAT32 was not yet available.

NTFS version 4.0 (also called NTFS 1.1) was used in earlier version of Windows NT up through NT 4.0. Starting with Windows 2000, an enhanced version of NTFS known as NTFS 5.0 was released and is the currently available version. Many features introduced in NTFS 5.0 were present in the structures used for earlier versions but not yet supported by the operating system. Enhancements such as file permissions and change logs offer additional features of use to the forensic examiner. Features such as compression and encryption also present new challenges during a forensic examination and require special handling. The forensic use of these will be detailed in this and the following chapter.

ALTERNATE DATA STREAMS

The NTFS file definitions support multiple $DATA attributes, each of which is referred to as an alternate data stream (ADS). The use of an ADS allows Windows programs to store additional information in the form of a separate stream, all within a single file. Secondary streams are not visible to most Windows applications, making them a great way to hide information in files.

Windows uses a colon to reference an ADS within a file. Each ADS is named, with the name be prefixed by the actual file name. Thus, an ADS called *financials* within a file innocuous.txt would be referenced as "innocuous.txt:financials." The data contained in the alternate stream would not be displayed by non-ADS aware applications. Likewise, the directory listing would only show the primary file name, not the financials stream. Even file size is not an indication. The file size displayed in Windows Explorer is only the size for the primary stream, allowing a multi-megabyte ADS to exist under a file showing a size of 1K.

Consider the following interaction, where the secret ADS is added to the file innocuous.txt:

```
C:\Test>echo This is a Test File > innocuous.txt


C:\Test>type innocuous.txt
This is a Test File


C:\Test>dir
 Volume in drive C has no label.
 Volume Serial Number is 00A8-1CDC


 Directory of C:\Test


09/20/2004  12:39 PM    <DIR>          .
09/20/2004  12:39 PM    <DIR>          ..
09/20/2004  12:39 PM                22 innocuous.txt
               1 File(s)             22 bytes
               2 Dir(s)   3,003,953,152 bytes free


C:\Test>echo Here is a second file > innocuous.txt:secret

C:\Test>dir
 Volume in drive C has no label.
 Volume Serial Number is 00A8-1CDC


 Directory of C:\Test


09/20/2004  12:39 PM    <DIR>          .
09/20/2004  12:39 PM    <DIR>          ..
09/20/2004  12:39 PM                22 innocuous.txt
```

```
              1 File(s)              22 bytes
              2 Dir(s)     3,003,953,152 bytes free

C:\Test>type innocuous.txt
This is a Test File

C:\Test>type innocuous.txt:secret
The filename, directory name, or volume label syntax is incorrect.

C:\Test>more < innocuous.txt:secret
Here is a second file
```

In the preceding example, the directory listing does not show the ADS in name or reflect the additional size of the data in either the bytes free or the total bytes listed. Likewise, the ADS cannot be accessed using the type command, as that command does not include ADS support. The more command, which is ADS-enabled, shows the data is present and accounted for, however. Likewise, DiskExplorer indicates the second $DATA attribute as being present as shown in the following figure.

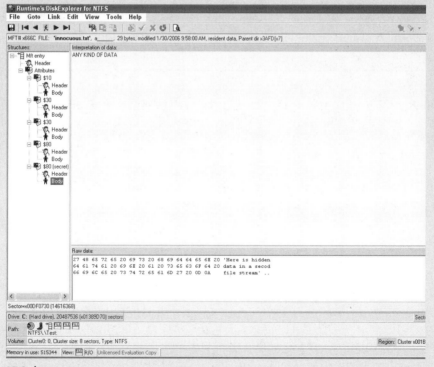

ADS data

(continued)

ALTERNATE DATA STREAMS *(continued)*

Although not viewable by general tools, ADSs will still be searched when a sector-level copy of the disk is examined for a given string. Likewise, ADSs can be identified by searching for other $DATA entries in a file, as done by the streams program available from Sysinternals. Using streams below shows the above-created stream in the innocuous.txt file.

```
C:\Test>streams *

Streams v1.5 - Enumerate alternate NTFS data streams
Copyright (C) 1999-2003 Mark Russinovich
Sysinternals - www.sysinternals.com

C:\Test\innocuous.txt:
        :secret:$DATA 24
```

Because streams allow recursive searching, an entire drive can be searched using the –s switch for any ADSs present on a given drive, for example, `streams -s c:\*.*.`

Streams are copied when a logical file is copied from one NTFS partition to a second NTFS partition. When a file is copied to a non-NTFS drive, however, any ADSs present are lost and only the primary $DATA stream retained. For the forensic examiner, a logical copy—using the copy command to duplicate files to a floppy, for example—should always include a preliminary check for the presence of ADSs.

Taking a cue from Unix systems, almost everything within an NTFS partition is a file, including files that contain meta-data about the partition itself. The exception to this is the partition boot sector which is referenced by the MBR and contains the basics of the partition and bootstrap code.

NOTE Technically, the partition boot sector is a file, $BOOT, as listed by the $MFT, but unlike other files cannot be relocated.

Table 4-7 shows the key features of the boot sector on an NTFS system which are of use in a forensic examination. (The full layout is included in Appendix E.)

The boot sector on an NTFS partition is mirrored on the last sector(s) of the disk as well, though it is not referenced as such.

Immediately following the boot sector is one of two mirrored copies of the main file used by NTFS, the master file table ($MFT). The master file table contains the information used to define the partition's file system and its contents, including metadata files. To accommodate all of this information, Microsoft reserves a significant portion (12.5 percent initially) of a disk to store this file. The space can be used, when necessary, by other applications but is initially set aside upon formatting.

Table 4-7 NTFS Boot Sector

OFFSET LOCATION	# OF BYTES	IDENTIFIER	NOTES
03h	8	OEM name	The name of the OS that formatted the partition. Can be used to determine legacy OS presence in the case of reformatted drives.
0Dh	2	Number of reserved sectors	The number of sectors reserved for the boot record. This number indicates the beginning of the actual NTFS file system.
15h	1	Media type	Should always be F8 for a hard drive. If the media type is changed, the device might not be recognized properly (although it may still contain valid data).
30h	8	Logical cluster number for the file $MFT	Starting cluster of the $MFT file (see below).
38h	8	Logical cluster number for the file $MFTMirr	Starting cluster of the $MFTMirr file (see below).
48h	4	Volume serial number	A unique number assigned to a partition at format time. Both Quick and Full formats reassign a serial number. This can be used to uniquely identify a partition on a given drive.

Each entry within the $MFT is referred to as an inode. Each inode is made up of attributes, defined in the $AttrDef metafile (a list of all Metafiles in NTFS is included as an appendix). The key inode attributes are as follows:

- $Standard_Information. The basic file attribute information (similar to FAT file information) is stored here. The information in the Standard Information includes the times and dates used by Windows for tracking file system additions, updates, and changes.

- $Attribute_List. A listing of all file attributes that are non-resident.

- $File_Name. The long and short names of the file.

- $Object_ID. A unique identifier assigned to each object.

- $Security_Descriptor. The attribute containing the file owner and access control list (ACL) information.

- $Data. The actual content of the file, or pointers to the content of the file (for most files, this will be a pointer to content. Only very small files store the data resident). NTFS supports multiple data streams per file, with one $DATA attribute per stream (see "Alternate Data Streams" later in this chapter).

The $Standard_Information attribute has the fields shown in Table 4-8.

Table 4-8 $Standard_Information Attribute Fields

OFFSET LOCATION	# OF BYTES	IDENTIFIER	NOTES
00h	8	File creation	The date and time the MFT record for the file was initially created.
08h	8	File modified	The date and time the file was last changed.
10h	8	MFT modified	The date and time the file's MFT entry was last altered.
18h	8	File accessed	The date and time the file was last read.
20h	4	DOS attributes	The DOS attribute settings for the file.
24h	4	Maximum versions	The maximum number of versions permitted for a file (0 if versioning is disabled for the file).
28h	4	Current version	The current, latest version number.
2Ch	4	Class ID	Used to point back to the class identifiers.
30h	4	Owner ID	The Owner ID contains a pointer to the $Quota metafile referencing the owner of the file for quota purposes.
34h	4	Security ID	The Security ID contains a pointer to an entry in the $Secure metadata file.

Table 4-8   *(continued)*

OFFSET LOCATION	# OF BYTES	IDENTIFIER	NOTES
38h	8	Quota charge	The number of quota bytes charged – includes the sum of all data streams in the file. Because only the primary stream size is shown by most applications, the quota charge may be different than the displayed file size values.
40h	8	USN	The update sequence number (USN) contains a pointer into the NTFS journal metadata used for file system transactional integrity.

The individual DOS file permissions expand on the basic file permissions assigned to files in the FAT file system. The permissions are shown in Table 4-9.

Table 4-9   NTFS DOS File Permissions

GROUP/BIT	IDENTIFIER	NOTES
1/1	Read-Only	The file system won't allow writing to the file.
1/2	Hidden	The file won't be displayed in standard directory listings.
1/3	System	Bit set for system (OS) files.
1/4	Directory	File is a directory.
2/2	Archive	Used for backups; set to indicate the file needs archiving.
2/3	Device	Special attribute to indicate the file is a device that mimics a file for operations.
2/4	Normal	File is a standard file.
3/1	Temporary	File is a temporary file that can be cleaned on system cleanup tasks.
3/2	Sparse file	File is a sparse file (a special type of file that is large in size but has small amounts of initial data).

(continued)

Table 4-9 *(continued)*

GROUP/BIT	IDENTIFIER	NOTES
3/3	Reparse point	File is a reparse point indicating another file system is mounted at this location.
3/4	Compressed	File is compressed by Windows.
4/1	Offline	File is not available (online) on the current media.
4/2	Encrypted	The file is encrypted by Windows.

Like the $Standard_Information attribute, the $File_Name attribute also contains information that may be of interest to the examiner. The $File_Name attribute is defined as shown in Table 4-10.

Table 4-10 $File_Name Attribute Definition

OFFSET LOCATION	# OF BYTES	IDENTIFIER	NOTES
00h	8	..	The pointer to the parent directory of the file.
08h	8	File creation	The date and time the MFT record for the file was initially created.
10h	8	File modified	The date and time the file was last changed.
18h	8	MFT modified	The date and time the file's MFT entry was last altered.
20h	8	File accessed	The date and time the file was last read.
28h	8	Allocated size	Allocated size of the file.
30h	8	Real size	Real size of the file
38h	4	DOS attributes	The DOS attribute settings for the file.
3Ch	4	EA size	The size of extended attributes buffer.
40h	1	File name length	The number of characters used by the file name.
41h	1	File name namespace	The namespace defining which characters are valid for the file.

The attributes in the $File_Name tag are not updated unless that attribute itself changes. The attributes in $Standard_Information are updated whenever the file or MFT entry changes and are therefore the accurate items to use in most investigations. If it is suspected that the user changed the name of the file intentionally to hide it, that attribute will then have a date different from the initial creation date.

The easiest way to view MFT entry information directly is through the use of a third-party tool. DiskExplorer from Runtime Software has a great interface for doing this. A view of the $Standard_Information attribute for the pagefile.sys file is shown in Figure 4-4.

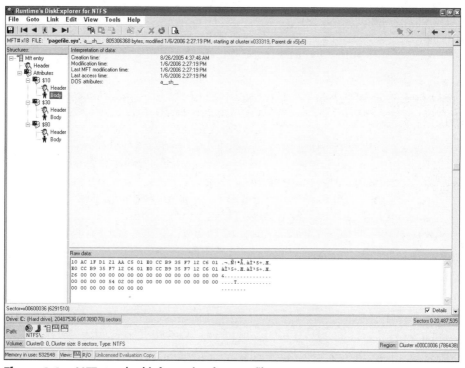

Figure 4-4: MFT standard information for pagefile.sys

NTFS has three additional special types of files of interest from a forensic standpoint:

- **Directories.** NTFS treats directories as files as well. A file defined as a directory contains three additional attributes, $Index_Root, $Index_Allocation, and $Bitmap. These three attributes contain entry information allowing for the linking to the $MFT file entries or subdirectory entries.

- **Sparse files.** Sparse files were designed to allow for very large files to reserve space with minimal amounts of actual storage allocated. A multi-gigabyte file with large runs of zeros may only take up a few megabytes if defined as a sparse file on NTFS. Be aware when conducting an examination using a native NTFS file system that copying a sparse file to another file system (for example, FAT) will result in the full-size file being generated and copied, requiring significantly more storage space or an NTFS drive to be used.

- **Reparse points.** Reparse points permit the redirection of access to a file using set criteria. Individual applications can define their own reparse point information but NTFS used reparse points for a few key items of interest to the investigator. Symbolic links provide Unix-like redirects from one file (or directory, in the case of junction points) to another. The other items of interest are volume mount points. These permit an entry to point to another system or partition and appear to be part of the same logical directory structure. The Windows Mountvol command will show all volume mount points present.

The NTFS file system supports two key features not found in FAT-based file systems: compression and encryption. Both present challenges for the investigator for searching, accessing, and copying files.

BYPASSING NTFS PERMISSIONS

NTFS allows for an individual user to claim ownership of a file or directory. That individual, designated as the owner, has the ability to assign access rights to Windows users and groups to that file or directory. These rights are stored along with the entity and can include any number of file permissions including reading, changing, and deleting a given file.

When accessed through a Windows environment, the NTFS driver checks the security permissions on a given file before permitting access to that file. If the individual currently logged on does not have rights to that file to perform the requested operation, access is denied. If the user has administrative rights over the system on which the NTFS partition resides, that user can take ownership of the entity and grant themselves rights to access it. If they do not have administrative rights, they must request that an administrator or the owner of the entity grant them the requested permissions.

Even though there are access control lists (ACLs) present on NTFS files, Windows relies on the individual NTFS driver to enforce those controls. Therefore, using a non-Microsoft NTFS drive such as the ones available for Linux or the read-only NTFSDOS driver that does not support ACL enforcement allows an individual to read any file on a drive regardless of permissions. Likewise, any utility that performs a raw, sector-by-sector copy of a drive (such as EnCase or SafeBack) will likewise ignore file permissions as it is operating at a level below that of file system when copying.

To access files on a machine for which the investigator does not have an account or the necessary permissions:

◆ Create a Windows 98 boot disk. Insert a blank disk into a Windows 98 machine and from the command prompt type `format a: /s`. This will create a bootable DOS disk with the Windows 98 file on it.

- If a boot CD is needed (for example, if there is no floppy drive on the system in question), Linux may be the best choice. Both Helix (available at www.e-fense.com/helix/) and F.I.R.E. (available at biatchux.dmzs.com) are forensic-specific bootable CDs, which include NTFS support.

◆ Download the NTFSDOS Professional driver from SysInternals at www.sysinternals.com/files/NTFSProR.exe to a Windows NT, 2000, or XP machine. Run the executable to install the disk creator.

◆ Run the installed NTFS Professional Boot Disk Wizard to copy the necessary system files to the newly created boot disk.

- To save time, create an ISO image of the NTFSDOS bootable floppy with the NTFSDOS executable called from the autoexec.bat file. These new images can be copied directly to a boot disk without needing to go through the first three steps.

◆ Boot the suspect's machine with the new floppy. Insert the new disk into the floppy drive of the target machine and ensure that the floppy drive is the first boot choice from the setup menu.

◆ Start NTFSDOS and browse the hard disk. Run NTFSDOS from the directory where the files are placed with the wizard. Browse the target NTFS file system in read-only mode and use other floppy disks or create a boot disk with network or null modem cable drivers to copy target files to a non-NTFS partition, bypassing any permissions.

Compression

NTFS permits the compression of files, directories, and volumes to save space. The compression used is lossless compression. There is no data lost in shrinking the file size. The specific algorithm used is an older Lempel-Zip (LZ) algorithm which searches for repeating strings of variable lengths and replaces them with smaller, fixed-length placeholder codes. While not optimal in terms of storage reduction (the algorithms used by programs such as PKZip and WinRAR do a much better job of compressing information to smaller sizes), the algorithm is fairly fast, allowing for a minimal time difference when accessing compressed files.

NOTE Algorithms such as JPEG and MPEG-2 are examples of lossy compression. Information is lost when these algorithms are used.

When a program accesses a file that is compressed using NTFS compression, the operating system compresses and decompresses the file on the fly. This is accomplished automatically when programs access NTFS-compressed files (Windows filters out system calls to files with compressed data and performs the decompression first then passed the decompressed data to the calling program.)

NOTE Windows XP also supports ZIP files. This is a separate function from NTFS compression, but the compression and decompression are still handled by the operating system, just a different set of library functions.

Because the act of compression changes the data stored on the disk, compressed files cannot be searched accurately within a sector-by-sector image. These files need special treatment to be accurately searched, as do all compressed files. They need to be decompressed and searched at a logical file system level instead of a sector level. Additionally, searches for file headers (for example, tools that search for deleted files with no MFT record), will likely be unsuccessful on compressed data.

Figure 4-5 shows the actual data stored in the compressed (bottom) and uncompressed (top) versions of a text file containing the words to the United States Constitution. The lower, compressed image is not likely to find keywords or strings when a basic search is performed.

The Microsoft command line tool compact allows the investigator to search a logical volume for, and uncompress, NTFS-compacted files that are present. The `compact /S` command can be used to recursively search all folders for compressed files. Any files with a "C" in front of the file name are compressed. The compact command also allows the investigator to both compress and decompress files and view the compression ratios. The `compact /C` command allows for a file to be compressed, and the `compact /U` command allows for decompression.

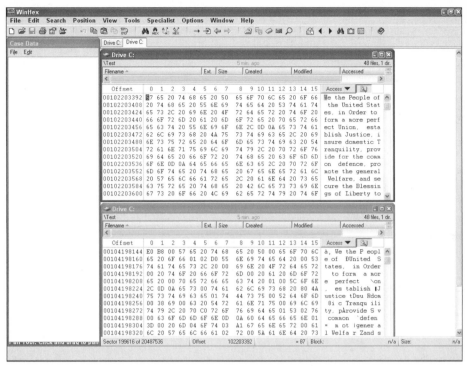

Figure 4-5: Compressed and uncompressed file comparison

The commands that follow compact the file report.htm, which is highly compressible due to extensive whitespace and repeating text being present. In fact, it compacts at a 2.6:1 ratio, allowing for it to be stored in less than half of the original space used. Note, however, the file size has not changed in the directory listing although the space used on disk has. This is of interest when copying files to a non-NTFS partition. Any files that were compressed will be decompressed when copying to a floppy or tape if a logical copy operation is used. This may require more storage space than was originally used on the source drive based on the compression ratios.

NOTE Windows also supports .cab compression. These files are usually distributed with software, and the format is not commonly used for end-user compression (and therefore less likely to contain evidence in a forensic investigation). To extract the files from a compressed .cab archive, the expand −F:* command can be used.

```
C:\Test>dir
 Volume in drive C has no label.
 Volume Serial Number is 00C9-1BDC

 Directory of C:\Test

09/21/2004  10:03 AM     <DIR>          .
09/21/2004  10:03 AM     <DIR>          ..
06/01/2004  09:38 AM              43,279 report.htm
               1 File(s)         43,279 bytes
               2 Dir(s)  2,492,268,544 bytes free

C:\Test>compact /C report.htm

 Compressing files in C:\Test\

report.htm              43279 :      16384 = 2.6 to 1 [OK]

1 files within 1 directories were compressed.
43,279 total bytes of data are stored in 16,384 bytes.
The compression ratio is 2.6 to 1.

C:\Test>dir
 Volume in drive C has no label.
 Volume Serial Number is 00C9-1BDC

 Directory of C:\Test

09/21/2004  10:03 AM     <DIR>          .
09/21/2004  10:03 AM     <DIR>          ..
06/01/2004  09:38 AM              43,279 report.htm
               1 File(s)         43,279 bytes
               2 Dir(s)  2,492,100,608 bytes free
```

Encryption

NTFS version 5, introduced with Windows 2000, brought the concept of encrypting the data within a file, directory, or volume as a native service provided by Windows. This encryption is supported in Windows 2000, XP Professional, and 2003 under the name Encrypting File System (EFS).

EFS permits an individual user to encrypt any files for which they are the owner. The act of encryption is fairly complex and uses both symmetric and public-key encryption. When encrypting a file, the file owner specifies who has access. By default, only the individual performing the encryption and any designated data recovery agents (DRAs) are permitted access, but other users can be added by the individual.

NOTE Data recovery agents are defined by policy as accounts that can be used to decrypt a file if the original account's encryption keys are lost or damaged or the original account holder is unavailable. Most organizations designate their security group as one of the DRAs.

To encrypt a file, the following steps take place:

1. Windows generates a random 128-bit key called the file encryption key (FEK) specifically for that file.

2. The current user's public key is accessed through the registry.

3. If this is the first time the user encrypts a file, Windows generates a public and private key for the user. The private key is stored in an encrypted form (encrypted with a master key generated by Windows from user-specific credentials) with the individual user's profile.

4. A data decryption field (DDF), containing the user's information and a copy of the FEK encrypted with the user's public key is generated and added to the file header.

5. Additional DDFs for each additional user granted access likewise contain FEKs encrypted with that user's public key and placed in the file header.

6. Any DRA fields are generated the same way as the DDFs and stored in the header.

7. The original data is symmetrically encrypted using DESX (an RSA enhancement to the data encryption standard algorithm) or TripleDES (another enhancement, available as an option with XP Professional and 2003) and copied to the $DATA attribute of the newly created header.

8. The original data file is removed.

SYMMETRIC AND PUBLIC KEY ENCRYPTION

Symmetric encryption relies on a single key that can be used to both encrypt and decrypt a file. An example is XOR'ing a file against a given set of binary digits and storing the result. A second XOR operation against the encrypted result with the same key will return the original data.

Public key encryption relies on two keys: a public and a private key. Public key algorithms use one-way functions, which are based on computationally hard problems (for example, factoring of large numbers) where a different key is used to encrypt (public) than to decrypt (private). With public key encryption, the encryption cannot be reversed with knowledge the public key in a reasonable timeframe, allowing that key to be published widely.

When a forensic investigator encounters an EFS-encrypted file, directory, or volume, he will not be able to read its contents using standard disk viewing tools at either a logical or physical level. The contents can actually be read, but they will be unintelligible as they are encrypted. To recover the information from an EFS-encrypted file, the investigator has a few primary options:

Obtain the user's credentials and log in as the user. This will potentially alter forensic evidence (for example, login times and profile information) and should only be performed after a full forensic duplicate of all information has been made. If EFS or other encryption is suspected and the user is logged in when the computer is found, a live system analysis should be performed in lieu of powering off the machine. The users' credentials can be obtained through social engineering, password guessing (of that or other passwords), or any other technique used to obtain user passwords.

- Use a designated DRA account to access the files. If the security group is registered as a DRA or has access to a DRA account, this account can be used to decrypt the files in question. The DRAs can be identified using a tool such as EFSDump as shown below:

```
C:\Test\report.htm:
DDF Entry:
    SECURITY\Chad M.S. Steel:
        Chad M.S. Steel(Chad M.S. Steel@SECURITY)
DRF Entry:
    SECURITY\Administrator
      Administrator(Administrator@SECURITY)
```

- After a DRA on a file has been identified, that account, if available, can be used to decrypt the contents.

- Obtain a certificate file for either the DRF or DDF entries as listed above. Certificate files with the private key included can be exported from Windows with a default extension of .PFX. These files can then be imported into the certificate store on the system used for analysis to permit access to files encrypted by those users. Some users will export .PFX files to either have a backup copy of their certificate or to use the same certificate on multiple systems. Searching the suspect's drives for .PFX files may yield the needed certificate. The Certificate Manager of the Microsoft Management Console can be used to view and import certificates. A sample Certificate Store is shown below in Figure 4-6. To import a new certificate, right-click the existing store and select All Tasks → Import. The wizard will then walk the user through importing a certificate. (In most Windows builds, double-clicking a .PFX file will automatically import it.)

NOTE The Certificate Management option may be available directly from the Control Panel. If it is not, open the Management Console by typing mmc; then select Add/Remove Snap-In from the File menu and select the Certificates snap-in to add.

■ Search for the unencrypted data at a physical level. Even though a file may be encrypted, remnants of the file or the whole file may exist on the drive. When an encrypted file is created, the original data is duplicated into an encrypted form. The original data may still be present from this process. Likewise, the file itself may be recoverable from the paging file, from temp files or from other unallocated sectors where fragments or old versions may reside.

TIP When an encrypted file is opened by an application, unencrypted temp copies may be generated by that application.

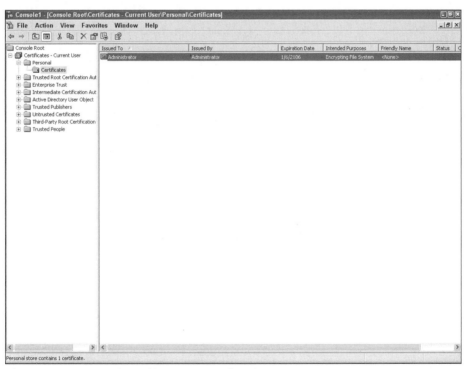

Figure 4-6: Microsoft Certificates storage location

Identifying encrypted files can be down with the Windows `cipher` command. This command also allows for the command line encryption and decryption of files. The `cipher` command can be used to encrypt, list, and then decrypt a file as follows:

```
C:\Test>cipher

 Listing C:\Test\
 New files added to this directory will not be encrypted.

U report.htm

C:\Test>cipher /E /A

 Encrypting files in C:\Test\

report.htm          [OK]

1 file(s) [or directorie(s)] within 1 directorie(s) were encrypted.
```

Converting files from plaintext to ciphertext may leave sections of old plaintext on the disk volume(s). It is best to use the command `cipher /W:directory` to clean up the disk after all converting is done.

```
C:\Test>cipher

 Listing C:\Test\
 New files added to this directory will not be encrypted.

E report.htm

C:\Test>cipher /A /D

 Decrypting files in C:\Test\

report.htm [OK]

1 file(s) [or directorie(s)] within 1 directorie(s) were decrypted.
```

In the preceding example, the "E" next to the file name indicates an encrypted file. To find all encrypted files on a drive, the command `cipher /S:C: /N` can be used. The `/S:C:` switch denotes a recursive search of the C: drive. The `/N` switch denotes a "no touch" search—DDF and DRFs will not be updated with the search.

As with compression, encryption is an NTFS-specific feature. When the encrypted file or directory is moved to a non-NTFS partition by a user with the appropriate access rights, the encryption will be turned off.

CASE STUDY: FTP HACKER

While running a web development organization, one of my team's tasks was to build and install development and staging servers for client projects. The servers were generally built by systems engineers, but occasionally a developer would build a box when resources were tight. One of the developers built a Windows NT 4.0 box with IIS for development then imaged that same build and deployed it on our external gateway for staging (we utilized our staging environment for customer acceptance testing as well as internal testing).

One of the common criticisms of Windows and security is its poor installation choices out-of-the-box. This was a conscious choice by Microsoft. (Microsoft Windows 2003 represents a shift in strategy; this operating system defaults to having everything off and requires the user to explicitly install needed functionality.) Users did not want to install functionality piecemeal; they wanted it all installed and would theoretically turn off functionality they did not need when they hardened the system, although in reality this rarely happened. Because of this, unused and exploitable functionality was frequently present on systems built by the less security conscious. The default installation of IIS is no exception to this rule. FTP, installed with the web server, allows anonymous access to the machine. Anonymous access and an Internet-accessible server was a recipe for disaster.

Our system engineers responded to developer complaints of disk space issues on the client staging server. As part of our build procedures, we would create a separate partition that only contained the wwwroot and ftproot directories, the locations where web and FTP traffic were located. A complaint of space being in short supply generally meant that one of the developers had started using the partition to share their MP3s. A routine cleansing of the offending directories would generally do the trick.

When the system engineer arrived at the machine, there were only two directories present on the partition and free space was at 10KB out of 20GB available. The developers did not generally use that much space. A quick check of directories in Windows Explorer showed the wwwroot directory was using 12MB and the ftproot directory had the remainder of that space used. Looking into the ftproot directory there was a single subdirectory present titled PRN. A check revealed a directory size of zero, with zero files present (the number of files and folders was not even visible) similar to that shown in the following figure. This was very unusual since the parent directory had hundreds of files and almost 20GB of used space.

Looking under the PRN subdirectory revealed an entire subdirectory after subdirectory, all with names like "COM1;PRN", "+--TAGGED BY PYRO--+", and "(((1 M 3LEET)))." Following the chain revealed directories containing DIVX version of several recent movies, cracked version of popular software, and some pornographic images. Fearing the machine had been hacked, the security team was called in.

(continued)

CASE STUDY: FTP HACKER *(continued)*

PRN Properties

General | Customize

PRN

Type of file: File Folder

Description: PRN

Location: C:\ftproot

Size: 0 bytes

Size on disk: 0 bytes

Created:

Modified:

Accessed:

Attributes: ☐ Read-only   ☐ Hidden   Advanced...

OK   Cancel   Apply

PRN directory size

When we arrived, we first took a look at the upstream router and noted several current FTP connections. We took the machine off the network to prevent further damage and began our analysis. A quick look at the FTP logs revealed several independent IP addresses had attempted anonymous connections, succeeded in connecting, then copied and deleted a filed labeled *1ktest*. A day after the first of these connections, the same IP address reconnected and created the directory structure present then proceeded to upload several pieces of the offending content. Over the next several days, another individual had found and uploaded content as well. This was followed by a massive downloading by hundreds of different IP addresses.

A check on the development box (which was never Internet accessible) showed that anonymous FTP was enabled. Since the staging server was built from the development image, this was likely how it had been configured as well. A hash comparison of the system partition to the development box to the system partition on the staging server showed no unusual discrepancies. The machine itself was not compromised, only its FTP partition.

The IP addresses which were primarily responsible for uploading returned addresses in several foreign countries with somewhat lax intellectual property and computer intrusion laws. Given the low likelihood of finding the offenders, the embarrassment at disclosing the intrusion, and the lack of permanent damage, the company made the decision to delete the offending content, lock down the configuration, and bring the servers back online.

Initial attempts to delete the offending PRN directory hierarchy using Windows Explorer were unsuccessful, returning the infamous message displayed in the following figure.

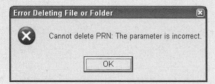

Error when deleting the PRN subdirectory

Similarly, attempts to delete the folder using the command prompt also failed:

```
C:\ftproot>dir
 Volume in drive C has no label.
 Volume Serial Number is 8C9D-6FEA

 Directory of C:\ftproot

03/01/2005  05:36 PM    <DIR>          .
03/01/2005  05:36 PM    <DIR>          ..
03/01/2005  05:16 PM    <DIR>          PRN
              0 File(s)            0 bytes
              3 Dir(s)     12,832 bytes free

C:\ftproot>rmdir PRN
The directory name is invalid.
```

A quick refresher on Windows file naming conventions revealed the directories that violated those conventions. The ftp interface used the full UNC paths when creating them, bypassing the Windows checks for domain names. By doing so, PRN (a reserved name for the printer device) and COM1 (a reserved name for the first serial port) were able to be used as names for the directories. To delete them, the respective UNC names had to be used from the command prompt:

```
C:\ftproot>rmdir \\.\C:\ftproot\PRN
```

After the folders had been removed, the machine was brought back online and new build requirements, including a security signoff by a systems engineer, were put in place.

Additional Resources

Refer to the following list for additional resources:

Darik's Boot and Nuke
   `dban.sourceforge.net`

FIRE Forensic Incident Response Environment
   `biatchux.dmzs.com`

Helix Bootable Forensics Environment
   `www.e-fense.com/helix/`

NTFS Filesystem Details From SourceForge
   `linux-ntfs.sourceforge.net/ntfs`

NTFS Professional Driver From SysInternals
   `www.sysinternals.com/ntw2k/freeware/ntfsdospro.shtml`

Secure Deletion From Magnetic Media
   `www.usenix.org/publications/library/proceedings/`
   `sec96/full_papers/gutmann/`

Streams ADS Viewer From SysInternals
   `www.sysinternals.com/ntw2k/source/misc.shtml#streams`

CHAPTER 5

Directory Structure and Special Files

When Microsoft Windows is installed on a personal computer, various directories and special files are created. An understanding of where each version of Windows places key files of note to a forensic examination and the underlying directory structures provides the basis for forensic analysis of the file system at the logical level.

Each of the different versions of Windows uses a slightly different directory structure with different names for key files. I will examine the specific directories and files created in Windows 9x/NT//2000/2003/XP with an emphasis on their forensic value.

Windows NT/2000/XP

The Windows NT and 2000 operating systems provided the first structural break from the prior MS-DOS directory and file structures used by the Windows 9x family. There are minimal differences from a file and directory standpoint between the various workstation and server versions of the operating systems. The server versions generally include a few additional files but have the same basic structure as the workstation versions. Additionally, the specific directories installed will vary slightly based on individual installation options. The items below reflect a default installation, with directories of special forensic interest installed as optional features noted.

Directories

The primary directories are created under the root on the partition the operating system was installed to (generally the partition assigned to the C: drive):

- **Documents and Settings.** The subdirectories under this directory provide individual user profile information. User profiles are specific to an account and store individual application settings, desktop information, documents, and other details. This information is found under %SYSTEMROOT%/profiles on Windows NT machines.

- **Inetpub.** The Windows Internet Information Services hierarchy is stored under subdirectories below this heading.

- **Program Files.** The default installation location for software installed under Windows is the Program Files directory. Individual applications will create their own subdirectories under this hierarchy.

- **Recycler.** On each drive, the Recycling Bin creates a Recycler folder with individual subfolders, labeled by the Security Identifier of their owners, for each user that has deleted a file on that drive. Recycling Bin analysis is covered in Chapter 10.

- **System volume information.** This is a hidden system directory. It provides information on restore points. Although not commonly looked at in forensic analysis, they can include fragments of information (sometimes SAM information), and they are a favorite hiding spot for hackers to place hidden directories. Windows NT does not have restore points and therefore does not have a System Volume Information folder.

- **Temp.** On Windows NT, a root level Temp folder was created for use by the operating system and applications for storage of temporary files.

- **WINNT/Windows.** The primary operating system directory for the installation of the Windows system files. Most of the system-based forensic information is likely to be present in subdirectories of this directory.

NOTE The core Windows directory defaults to WINNT under 2000 and earlier versions, and WINDOWS for later versions. It can be set to any directory name, however, and the best way to identify the valid directory (if a multiboot machine is used) is to review the %SYSTEMROOT% environment variable by typing its name at the command prompt (or typing set).

WINDOWS STARTUP INFORMATION

To access startup configuration information in one location with Windows 98/ME/2003/XP, Microsoft provides the MSConfig utility. To start MSConfig, select Start → Run and type `msconfig` in the text box.

The MSConfig utility enables the viewing and editing of the WIN.INI, SYSTEM.INI, and BOOT.INI files. Additionally, any services set to start automatically or registry entries that execute automatically—a favorite way for viruses to re-infect after a re-boot—are displayed under the Services and Startup tabs, respectively.

The following screenshot shows a list of programs set to run automatically when Windows is started.

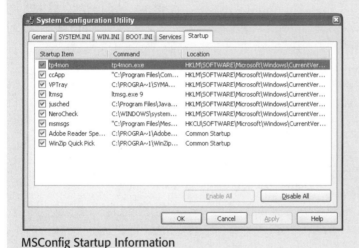

MSConfig Startup Information

Under each of these directory structures are further directories of interest in a forensic examination. Table 5-1 details several key directories and their forensic value.

Table 5-1   Key Windows NT/2000/2003/XP Directories

MAIN DIRECTORY	SUBDIRECTORY	CONTENTS
Documents and Settings	All Users/Desktop	Stores items shown on the desktop as icons for all users. May be used with an individual profile to indicate whether an individual user added an item or someone else added it.

(continued)

Table 5-1 *(continued)*

MAIN DIRECTORY	SUBDIRECTORY	CONTENTS
Documents and Settings	All Users/Documents	Stores any shared documents between machine users. Likewise, some applications will create individual user subdirectories under this directory.
Documents and Settings	All Users/Start Menu	Stores any items that appear on all Start menus. The Programs/Startup subfolder contains shortcuts to files that start automatically when the user logs in.
Documents and Settings	Default User	Stores the default profile which is copied to an individual profile upon adding an account to the system. Social-engineering and access to this folder have been used by hackers looking to exploit a specific account.
Documents and Settings	<Profile Name>/ Application Data	Contains application data for each individual profile. Configurations, log files, and general data may be stored under application subdirectories in this hierarchy.
Documents and Settings	<Profile Name>/ Cookies	Contains text files of individual cookies for a particular user.
Documents and Settings	<Profile Name>/ Favorites	Contains the individual's Internet Explorer favorites.
Documents and Settings	<Profile Name>/ Local Settings/ Application Data	Contains any application data specific to the computer.
Documents and Settings	<Profile Name>/ Local Settings/ History	Contains the individual's Internet Explorer browsing history. This directory is treated as special for display purposes in Windows Explorer.

Table 5-1   *(continued)*

MAIN DIRECTORY	SUBDIRECTORY	CONTENTS
Documents and Settings	<Profile Name>/ Local Settings/Temp	Stores any temporary files created or downloaded using Internet Explorer. This is used for temporary purposes (for example, installers) as opposed to caching.
Documents and Settings	<Profile Name>/ Local Settings/ Temporary Internet Files	Contains the individual's Internet Explorer–cached files.
Documents and Settings	<Profile Name>/ Local Settings/ My Documents	Acts as the default storage location for all user-created documents. My Pictures and My Music are also located under this subdirectory. This is one of the most common locations for forensic recovery.
Documents and Settings	<Profile Name>/ Nethood	Contains all Network Neighborhood shortcuts. Good for showing an individual knew about and accessed a particular network computer.
Documents and Settings	<Profile Name>/ Printhood	Shows all installed printers. If an individual printer is mapped in this directory, the associated profile had that printer installed.
Documents and Settings	<Profile Name>/ Recent	Shows recently opened items, including shortcuts to previously removed items. One of the best locations for evidence.
Documents and Settings	<Profile Name>/ SendTo	Contains items that appear on the Send To right-click menu. Frequently, shortcuts to removable drives or CD-burning software install items here.

(continued)

Table 5-1 *(continued)*

MAIN DIRECTORY	SUBDIRECTORY	CONTENTS
Documents and Settings	<Profile Name>/ Start Menu	Contains the applications an individual profile has installed. These are in addition to the All Users items. The Programs/Startup subfolder contains shortcuts to files that start automatically when the user logs on.
Inetpub	Ftproot	Acts as the default location for an IIS FTP server's files.
Inetpub	Mailroot	Acts as the default location for an IIS SMTP server's files.
Inetpub	Wwwroot	Acts as the default location for an IIS web server's files.
%SYSTEMROOT%	$NtUninstallxxxxxxx$	Indicates installation of various patch files. The directory date can be used to indicate when a particular patch was applied, to prove whether an infection was possible at a point in time. You can use the xxxxxxx code to search on www.microsoft.com for particulars.
%SYSTEMROOT%	Addins	Shows any installed local ActiveX control files. Given recent ActiveX exploits, this is a possible malicious code location.
%SYSTEMROOT%	Downloaded Installations (and Installer)	Contains MSI installers (Microsoft's installer files). Even after removal, the installer for a piece of software may still be present in a subdirectory here.
%SYSTEMROOT%	Downloaded Program Files	Contains Internet Explorer add-ins (such as the Shockwave Flash Object). If a particular site requires a special download, this is a potential location to examine whether the site has been visited.

Table 5-1 *(continued)*

MAIN DIRECTORY	SUBDIRECTORY	CONTENTS
%SYSTEMROOT%	Driver Cache	Contains specific drivers files previously used by Windows. Of particular interest are files that indicate a specific device has been connected (such as the usbxxxx.sys files for USB Devices).
%SYSTEMROOT%	Offline Web Pages	Shows any web pages stored for later offline browsing using Internet Explorer.
%SYSTEMROOT%	Profiles	Shows the same items as the Documents and Settings hierarchy on Windows NT systems or systems upgraded from NT.
%SYSTEMROOT%	Repair	Contains backups of the registry files. This is an excellent location for old registry files and SAM information.
%SYSTEMROOT%	System32	Contains essential system files, including .DLL and EXE files used by the operating system. Any infected operating system files are likely to be under this directory tree.
%SYSTEMROOT%	System32/Config	Contains the registry files and the event logs (except User hive information). This is a frequently visited directory in forensic analyses.
%SYSTEMROOT%	System32/Drivers	Indicates specific devices that have been installed on a system by the drivers referenced (like the Driver Cache folder).

(continued)

Table 5-1 *(continued)*

MAIN DIRECTORY	SUBDIRECTORY	CONTENTS
%SYSTEMROOT%	System32/ Drivers/Etc	Contains the hosts and lmhosts files, which provide local hostname resolution services. These are processed before DNS and WINS lookups, and therefore the entries here override these services.
%SYSTEMROOT%	System32/ Spool/Printers	Shows Print spool files. These are files that have been printed or failed printings.
%SYSTEMROOT%	Tasks	Lists any scheduled tasks using the Windows Scheduler. The scheduler has been used for escalation of privileges as well as "logic bomb" scheduling in the past.
%SYSTEMROOT%	Temp	Contains a grab bag of items for forensic analysis. Log files, temporary files, and other miscellaneous items appear here. The Temp directory for individuals is generally Documents and Settings\<PROFILE NAME>\Local Settings\Temp.

NOTE In Windows, each account has an associated profile. The profile stores information about the individual user, including application data, documents, and configuration settings. Microsoft also introduced the concept of Roaming Profiles to allow users to access their data from any machine on a given domain. With roaming profiles enabled, all of the user's information—except for the Application Data, Local Settings, Nethood, and Printhood—are stored on a network drive instead of the local computer.

The above directories represent only a few of the many locations forensic evidence may reside. Users and applications can create their own directory hierarchies, rename an existing hierarchy, or use little-visited branches of the hierarchy to store information away from investigative prying eyes.

ENVIRONMENT VARIABLES

When an application wants to find the default directory where Windows was installed or a user types a command that is not in the current directory, the locations are looked up in memory where they are stored as environment variables.

Environment variables may be added or changed using the set command along with the variable name. Typing set without a variable name will return all of the environment variables present on a given system. Here is an example of the environment variables present:

```
C:\Documents and Settings\Administrator>set
ALLUSERSPROFILE=C:\Documents and Settings\All Users
APPDATA=C:\Documents and Settings\Administrator\Application Data
CLIENTNAME=MYSECURITY
ClusterLog=C:\WINDOWS\Cluster\cluster.log
CommonProgramFiles=C:\Program Files\Common Files
COMPUTERNAME=CMSSWEB
ComSpec=C:\WINDOWS\system32\cmd.exe
HOMEDRIVE=C:
HOMEPATH=\Documents and Settings\Administrator
LOGONSERVER=\\CMSSWEB
NUMBER_OF_PROCESSORS=1
OS=Windows_NT
Path=C:\WINDOWS\system32;C:\WINDOWS;C:\WINDOWS\System32\Wbem;C:\Progra
m Files\Ex
ecutive Software\Diskeeper\
PATHEXT=.COM;.EXE;.BAT;.CMD;.VBS;.VBE;.JS;.JSE;.WSF;.WSH
PROCESSOR_ARCHITECTURE=x86
PROCESSOR_IDENTIFIER=x86 Family 6 Model 8 Stepping 3, GenuineIntel
PROCESSOR_LEVEL=6
PROCESSOR_REVISION=0803
ProgramFiles=C:\Program Files
PROMPT=$P$G
SESSIONNAME=RDP-Tcp#1
SystemDrive=C:
SystemRoot=C:\WINDOWS
TEMP=C:\DOCUME~1\ADMINI~1\LOCALS~1\Temp\1
TMP=C:\DOCUME~1\ADMINI~1\LOCALS~1\Temp\1
USERDOMAIN=CMSSWEB
USERNAME=Administrator
USERPROFILE=C:\Documents and Settings\Administrator
windir=C:\WINDOWS
```

(continued)

ENVIRONMENT VARIABLES *(continued)*

Of key importance to the forensic analyst are the following environment variables:

◆ **COMPUTERNAME.** The actual name assigned to the computer in the currently running version of Windows. (You didn't trust the P-Touch label with the computer name on it, did you?)

◆ **COMSPEC.** The location of the command interpreter. If this is anything other than the expected %SYSTEMROOT%\Command.com (Windows 9x) or %SYSTEMROOT%\System32\cmd.exe (Windows NT) this may indicate malicious code is present.

◆ **HOMEDRIVE/HOMEPATH.** The home drive and path for the current user. Any user-specific files are likely to be under this hierarchy.

◆ **LOGONSERVER.** The name of the domain controller that validated the credentials of the system at logon. The controller is likely to have log event information on this system.

◆ **OS.** The name of the OS; NT will be displayed for Windows NT/2000/2003/XP.

◆ **PATH.** The search path for executable files. They are searched in the order present. If multiple executables with the same name are found (for example, another cmd.exe file), check the PATH statement to see which one will be executed first.

◆ **PATHEXT.** A list of the file extensions that Windows will treat as executable. Unusual extensions may indicate hidden files with those extension names on the system.

◆ **SYSTEMDRIVE/SYSTEMROOT.** The default location of the Windows directory and system files. If this is different from the Windows/WINNT directories, multiple versions of an OS may be present.

◆ **TEMP/TMP.** The location for the individual user's temporary files. A great place to check for copies of deleted files or transient files that were viewed or printed but not saved.

◆ **USERDOMAIN/USERNAME.** The domain and the name of the user currently logged in. This information is useful in a live analysis when determining who was on the system at the time.

◆ **WINDIR.** The location of the Windows directory. This takes the place of SYSTEMROOT on 9x machines and is present on other Windows versions for backward compatibility.

Files

As with directories, there are a few special Windows files which are frequently accessed as part of computer investigations. These files contain information pertinent to a broad range of forensic analyses. This section covers the locations and purpose of these files. The analyses of these files are covered in Chapter 10. Some of the most frequently accessed files are noted in Table 5-2.

CASE STUDY: ALTERED HOSTS FILE

An unusual user problem prompted a security incident at one of the companies where I worked. The user reporting the problem consistently visited several well-known websites such as yahoo.com and google.com only to have pornography appear on her system. When asked how the user went to the websites, she indicated that she typed the individual site names into her web browser (as opposed to clicking email links or other mechanisms which may have created a similar problem).

The company had a proxy server setup, so an initial review of the proxy logs was done remotely. The proxy logs showed no requests for yahoo.com or google.com from the user reporting the problem. However, it did show requests based on IP addresses to two well-known sites containing hardcore pornography.

Initially, the evidence pointed to spyware or malware installed on the user's system which was redirecting web requests to the other sites. I had made the mistake of looking for a zebra before a horse. The Internet Explorer files did not match. The TypedURLs showed the Yahoo! and Google sites, but the Temporary Internet Files location showed the inappropriate content. No unusual plug-ins or ActiveX controls were found and both a virus and spyware scan turned up nothing.

To rule out the browser itself, I performed an nslookup on the command line, which returned the proper addresses for the hostnames. A ping, however, was sent to the offending IP addresses. This ruled out any Internet Explorer specific calamities.

As the resolution of the domain name from the company's server was correct, I looked for local resolution issues in the Hosts file. Opening this file revealed entries for several commonly typed websites, with the IP addresses of the inappropriate sites observed.

After interviewing her co-workers (not all computer investigation work involves sitting in front of a keyboard), one admitted that another person in the group had decided to play a joke on the user. The new suspect had altered the Hosts file while the user was away from her computer (she did not lock the system) to point her requests for innocent websites to the inappropriate material.

(continued)

CASE STUDY: ALTERED HOSTS FILE *(continued)*

Because I could not prove who changed the file from the local evidence (the suspect performed the actions while logged in as the user), I reasoned how the suspect would have committed the act. Since most users do not know the IP addresses of websites by heart, I surmised the individual may have done a DNS lookup immediately before the last changed date on the Hosts file.

Sure enough, a review of the DNS server logs revealed the IP address of the requests. Matching that to DHCP logs (to determine who had the IP address) and then Event logs (to determine who was logged in to the machine at the time), I was able to identify and appropriately discipline the actual perpetrator for violating company policies on both appropriate usage and sexual harassment.

Table 5-2   Common Windows Files

FILE NAME	DEFAULT LOCATION	DESCRIPTION
Thumbs.db	Any	Any folder which displays its contents in the Thumbnails view (for XP/2003) will cache small copies of the current and past images and movies present in the thumbs.db file. EnCase is able to read these files to extract file names as well as images.
Index.dat	Multiple	The index.dat files catalog various aspects of Internet-browsing history. Found under individual profile subdirectories, the analysis of these files is covered in Chapter 12.
Autoexec.bat	Root	The Autoexec.bat file is a legacy batch file set to run on startup with older versions of Windows. Any Windows version later than Windows 95 should only have a PATH statement present.
Boot.ini	Root	Any multi-boot information handled by Windows is found in this file, including the default boot device.
Config.sys	Root	The config.sys file is a legacy configuration file that previously contained driver loading instructions. This should no longer be used in current versions of Windows.

Table 5-2 *(continued)*

FILE NAME	DEFAULT LOCATION	DESCRIPTION
Pagefile.sys	Root	The pagefile is where Windows swaps out unused data from memory to the local drive to conserve RAM for program use. Because of this, fragments of information from programs are frequently found in this file—even those never saved to disk. This is probably the most useful file to search for text strings on a Windows machine.
Hiberfil.sys	Root	On machines that have a hibernation mode (Windows 2000/ 2003/XP), the hiberfil.sys stores the hibernated configuration. This configuration consists primarily of the entire contents of RAM. When a machine goes into sleep or hibernation mode, the contents of RAM are saved to allow for restoration of all current programs, making this as fruitful as the pagefile.sys for text searches when present.
NTUser.dat	Documents and Settings\ <Profile Name>	The HKEY_Current_User registry hive is stored in the main profile folder of each user. The Default User directory contains the basic hive file for new users. The .log versions of the registry files store changes made in the session to those files. The .sav files are backups of the files created at system setup time, and their datestamps are one of the mechanisms to identify when the system was initially built.
Default	%SYSTEMROOT%\ System32\Config	The HKEY_Users .Default profile is stored in this file.
Sam	%SYSTEMROOT%\ System32\Config	The HKEY_LocalMachine\SAM hive, used for Windows account management, is stored here.
Security	%SYSTEMROOT%\ System32\Config	The HKEY_LocalMachine\Security hive, used for network security, is stored here.
Software	%SYSTEMROOT%\ System32\Config	Any software-specific settings from HKEY_LocalMachine\software are stored in this file.

(continued)

Table 5-2   *(continued)*

FILE NAME	DEFAULT LOCATION	DESCRIPTION
System	%SYSTEMROOT%\System32\Config	The HKEY_Current_Config hive information is stored in this file.
AppEvent.evt	%SYSTEMROOT%\System32\Config	The Application event log file information is located here. Recovery of Event Logs is covered in a later chapter.
SecEvent.evt	%SYSTEMROOT%\System32\Config	The Security event log file information is located here. Recovery of event logs is covered in Chapter 11.
Hosts	%SYSTEMROOT%\System32\Drivers\Etc	Contains a mapping of DNS hostnames to IP addresses. Used before DNS lookups on Windows systems.
LMHosts	%SYSTEMROOT%\System32\Drivers\Etc	Contains a mapping of NetBIOS hostnames to IP addresses. Used before WINS lookups on Windows systems.
System.ini	%SYSTEMROOT%	Provides driver information to the operating system. Some of the functionality of this file has been transported to the Registry as Windows has evolved.
Win.ini	%SYSTEMROOT%	Provides operating system and application information to the operating system. Some of the functionality of this file has been transported to the Registry as Windows has evolved.

TIP   When entering into the command line a value that has spaces in it, surround the value with double quotes.

SECURITY IDENTIFIERS

Microsoft uses a unique Security Identifier (SID) to link assets to user accounts. Every user account has an SID generated when it is created based on both the user name and the domain. Because the SID includes domain information, it will be unique for that particular domain/user combination (that is, the user name ihack on the domain CORPORATE will be different than ihack on the domain AUTHORIZED).

The SID is frequently used in computer investigations. By searching a drive for the SID of a particular user, files created by that user or profile information related to that user can be found. Likewise, by performing a reverse lookup of a SID, the user name associated with a given SID can be ascertained.

To facilitate this, there are two freeware tools, sid2user and user2sid. By running the tools on a known user name or SID (the relevant domain needs to be available), the analyst can determine their counterparts. As an example, looking at the Recycler folder shows an associated SID (the /a is needed, as the folder is hidden):

```
C:\RECYCLER>dir /a
 Volume in drive C has no label.
 Volume Serial Number is 0401-17DD

 Directory of C:\RECYCLER

09/08/2003  05:58 PM    <DIR>          .
09/08/2003  05:58 PM    <DIR>          ..
09/13/2004  04:39 PM    <DIR>          S-1-5-
21-117609710-764733703-842925346-1003
               0 File(s)              0 bytes
               3 Dir(s)     231,620,608 bytes free

C:\RECYCLER>C:\temp\sid2user 5 21 117609710 764733703 842925346

Name is
Domain is CLASS
Type of SID is SidTypeDomain

C:\RECYCLER>C:\temp\sid2user 5 21 117609710 764733703 842925346 1003

Name is Chad M.S. Steel
Domain is CLASS
Type of SID is SidTypeUser

C:\RECYCLER>C:\temp\user2sid "Chad M.S. Steel"

S-1-5-21-117609710-764733703-842925346-1003

Number of subauthorities is 5
Domain is CLASS
Length of SID in memory is 28 bytes
Type of SID is SidTypeUser

C:\RECYCLER>C:\temp\user2sid Administrator

S-1-5-21-117609710-764733703-842925346-500

Number of subauthorities is 5
```

(continued)

SECURITY IDENTIFIERS *(continued)*

```
Domain is CLASS
Length of SID in memory is 28 bytes
Type of SID is SidTypeUser


C:\RECYCLER>C:\temp\user2sid Guest


S-1-5-21-117609710-764733703-842925346-501


Number of subauthorities is 5
Domain is CLASS
Length of SID in memory is 28 bytes
Type of SID is SidTypeUser
```

In the preceding example, first the domain and then the individual user of the SID are looked up. The domain is everything except the generic S-1 and the final number and returns the name CLASS in this case. The user name in the domain, specified by 1003, returns the name Chad M.S. Steel. Performing a reverse lookup returns on the name returns the SID value.

Even if the domain is not available, some information can be obtained from the last group of numbers in the identifier. Specifically, any identifier ending in -500 will always refer to the Administrator account, even if that account is renamed. Likewise, any identifier ending in -501 always refers to the Guest account.

Windows 9*x*

The Windows 9*x* systems contain legacy MS-DOS structures and as a result have a few differences in directory and file structure from the NT series of operating systems. This section covers the key differences, from a forensic standpoint, in the default directory structures and files between the operating system versions.

Directories

The default system root directory in Windows 9*x* is the Windows directory as opposed to WINNT. The Program Files directory functions the same as other versions of Windows.

Because Windows 9*x* was designed initially as a single user system, the concept of profiles are not as well embedded. Therefore, there is no Documents and Settings hierarchy present when first installed. The My Document directory off the root is the main repository for user information on a default installation. Likewise, temporary internet files and other data are stored directly off the %SYSTEMROOT% folder instead of in individual profiles.

If an additional user account is added to a Windows 9x system, the operating system does create a profile hierarchy containing the desktop, documents, application, and Internet files for each user. This hierarchy is stored under %SYSTEMROOT%/Profiles/<Profile Name>. Other key directory changes include:

- Printer spool information is kept in %SYSTEMROOT%/Spool/Printers.

- The Temporary directory is %SYSTEMROOT%/Temp.

- The System32 directory hierarchy is greatly reduced and does not contain the detailed configuration information.

- Since System Restore Points are not present, a System Volume Information folder is not created.

- The main registry files are simplified and reside directly in the %SYSTEMROOT% directory.

Files

Windows 9x contains fewer overall files and a more simplified file organization than the NT variants. This, along with a less complicated security model for files (there is effectively no security), makes analysis easier, although more likely to be necessary. The key file differences in Windows 9x over what is noted previously are as follows:

- There is no thumbs.db file as thumbnail-based views are not present (except in Windows ME).

- The paging file is referred to as a swap file and is located under the %SYSTEMROOT% directory in a file called Win386.swp.

- The registry is stored in three files instead of the multiple files noted above:

  - %SYSTEMROOT%/System.dat stores system-based registry information.

  - %SYSTEMROOT%/User.dat stores user-based registry information. This file will be in the individual profiles if multiple users are present on the system.

- The HOSTS and LMHOSTS files are located in the %SYSTEMROOT% directory.

- There are no event viewer logs, because there is no event viewer.

Additional Resources

Refer to the following list for additional resources:

Ad-aware Antispyware
 `www.lavasoftusa.com/software/adaware/`

Microsoft SID Reference
 `msdn.microsoft.com/library/default.asp?url=/library/`
 `en-us/secauthz/security/well_known_sids.asp`

SpyBot Search and Destroy
 `www.safer-networking.org/`

User2Sid and Sid2User
 `www.chem.msu.su/~rudnyi/NT/`

The Registry

The Microsoft Windows registry is the core repository for both operating system and application-specific settings. Information pertaining to the configuration and customization of Windows is stored in a series of hierarchical structures, accessible through a common interface. For the computer investigator, the registry provides a rich source of information on computer settings and activities ranging from identifying installed software to finding website passwords.

History

Legacy DOS operating systems stored their small amounts of configuration and customization information in two files: config.sys and autoexec.bat. Both of these files still exist, even in Windows 2003, for backwards compatibility. Early versions of Microsoft Windows built upon this configuration structure by storing additional configuration information for the operating system and applications as text-based settings stored in INI files. Like the autoexec.bat and config.sys files, INI files still exist in all versions of Windows.

To consolidate the information stored in these locations as well as provide structure to it (there were no hierarchical relationships between settings in the INI files), Microsoft introduced the registry in Windows 3.1 and expanded it to be the primary source of Windows settings in Windows 95. The registry provided structure as well as consolidation for the various operating system and application settings. A pre-defined hierarchy of *keys* was introduced, and applications could create their own subhierarchies as needed.

Since Windows 95, the registry has evolved considerably. The latest versions of the registry in Windows XP and 2003 are complex structures, and finding specific pieces of information in them relevant to an investigation can be challenging. Because of Microsoft's reliance on the registry for both information storage and retrieval, understanding the registry structure is essential to conducting a complete forensic analysis.

Registry Basics

The Windows registry is a hierarchical database of configuration values stored in a proprietary file format. Within the files are an organized set of hives that form the building blocks of the registry. Under each hive is a list of keys. All keys have a name and may contain multiple name/value pairs and subkeys. All of the keys are located beneath one of five root hives:

- HKEY_CLASSES_ROOT. Stores file association (associating file extensions with applications) and Microsoft Component Object Model (COM) information. This key is actually a pointer to HKEY_LOCAL_MACHINE\SOFTWARE\Classes. In Windows XP and 2003, this also contains information from HKEY_CURRENT_USER\SOFTWARE\Classes.

- HKEY_CURRENT_USER. Stores any user-specific information, including profile details, application usage information, and an individual's Internet activity details. This key and the HKEY_LOCAL_MACHINE key below are the two most important in an investigation. This key is actually a pointer to HKEY_USERS\SID, where SID is the unique security identifier for the currently logged-in user.

- HKEY_LOCAL_MACHINE. Stores the hardware and software settings as well as the security settings for the system. This is one of the two most critical keys in a computer investigation.

- HKEY_USERS. Stores all of the configuration information for all system users. The current user, pointed to by HKEY_CURRENT_USER, is generally (but not always) the most important in an investigation.

- HKEY_CURRENT_CONFIG. Stores any information on the current hardware configuration. It is not frequently used in an investigation. The key is actually a pointer to HKEY_LOCAL_MACHINE\SYSTEM\CurrentControlSet\Hardware Profiles*xxxx*, with *xxxx* being one of the numeric profiles (whichever one is the current one) listed.

NOTE A sixth hive, HKEY_DYN_DATA, is generated automatically in Windows 9x and NT. This key contains dynamic data such as performance measures and is not generally analyzed as part of a computer investigation.

The registry is primarily accessed through the Windows Registry Editor program. You can access it by typing regedit from the command line. The Registry Editor provides several functions of interest in an investigation. Primarily, it enables the investigator to both browse and search the registry for information. Secondarily, the Registry Editor gives the investigator the ability to export registry information for external analysis. The Registry Editor is shown in Figure 6-1.

A better choice for viewing the Windows XP/Server 2003 registry is the Registry Viewer from the 2003 resource kit, available for download from the Microsoft website. For Windows 2000, the Regedt32 program (an alternative Registry Editor) has a read-only mode as well.

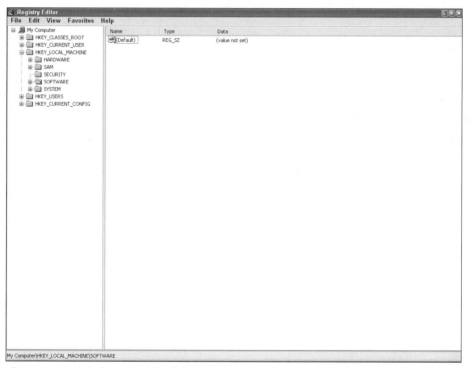

Figure 6-1: Windows Registry Editor

For command prompt–based analysis, a second Windows NT tool is also useful: the Microsoft Console Registry Tool (CRT), accessible with the reg command. The CRT provides an investigator with the capability of querying and exporting registry key information using reg query and reg export, respectively. An example of the use of the CRT to query the Run key (used to automatically run programs at startup) and all of its subkeys and name/value pairs (the /s switch does this recursively) is as follows:

```
C:\>reg query HKLM\Software\Microsoft\Windows\CurrentVersion\Run /s

! REG.EXE VERSION 3.0

HKEY_LOCAL_MACHINE\Software\Microsoft\Windows\CurrentVersion\Run
     ccApp       REG_SZ   "D:\Program Files\Common Files\Symantec
Shared\ccApp.exe"
     vptray      REG_SZ   C:\PROGRA~1\SYMANT~1\VPTray.exe
     epgcfsiscpe REG_SZ   D:\WINDOWS\System32\jslfde.exe
     Win Server Updt    REG_SZ   D:\WINDOWS\wupdt.exe
     NeroFilterCheck    REG_SZ   D:\WINDOWS\system32\NeroCheck.exe

HKEY_LOCAL_MACHINE\Software\Microsoft\Windows\CurrentVersion\Run\Optiona
lComponents

HKEY_LOCAL_MACHINE\Software\Microsoft\Windows\CurrentVersion\Run\Optiona
lComponents\IMAIL
     Installed   REG_SZ   1

HKEY_LOCAL_MACHINE\Software\Microsoft\Windows\CurrentVersion\Run\Optiona
lComponents\MAPI
     Installed   REG_SZ   1
     NoChange    REG_SZ   1

HKEY_LOCAL_MACHINE\Software\Microsoft\Windows\CurrentVersion\Run\Optiona
lComponents\MSFS
     Installed   REG_SZ   1
```

Another useful tool for analyzing a specific program for operational use is Regmon a real-time registry access monitor available from Sysinternals. Regmon is used to determine what keys are read from or written to. It is exceptionally useful in identifying specific registry keys that an individual application stored information in, such as recently used files, usage statistics, or installation times. It is also used for malicious code analysis to see where a virus or worm plants itself to start automatically. Figure 6-2 shows a screenshot of an active Regmon session.

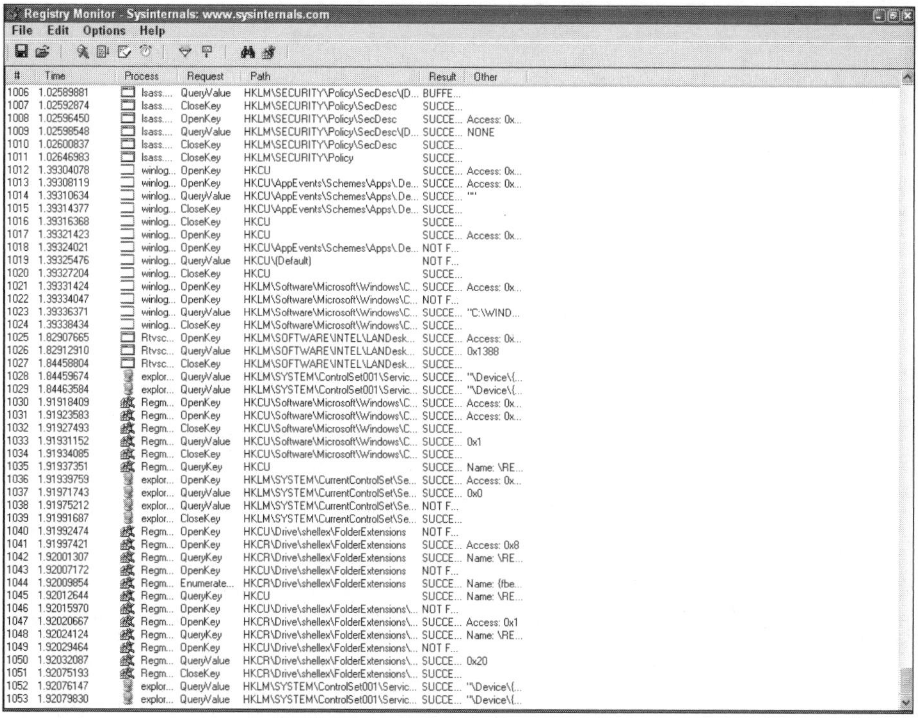

Figure 6-2:   Registry activity viewed with Regmon

Microsoft protects registry keys through permissions (on the NT side), because they can contain personal user information as well as critical Windows security details (and dangerous settings that can drastically alter Windows behavior). An individual's hives under HKEY_USERS are protected for access by that user. Likewise, certain subkeys are even protected from administrator viewing (such as the SAM and SECURITY subkeys under the HKEY_LOCAL_MACHINE hive) by default. In a locked-down environment, permissions can be set for individual keys.

WINDOWS REGISTRY FILE LOCATIONS

The standard Windows registry file locations vary based on operating system. Additional versions of the registry that may contain legacy information prior to cleaning in the case of user-wiped registries may be present in several locations. The default registry files are located as follows:

Windows NT/2000/XP/2003

◆ **HKEY_CURRENT_USER—Located under the user's profile directory (Documents and Settings\Profilename\NTUser.dat on 2000/XP/2003 or %SYSTEMROOT%\profiles\Profilename\NTUser.dat on NT)**

(continued)

WINDOWS REGISTRY FILE LOCATIONS *(continued)*

- ◆ HKEY_CURRENT_CONFIG—Taken from the HKEY_LOCAL_MACHINE\ SYSTEM file

- ◆ HKEY_CLASSES_ROOT—Taken from the HKEY_CURRENT_USER and HKEY_LOCAL_MACHINE\SOFTWARE files

- ◆ HKEY_LOCAL_MACHINE\

  - ■ HARDWARE—A dynamic key built by Windows at startup

  - ■ SAM—%SYSTEMROOT%\System32\Config\SAM

  - ■ SECURITY—%SYSTEMROOT%\System32\Config\SECURITY

  - ■ SOFTWARE—%SYSTEMROOT%\System32\Config\SOFTWARE

  - ■ SYSTEM—%SYSTEMROOT%\System32\Config\SYSTEM

  - ■ HKEY_USERS—Built from the individual user profile NTUser.dat files

Windows 9x

- ◆ HKEY_CURRENT_USER—%SYSTEMROOT%\Profiles\Profilename\User.dat

- ◆ HKEY_CURRENT_CONFIG—Taken from System.dat

- ◆ HKEY_CLASSES_ROOT—Taken from System.dat

- ◆ HKEY_LOCAL_MACHINE—%SYSTEMROOT%\System.dat

- ◆ HKEY_USERS—Built from the individual user profile User.dat files

- ◆ HKEY_DYN_DATA—Generated dynamically on system startup

In addition to the default file locations, the registry hive files or their data may be located in other areas. In addition to searching for hive files, the following are likely spots for the same information:

- ◆ *System.alt.* On Windows NT and 2000 systems, the System.alt file is a backup of the system file and the associated hives. The System.alt file is located in the same directory as the standard files.

- ◆ **.sav.* On the initial system build, a copy of the raw registry file is created as a SAV file. While it may not contain information added to a system, it may provide other guidance (such as the version of the software installed, the install date/time). The SAV files are located in the same directory as the standard files.

- ◆ *%SYSTEMROOT%\Sysbckup*. Windows 9x systems store backups of the registry files in CAB archives labeled rb00n.cab, where *n* is the number of the backup. These can be extracted using the command extract /e rb00n.cab and copies of the registry at a specific period viewed.

- ◆ *%SYSTEMROOT%\Repair*. On NT-based systems, copies of the initial registry files are made to this directory upon initial system installation.

◆ **%SYSTEMROOT%\Repair\Regback.** **When an Emergency Repair Disk is created on NT-based systems, copies of the registry files are put in this directory. They are too large to fit on a disk.**

◆ **C:\System Volume Information\restore_{xxx-xxx}\RPnn\.** **Under Windows XP and later systems, any system restore points may have registry information. Search under the various _restore directories and associated RPnn directories for files labeled:**

- **_REGISTRY_USER_.DEFAULT**
- **_REGISTRY_MACHINE_SECURITY**
- **_REGISTRY_MACHINE_SOFTWARE**
- **_REGISTRY_MACHINE_SYSTEM**
- **_REGISTRY_MACHINE_SAM**

Each of these files can be restored to the respective registry file by renaming the file to correspond with the original name (for example, _REGISTRY_MACHINE_SYSTEM becomes SYSTEM).

Registry Analysis

There are four primary methods of analyzing the registry in a forensic analysis of a system (five if the real-time analysis provided by Regmon is included):

- Perform a live system analysis graphically. This method is the easiest but the least forensically sound. Opening the registry using regedit on the target system will show the easiest to traverse view of the registry, but allows for the accidental or intentional altering of data when viewing, in addition to a very small amount of memory overwrite (or paging file) to run the program (around 250K).

- Perform a live system analysis using the command line. Command line analysis allows for a lower profile (and less risky) gathering of registry information, with some loss of interactivity. The reg command can be used to gather specifics on a given set of keys determined beforehand and placed in a batch file or an entire registry section (recursively printing values) as needed.

- Perform a live systems analysis remotely. Regedit provides the ability to connect to a remote registry, provided the appropriate permissions are present. This enables an administrator to examine a registry on a remote system without directly alerting the user. Likewise, the use of a Null session connection (such as that used by Superscan from Foundstone) will allow the enumeration of several registry keys, including user lists and information on current users.

■ Perform an offline analysis on registry files. EnCase is able to parse the raw registry files on acquired drives. This allows for the offline analysis of registry information in a completely forensically sound manner. Although this is the most sound mechanism, it is also the least fruitful. Any dynamic information is lost, the structure is more difficult to navigate, and the links are missing (for example, the HKEY_CURRENT_USER linkage).

When analyzing the registry, numerous values are relevant to a wide range of investigations. A few of the key values, and the types of investigations they are relevant in, are detailed in the following sections.

General

Several registry keys are examined in numerous types of investigations. They are not necessarily specific to a given area; however, they are relevant to a number of investigations. These keys include basic system information (who used the system and what applications are installed) and more detailed information on key system areas (what hardware was installed and what drives were mounted). Table 6-1 lists these general registry keys.

Table 6-1   General Registry Keys

NAME	DESCRIPTION
HKCR*\(Default)	Provides the name of the application handler associated with a file extension. Looking up the application handler name may provide the associated executable. When unknown file extensions are encountered (or extensions appear to be mapped oddly), they can be traced to an executable here.
HKCU\Control Panel*	Stores all of the control panel settings under subkeys. If a particular control panel setting needs to be known for an investigation (such as whether or not the Wallpaper setting under Desktop points to a Victoria's Secret image), this is the location to check. All of the entries under HKEY_CURRENT_USER apply to all of the subkeys of HKEY_USERS.
HKCU\Network*	Lists drives mapped as persistent (restored at login). Each drive letter under Network refers to a mapped drive on the system. Non-persistent drives are not.

Table 6-1   *(continued)*

NAME	DESCRIPTION
HKCU\Printers\ DevModePerUser	Shows any printers defined by the system for the current, including network printers. If this key is not present, no Printers have been added to the system.
HKCU\Volatile Environment	Stores environment variables for the current session on XP/2003.
HKCU\Software* and HKLM\Software*	Refer to software installed on the system. Software that has been deleted or uninstalled frequently leaves registry keys with user settings or machine settings after removal.
HKCU\Software\Microsoft\ Internet Account Manager\ Accounts*	Stores the settings for Outlook Express mail accounts under the numbered subdirectories. SMTP and POP3 servers as well as user names and email addresses are present.
HKCU\Software\Microsoft\ NTBackup	Provides details, in log file subkeys, on the last time a backup was run on the NT line of software. This data indicates the possible presence and timeframe for tapes or other media to be present.
HKCU\Software\ Microsoft\Windows\ CurrentVersion\Explorer\ ComputerDescriptions	Caches comments of servers the user has browsed (but not necessarily connected. Windows XP and 2003 machines include additional comments about a server in addition to the server name in a browse list.
HKCU\Software\Microsoft\ Windows NT\CurrentVersion\ Devices and \PrinterPorts and \Windows and HKLM\ Software\Microsoft\ Windows NT\CurrentVersion\ Print\Printers	Lists printers set up under the current system for Windows NT-based systems.
HKLM\Hardware\ Devicemap\Scsi\	Contain individual entries for peripheral devices attached to both the SCSI and IDE bus on NT-based systems, including CD-ROM, Zip, and hard disks.
HKLM\Network\Logon\	Lists the different logon profiles that appear on the startup screen for a given machine on Windows 9x machines.
HKLM\SAM\SAM\ Domains\Account\	Lists names for Users and Groups (under the /Names subkey of their respective areas, if permissions allow viewing the SAM key on NT-based systems.

(continued)

Table 6-1 *(continued)*

NAME	DESCRIPTION
HKLM\Software\ Microsoft\Updates	Lists the installed updates with installation dates for Windows XP and 2003re. This can be useful in disproving virus or worm susceptibility, or showing a pattern of regular security updating.
HKLM\Software\ Microsoft\Windows\ CurrentVersion\Uninstall	Lists all installed programs under subkeys. Sometimes uninstalled programs will leave remnants here for the investigator to find.
HKLM\Software\Microsoft\ WindowsNT\CurrentVersion\ Network Cards	Shows network cards the system is aware of on NT-based systems. Previously removed network cards may still be listed.
HKLM\System\ CurrentControlSet\Control\ ComputerName	Lists the name of the computer assigned by the user.
HKLM\System\ CurrentControlSet\Control\ Print\Printers	Displays printer information on installed printers for all Windows versions.
HKLM\System\ CurrentControlSet\Control\ TimeZoneInformation	Shows the time zone set for the computer. For large enterprises, this may indicate the nationality or location of the user.
HKLM\System\ CurrentControlSet\Enum	Lists information on current and previously installed hardware.
HKLM\System\ CurrentControlSet\Enum\ USBSTOR	Lists any USB storage devices (for example, DVD-Rs or flash drives), even after the device has been disconnected.
HKLM\System\ CurrentControlSet\Services	Lists all of the current services installed. A Start value of 2 indicates automatic startup, 3 indicates manual.
HKLM\System\ MountedDevices	Lists the mounted drive letters and volume names, including those of previously mounted devices.

TIP Common file types to search for when looking for burned CDs include RCL for Roxio EZ-CD Creator compilations, ISO, IMG, .BIN for actual images, and CUE files for tables of contents. To view the files without burning a CD, WinISO from www.winiso.com can be useful.

CASE STUDY: CD BURNING

One of our department managers made allegations that an individual from IT was copying confidential company information to DVD-R and removing if from the company. We were asked to confirm the individual had a DVD burner and had made copies, in addition to confirming the contents of what may have been copied.

Searching the corporate asset management records produced no CD or DVD burner issued to the suspect or his department. A subsequent physical search of the suspect's area likewise turned up no burners. The suspect's laptop was acquired forensically and brought back to the lab for analysis.

Prior to analyzing the laptop, the subject was questioned regarding the use of a CD or DVD burner on his laptop. He denied ever possessing a CD or DVD burner or connecting one to his laptop.

The registry of the laptop was viewed and showed a USB device in the list of prior connections with a device name of PLEXTOR DVDR PX-708A USB Device under HKEY_LOCAL_MACHINE\System\CurrentControlSet\Enum\USBSTOR. Likewise, a search of the software keys indicated a key labeled HKEY_LOCAL_MACHINE\Software\Ahead\Nero - Burning Rom, which corresponded with the name and company of a popular CD/DVD authoring tool: Nero Burning ROM.

A search for Nero compilation files (.nrc) found numerous files presents. Likewise, a search for other compilation and disk files turned up numerous volumes, including several dozen ISO image files.

Opening the compilation files in the respective programs revealed numerous DVD-R movies had been burned to CD. Likewise, opening the actual image files found they contained both DVD-format and AVI format versions of copyrighted movies.

There was no evidence of company information being burned to disk. That said, the employee's use of company equipment to download and subsequently burn copyrighted material, coupled with his decision to lie about using a CD/DVD burner, resulted in his termination.

Folder Locations

The key folders on Microsoft systems are the most likely location for files of interest in an investigation. These folders include the My Documents folder (and My Music/My Pictures folders), the Startup folder, the Recent folder, and the Internet folders (Cache, History, Favorites and Cookies).

The default locations of these folders are noted in the previous chapters. By altering registry settings, an individual user can change these folders, generally for legitimate reasons (for example, storing My Documents on a separate partition). By confirming the locations of these folders, an investigation can be directed at target locations for initial analysis. Table 6-2 lists the folder location registry keys.

Table 6-2 Folder Location Registry Keys

NAME	DESCRIPTION
HKCU\Environment\ Tmp & Temp	Identifies the environment variables that provide the location of the Windows temp directories. The temp directories are likely locations for temporary copies of files that may or may not exist elsewhere.
HKCU\Software\Microsoft\ Windows\CurrentVersion\ Explorer\Shell Folders*	Enables users to change the locations of specific folders, such as My Documents, Recent, and Startup through the various subkeys. Changing these folder locations changes the links from all locations that point to the particular special folder. When conducting an investigation, the computer investigator needs to confirm the contents of the folder in addition to confirming what that folder is associated with (for example, if the Startup folder is redirected, programs may be executing at startup from that new location).
HKLM\Software\Microsoft\ Windows\CurrentVersion\ Explorer\Shell Folders*	Contains the links relevant to folders used by All Users. These can likewise be redirected to point to alternate file system locations for malicious or legitimate reasons.
HKLM\System\ CurrentControlSet\Control\ Hivelist	Identifies the locations of registry hive files on Windows XP and 2003.

Determining what files, folders, or applications were most recently used is a key task in investigations. Showing that an individual opened a file, saved a file, or searched for a file can prove the suspect knew the file existed (or even created the file, in the case of Save As lists). Sometimes a suspect will delete a file after viewing it. Unless explicitly cleared, the file name may still appear in the Most Recently Used (MRU) registry keys.

Many of the MRU listed in Table 6-3 contain subkeys with single letter names in addition to a key called MRUList with a list of letters. For the MRUList key, the most recently opened item will be designated by the first letter listed on the left, with the next most recent following, through the end of the list.

In addition to the Microsoft-specific MRU lists, installed applications may have their own most recently used keys. The most likely location for these is under the HKEY_CURRENT_USER\Software*AppName* hierarchy.

Table 6-3   Recently Used Item Registry Keys

NAME	DESCRIPTION
HKCU\Software\Microsoft\ Internet Explorer\TypedURLs	Shows any URLs typed into the address bar in Internet Explorer, including local links. These URL's have been typed by a user (as opposed to being clicked on or generated by spyware), and can be used to disprove spyware defenses.
HKCU\Software\Microsoft\ Windows\CurrentVersion\ Applets\Wordpad\ Recent File List	Displays the most recent files opened up in Wordpad. Notepad does not have a specific MRU list.
HKCU\Software\Microsoft\ Windows\CurrentVersion\ Applets\Paint\ Recent File List	Shows the most recent files opened in Paint.
HKCU\Software\Microsoft\ Windows\CurrentVersion\ Explorer\RunMRU	Lists the most recently typed items in the Run box. Any programs run directly from the command line instead of the Run dialog box are not shown. Programs a suspect may have launched and then deleted might be listed in this key.
HKCU\Software\Microsoft\ Windows\CurrentVersion\ Explorer\RecentDocs*	Lists, under subkeys, the most recently opened documents from Explorer associated with a specific extension. Separate from the Recent Documents Start Menu item, searches for a given file or files of a particular extension may show the user recently opened files here.
HKCU\Software\Microsoft\ Windows\CurrentVersion\ Explorer\StreamMRU	Stores the windows size and location of the most recently used files. Although the size and location may not matter, the file name associated with the Window may show that file was present and opened on a specific machine. This key is rarely cleaned, even when users go through the registry to delete items. Likewise, because the file names are sometimes padded with other characters, a simple text search in RegEdit will not turn them up.
HKCU\Software\Microsoft\ Windows\CurrentVersion\ Explorer\ComDlg32\ LastVisitedMRU	Shows the most recently opened folders for a given executable (opened from a common dialog box). Showing what folders an application was using can indicate that a user was aware of their existence and opened something from them, although what was opened is not listed.

(continued)

Table 6-3   *(continued)*

NAME	DESCRIPTION
HKCU\Software\Microsoft\ Windows\CurrentVersion\ Explorer\ComDlg32\ OpenSaveMRU	Lists the most recently opened files from a common dialog box, grouped by extension. A list of the most recently opened files with any extension are listed under the * key. The presence of a given file here indicates that the user knowingly opened that file for use, viewing, or editing. These keys are not available on Windows NT.
HKCU\Software\Microsoft\ MediaPlayer\Player\ RecentFileList	Shows the most recent files opened by Media Player. Media Player can be used to play songs, videos, and other content (such as DVDs).
HKCU\Software\Microsoft\ MSPaper\Recent File List	Lists all recent faxes or images with a .tif extension opened by Microsoft Picture and Fax Viewer. The Microsoft Picture and Fax Viewer is the default viewer for TIF images on XP.
HKCU\Software\Microsoft\ Search Assistant\ACMru	Contains the most recently typed items from the Search Assistant dialog box. Items searched for using the older Find Files or Folders dialog box are located in HKCU\Software\Microsoft\Windows\ CurrentVersion\Explorer\Doc Find Spec MRU.
HKCU\Software\Microsoft\ Office\<Version Number>\ Common\OpenFind*	Under each of the applications will be a list of the most recently opened and saved files for each Microsoft Office application. Additionally, under the HKCU\Software\Microsoft\Office*Version Number\App Name* key, there may be an additional Recent Files key, which lists the most recent files opened by that application depending on the Office version.
HKCU\Software\Microsoft\ Windows\CurrentVersion\ Explorer\ Map Network Drive MRU	Shows the most recent network drives mapped by the computer.

Startup Items

Spyware, viruses, and other malicious code will frequently continue to infect a computer after a reboot. To accomplish this, the code needs to be run automatically unless it is associated with a file the user is expected to reopen frequently, such as a mail file or common executable. The Windows Registry contains numerous locations from which code can automatically be run; the most common of these locations are detailed in Table 6-4. Anything suspicious found in these keys may require further investigation, but many legitimate programs also make use of these keys.

Table 6-4   Startup Item Registry Keys

NAME	DESCRIPTION
HKCU\Software\Microsoft\ Windows\CurrentVersion\ Run\	Identifies any user-specific software set to run the next time that individual logs in. This is less frequently used than the HKEY_LOCAL_MACHINE keys, as it is user-dependent.
HKLM\Software\Microsoft\ Windows\CurrentVersion\ Run\	Shows the items that are automatically executed on every system logon. This is the old favorite location for malware to start but is becoming less commonly used as malware authors are hiding their software in more obscure key locations.
HKLM\Software\Microsoft\ Windows\CurrentVersion\ RunOnce\	Lists executables set to be run once and then deleted from the registry. This is frequently used by two-part installers requiring a reboot between each part. Malware can use this key by placing a link to the offending code in it, then adding it back after automatic removal.
HKLM\Software\Microsoft\ Windows\CurrentVersion\ RunOnceEx	Lists executables set to be run once and then deleted from the registry. Generally used for unattended system installations on Windows XP, RunOnceEx can be used for malicious code the same was as the above RunOnce key.
HKCU\Software\Microsoft\ Windows\CurrentVersion\ RunServices HKCU\Software\Microsoft\ Windows\CurrentVersion\ RunServicesOnce HKLM\Software\Microsoft\ Windows\CurrentVersion\ RunServices HKLM\Software\Microsoft\ Windows\CurrentVersion\ RunServicesOnce	Lists services set to run automatically at startup either once or every time. These keys can be used to trigger executables before a user logs on. These keys are not always present, but can be created by the programs taking advantage of them.
HKCU\Software\Microsoft\ WindowsNT\CurrentVersion\ Windows\Load	This is a lesser-known key. It is used sometimes, because it does not require the creation of a new subkey and is less frequently examined.
HKLM\Software\Microsoft\ Windows\CurrentVersion\ Policies\Explorer\Run HKLM\Software\Microsoft\ Windows\CurrentVersion\ Policies\Explorer\Run	Lists programs associated with Windows Explorer that are permitted to run automatically when the users logs in. The HKEY_CURRENT_USER key is associated with a particular user, while the other key runs with any user.

(continued)

Table 6-4 *(continued)*

NAME	DESCRIPTION
HKLM\Software\Microsoft\ WindowsNT\CurrentVersion\ Winlogon\Userinit	Contains the userinit.exe executable (which is legitimate). However, it can also contain other names separated by commas. As this key is not generally used by legitimate programs, any entry other than userinit.exe should be viewed with suspicion.
HKLM\Software\Microsoft\ Windows\CurrentVersion\ Explorer\SharedTaskScheduler	Shows tasks scheduled to be run at startup on the Windows NT–based operating systems (not Windows 9x). There are generally a few legitimate Windows-generated keys in this hierarchy.

AUTOSTART LOCATIONS

Windows has numerous locations from which programs can be launched automatically at startup. In addition to the standard registry locations detailed earlier, there are numerous other points from which an application can be launched. These include:

- ◆ The Startup folders under individual user profiles:
  - ■ C:\Documents and Settings*Profile Name*\Start Menu\Programs\Startup by default on Windows 2000/XP/2003
  - ■ %SYSTEMROOT%\Profiles*Profile Name*\Start Menu\Programs\ on Windows NT
- ◆ The Startup folders for all profiles:
  - ■ C:\Documents and Settings\All Users\Start Menu\Programs\Startup by default on Windows 2000/XP/2003
  - ■ %SYSTEMROOT%\Profiles\All Users\Start Menu\Programs\ on Windows NT
  - ■ %SYSTEMROOT%\Start Menu\Programs\ on Windows 9x
- ◆ The legacy DOS program and driver autoload locations:
  - ■ C:\autoexec.bat
  - ■ C:\config.sys
- ◆ The Windows autostart files:
  - ■ %SYSTEMROOT%\winstart.bat
  - ■ %SYSTEMROOT%\wininit.ini
- ◆ The Windows configuration files:
  - ■ %SYSTEMROOT%\win.ini (listed under load and run in the [windows] key)
  - ■ %SYSTEMROOT%\system.ini (listed under shell and scrnsave.exe in the [boot] key)

◆ **The legacy DOS-mode startup file (on Windows 9x):**

■ **%SYSTEMROOT%\dosstart.bat**

◆ **The application environment files for 16-bit applications (on Windows NT–based systems):**

■ **%SYSTEMROOT%\System32\autoexec.nt**

■ **%SYSTEMROOT%\System32\config.nt**

◆ **As Windows Services:**

■ **Any services with a Startup type of Automatic in the Services list**

In addition to the above locations, applications can be automatically started from other applications, from other application shortcuts, and through component controls (such as those in Internet Explorer).

To easily view the majority of programs that start automatically, SysInternals provides the program Autoruns. A screenshot of Autoruns output is shown in the following figure. Additionally, for live system forensic analysis, a command line version (autorunsc) is included.

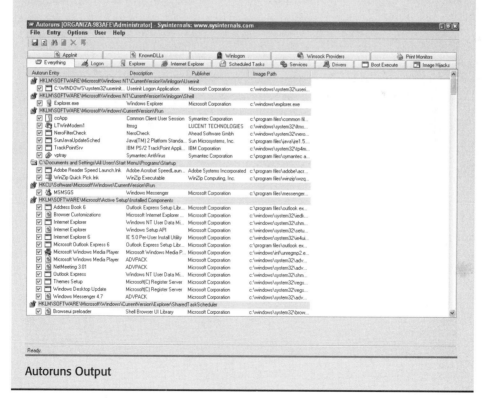

Autoruns Output

Intelliforms

Microsoft Internet Explorer 5.0 introduced the Autocomplete feature to allow users to easily store and automatically fill out form entries online. Autocomplete uses a Microsoft technology called Intelliforms. The technology itself matches the name on a form input field to a group of values stored in the registry. These registry entries are then queried when a website with similar fields is opened.

Intelliforms can store all information typed into forms on a web browser. This includes credit card numbers, passwords, addresses, and other pieces of information critical to an investigation. To protect this information, Microsoft encrypts any registry entries stored for Intelliforms use and places them under the registry key HKEY_CURRENT_USER\Software\Microsoft\Protected Storage System Provider\. This key is accessible only to the SYSTEM account by default, and the data is not viewable except in encrypted form even with the proper permissions granted.

To access Intelliforms information as well as other encrypted registry entries, the investigator can refer to a few products, including Windows Secret Explorer, which works on both live systems and registry files (see Figure 6-3).

Figure 6-3: Windows Secret Explorer decryption

The entries shown correspond to the field firstname and the different entries typed into fields of that name. If an investigator needs to find out what was typed into a particular field on a URL and Autocomplete was turned on, the investigator can open the page in question, view the HTML code, and find the name of the relevant text box (which should be a tag labeled `<input type="text" name="nnnn">` where *nnnn* is the name of the field). The `textarea` tags are also common form elements, which may have names associated with them. Armed with the name of the tag, Windows Secret Explorer can then be used to directly view the values typed into that field.

Advanced Registry Analysis

The registry keys above provide guidance on how to analyze a registry file when the target keys are known. Many analyses, however, involve finding unknown values in the registry for very specific software packages, including web browsers, peer-to-peer software, spyware, and CD/DVD authoring software.

To find the appropriate registry keys associated with a specific piece of software, there are two mechanisms: using static registry analysis (snapshots) and dynamic registry analysis (monitoring). Static analysis is generally easier to analyze because monitoring produces large amounts of data and requires filtering to be useful. Dynamic analysis provides information that cannot be provided by static analysis such as registry reads (for example, to find licensing information).

Static analysis is performed as follows:

1. The investigator creates a clean operating system installation. VMWare and Microsoft Virtual PC are great for these as the image files for a new build can simply be copied every time a new machine is needed.

2. A copy of the registry is taken using a registry snapshot tool such as RegShot (shown in Figure 6-4).

Figure 6-4: RegShot registry snapshot tool

3. The software package to be analyzed is installed.

4. A second copy of the registry is taken.

5. The first and second copies of the registry are compared and any new or changed entries are noted.

The following listing is a sample output of the keys added from the installation of Firefox version 1.0PR taken with RegShot:

```
REGSHOT LOG 1.60
Comments:
Datetime:2004/10/19 18:06:27  |  2004/10/19 18:17:07
Computer:SECURITY | SECURITY
Username: |


----------------------------------
Keys deleted:1
----------------------------------
HKEY_USERS\S-1-5-
21-448539723-1563985344-1202660629-1003\Software\Microsoft\Windows\Curre
ntVersion\Explorer\Discardable\PostSetup\ShellNew


----------------------------------
Keys added:17
----------------------------------
HKEY_LOCAL_MACHINE\SOFTWARE\Classes\CHROME\shell\open\ddeexec
HKEY_LOCAL_MACHINE\SOFTWARE\Classes\CHROME\shell\open\ddeexec\Application
HKEY_LOCAL_MACHINE\SOFTWARE\Classes\CHROME\shell\open\ddeexec\Topic
HKEY_LOCAL_MACHINE\SOFTWARE\FullCircle\TalkBack\MozillaOrgFirefox10
Win322004100109
HKEY_LOCAL_MACHINE\SOFTWARE\Microsoft\Windows\CurrentVersion\Uninstall\
Mozilla Firefox (1.0PR)
HKEY_LOCAL_MACHINE\SOFTWARE\Mozilla\Mozilla Firefox\1.0PR (en-US)
HKEY_LOCAL_MACHINE\SOFTWARE\Mozilla\Mozilla Firefox\1.0PR (en-US)\Main
HKEY_LOCAL_MACHINE\SOFTWARE\Mozilla\Mozilla Firefox\1.0PR (en-US)\
Uninstall
HKEY_LOCAL_MACHINE\SOFTWARE\Mozilla\Mozilla Firefox 1.0PR
HKEY_LOCAL_MACHINE\SOFTWARE\Mozilla\Mozilla Firefox 1.0PR\bin
HKEY_LOCAL_MACHINE\SOFTWARE\Mozilla\Mozilla Firefox 1.0PR\Extensions
HKEY_USERS\S-1-5-21-448539723-1563985344-1202660629-1003\Software\
Mozilla\Mozilla Firefox\1.0PR (en-US)
HKEY_USERS\S-1-5-21-448539723-1563985344-1202660629-1003\Software\
Mozilla\Mozilla Firefox\1.0PR (en-US)\Main
HKEY_USERS\S-1-5-21-448539723-1563985344-1202660629-1003\Software\
Mozilla\Mozilla Firefox\1.0PR (en-US)\Uninstall
HKEY_USERS\S-1-5-21-448539723-1563985344-1202660629-1003\Software\
Mozilla\Mozilla Firefox 1.0PR
HKEY_USERS\S-1-5-21-448539723-1563985344-1202660629-1003\Software\
Mozilla\Mozilla Firefox 1.0PR\bin
HKEY_USERS\S-1-5-21-448539723-1563985344-1202660629-1003\Software\
Mozilla\Mozilla Firefox 1.0PR\Extensions
```

For dynamic registry analysis, a tool such as Regmon can be used to perform real-time analysis. Dynamic analysis steps are similar to those in static analysis:

1. The investigator creates a clean operating system installation. VMWare and Microsoft Virtual PC are great for these as the image files for a new build can simply be copied every time a new machine is needed.

2. The registry monitoring tool is started.

3. The registry monitoring tool filter is configured to include the process in question.

4. The software package to be analyzed is installed.

5. The registry monitoring results are analyzed. A sample analysis is shown in Figure 6-5.

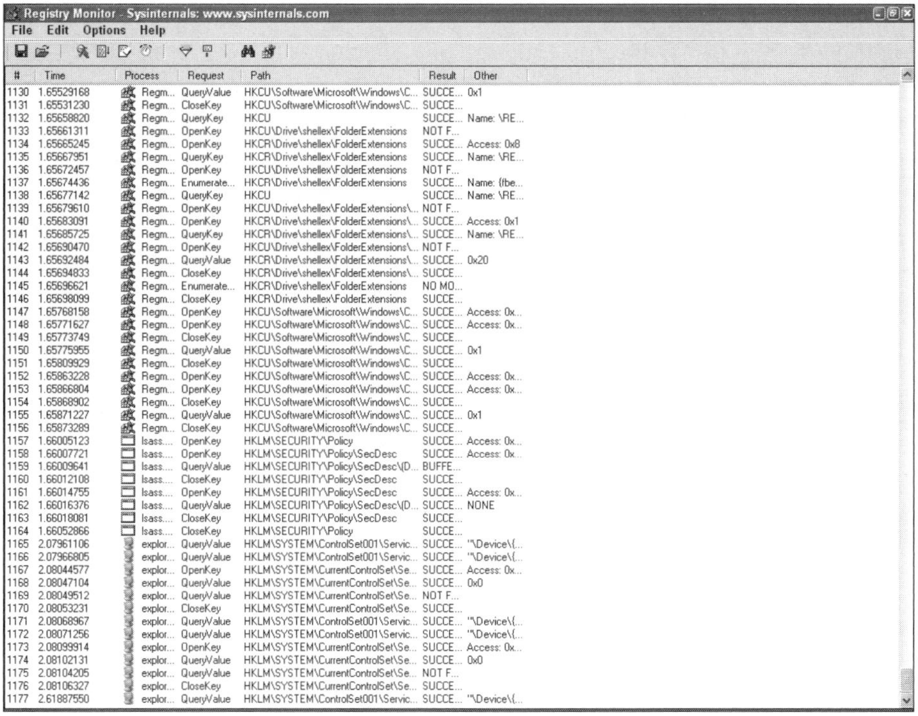

Figure 6-5: Regmon dynamic analysis

Additional Resources

Refer to the following list for additional resources:

Autoruns Autostart Viewer From SysInternals
`www.sysinternals.com/ntw2k/freeware/autoruns.shtml`

FileMon File Monitor From SysInternals
`www.sysinternals.com/Utilities/Filemon.html`

Microsoft Registry Viewer
`www.microsoft.com/downloads/details.aspx?FamilyID=`
`9d467a69-57ff-4ae7-96ee-b18c4790cffd&displaylang=en`

RegMon Registry Monitor From SysInternals
`www.sysinternals.com/Utilities/Regmon.html`

RegShot Registry Snapshot Tool
`www.majorgeeks.com/download965.html`

Windows Secret Explorer
`lastbit.com/wse/default.asp`

WinISO CD Image Editor
`www.winiso.com`

Forensic Analysis

The previous chapters detailed the basics of the Windows environment that are relevant to a forensic investigation. Effective computer investigators put together that knowledge with recognized forensic techniques—that is one of the things that separate a computer investigator from an MCSE or other Windows professional. The following chapters use the building blocks of knowledge provided in the previous chapters and apply them to actual forensic activities.

TIP The Microsoft Certified Software Engineer (MCSE), specifically the MCSE: Security Certification, is an excellent baseline to start from when learning Windows forensics. MCSE courses are widely available and are a recommended addition to any security certifications held by a computer investigator focusing on Windows.

The techniques used in a computer investigation can be broken down into several categories:

- **Live system analysis.** These techniques are used before shutting down and imaging a system and can provide information on running programs, currently logged-in users, and other activities that may be lost in an off-line analysis.

■ **Forensic duplication.** Creating forensically sound images of content on a Windows system presents a host of challenges. Techniques for imaging content are varied and provide the basis for further analysis.

■ **File systems analysis.** Most forensic analysis involves looking at the file system—finding files, recovering files, providing details on file creation, ownership, and modification, and so on. Learning these techniques will provide the most frequently used tools in the computer investigator's arsenal.

■ **Internet analysis.** Almost all Windows investigations today involve the analysis of Internet activity to some degree. Looking at peer-to-peer, web browsing, and instant messaging usage can provide a detailed record of past Internet activity.

■ **Email forensics.** The identification and recovery of emails gives the computer investigator records of communication between the suspect and his associates. Microsoft Outlook, Outlook Express, and Lotus Notes are the most common Windows-based email applications encountered in investigations.

■ **Log file analysis.** Analyzing individual log files for data that was recorded on system, application, or user activity is important for both client and server analyses. Records of past actions can be found using Event Viewer, Microsoft's event log analysis application, as well as through the inspection of server logs.

■ **Network monitoring.** Although detailed network forensics is beyond the scope of this book, some knowledge of monitoring on Windows systems is useful to a forensic examiner. Effectively using network sniffing tools is a stealthy way to obtain evidence in real-time.

With a detailed understanding of the basic Windows forensic techniques, the computer investigator is equipped to handle a broad range of situations. Almost any computer investigation can be undertaken, from finding evidence of email fraud to showing inappropriate usage, by putting the same techniques to use in a logical manner.

CHAPTER 8

Live System Analysis

For several reasons, computer investigators analyze live Windows systems before powering them down. There are two mechanisms for performing live systems analysis: covert monitoring and overt acquisition.

Covert analysis attempts to examine or monitor the activities of users or programs. Analysis reviews existing information. Monitoring can take place at a computer or network level and can encompass current and future actions. The major covert analysis activities are:

- **Performing remote acquisition.** Remote acquisition or drive previewing using EnCase Enterprise enables an investigator to sneak a peek into a computer's file system or perform a full, remote drive image.

- **Determining system information using Windows Administrative tools.** Using common Administration tools such as the Computer Management console enables an examiner on a corporate network to review systems to which she has administrative rights.

- **Monitoring current keyboard/mouse activity.** Performing keystroke monitoring and other live system monitoring can provide play-by-play view into user actions currently taking place.

- **Monitoring current network activity.** Network-based monitoring provides a safe way to collect evidence of network-based activity prior to acquiring equipment. User or program activity can be monitored.

WARNING Although remote analysis can be performed in a covert fashion, unless a product like EnCase Enterprise is used there is a reasonable risk of detection.

Overt live system analysis is performed on the system itself through either a local or a remote connection. The analysis is done after the system has been secured and can be performed through the Windows GUI, the command line, or a remote command line. Overt analysis tasks include:

- **Proving system state at time of acquisition.** It may be necessary to show multiple pieces of information on the system state at the time of acquisition, including currently logged-on users (network and local), clipboard information (stored in memory), or current network connections (file share, FTP, HTTP, and others).

- **Obtaining information on currently running programs.** When the computer is powered down, the list of programs and their contents that were running at the time will be lost.

- **Finding information resident in main memory.** If information is expected to be present in RAM, that information needs to be collected before powering down the system and losing its contents.

- **Acquiring data from a production system.** Not all systems can be shut down for off-site acquisition or need to be imaged from a disk perspective locally. If there are simple tasks that need to be performed on a live system (for example, copying log files and seeing event information), these may be done in real time.

When a live system analysis is performed, there is almost always some system alteration, with the exception of network monitoring. Running any process will at a minimum alter the CPU registers in addition to some memory and possible disk space as well. The key to a successful live analysis from an investigative perspective is fourfold:

1. **Understand and document why a live analysis is being performed.** When you are making the decision to perform a live system analysis, one of the scenarios noted above should be relevant. Ideally, standard operating procedures are developed by your organization beforehand. These procedures detail when a live system analysis is warranted, who approves the analysis, and how it occurs. Any deviation from these procedures must be documented as part of the case file.

2. **Minimize the amount of alteration.** Some alteration is unavoidable in a live system analysis. When deciding on an approach to analyzing a live system, consideration must be given to the least disruptive way of accomplishing this. If the investigator wants to know what ports are accessible from a given IP address, an external port scan may be the least intrusive. If there is a further question on what applications those

ports are associated with, a small footprint program such as Foundstone FPort may be the most appropriate.

3. **Understand the alteration.** Understanding the impact caused by the programs you will be running is essential to a court presentation of actions. It is understood that all programs run on a given machine will alter memory in some fashion, but specific to the analyst's forensic suite, he will want to know, at a minimum, answers to the following: Does it write to the disk? Does it start any services? Will it alter file timestamps? Does it open network connections?

4. **Do not trust tools on the system.** Where possible, use tools that you provide to perform a live system analysis. If a system compromise is suspected, built-in tools may be altered to provide false data or hide specific system activities. Although this is more common on compromised Unix systems, the best practice is relevant for Windows as well.

A live system analysis is one of the most powerful tools in the forensic arsenal of a computer investigator. Using it appropriately can yield results unattainable through other means.

ORDER OF VOLATILITY

All data on a computer system is volatile to some degree. At the high end of volatility, network transmissions and information moving across the system bus can be considered extremely volatile. The information may exist and be able to be captured for a matter of milliseconds or even nanoseconds. At the lower end of volatility are permanent files stored to magnetic or optical media. This information may be present in an unaltered form for anywhere from several seconds to several decades (and potentially longer for archival quality optical media).

The difficulty in capturing data increases as the volatility of the data increases. CPU registers are difficult to read without altering their data — what instructions can one run from within the operating system that will not replace the registers by running them? Bus lines and custom chips may require specialized equipment (for example, an oscilloscope and logic probe) and internal chip caches may be internally managed and inaccessible externally. The greater difficulty comes from the very short duration of this information. Because of the timeframes, a priori knowledge of an incident is required. Specifically, monitoring has to be actively set up and occurring before an incident happens, making the most volatile contents of a system unavailable in response situations.

As anyone who has ever managed a large tape backup library can attest, even permanent storage is volatile in nature. Both magnetic media and optical media have life spans due to wear, environmental factors, and material limitations. Prior to the physical media wearing out, the logical contents can be erased as well. Files can be deleted and wiped, unused sectors overwritten, and

(continued)

ORDER OF VOLATILITY *(continued)*

temporary files cleaned by the operating system. Because of this, a rapid response capability is essential to any incident response program. Likewise, examiners should acquire the most volatile information they believe will be useful first, before moving to the next most volatile piece of information. The following table lists the volatility of various computer components useful in a forensic analysis.

LOCATION	PRIMARY ANALYSIS METHOD	LIFE OF DATA	USEFULNESS
CPU registers	Live	Milliseconds	Registers generally contain very small amounts of information, much of which is not broadly useful to investigations (for example, array offsets and intermediate calculation values).
CPU cache (on and off-chip)	Live	Seconds	The CPU cache(s) contain instructions and data, and as they become larger they contain more information. Because much of the cache information will also be stored in less-transient RAM, the effort to read the cache usually outweighs any benefits.
RAM	Live	Minutes	The computer's main memory stores information from current and previously running programs, including pieces of data that may be unavailable elsewhere. The data is not well structured to analysis, but can be searched for key words and phrases effectively. Investigations where a machine is still running after a user has purportedly performed recent actions of interest may yield information not stored in a more permanent fashion.

LOCATION	PRIMARY ANALYSIS METHOD	LIFE OF DATA	USEFULNESS
Disk cache	Live/offline	Hours	With larger amounts of RAM present in computers, the Disk Cache changes less rapidly but is still used. Even after a system is turned off, the cache file can be searched for strings of data to prove or disprove an allegation. The disk cache is one of the most common locations to find information that a user thinks she never saved to disk.
Temporary files	Live/offline	Hours	Many applications in addition to Windows itself create temporary files without the user's knowledge. Because these files frequently contain structured data in a complete fashion, they are of great value in an investigation. Temporary files can be cleaned by individual applications when a document is closed, or may reside in a temporary directory until system reboot or beyond.
Unallocated space	Offline	Days	Unallocated disk space is any location that does not currently have an addressable file. Fragments and even full files that were deleted can be present for years, depending on disk usage. Searching unallocated disk space (both file and RAM slack) is done on almost all disk-based forensic analyses.

(continued)

ORDER OF VOLATILITY *(continued)*

LOCATION	PRIMARY ANALYSIS METHOD	LIFE OF DATA	USEFULNESS
Permanent files	Offline	Years	Permanent files exist until they are deleted or the media is no longer viable. The best form of evidence when available, permanent files are data that has been saved to media that retains information even after losing power. Permanent files are generally stable enough for offline analysis.

Covert Analysis

Covert analysis is the mechanism by which activities can be monitored without alerting a suspect. Depending on the technique used and the sophistication (and wariness) of the user, covert system analysis may range from low risk to high risk. The risk levels of each covert action are detailed in the respective sections below.

Covert analysis is not limited to digital means. Hidden cameras are used extensively by physical security investigators and can even complement computer activity monitoring (it does not hurt to show that the suspect was sitting in front of his computer at the time the activity from his machine occurred). A frequent, non-digital covert action on corporate systems is a manual review (and sometimes imaging of drives, which is covered later in the "Main Memory Analysis" section) of the equipment and connections present, generally after hours.

Covert analysis activities can be broken in to two categories: actions taken to determine the current or prior state of a system and actions taken to monitor ongoing current or future system activity.

System State Analysis

Determining the current system state through covert analysis can provide pre-acquisition system details on what hardware or software clues to look for. It can also determine other potential investigation targets in case the investigation is larger than a single individual or device and can provide pre-investigation triage to rule out quickly potential suspects.

The current system state can be determined covertly and safely three different ways: using a forensic tool such as EnCase Enterprise, using remote administration tools such as Computer Management in Windows, or using Windows features to provide remote information. The use of EnCase Enterprise is covered in the "Main Memory Analysis" section later in the chapter. The other two techniques are covered here.

The easiest way to obtain remote information on a system covertly (when administrative rights to the machine are available) is to utilize Microsoft's remote management features. The primary remote management tool of use is the Computer Management console software, shown in Figure 8-1. Other Microsoft tools can be used to obtain remote information as well. Event Viewer and IIS Administrator are two other common, standalone tools with remote management capabilities.

The Computer Management console (CMC) is accessible as part of the Administrative Tools under the Control Panel on Windows 2000 and XP devices and has limited functionality to manage older Windows machines. The CMC can manage local or remote hosts. To manage a remote host, the Administrator chooses Action → Connect To Another Computer and then puts in the domain name or IP address of the remote system. To fully manage the system, administrative rights on the appropriate domain or local system are necessary.

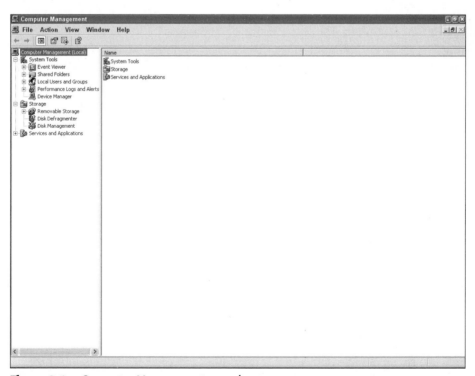

Figure 8-1: Computer Management console

The CMC provides access to both current configurations and currently running applications. By providing insight into who is on a system and what they are currently doing, the computer investigator is able to perform quick reconnaissance without the end users being aware of the investigator's actions. Since the CMC uses standard Microsoft ports, there should be no suspicious traffic to alert the remote computer user of the actions being taken. This provides a low-risk method of obtaining remote information. An exceptionally wary user running port mapping tools such as FPort or looking at currently connected users, however, may detect activity. The investigator should have a plan of action for her machine or account use being detected and a plausible answer should the user question her presence.

TIP Use a generic-sounding administrator account and machine for this — nothing labeled SecretInvestigationAdmin or the like.

The CMC is broken into three major sections: System Tools, Storage, and Services and Applications. Depending on what is installed on the remote system and the OS version, additional features for managing IIS, viewing DNS logs, or other actions may be present. The investigative items of interest from the three main features are noted in the following sections.

System Tools

The primary system tool for remote access to past actions is Event Viewer. The Event Viewer activity log operates the same as using Event Viewer locally. The Application, Security, and System Event logs from the remote are all present. Details on Event Viewer usage in Forensics are listed in Chapter 11.

Shared Folders is a listing of the share and remote session activity on the system. It is broken into three sections: Shares, Sessions, and Open Files. Shares lists all of the file shares, including the administrative shares. Sessions provides the computer and users information on any users currently mapped to the listed shared drives and how long they have been active or idle. Open Files lists the specific files those users have open, which is great if one catches a suspect in the act of having a forbidden file open.

Local Users and Groups provide details on the names of local system users and groups. The association of specific accounts (local accounts or domain accounts) with a local administrators group, or the presence of unusual local groups may signify inappropriate activity.

NOTE Windows automatically creates administrative shares (accessible to the Administrators group) for each drive in addition to an Admin$ (to the Windows directory), print$ (for sharing of printers) and IPC$ (for Inter-Process Communications) share. Administrative shares have a dollar sign as the last character of their share name and are not visible through Network Neighborhood when viewing the available shares on a system.

Performance Logs and Alerts are a remote view into the Performance Monitoring system in Windows if enabled. Performance logs are not generally used in an investigation unless a denial-of-service attack is suspected and currently occurring or a resource-intensive task (for example, transferring of large files over the network) may be occurring. Additional counters for different disk, processor, memory, or network activity can be added remotely as needed.

Device Manager lists all of the currently installed devices on a system. If a USB drive or external DVD burner is installed, a modem is connected, or a second network card is installed, it will appear here. Devices shown in device manager may not be present at a later date in the case of removable devices, making the information displayed in Device Manager very important in establishing remote user actions. An example of Device Manager with several sections expanded is shown in Figure 8-2. The Storage Volumes subcategory is also of forensic interest. USB flash drives as well as Zip disks will appear as volumes under this heading. View the properties of each Generic Volume entry for details.

Storage

The Storage section provides detailed information on fixed and removable storage known to Windows (non-Windows partitions will not be present). There are three key sections: Removable Storage, Disk Defragmenter, and Disk Management. Disk Defragmenter does not have an investigative use and running it can greatly alter disk information. However, both the Removable Storage and Disk Defragmenter sections are of interest to an investigator.

Removable Storage provides details on all devices with removable media except floppy disks. Note that USB and FireWire solid-state drives. Both flash- and hard-disk–based drives are listed in the Disk Management section. Listed devices include CD/DVDs, Zip disks, and tape drives. There are two sections: Media and Libraries. Media lists all currently mounted media, including tapes and optical media currently in the drives, which can show the presence of items that may later be removed. Libraries lists the actual devices themselves.

NOTE Although the terminology in Libraries appears to be specific to tape units, other removable media types will be listed as well.

Disk Management displays the current format and status of all drive partitions, including those on connected FireWire or USB drives. The physical drives as well as their associated partitions (and any unrecognized or unpartitioned space) will be listed. Each partition will have the associated file system type and size available as well as total size present, allowing for appropriate planning for future acquisition. The presence of a RAID 5 array with 1.5 terabytes of storage may require a different strategy than a single 20GB drive. As with the preceding items, USB drives and other removable devices that may not be present at a later day can also be noted here.

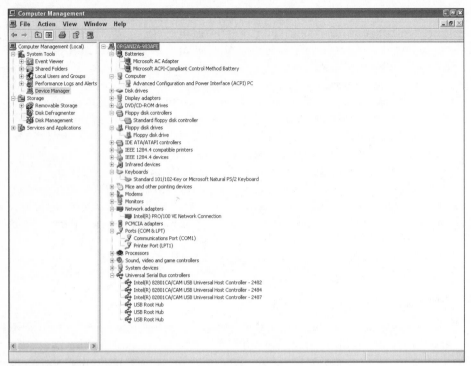

Figure 8-2: Device Manager

Services and Applications

All of the currently running services and their details are viewable through this interface. The section contains three primary areas: Windows Management Interface (which is not useful in an investigation), Services, and Indexing Service.

Services is straightforward. It provides details on running services as well as other installed services. Services can be remotely started from the interface and details about their startup options viewed as well. If a given application is service based, the presence of a running service associated with that application is a good indicator of its presence on the suspect machine.

The Indexing Service section is one of the single most powerful remote forensic tools available but receives little fanfare. Microsoft provides an indexing service which will index content in any files the service has an appropriate filter for. By default, this includes all text-based documents, including XML, HTML, and Microsoft Office documents. Included in the remote interface to this service is the ability to search the index. While this does not take the place of sector-level text searches, it is substantially faster (almost instantaneous) and provides results from Office format files like Excel that cannot be found in basic text searches.

The indexing service needs to be started and be provided time to parse the drive contents before any searching can occur. To start the service, right-click on the Indexing Service option in the CMC and select Start. The service will then begin actively indexing all of the drive's contents. Indexing can take anywhere from several minutes to several hours. The indexing service runs with a low priority and will not degrade the interactive performance, making it a low-risk endeavor. When indexing is complete the main Indexing Service screen will show no items in the Docs to Index column.

NOTE This number may never actually reach zero. If the system is actively being used, there may be open documents that are constantly being re-indexed. If a small number of documents are listed as open (under ten), this may be as close to zero as the system will get.

The specific drives and directories indexed are shown under the System → Directories submenu. By right-clicking on the window listing the directories and selecting New → Directory, additional directories can be added to the index. This allows for the addition of other drives (such as flash drives) which may be recently connected and not included in the default search. The System → Properties dropdown menu lists the various metadata properties found in the indexed files — these properties can be used in the search expressions in the Query the Catalog screen.

The least-known and most powerful feature of the indexing service for a computer investigation is the Query the Catalog option under System. This is a fully functionally, query-based search engine which allows for near-instantaneous searching of all indexed content. Searching can be done before all content has been indexed, but un-indexed items will not be included in the results. The Query option allows for complex SQL-based queries or queries using the Microsoft Indexing Service Query Language (MSISQL). The MSISQL provides complex Unix regular-expression based searching in addition to MS-DOS wildcard searching of full text or any of the associated properties of a file. For example, to run an advanced query of all JPEG image files, a syntax for an Advanced Query would be:

```
#filename = *.jpg
```

For free-text searches, the name of the term, with or without wildcards, can be typed using the Standard Query option. The search results will return all of the files which match the query. These files can then be opened to analyze their contents or the presence of the suspicious names used as probable cause to image the drive. An example of a search for the words *hack* or *crack* is shown in Figure 8-3.

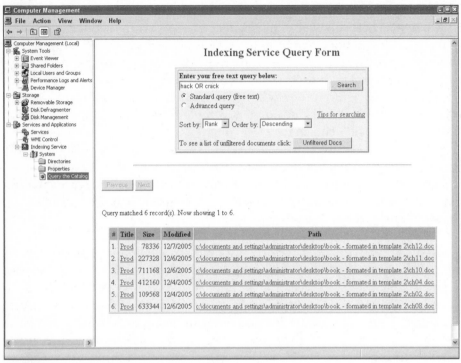

Figure 8-3: Indexing Service query results

Remote Enumeration

In addition to the CMC tool, the actual administrative shares for drives in use on the remote system may be mapped by an administrator with remote privileges using the Net Use command. To map a drive, the administrator types the following in the command line:

```
Net Use X: \\suspectcomputer\c$
```

The drive letter (X:) is the letter of the drive the share will be mapped to. C$ is the administrative share for the C: drive. Other shares will be named appropriately for their respective drives. When the drive is mapped, the investigator will be able to access it from Windows Explorer in a non-forensically sound way (the disk can be written to or altered). The investigator may then run tools against the drive (for example, search and analysis) or copy files from it as permissions allow.

Mapping of drives in this manner is not recommended for an extended analysis for several reasons:

- The connection will show up on the remote computer if the suspect knows where to look.

- The suspect may receive notifications that someone is still connected to her machine when she goes to shut down. A Net Use /Delete command needs to be run to unmap from the target drive.

- Accidental alteration of the file system can occur and it makes proving no intentional or unintentional alteration occurred.

If the suspect's machine is not part of a domain or administrative rights on the machine are not available, a covert remote analysis is more difficult but not impossible. The steps for a covert remote analysis when privileges are not available are as follows:

1. **Identify the operating system of the remote machine.** OS fingerprinting can be performed with a reasonable degree of accuracy using nmap. Nmap looks at open ports, packet construction, and other areas to identify what operating system the remote system is running. This enables the determination of the Windows version for the examination of potential options for further analysis. Here are the results of Nmap run against a Windows 2003 server:

```
C:\Tools>nmap -O www.chadsteel.com

Starting nmap 3.75 ( http://www.insecure.org/nmap ) at 2004-11-10
15:12 Eastern
Standard Time
Interesting ports on pcp08364727pcs.lndsd201.pa.comcast.net
(68.42.19.63):
(The 1642 ports scanned but not shown below are in state: closed)
PORT      STATE    SERVICE
21/tcp    open     ftp
25/tcp    open     smtp
80/tcp    open     http
110/tcp   open     pop3
135/tcp   filtered msrpc
136/tcp   filtered profile
137/tcp   filtered netbios-ns
138/tcp   filtered netbios-dgm
139/tcp   filtered netbios-ssn
445/tcp   filtered microsoft-ds
902/tcp   open     iss-realsecure-sensor
912/tcp   open     unknown
1025/tcp  open     NFS-or-IIS
1026/tcp  open     LSA-or-nterm
```

```
1027/tcp open       IIS
1029/tcp open       ms-lsa
1030/tcp open       iad1
1031/tcp open       iad2
1080/tcp filtered socks
1720/tcp filtered H.323/Q.931
3389/tcp open       ms-term-serv
Device type: general purpose
Running: Microsoft Windows 2003/.NET
OS details: Microsoft Windows .NET Enterprise Server RC2 (Version
5.2, build 371
8.dnsrv.021114-1947)

Nmap run completed -- 1 IP address (1 host up) scanned in 77.342
seconds
```

2. **Identify services running on the remote system.** Service identification can be performed by running a port scan (sending TCP or UDP packets to different ports on a system to gauge the response). The port banners are then reviewed and their port numbers compared to a list of well-known port numbers to determine what services are running and accessible on the remote machine. If the investigation hinges on a suspect running an FTP or IRC server, or if it is suspected that the individual has a mail server available, this will be reflected in the port scanning results. Nmap remains the predominant tool for port scanning. The preceding output shows the OS fingerprint results in addition to what ports are listening. A secondary tool for port scanning, which is useful in the enumeration step (Step 3) is SuperScan from Foundstone. The results of SuperScan run against the same system noted previously are shown in Figure 8-4. The details of the banner grab are viewable in the HTML report.

3. **Enumerate Windows information.** Depending on the suspect system configuration, a NULL Session connection can return information on Windows NT/2000/XP/2003 systems. NULL Session refers to connecting to a remote system without authentication (the NULL part) using the higher-level protocols, Server Message Block (SMB)/NetBIOS. These connections allow an investigator to enumerate information on the remote system, including shared drives, MAC addresses, user accounts, current users, services, and other details. SuperScan provides a Windows Enumeration function in addition to the port scanning function. The results of a NULL Session enumeration are shown in Figure 8-5. Note the SharedDocs file share.

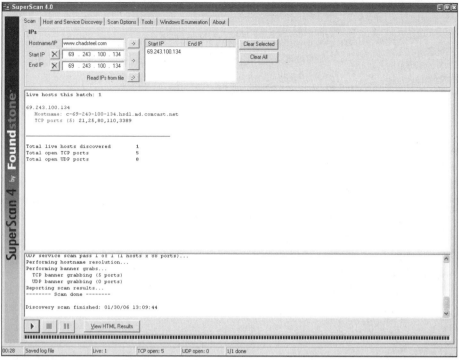

Figure 8-4: Port scan results

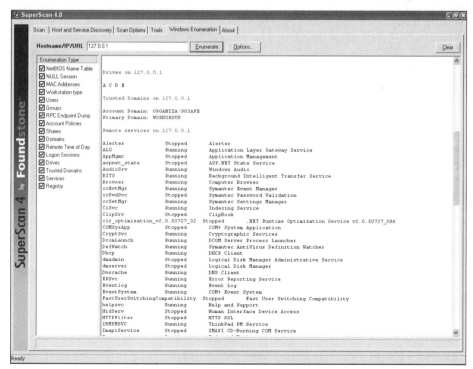

Figure 8-5: Windows Enumeration results

After the information has been completed, it can be used to further examine the system (for example, connecting to FTP and HTTP sites and mapping shared drives). The further examination will depend on the findings and may include finding owners of other system accounts that have privileges to perform the remote administration steps shown previously.

Port scanning, OS Detection, and Remote enumeration are fairly quick and will not generally alert the end user to any unusual activity. If these tasks are performed, make sure the originating IP address and system name are not readily associated with the investigation team. Calling the machine Network-Analysis and connecting from a visitor office works well. While no known convictions to date have been upheld for either port scanning or enumeration, they are bordering on trespassing for systems that the investigator does not own and are more appropriate for corporate investigations where the target PC is the property of the company.

WARNING Host-based intrusion detection systems integrated into popular firewalls may generate an alert to the user if a port scan is performed against his or her machine.

Monitoring

The second form of covert investigation is monitoring of user activities through the active recording of system activity. This can include monitoring of keystrokes, capturing network traffic, or interactively viewing system activity through screenshots or reports.

Monitoring can provide a broader, temporal view of user actions not available through snapshot-based activities like disk imaging and can be replayed to reconstruct specific user actions. Monitoring of computer activity by the provider of that service has generally been permitted and been exempt from one- or two-party consent laws on recordings, but the case law in this area is very fluid. The analyst must check the appropriate legal department before performing any active monitoring.

NOTE By placing an appropriate warning banner and requiring users to click an agreement on login, consent from one of the parties can be obtained when the system is started. Additionally, a good acceptable usage policy and user awareness training plan will alert users in a corporate environment that they can be monitored. Having them sign an agreement to this policy upon accepting employment is an additional plus.

Covert cameras and keystroke recorders are both physical mechanisms for obtaining evidence. Covert cameras can be disguised as smoke detectors, clocks, and sprinkler heads to easily blend in to an office environment. Placed with a view of the computer screen and keyboard (sometimes difficult with viewing angles on laptops), these can provide direct evidence of activity. Details on covert camera selection and placement are beyond the scope of this book. Consult a physical security team for guidance on their use.

Keystroke Recording

Keystroke recorders can be either physical objects or software based. They are useful for finding passwords, retrieving the text of documents created, and logging Instant Messaging sessions, although only half of the conversation is logged. Physical recorders sit between the keyboard itself and the computer. They can take several forms:

- **Adapters.** Keystroke recorders that look like AT-to-PS2 adapters or PS2-to-USB adapters sit right on the relevant port on the back of a system. They are the least likely connector to be noticed, especially on desktop systems.

- **Extension cables.** Appearing to be an extension to the keyboard cable, these adapters can generally hold slightly more keystrokes (up to two million). Extension cable–based adapters are more likely to be spotted by wary users but can replace existing adapters.

- **Keyboard replacements.** Full keyboard replacements resemble their respective manufacturer's models. These can replace the existing keyboard and show no external signs of logging hardware, but a ruse for putting in a replacement keyboard is necessary (generally damaging the existing keyboard and providing the logging keyboard as a replacement).

- **Altered keyboards.** The most effective and least likely to generate suspicion, altering the existing keyboard is the best approach. An adapter or extension-based keyboard logger is placed within the keyboard itself by cutting the wire internally and attaching it to the logger at both ends.

Hardware keystroke logging has inherent limitations. There is a detectable piece of equipment that is used, although the likelihood varies and is very low for altered keyboards. Additionally, physical access to the system is required, and some systems cannot use hardware keystroke loggers (for example, laptops). Finally, hardware logging only shows what was typed, not where it was typed. If a mouse click is used to add addresses to an email, for example, this will not be part of the recording.

Software keystroke logging provides an alternative to hardware solutions and can be deployed locally or remotely using SMS, PSExec, or by tricking the user into running an executable. The software runs in the background and if all goes well, does not provide any indication to the suspect that it is running.

Keystroke logging software suffers from some of the same problems as hardware-based solutions in addition to having some problems of its own. Knowledgeable users may notice an additional service or process running, network traffic or disk traffic if the data is stored locally, and that software will not work outside of the environment in which it was installed (for example, on a dual-boot system). Finally, like hardware logging solutions, the basic software only logs what was actually typed on the keyboard.

More advanced software has become available for Windows-based active surveillance than basic keystroke logging. Advanced monitoring software, such as Spector Pro, can record application access, take screenshots of activity, and even send networked alerts based on keywords that are entered. The CNE version of Spector Pro is even network-compatible; content that would be stored on a local drive for later retrieval can now be accessed in real time from a networked PC. The downside is a slightly larger application footprint and possible suspicious network traffic generated, limiting the usefulness for investigating a network administrator or other professional that may be using sniffing software as part of his job. Figure 8-6 shows a screenshot of the keystroke capture capability in Spector Pro.

Figure 8-6: Spector Pro keystroke capture

Network Monitoring

Network-based monitoring of the activity on a suspect machine can be accomplished with a very low risk or discovery if performed properly. The monitoring of network activity can occur anywhere between the suspect machine and the target machine. Popular places to monitor include switching closets (if the suspect does not have access to the associated switches either physically or logically), local cables (for in-line taps) and firewalls or routers (for basic connection information).

Because it is a passive act, network monitoring is relatively safe. If proper precautions are taken, and unless the physical device is discovered or access to the network equipment is available, the monitoring can go unnoticed. Similarly, sniffing the network and performing packet captures is a common system administration task that in itself is not necessarily suspicious.

There are four primary methods for performing network monitoring, excluding IDS alerting based on specific activities:

- **In-Line Tap.** An in-line tap (sometimes called a vampire tap) is used to sniff traffic directly from a specific cable. Fiber-based in-line taps clamp on to the cable with part of the sheathing removed and read a portion of the light transmitted through the exposed cable and amplify it. Copper-based in-line taps are more complex in operation (since the CAT5 Ethernet has two read and two write cables, requiring traffic to be put back together with a direct tap). As a result, most copper taps are now end taps. They plug in to the end of an Ethernet cable and provide full access to reconstructed traffic from both sides of the conversation. End tap–based fiber taps that regenerate the network traffic are also available.

NOTE A vampire tap more accurately refers to an older style of tap popular with Thicknet and Thinnet Ethernet that used coaxial cables. With these, an actual metal spike was inserted (like a vampire's fangs) through the sheathing of the cable to allow a conductor to be clamped to the inner, copper cable. In-line taps also encompass other products that do not alter the wire.

- **Hub and sniffer cable.** Unlike a switch, a hub repeats all traffic to every port. Because of this, connecting a hub in between the machine to be monitored and a switch allows for all traffic to be monitored with an inexpensive piece of hardware (4 port, 10/100 Ethernet hubs can be purchased for less than US$25 at the time of this writing) and a simple sniffer cable can be built inexpensively.

TIP When connecting the hub to a switch, remember to use a crossover cable unless an uplink port is available on one of the devices.

- **Switch SPAN ports.** Switch Port Analyzer (SPAN) ports receive all of the traffic generated on the other switch ports. Most corporate switching products from major vendors include the capability of defining one of the ports as a SPAN port. The sniffer box can then be plugged directly into this port and receive all of the traffic from the end station. To be effective, the traffic received by this port needs to be filtered to remove any information not sourced from or destined to the suspect machine. Many products additionally make the SPAN-defined port receive-only, reducing the risk of discovery.

TIP Some switches include a port-mirroring capability instead of (or in addition to) a SPAN port. Port mirroring replicates the traffic from a single port in the switch to another port in read-only mode. This is ideal for ensuring all traffic to and from a single port is analyzed without the need for extensive filtering.

- **ARP spoofing.** Address Resolution Protocol (ARP) is used to translate IP addresses to Ethernet MAC addresses. Since a Windows machine sends all of its non-local packets to a default gateway IP address, poisoning the ARP cache of the target machine to send all packets to the sniffer box (instead of the gateway) allows sniffing on a switched network. To be effective, the ARP cache on the target machine or a router in between needs to be spoofed and the sniffer box needs to forward IP packets to the real gateway. The primary tool for ARP spoofing is dsniff from Dug Song. A GUI-based Windows tool, Win ARP Spoofer, is also available from NextSecurity. Figure 8-7 shows a screenshot of Win ARP Spoofer. ARP spoofing is more difficult than the other techniques but has the advantage of not requiring direct access to the suspect's cable or the switch itself.

For all of the methods, an Ethernet card capable of operating in promiscuous mode (almost all available cards should be able to) is a requirement for monitoring. Generally, an Ethernet card only receives traffic that is associated with its own Media Access Control (MAC) address, a unique identifier hardcoded into every card, and broadcast traffic. By placing an Ethernet card in promiscuous mode, the card received all network traffic and passes it up the stack.

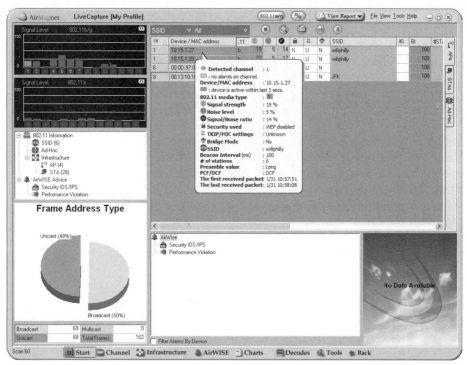

Figure 8-7: Win ARP spoof software

There are two primary forms of monitoring: full-packet capture and header capture. Full-packet capture stores the entire contents of all packets traversing a given segment. Both the header portion of the packet and the associated data are collected. The advantage of full-packet capture is the ability to fully reconstruct and recover the content from all unencrypted communications. The disadvantage is the amount of space required; full-packet capture requires an amount of space proportional to the bandwidth used. For a 100 Mb/s connection that is fully utilized, this can amount to tens of gigabytes of uncompressed data per hour, which will quickly fill even large disk drives, although most connections will not utilize anywhere close to the full bandwidth for a sustained period.

Header capture stores only the header information, not the contents. This is the electronic equivalent of a pen-register. It enables the investigator to determine the source, destination, and duration of all communications between the suspect machine and other machines. Although it is not as thorough as a full-packet capture, a header capture requires significantly less disk space and can be parsed fairly quickly.

WIRELESS MONITORING

Sniffing a wireless network connection can be difficult, especially on Windows devices. The reason for the difficulty lies in the availability of drives that support the wireless cousin to promiscuous mode: RFMON. RFMON is widely supported on a few chipsets in the Linux environment where custom drivers have been written and made available as open source, but it is difficult to find similar drivers in the Windows world. Because of this many popular sniffing utilities such as Kismet and Wellenreiter are unavailable or crippled on the Windows platform. In general, the chipsets used by the ORiNOCO Gold cards from Proxim and the Cisco Aironet cards have been the most widely supported on Linux, but others are now available.

Due to a lack of available drivers, common sniffing tools such as Ethereal and TCPDump are not effective on Windows. They still function, but because the driver does not provide any network data other than broadcasts and directed traffic to the programs, sniffing the network itself is not truly occurring.

Commercial wireless sniffers that mimic the features of their wired counterparts and expand upon them are available, notably from Network Associates (with Sniffer Wireless) and AirMagnet. These sniffers provide full-packet monitoring capabilities on a limited number of wireless cards through custom drivers distributed with the software itself. The following figure shows the AirMagnet interface for deep packet inspection.

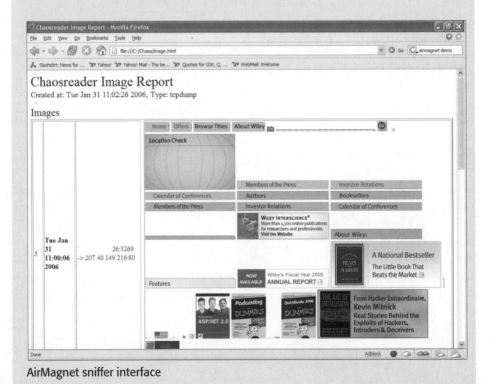

AirMagnet sniffer interface

In addition to network sniffing, an investigator may be required to find a wireless access point or card. Both the Sniffer and AirMagnet products provide this functionality as well using a direction antennae and signal strength readings (AirMagnet provides a triangulation capability as well with the right setup). By pointing the directional antenna and watching the signal strength, the relative position and distance of the device can be determined. See www.turnpoint.net/wireless/cantennahowto.html for instructions on how to build a homebrew directional antenna. I have had better experience with my own antenna built from these specifications and a coffee can than with either my commercial antenna or a Pringles cantenna.

One common misconception is that NetStumbler can provide the same functionality as the previously mentioned tools in tracking down wireless violators. In reality, NetStumbler is an excellent survey tool for finding access points that broadcast their SSID, but it is not a passive monitoring tool. NetStumbler and similar products broadcast request packets and read the responses. They do not sniff frames not directed toward the machine performing the monitoring (which is not possible without RFMON driver support), and they reveal their presence with broadcast packets (which AirMagnet will actually pick up as an alert).

With the widespread availability of open access points, tracking down a wireless user and monitoring wireless traffic will become more frequent occurrences for the IT investigator.

TIP Apply a filter to only capture packets sent to and from the suspect machine when connecting to a hub shared by other machines. If it is suspected that the machine is spoofing both the IP and MAC address of packets, all packets may need to be collected or a switch inserted into the monitoring path to collect all relevant information.

Sniffer software varies in price and quality. At the low end are free and easy-to-use tools like Windows Network Monitor. On the high end are commercial products such as the Network General Sniffer line of software. Since many of the protocol analysis features present in the higher-end tools are geared toward network troubleshooting (as opposed to computer investigations), a freeware tool Ethereal covers the bases for security monitoring needs while providing advanced functionality where it is necessary.

NOTE Formerly known as Network Associates Sniffer, the Network General spinoff is one of the more fully functional and well-known sniffing packages.

To perform a basic capture with Ethereal, start the executable and choose Capture → Start from the menu. The standard options should be sufficient for a basic capture. Make sure that all of the Name Resolution options are checked. These resolve the computer name based on the MAC as well as higher network protocol name resolution options. As the IP addresses of machines may change from the time of the capture, MAC address and computer name may be of later value. Click OK to begin the capture.

Ethereal captures all packets with full packet payloads by default. If an investigation is targeting a specific machine (for example, a warrant is issued to track only traffic to and from a specific device), a capture filter can be used to reduce the storage space required. Alternatively, all information can be captured and the filter applied later. This has the advantage of a lower likelihood of missing data but the disadvantage of requiring potentially large amounts of storage space. Likewise, capture filters can be used to return only certain types of traffic (for example, all HTTP requests), allowing for even more granular targeting of data collection.

To capture just headers, Ethereal allows the user to set the maximum size captured for each packet. The default size of 68 bytes is generally sufficient to capture the link layer and TCP/IP headers but not the headers for higher-level protocols such as HTTP headers.

When a target group of packets is identified within Ethereal, the product has the ability to follow the packet stream and decode the results as a whole. Figure 8-8 shows a decoded FTP data stream and the associated user name and password, as well as the commands typed. This was obtained by selecting one of the FTP packets, right-clicking, and selecting Follow TCP Stream. Unless data has been encrypted (for example, using SSL), it can be decoded in the network capture. If it is encrypted properly, one of the local capture techniques mentioned will need to be used on the source or destination machines to get the raw data.

NOTE The data packets are sent separately in an FTP connection and are listed as TCP packets with the first part of the Info field containing the word ftp-data in Ethereal. These can also be decoded to recover transmitted files and directory listings. FTP sends all credentials in plain text unless SFTP or other software is used. Do not bother trying the password in the example — it has long since been changed.

NETWORK TRAFFIC RECONSTRUCTION

Obtaining raw network output from a sniffer can show connection histories, support text searching, and enable protocol-level analysis. Frequently, an IT investigator wants to see the specifics of what was transferred in a given connection graphically. This can include detailed data on file or terminal sessions, the reconstruction of images or files that were transmitted, and details on web activity. This information can be obtained from an Ethereal sniffer log (or any log in libpcap format) using a Perl program called ChaosReader.

ChaosReader takes a raw log output file and parses it for specific TCP streams. These streams are then reconstructed into their individual components and indexed as an HTML file. The use of ChaosReader is simple. First, obtain a valid sniffer log. This can be an existing log or Ethereal, TCPDump, and other sniffers can be used to save the output to a file-based format. Next, the output file is copied to an examination directory where the ChaosReader-created files will be located. Finally, ChaosReader is run on the sniffer log and the output generated:

```
C:\Tools>Chaosreader.pl sniffer.out
```

After ChaosReader completes, the index.html file can be opened with a web browser. This file contains links to individual communications, as well as reports on web usage and file/image activity. The individual links can be followed to see reconstructed session data in a visual manner. The following figure shows an image results page from a sample capture. The individual web page and associated images viewed are clearly visible in the output.

Web browsing session output

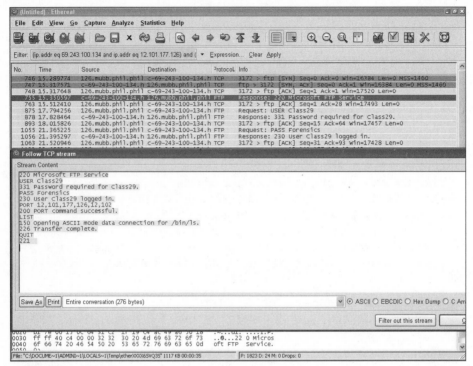

Figure 8-8: FTP packet capture

SNIFFER CABLE CONSTRUCTION

A sniffer cable provides a stealthier way of network monitoring. Because a proper sniffer cable does not have transmit lines from the monitoring box, inappropriate traffic (for example, DHCP packets and ARP packets) will not inadvertently give the monitoring box away if the suspect happens to be running sniffing software himself. Simple sniffer cables are inexpensive to construct and do not require anything more than a single CAT5 Ethernet cable, a wire stripper, and a pair of wire connectors.

While easy to make, building a sniffer cable is not as simple as just cutting the transmit wires from an Ethernet cable. If the transmit wires are cut, the hub the machine connects to will not sense any signal and will assume the port is off, thereby sending no traffic to that port. To remedy that, the network cable design that follows transmits back an inverted version of the signals generated from the hub itself or other machines connected to its ports. Inverted signals are a better solution than raw signals. They avoid the possibility of legitimate, duplicate traffic appearing on the device that keeps the signal alive.

The sniffer cable can be constructed as follows:

1. Obtain a standard UTP CAT5 cable of three to five feet in length. (For best results, purchase a CAT5e or CAT6 cable in an obscure color to prevent confusing the cable with others.)

2. Remove approximately eight centimeters of the outer sheathing in the center of the cable.

3. Clip the orange, orange-stripe, green, and green-stripe wires.

4. Choose one end of the cable as the end to be connected to the sniffer box. Clip one side of the orange and orange-stripe (transmit) wires to the edge of the sheathing. Label the clipped end with a Sharpie or similar pen as the end for the sniffer itself.

5. Strip approximately one centimeter of the inner sheathing from each remaining side of the green, green-stripe, orange, and orange-stripe wires.

6. Twist together both green wire ends and the remaining orange stripe wire end in one wire cap or solder all three together and cover with electrical tape.

7. Twist together both green-stripe wire ends and the remaining orange wire end in a second wire cap or solder all three together and cover with electrical tape.

8. Using electrical tape, secure the uncovered wires (the area missing the outer sheathing).

To test the cable, plug the sniffer box into the hub using the cable. Plug a second machine (simulating a suspect machine) into the hub. Running ethereal on the suspect machine, no traffic generated from the sniffer box should be viewable.

The following figure shows a diagram of the connections for the sniffer cable.

Sniffer Box		Hub	
1 TX+	Orange Stripe	TX+	1
2 TX-	Orange	TX-	2
3 RX+	Green Stripe	RX+	3
4 Unused	Blue	Unused	4
5 Unused	Blue Stripe	Unused	5
6 RX-	Green	RX-	6
7 Unused	Brown Stripe	Unused	7
8 Unused	Brown	Unused	8

Sniffer cable layout

Overt Analysis

Overt analysis is performed on a running system to obtain volatile information. Currently running processes and services, open documents and applications, inbound and outbound network connections, and the contents of memory are all transient data that may need to be acquired before system shutdown. Likewise, the acquisition of volatile information can be used as an initial triage (for example, to determine whether a worm infection is present) or to perform an investigation on a machine that cannot be taken offline.

There are three primary methods of overt analysis: using the Windows GUI, using a local command line, and using a remote command line. There are additional variations on each of these techniques as well.

GUI-based Overt Analysis

The most invasive (in terms of likelihood of altering information) analysis is to perform an analysis from the Windows GUI. This analysis entails using existing Windows management programs (for example, Regedit, the registry editor) or third-party graphical tools (for example, Sysinternals Process Explorer).

WARNING All of the overt analysis techniques noted in this section rely on the system being unlocked. Unlocking by an administrator will change the user context. If the system is locked by a particular user, either that user's password needs to be entered or the password reset centrally by an administrator to unlock the system. If the system cannot be unlocked, the techniques described in the covert analysis section may provide some information on the live environment.

GUI tools provide an advantage over command line tools in that information can be viewed and retrieved interactively in a graphical fashion. Hierarchies as well as complex correlations can be presented in a more concise fashion with graphical tools, and the viewing of certain files (for example, images and movies) require the use of the GUI. While these are compelling reasons to utilize GUI tools in an overt analysis, there are several reasons to avoid GUI tools on a live system unless the specific situation dictates it:

- **GUI tools alter the system to a greater degree.** The typical GUI tool utilizes more memory, which potentially overwrites evidence in RAM and in the cache, and calls more libraries for the generation of the GUI in addition to the collection of the data than the corresponding command line tool. This results in greater system alteration when using a graphical tool instead of an equivalent non-graphical tool.

■ **GUI tools may be altered.** Utilizing a built-in GUI tool on the target system has the same disadvantage of using any un-trusted binary. The tool itself may be altered. Although rootkits, which replace key binaries, are less frequently seen on Windows systems than on Unix, they do exist. If the binary has been replaced, the GUI tool used may intentionally hide the specific information you are looking for! Even if the binary for the tool is confirmed valid, any libraries dynamically linked to that tool may also be suspect.

■ **Scripting is easier with non-graphical tools.** Command line tools are built for scripting and used in batch files. By pre-scripting an analysis, the amount of time spent on a given system is minimized and the likelihood of accidental alteration reduced, providing another advantage for command line tools.

With the disadvantages given previously, there is still one primary use of the GUI in an overt analysis: viewing open applications from the taskbar. Information on what is open in terms of both applications and files from an end-user perspective, as opposed to from a background process, can be determined easily without touching the keyboard.

As the first step in overt analysis, the investigator may move the mouse (not click any buttons, just move the mouse) to disengage power saving mode or screensavers. A picture of the screen can then be obtained from a camera. After the initial screen picture is obtained, if evidence is suspected of being present in one of the applications shown in the task bar, each of those applications can be maximized and another picture taken of each.

WARNING Full-screen captures can be done on Windows systems using the Print Screen key or ALT-Print Screen for just the selected window. This is not recommended, however, as the captured screen overwrites part of memory, changes the contents of the clipboard, and requires another program to paste into and then save.

ROOTKITS

Clever rootkits leave the binaries and replace the core files, including Dynamic Link Libraries or DLLs. If the core libraries are replaced, any third-party tools that take advantage of these libraries will also be affected. Static linking (including normally shared libraries in the executables) is used when a rootkit infection is suspected.

Although a best practice to avoid using on system DLLs, the number of Windows incidents involving DLL-level compromise remains small at the time of writing but is growing with the introduction of packages like Hacker Defender, FU, and Vanquish. Microsoft makes a detection tool for rootkits called Strider Ghostbuster, available from Microsoft Research, which can be used to scan systems if a rootkit installation is suspected.

One final task that can be done easier from the GUI is viewing the contents of the clipboard. Windows uses the clipboard to store information for pasting. The contents of the clipboard or clipbook in later version of Windows can be viewed by selecting Program Files → Accessories → Clipboard Viewer on Windows 9*x*/NT/ME or by selecting Start → Run and typing Clipbrd in the text box on Windows 2000/2003/XP. For a better solution, a copy of the clipbrd.exe executable known to be good for the specific version of Windows being analyzed can be run from a secure CD or floppy disk. Figure 8-9 shows the results of viewing the clipboard on a system and reveals a screen capture still present.

TIP   Later versions of Microsoft Office contain an even more robust clipboard, which can store up to 24 items at once. These can be viewed by selecting Edit → Office Clipboard from the menu in any Office application, even if the contents were copied in a different application.

Figure 8-9: Clipboard contents

Local Command Line Analysis

Analyzing a live system locally from the command line is the most common (and least impactful) form of live system analysis noted. Performing a command line analysis requires familiarity with the Windows command line options, a proven command interpreter, and copies of other command line–based programs that provide information in a more adaptable format than is available with the standard Windows commands.

TIP The Helix CD, in addition to providing an excellent bootable Linux forensics environment, already contains a trusted command shell as well as other Windows forensic response tools and the ISO can be modified to include any additional tools you frequently use.

Command line analysis is best performed offline on a non-evidentiary system first, then performed on the target system. The steps for performing a local command line analysis of a running system are as follows:

1. Build a functionally identical system (with the same Windows version and as similar an environment as possible).

2. Acquire the necessary command line tools for the analysis as well as the command interpreter (cmd.exe) and place them on CD (or floppy is a CD is not accessible on the machine in question).

3. Attempt and record the individual commands needed to obtain the data from each specific tool.

4. Place the individual commands into a batch file, and then run the batch file and note the results.

5. Take a floppy or CD with the batch file to the live machine and run it.

6. Save the evidence generated to a networked using netcat (see the section "Remote Command Line Analysis" later in this chapter) or local storage location.

7. Generate an md5 hash of the stored evidence.

8. Burn the evidence to CD or other non-rewritable media.

WARNING Microsoft includes two versions of its command interpreter in later Windows releases — command.com and cmd.exe. The command.com interpreter is provided for backward compatibility and should not be used for forensic purposes (for example, by selecting Start → Run and typing command in the text box) as it does not fully support key features such as long file names. Always use cmd.exe (for example, by selecting Start → Run and typing cmd).

The specific commands necessary for a basic live machine analysis are detailed in the individual sections that follow.

When receiving the output from a command line tool, the standard approach for forensics is to redirect to a file. Redirection from the command line is done using the greater-than sign (>). To redirect the output of the directory command to a file called output.txt, the following command line would be used:

```
C:\>dir > output.txt
```

This preceding command creates a new file called output.txt in the root directory of the C: drive. Another location for the output can be specified (for example, dir > a:\evidence\output.txt will create a file with the output of the command in the evidence directory of the A: drive).

Because the greater-than sign overwrites a file if it already exists, a better option is to use the append redirect, which consists of two greater-than signs (>>). The same command here using an append is as follows:

```
C:\>dir >> output.txt
```

By using the append characters, a new file is still created if one does not already exist, but any output from the command will be appended to the file if it does exist, preventing the accidental overwriting of existing evidence.

Depending on the size of the output, the evidence can be stored directly to a floppy disk. Alternatively, the evidence can be stored on a USB-attachable drive as well. Never store the evidence to any of the drives on the evidence machine. Doing so will overwrite potential evidence. Finally, the data can be sent over a network and stored to an external forensic machine (see the following section for details).

WARNING Plugging in a USB drive (hard disk or flash drive) to a machine under investigation does involve the loading of drivers in the background and may alter information on existing drives in the registry. If using a USB-based drive, collect the registry data before connecting the USB device.

Remote Command Line Analysis

A final alternative to performing a local command line analysis is to use a remote command line. A remote command line may be used in two ways: pulling from the forensic workstation or pushing to the forensic workstation. Both methods can be accomplished using a small, free tool called NetCat.

TIP If encryption is required (when the data is being transmitted over an unsecured network connection), a version of NetCat that uses encryption, CryptCat, can be used instead. CryptCat is available from farm9.org.

Using the Pull method, a NetCat listener is started on the evidence machine. The listener opens a local command shell, which can then be used remotely to type the same commands as the local command shell. Instead of redirecting output to a file, however, the output can be captured in the connection logs and parsed out at a later point. The NetCat listener support connections from both NetCat itself as well as from standard Telnet clients. An excellent Telnet client for forensics (as well as an SSH client) is available in PuTTY and includes full logging capabilities.

To start a NetCat listener, the following command line can be used:

```
D:\forensic_tools>nc -L -p 23 -t -e cmd.exe
```

TIP The command line provided keeps the DOS window that it was started in open. To run NetCat in the background, the −d option can be used.

The preceding command is run from the D: drive (in this case a CD-ROM containing known-good versions of both the NetCat program and the cmd.exe file in the forensic_tools directory), but could be run from a floppy as well. The −L option initiates a persistent listener (−1 initiates a single-use listener that terminates after a single connection) on the suspect's machine and waits for an incoming connection. To bind it to a port, the −p option is used with port number 23 (the standard Telnet port). This could be changed to any port number to hide the connection and/or tunnel through a firewall. The −t option indicates a Telnet negotiation should be engaged with the client, allowing standard Telnet clients to connect in addition to NetCat itself. Finally, the −e option binds the command prompt input and output to NetCat.

When the session has finished, typing **exit** from the remote machine will close the connection. Figure 8-10 shows the results of typing netstat from a remote command shell (PuTTY was used as the Telnet client).

NOTE PuTTY also has SFTP and SCP programs available for securely copying files.

The more common Push method of using a remote command line requires that commands be run on the local command line but that their output be redirected to a remote shell. In this case, a NetCat listener is started on the box where the evidence will be stored using a persistent listener:

```
C:\evidence\nc -L -p 23 >> evidence.txt
```

TIP Use a non-persistent listener (the −l switch instead of −L) and change the file name before each command sent. This removes the need to later break apart the evidence file by command.

```
10.2.2.1 - PuTTY

Microsoft Windows XP [Version 5.1.2600]
(C) Copyright 1985-2001 Microsoft Corp.

C:\>netstat -An
netstat -An

Active Connections

  Proto  Local Address          Foreign Address        State
  TCP    0.0.0.0:135            0.0.0.0:0              LISTENING
  TCP    0.0.0.0:445            0.0.0.0:0              LISTENING
  TCP    10.2.2.1:23            10.2.2.1:3559          ESTABLISHED
  TCP    10.2.2.1:139           0.0.0.0:0              LISTENING
  TCP    10.2.2.1:3559          10.2.2.1:23            ESTABLISHED
  TCP    127.0.0.1:1025         0.0.0.0:0              LISTENING
  TCP    127.0.0.1:1064         0.0.0.0:0              LISTENING
  TCP    127.0.0.1:3179         127.0.0.1:3180         ESTABLISHED
  TCP    127.0.0.1:3180         127.0.0.1:3179         ESTABLISHED
  TCP    127.0.0.1:4664         0.0.0.0:0              LISTENING
  UDP    0.0.0.0:445            *:*
  UDP    0.0.0.0:500            *:*
  UDP    0.0.0.0:1026           *:*
  UDP    0.0.0.0:1154           *:*
  UDP    0.0.0.0:1496           *:*
  UDP    0.0.0.0:2097           *:*
  UDP    0.0.0.0:2106           *:*
  UDP    0.0.0.0:2877           *:*
  UDP    0.0.0.0:2878           *:*
  UDP    0.0.0.0:4237           *:*
  UDP    0.0.0.0:4500           *:*
  UDP    10.2.2.1:123           *:*
  UDP    10.2.2.1:137           *:*
  UDP    10.2.2.1:138           *:*
  UDP    10.2.2.1:1900          *:*
  UDP    127.0.0.1:123          *:*
  UDP    127.0.0.1:1900         *:*
  UDP    127.0.0.1:3532         *:*

C:\>
C:\>
```

Figure 8-10: PuTTY connection to NetCat

The preceding command line starts a standard listener with the output directed to the file evidence.txt. Note the append characters are used. This is critical because NetCat will actually restart the listener after each command. If the append characters are not used, the file will be overwritten each time.

TIP When using PuTTY, don't use the −t switch for the NetCat listener and select Raw Mode for the connection type and Log All Session Output from the PuTTY connection screen.

After the listener is started on the remote system, the commands are typed or the batch file run on the local system and the output redirected to NetCat using the pipe character (|). The pipe character takes the output from one program and uses it as input to another program. To send output to the listener, the information is redirected as follows, typed on the suspect's machine:

```
C:\>fport | nc 10.0.0.1 23
```

This command sends the output of the forensic tool fport to the NetCat listener at IP address 10.0.0.1 on port 23. There are problems with this method, however. It requires a break to be issued (Control-C) on the suspect's machine to let NetCat know the connection is over, requiring user interaction as well as advanced knowledge of when the program is actually complete. There are two solutions to this. The first is to use the timing option of NetCat, -w, which takes a given time in seconds before closing the connection. This relies on an approximation of how long the operation will take, for example, fport | nc 10.0.0.1 23 -w 5 will wait five seconds before automatically terminating the connection. The second is to write the code to a temporary file locally (on the A: drive or other removable media) and then to send it to NetCat, delete it, and move it to the next statement. This allows for safer batch file generation but requires no command to output more than the available space on a floppy drive. The chained commands would be as follows (instead of deleting, the next command can also just use a single greater-than sign to overwrite the last file):

```
C:\>fport > a:\evidence.txt
C:\>type a:\evidence.txt | nc 10.0.0.1 23 -w 5
C:\>del a:\evidence.txt
```

TIP Looking at the output file in a read-only viewer can give a good indication of when the program is complete. Windows ports of the Unix tail command are excellent for this task.

Basic Information Gathering

Before any specific live system information can be obtained, most investigations will gather basic information about the system and enable the appropriate logging to ensure the accuracy and repeatability of the steps taken.

The first step in command line live system analysis is to enable local logging (if connecting via a remote command line, the logging feature of the relevant Telnet client can be used in place of or in addition to local logging). Unlike the built-in logging command on a Unix system, Windows logging of commands is limited to the command itself and any switches associated with the command. Output is not logged using the basic logging features but is logged with Telnet session logs.

The primary command for logging, which should be the first command in the batch file (or typed) during a live system analysis, is DOSKEY. DOSKEY enables all commands typed to be logged as discrete entries in the order they were entered and allows the use of the up arrow to recall commands. To enable DOSKEY, the name is typed from the command line:

```
C:\> DOSKEY
```

In addition to being the first command typed, DOSKEY is also the last command typed in a live analysis, along with the /HISTORY switch to display all of the command entered during the session. The sample output of DOSKEY /HISTORY from a forensic session is as follows:

```
C:\>DOSKEY /HISTORY
date /t | nc www.chadsteel.com 23
time /t | nc www.chadsteel.com 23
cd Tools
dir
net session | nc www.chadsteel.com 23
fport | nc www.chadsteel.com 23
dir > output.txt
type output.txt | nc www.chadsteel.com 23
DOSKEY /HISTORY

C:\>
```

The second and third commands typed are generally the same as well. They establish the date and time the investigation was performed. The date and time need to be recorded both electronically and offline. The electronic time should be added to the output file using the date and time commands:

```
C:> DATE /T >> A:\Evidence.txt
C:> TIME /T >> A:\Evidence.txt
```

> **TIP** Have the second command be an ECHO command in the batch file which labels the evidence file with details such as the examiner name and location.

The /T switch prints out the date and time. By default, the DATE and TIME commands are interactive and allow the changing of the local DATE and TIME as well. As soon as the date and time are recorded electronically, the date and time should also be read from a known-good time source. Cell phones are generally a reasonable quick solution. The difference is noted in the log book.

When the date and time are established and logging has started, specific details about system components can be gathered. The PsInfo tool from SysInternals is the first stop in gathering basic system information. PsInfo provides information on the operating system, hardware, and software installed on the system. The PsInfo tool is used with the –h, –s, and –d switches to return the list of installed hotfixes (for proving that the system was inoculated and refuting a "worm did it" defense), a list of installed software, and information on the system volumes respectively. The information generated is gathered from the HKLM\SYSTEM registry key. Sample output of PsInfo (truncated) is as follows:

```
C:\>PsInfo -h -s -d

PsInfo v1.63 - Local and remote system information viewer
Copyright (C) 2001-2004 Mark Russinovich
Sysinternals - www.sysinternals.com

System information for \\CMSSWEB:
Uptime:                    23 days 12 hours 37 minutes 10 seconds
Kernel version:            Microsoft Windows Server 2003, Uniprocessor
Free
Product type:              Standard Edition
Product version:           5.2
Service pack:              0
Kernel build number:       3790
Registered organization:   Personal
Registered owner:          Chad M.S. Steel
Install date:              8/5/2003, 6:09:29 PM
Activation status:         Activated
IE version:                6.0000
System root:               C:\WINDOWS
Processors:                1
Processor speed:           865 MHz
Processor type:            Intel Pentium III
Physical memory:           510 MB
Video driver:              Intel(R) 82815 Graphics Controller (Microsoft
Corporation)
Volume Type      Format    Label          Size      Free    Free
     A: Removable                                            0%
     C: Fixed    NTFS                      11.7 GB   7.9 GB  68%
     D: CD-ROM                                               0%
     E: Fixed    NTFS                      19.5 GB   19.5 GB 99%
     F: Fixed    NTFS                      9.8 GB    9.5 GB  97%
     G: Fixed    NTFS                      9.8 GB    6.0 GB  61%
     H: Fixed    NTFS                      61.0 GB   9.5 GB  16%


OS Hot Fix     Installed

KB282010       8/6/2003
KB818529       8/5/2003
KB819696       8/5/2003
Q819639        8/5/2003
Q828026        10/4/2003
Applications:
Adobe Reader 6.0 6.0
DirectX 9 Hotfix - KB839643
Diskeeper Server Enterprise Edition 8.0.459
Dynamic DNS Client .NET Edition - Service 1.1.0
Ethereal 0.10.7 0.10.7
Google Toolbar for Internet Explorer
LiveUpdate 1.80 (Symantec Corporation) 1.80.19.0
```

```
Microsoft Data Access Components KB870669
Mozilla Firefox (1.0)
PGP 8.0
Symantec AntiVirus Client 8.1.0.821
WinHex
WinISO 5.3
WinRAR archiver
WinZip  9.0
Windows Media Player Hotfix [See KB837272 for more information]
Windows Media Player Hotfix [See wm819639 for more information]
Windows Media Player Hotfix [See wm828026 for more information]
Windows Server 2003 Hotfix - KB 818529 200311.111
Windows Server 2003 Hotfix - KB 822925 20030805.182229
Windows Server 2003 Hotfix - KB 823182 20030710.124724
Windows Server 2003 Hotfix - KB 823353 20040622.155431
Windows Server 2003 Hotfix - KB 823559 20030629.162850
```

After running PsInfo, a second tool from Sysinternals is useful in obtaining the Security Identifier for later searching: PsGetSID. Sample output from PsGetSID is as follows:

```
C:\>PsGetSID

PsGetSid v1.41 - Translates SIDs to names and vice versa
Copyright (C) 1999-2004 Mark Russinovich
Sysinternals - www.sysinternals.com

SID for \\CMSSWEB:
S-1-5-21-985051243-3901857598-654521942
```

The final piece of basic evidence collected is a general listing of all files on the system. While the file contents are not necessarily captured, the listing of the files can be examined to determine specific files to copy (in the event that a full image cannot be obtained or is not necessary) or to look for MAC dates and times on specific files.

Listing all of the files on the system is generally performed three times: once sorted by modified, once sorted by accessed, and once sorted by created times. The listings can also be imported into other programs to re-sort offline by name and folder. The three commands are as follows:

```
C:\> DIR /T:W /A /S /O:D
C:\> DIR /T:A /A /S /O:D
C:\> DIR /T:C /A /S /O:D
```

The /T switch indicates the date/time used for sorting, /T:W for Written (Modified), /T:A for Accessed, and /T:C for Created. The /A option lists all files (hidden and system as well). /S recursively traverses all directories. These commands should be run once from each of the drives' root directories. /O:D indicates as sort order by Date.

TIP All of the evidence files noted in the examples are given generic labels, but in practice the name of the evidence file can be important for differentiation at a later point. As a best practice, name the evidence file Case#-Evidence#-Item#.txt, where Case# is the number of the case, Evidence# is the evidence label number for the specific machine being examined, and Item# is the specific item being collected for that machine (all of which should be recorded in the log book with details on their contents). A typical evidence file number might be C2006001-001-001.txt, for the first case in 2006 C2006001, the first piece of evidence in that case (001) and the first item in that evidence (001).

System State Information

Overt gathering of information on the current system state has multiple associated tasks: establishing the current user of the system, determining the networked state of the computer, and obtaining the contents of the clipboard (detailed above as part of the GUI analysis).

The current users of the system are an important link in the chain of evidence. They allow the investigator to show what account or accounts are currently active to facilitate the association of specific actions (for example, having a network connection open) with a specific account. Obtaining the information on the currently active accounts is more relevant for Windows NT/2000/XP/2003 systems because activities are tied to specific accounts on these machines. An effective command line tool to determine the current users is PsLoggedOn, from SysInternals.

```
C:\Tools>psloggedon

PsLoggedOn v1.31 - Logon Session Displayer
Copyright (C) 1999-2003 Mark Russinovich
Sysinternals - www.sysinternals.com

Users logged on locally:
     <Unknown> NT AUTHORITY\LOCAL SERVICE
     <Unknown> NT AUTHORITY\NETWORK SERVICE
     12/16/2005 10:58:44 AM    CMSS\Chad M.S. Steel
     <Unknown> NT AUTHORITY\SYSTEM

No one is logged on via resource shares.
```

As noted in the preceding output, four accounts are active. The Local Server, Network Service, and System accounts are standard Windows machine accounts. The account with the name Chad M.S. Steel is active and registered under the domain CMSS (and has been logged in since December 16, 2005\). Any individuals currently connected to resource shares (for example, shared drives) would be shown with this command as well.

Determining the network state of the system is threefold: determining the current network configuration, obtaining information on current network connections, and obtaining information on programs listening for new incoming connections.

The current network configuration can be obtained with the built-in Windows command ipconfig. Windows 95 machines don't have an equivalent command line option. On those systems, winipcfg brings up a graphical version of the same information. The ipconfig command returns information on all adapters and their associated network address information, as well as their other network configuration settings. The results of typing ipconfig are as follows:

```
C:\Tools>ipconfig /all

Windows IP Configuration

        Host Name . . . . . . . . . . . . : CMSS
        Primary Dns Suffix  . . . . . . . :
        Node Type . . . . . . . . . . . . : Hybrid
        IP Routing Enabled. . . . . . . . : No
        WINS Proxy Enabled. . . . . . . . : No

Ethernet adapter Local Area Connection:

        Connection-specific DNS Suffix  . :
        Description . . . . . . . . . . . : 3Com EtherLink XL 10/100 PCI
For Complete PC Management NIC (3C905C-TX)
        Physical Address. . . . . . . . . : 00-01-22-4A-D8-96
        Dhcp Enabled. . . . . . . . . . . : No
        IP Address. . . . . . . . . . . . : 68.42.19.63
        Subnet Mask . . . . . . . . . . . : 255.255.255.0
        Default Gateway . . . . . . . . . : 68.42.19.1
        DNS Servers . . . . . . . . . . . : 4.2.2.1
```

Several key pieces of information can be obtained from the output of the ipconfig command. First, the name of the host and the DNS suffix to find the fully qualified domain name are shown. Second, the current IP address and MAC address are provided. Matching any of these addresses to network traffic is a key step in identifying an offending machine. If the machine is suspected of being an intermediary in attack, IP Routing may be enabled, allowing an attacker to forward packets through the device as if it were a router itself.

To look for additional log information on computer usage, any listed WINS, DNS Servers and Gateway devices can be good sources. Likewise, if DHCP is listed as being enabled, a DHCP server will be listed as a source for log files. The current lease date and expiration for the IP address should also be listed for dynamically assigned addresses.

TIP To find out the MAC and IP addresses of other devices on the same subnet, a broadcast ping can be used with `arp -a`. Pinging the subnet's broadcast address (for example, 68.42.19.255 for the CIDR Class C above based on the subnet mask) and typing `arp -a` will show any devices which respond to pings.

Another location for network information is the ARP cache. The ARP cache retains the MAC addresses of recently accessed machines on the local subnet. Obtaining the MAC address of recent connections will show potential sources and/or destinations for machines previously connected. The ARP cache can be listed with the `arp -a` command:

```
C:\Tools>arp -a

Interface: 68.42.19.63 --- 0x2
  Internet Address        Physical Address       Type
  68.42.19.63             00-01-22-4A-D8-96       dynamic
  68.42.19.1              00-03-32-7F-99-1B       dynamic
  68.42.19.24             00-F3-A7-9B-DF-CD       dynamic
```

Any current network connections are available through two basic Windows commands as well: netstat and nbtstat. The netstat command returns any TCP/IP connection statistics, and nbtstat does the same for NetBIOS connections. The netstat command use is as follows:

```
C:\Tools>netstat -an

Active Connections

  Proto  Local Address           Foreign Address         State
  TCP    0.0.0.0:135             0.0.0.0:0               LISTENING
  TCP    0.0.0.0:445             0.0.0.0:0               LISTENING
  TCP    0.0.0.0:3389            0.0.0.0:0               LISTENING
  TCP    68.42.19.62:23          68.42.19.63:3961        CLOSE_WAIT
  TCP    68.42.19.62:139         0.0.0.0:0               LISTENING
  TCP    68.42.19.62:1035        207.46.107.3:1863       ESTABLISHED
  TCP    68.42.19.62:3899        209.170.119.71:80       CLOSE_WAIT
  TCP    127.0.0.1:1028          0.0.0.0:0               LISTENING
  TCP    127.0.0.1:1036          0.0.0.0:0               LISTENING
  TCP    127.0.0.1:1241          0.0.0.0:0               LISTENING
  TCP    127.0.0.1:1242          0.0.0.0:0               LISTENING
  TCP    127.0.0.1:3310          127.0.0.1:3311          ESTABLISHED
  TCP    127.0.0.1:3311          127.0.0.1:3310          ESTABLISHED
  UDP    0.0.0.0:445             *:*
  UDP    0.0.0.0:500             *:*
  UDP    0.0.0.0:1029            *:*
  UDP    0.0.0.0:1118            *:*
  UDP    0.0.0.0:4500            *:*
  UDP    12.101.177.126:123      *:*
  UDP    12.101.177.126:137      *:*
```

```
UDP       12.101.177.126:138      *:*
UDP       12.101.177.126:1900     *:*
UDP       127.0.0.1:123           *:*
UDP       127.0.0.1:1037          *:*
UDP       127.0.0.1:1900          *:*
UDP       127.0.0.1:3410          *:*
UDP       127.0.0.1:62515         *:*
UDP       127.0.0.1:62517         *:*
UDP       127.0.0.1:62519         *:*
UDP       127.0.0.1:62521         *:*
UDP       127.0.0.1:62523         *:*
UDP       127.0.0.1:62524         *:*
```

The –a option shows all current connections as well as listening ports. The –n option shows the port name into a number. If the port is listed in the Windows list of well-known ports, leaving off the –n will show the associated protocol. The above listing displays numerous connections open, including several to the loopback (127.0.0.1) address. Recently terminated connections in the CLOSE_WAIT state to the Telnet port and HTTP ports respectively above may be of forensic interest. Likewise, the ESTABLISHED connection on port 1035 to the MSN servers is of potential interest as well. Less frequently used is the netstat –r option, which displays the routing table. If IP routing is enabled, or it is suspected an individual has static routes included on their computer, the routing table should be examined.

TIP The XP and 2003 versions of netstat also include an option –b, which will return the program associated with each connection. Earlier versions of Windows require another tool such as FPort to accomplish this.

NetBIOS information similar to that available from netstat can be obtained with the nbtstat command, using both the –s and the –S options. The lowercase version shows the destination by NetBIOS name, the uppercase version lists the IP address associated with that name. Sample output of nbtstat –s showing a connection to CMSPRINT4 which has transferred a small amount of information in two directions is as follows:

```
C:\Tools>nbtstat -s

Local Area Connection:
Node IpAddress: [68.42.19.62] Scope Id: []

                    NetBIOS Connection Table

Local Name               State      In/Out   Remote Host      Input    Output
----------------------------------------------------------------

    CMSS   <00>  Connected      Out      CMSPRINT4 <20>   162KB    144KB
    CMSS   <1F>  Listening
```

The current NetBIOS connection shown was established outbound, and there is an additional NetBIOS listener on the system shown above. A total number of bytes sent and received are shown in Input/Output respectively. A large number of bytes in one direction may indicate a file transfer or other high-bandwidth connection.

Two additional nbtstat options, –n and –c, are also useful. –n shows the local NetBIOS name resolution table, including any names that resolve differently on the specific machine being examined either maliciously or otherwise, such as the scenario where two machine with identical names are placed on the same network. The –c option displays the NetBIOS cache, which includes recent connections as well as the names of the domain controllers used by the machine, which provide an additional location to obtain log files outside of the system itself.

To find any current connections as well as listeners attached to unusual programs (for example, a port 80 listener attached to svchost), Foundstone produced the fport tool. Fport lists all of the open ports on a system as well as the program that is associated with that port (where applicable). The following is the output of running fport on a sample system:

```
C:\Tools>fport
FPort v2.0 - TCP/IP Process to Port Mapper
Copyright 2000 by Foundstone, Inc.
http://www.foundstone.com

Pid    Process          Port  Proto Path
3196                ->  23    TCP
1924                ->  135   TCP
4      System       ->  139   TCP
4      System       ->  445   TCP
1544                ->  1028  TCP
1688   FIREFOX      ->  3310  TCP   C:\PROGRA~1\FIREFOX\FIREFOX.EXE
1688   FIREFOX      ->  3311  TCP   C:\PROGRA~1\FIREFOX\FIREFOX.EXE
1792   svchost      ->  3389  TCP   D:\WINDOWS\system32\svchost.exe
1552                ->  3925  TCP
1552                ->  137   UDP
1544                ->  138   UDP
1924                ->  445   UDP
4      System       ->  500   UDP
1792   svchost      ->  1029  UDP   D:\WINDOWS\system32\svchost.exe
3196                ->  1118  UDP
1688   FIREFOX      ->  1900  UDP   C:\PROGRA~1\FIREFOX\FIREFOX.EXE
1688   FIREFOX      ->  3410  UDP   C:\PROGRA~1\FIREFOX\FIREFOX.EXE
4      System       ->  4500  UDP
0      System       ->  62515 UDP
0      System       ->  62517 UDP
0      System       ->  62519 UDP
0      System       ->  62521 UDP
0      System       ->  62523 UDP
0      System       ->  62524 UDP
```

A final built-in program that represents a Swiss army knife of commands for obtaining network information (both local and remote) is the net command. The net command is a series of network utilities available natively in Windows that provide information on network connections ranging from share information to current sessions. The most useful net commands for forensics are as follows:

- net localgroup. Returns a list of the local Windows groups on the current machine.
- net session. Returns information on any currently connected (to the suspect machine) network sessions.
- net share. Returns the list of shared directories on the current machine, including administrative shares.
- net use. Returns the list of shared drive mappings on the machine, including both source (local drive letter) and destination (UNC name).
- net user. Returns the list of Windows user accounts on the current system.
- net view. Returns the browse list for the local domain, listing all machines that are immediately known to the suspect's machine.

Sample output from the net share command follows. Administrative, user, and printer shares are all listed.

```
C:\Tools>net share

Share name    Resource                              Remark

-------------------------------------------------------------------
D$            D:\                                   Default share
print$        D:\WINDOWS\System32\spool\drivers
                                                    Printer Drivers
G$            G:\                                   Default share
ADMIN$        D:\WINDOWS                            Remote Admin
C$            C:\                                   Default share
IPC$                                                Remote IPC
SharedDocs    D:\DOCUMENTS AND SETTINGS\ALL USERS\DOCUMENTS
Printer       DOT4_001            Spooled  HP LaserJet 895 Series PCL
The command completed successfully.
```

Running Program Information

Knowing what a suspect machine is running (in terms of programs) at a specific time can prove or disprove malicious activity. Windows systems have two basic classes of running programs: interactive programs and services. Interactive programs are started from the command line or GUI and show up in the list of running processes, viewable from the GUI by pressing Ctrl+Alt+Del. Services may be started automatically and run in the background without user interaction (or even knowledge).

NOTE Interactive programs can also be called from other programs or loaded automatically as noted in the Registry analysis chapter.

Finding a list of running processes on Windows NT/2000/XP/2003 systems can be done with the PsList tool from Sysinternals. The software provides a listing of all running programs, their CPU usage (useful in identifying programs which are exhausting resources or actively scanning), and any associated threads.

NOTE A thread is a lightweight process that runs subservient to a main process. Many large programs are multi-threaded, but so are many worms that spawn numerous scan threads.

There are two PsList options of use in an examination, -x and -t. The -x command line switch returns all information on running processes and their specific threads. This listing is useful for in-depth analysis of a specific program, or overall usage details on all running programs. The second option, -t, lists all running processes in a tree-like fashion. This permits a quick evaluation of which programs launched another program, and of program hierarchies. PsList -t results from an example system are as follows:

```
C:\Tools>pslist -t

PsList 1.26 - Process Information Lister
Copyright (C) 1999-2004 Mark Russinovich
Sysinternals - www.sysinternals.com

Process information for CMSS:

Name          Pid Pri Thd  Hnd     VM     WS   Priv
Idle            0   0   1    0      0     16      0
 System         4   8  59  506   1876     28      0
  smss       1444  11   2   22   3544    124    144
   csrss     1548  13  12  567  28344   2316   1888
  winlogon   1572  13  18  553  53992    872   7344
   services  1616   9  15  303  36300   1212   1924
    svchost   240   8   6   82  29660    920   1228
    svchost   340   8  14  206  37484    348   1616
    spoolsv   568   8  11  120  42756   1116   3028
    ccSetMgr  672   8   7  185  33752    100   2408
    cvpnd     708   8   3   61  19864    612    896
    DefWatch  780   8   3   27  16396     40    316
    DkService 796   8   4   90  40220    780   1316
    mdm       848   8   4   85  33044    440    844
```

nmapserv	880	8	2	36	25960	224	604
Rtvscan	928	8	44	339	107024	3312	11208
newtd	1068	8	3	99	23388	324	2236
MsPMSPSv	1128	8	2	43	13224	40	364
ccEvtMgr	1160	8	14	218	41012	48	2400
alg	1544	8	5	110	32292	212	1024
svchost	1792	8	21	229	65240	1576	2796
wisptis	756	13	3	102	28752	400	2196
LUCOMS~1	1552	8	3	200	47576	2496	5400
svchost	1924	8	10	396	37444	1116	1784
svchost	2036	8	61	1580	118064	10588	16128
lsass	1628	9	14	313	37064	892	2128
cmd	476	8	1	36	30048	252	1920
explorer	1692	8	19	788	113812	11000	23408
ccApp	908	8	9	234	52028	324	3240
cmd	996	8	1	30	30048	752	1944
iexplore	1412	8	11	920	131244	13784	25444
VPTray	1632	8	2	121	37788	436	2224
firefox	1688	8	11	247	138988	30184	40600
POWERPNT	464	8	4	186	113916	972	3756
msmsgs	2052	8	8	327	52676	2640	3168
ctfmon	2064	8	1	66	29536	468	760
WZQKPICK	2348	8	1	29	25676	180	528
cmd	2496	8	1	31	30048	996	1944
pslist	2448	13	2	81	17620	1620	712
EXCEL	3000	8	4	224	88348	2880	4336
WINWORD	3192	8	8	400	204712	23980	17692
Virtual PC	3312	8	14	326	110196	6752	13244
helix	3888	8	7	160	47188	956	10020
devldr32	2656	8	4	80	29408	220	1804
realsched	2948	8	4	111	35380	124	824

In the preceding listing, individual programs are generally listed as running one of three ways: as root programs, which are generally run at startup automatically or directly from the Run command window, such as cmd; as a subprocess to Windows Explorer, launched from the GUI; or as a service, listed under SMSS, the Session Management Subsystem, which processes user logons and the associated programs and services run from them. The PsList program itself can be seen as a subprocess to the command shell (cmd) which was launched via an Explorer shortcut (under the Explorer process). A second command shell, run from the Run command, is shown as a peer of the Explorer process under its own hierarchy.

Windows programs can also run as services roughly equivalent to daemons in the Unix world. Services are programs that run without the need for direct user interaction and can be started manually or automatically. Recent worms (for example, Nachi) as well as software of interest (for example, nmap) frequently run as services. The easiest way to display all running services is using the PsService program from SysInternals. Executing the command without any options returns all running services. Using the config option (no dash) returns the detailed settings for those services, including startup values (for example, auto or manual start). Truncated output detailing a few services from PsService is shown here:

```
C:\Tools>psservice | more

PsService v2.12 - local and remote services viewer/controller
Copyright (C) 2001-2004 Mark Russinovich
Sysinternals - www.sysinternals.com

SERVICE_NAME: Alerter
DISPLAY_NAME: Alerter

Notifies selected users and computers of administrative alerts. If the
service is stopped, programs that use administrative alerts will not
receive them. If this service is disabled, any services that explicitly
depend on it will fail to start.

        TYPE              : 20 WIN32_SHARE_PROCESS
        STATE             : 1  STOPPED
                            (NOT_STOPPABLE,NOT_PAUSABLE,IGNORES_SHUTDOWN)
        WIN32_EXIT_CODE   : 1077 (0x435)
        SERVICE_EXIT_CODE : 0  (0x0)
        CHECKPOINT        : 0x0
        WAIT_HINT         : 0x0

SERVICE_NAME: ALG
DISPLAY_NAME: Application Layer Gateway Service
Provides support for third party protocol plug-ins for Internet
Connection Sharing and the Windows Firewall.

        TYPE              : 10 WIN32_OWN_PROCESS
        STATE             : 4  RUNNING
                            (STOPPABLE,NOT_PAUSABLE,IGNORES_SHUTDOWN)
        WIN32_EXIT_CODE   : 0  (0x0)
        SERVICE_EXIT_CODE : 0  (0x0)
        CHECKPOINT        : 0x0
        WAIT_HINT         : 0x0

SERVICE_NAME: AppMgmt
DISPLAY_NAME: Application Management

Provides software installation services such as Assign, Publish, and
Remove.

        TYPE              : 20 WIN32_SHARE_PROCESS
        STATE             : 1  STOPPED
                            (NOT_STOPPABLE,NOT_PAUSABLE,IGNORES_SHUTDOWN)
        WIN32_EXIT_CODE   : 1077 (0x435)
        SERVICE_EXIT_CODE : 0  (0x0)
        CHECKPOINT        : 0x0
        WAIT_HINT         : 0x0
```

The config option includes the START_TYPE variable, indicating the autostart settings of a particular service. The START_TYPE, which follows shown as having a value of 4 for the ClipSrv service, indicates the service is Disabled (not startable without changing the setting). A START_TYPE of 3 indicates the service needs to be manually started and 2 that the service is started automatically (1 represents a service started by the system when the kernel loads and 0 by the bootloader).

```
SERVICE_NAME: ClipSrv

Enables ClipBook Viewer to store information and share it with remote
computers. If the service is stopped, ClipBook Viewer will not be able
to share information with remote computers. If this service is disabled,
any services that explicitly depend on it will fail to start.

        TYPE               : 10 WIN32_OWN_PROCESS
        START_TYPE         : 4  DISABLED
        ERROR_CONTROL      : 1  NORMAL
        BINARY_PATH_NAME   : D:\WINDOWS\system32\clipsrv.exe
        LOAD_ORDER_GROUP   :
        TAG                : 0
        DISPLAY_NAME       : ClipBook
        DEPENDENCIES       : NetDDE
        SERVICE_START_NAME: LocalSystem
```

A final command of use when analyzing programs is at, which accesses the command-line scheduler. Similar to Unix cron jobs, at returns the full list of scheduled programs and when they are scheduled to run. The output here shows an executable, generate.exe, is scheduled to run at 23:00:

```
C:\Tools>at
Status ID   Day                    Time           Command Line
-------------------------------------------------------------------
        1   Today                  11:00 PM       generate.exe
```

Main Memory Analysis

The computer's RAM contains information on running programs, including data, instructions, and fragments from older programs. Searching main memory can yield data that was not written to disk but was generated as part of the current work session on a computer. There are three ways to analyze main memory: using Winhex, using process-specific tools such as PMDump, and dumping all of main memory to an image file for later analysis. The use of Winhex is detailed in the section on file systems. The same techniques apply to analyzing memory. The other two options are available through the command line.

The imaging of main memory causes an issue with storage. File copies of main memory can be very large. With current RAM amounts ranging into the Gigabyte range, storage of the RAM images must be done on a large removable media source (for example, USB hard disk) or transmitted across the network to an off-machine storage location. Examples of offline storage using NetCat are shown later in this section.

When determining how to image memory, the investigator needs to look toward the scope of the investigation. If there is a need to identify a single rogue process (an unreported worm, for example), dumping of a single process will result in less data to analyze. Likewise, if a single, running application is the sole target, obtaining the contents of that application's memory usage may be sufficient. For broader searching where text fragments from past data may be present, imaging the entire contents of RAM will be the most fruitful. When in doubt, imaging all of RAM and analyzing later is a prudent choice. Mapping back individual memory sections to a specific application may not be possible.

PMDump, from Arne Vidstrom, returns the contents of memory for a specific process using the process ID (PID). PMDump functions on all NT-based Windows systems but not on Windows 9*x* systems. The PID for individual processes is returned by the PsList command noted above, or by using the –list switch with PMDump. PMDump produces a raw file that can be read offline with a hex editor like WinHex (or through a string searching program on the command line). The size of the file depends on the amount of memory allocated to the process being imaged. A sample PMDump command line for dumping the memory used by a WINWORD process (PID 2320) to a file dump.img is as follows:

```
C:\Tools>pmdump 2320 G:\dump.img

pmdump 1.2 - (c) 2002, Arne Vidstrom (arne.vidstrom@ntsecurity.nu)
         - http://ntsecurity.nu/toolbox/pmdump/
C:\Tools>
```

For dumping the entire contents of memory, a large USB-based drive or network connection is required. The dd.exe executable, a Windows port of a program available for Unix systems that performs physical sector-by-sector duplications on disks, can be used to dump the entire contents of memory to an image file. The custom version of dd was developed by George Garner and works well for both disk and memory imaging and works on NT-based Windows systems.

Using the dd command requires the assignment of an input file (if) and output file (of). For memory, the input file is \\.\PhysicalMemory (the UNC name used for referencing the computer's RAM). The output file is either the name of an image file to be stored locally on a USB or similarly connected device, or piped to NetCat for remote storage. The version of dd.exe shown additionally supports the generation of MD5 hashes at the time of acquisition. Generating an MD5 hash of the contents, verifying it, and saving it to a file can be performed using the `--md5sum`, `--verifymd5` and `--md5out` respectively as part of the duplication command. A sample duplication of RAM using dd is shown here:

```
C:\Tools>dd.exe if=\\.\PhysicalMemory of=G:\RAM.img bs=4096 conv=noerror
--md5sum --verifymd5 --md5out=G:\RAM.img.md5
Forensic Acquisition Utilities, 1, 0, 0, 1035 dd, 3, 16, 2, 1035
Copyright (C) 2002-2004 George M. Garner Jr.

Command Line: dd.exe if=\\.\PhysicalMemory of=G:\RAM.img bs=4096
conv=noerror --md5sum --verifymd5 --md5out=G:\RAM.img.md5
Based on original version developed by Paul Rubin, David MacKenzie, and
Stuart Kemp
Microsoft Windows: Version 5.1 (Build 2600.Professional Service Pack 2)

13/01/2005  13:41:43 (UTC)
13/01/2005  08:41:43 (local time)

Current User: CMSS\Chad M.S. Steel

Total physical memory reported: 392740 KB
Copying physical memory...
Physical memory in the range 0x00004000-0x00004000 could not be read.
C:\Tools\dd.exe:
        Stopped reading physical memory:

\ca1215ea5bd0d21f2fafa3813e53aa69 [\\\\.\\PhysicalMemory] *G:\\RAM.img

Verifying output file...
\ca1215ea5bd0d21f2fafa3813e53aa69 [G:\\RAM.img] *G:\\RAM.img
The checksums do match.
The operation completed successfully.

Output G:\RAM.img 402649088/402649088 bytes (compressed/uncompressed)
98303+0 records in
98303+0 records out
```

In the listed duplication, a read block size (in bytes) is specified with the `bs` switch, and `conv=noerror` directs the program to ignore errors and continue to run. Portions of RAM may be protected by the operating system and inaccessible to direct reads. These will be skipped as necessary with this switch. The total number of bytes read or written is shown, as are any skipped portions of memory. The preceding example represents close to half a gigabyte of memory, too large to fit on a floppy disk even if greatly compressable. The number of records represents the number of blocks (blocks × blocksize = number of bytes). The resultant image file (RAM.img) and hash file (RAM.img.md5) can now be stored as evidence.

As with all forensic duplication, the copy of RAM is a snapshot in time. The act of running dd itself changes a portion of RAM. Indeed, searching for dd.exe will yield results as the process itself is utilizing memory. This is unavoidable, but the amount of alteration to memory can be minimized by not running additional programs simultaneously. Likewise, the percentage of RAM affected is minimal compared to the overall size of RAM in an average system. Analysis of the RAM is the same as that of disks. It is generally analyzed with a text editor or a search utility. These analysis techniques are covered in the Disk Analysis section.

As with the other command line options, the raw output from a large image can be piped over NetCat for storage on a remote system. The NetCat listener can be started on the remote system with the same command as before. Note the −l for the non-persistent listener, as only one file will be transferred:

```
C:\Tools>nc -l -p 23 >> RAMImage.img
```

NOTE The output can be passed on the remote machine to an md5sum program as well to obtain the immediate hash value. Alternatively, it can be stored to disk and a hash value calculated after the storage.

The dd command can then be run on the local system and the image itself sent across through the NetCat pipe by leaving out the output file (of) option:

```
C:\Tools>dd if=\\.\PhysicalMemory bs=4096 conv=noerror | nc
www.chadsteel.com 23
```

The error messages and diagnostic information will still be passed to standard output (the monitor) on the suspect's machine, but the data will be transmitted over the NetCat pipe. Depending on the size of the memory and the bandwidth available, transmission can take several minutes. The easiest way to monitor completeness is to watch the file size on the remote system.

Additional Resources

Refer to the following list for additional resources:

ActivePERL Windows PERL Interpreter From ActiveState
   www.activestate.com/Products/ActivePerl/

Cantenna Wireless Antenna Construction
   www.turnpoint.net/wireless/cantennahowto.html

ChaosReader Traffic Reconstruction
   users.tpg.com.au/bdgcvb/chaosreader.html

CryptCat for Windows
  `farm9.org/Cryptcat/GetCryptcat.php`

DSniff by Dug Song
  `www.monkey.org/~dugsong/dsniff/`

Ethereal
  `www.ethereal.com/distribution/win32/`

FPort from FoundStone
  `www.foundstone.com/index.htm?subnav=resources
  /navigation.htm&subcontent=/resources/proddesc
  /fport.htm`

Helix Bootable Forensic Environment
  `www.e-fense.com/helix/`

KeyGhost Physical Keystroke Loggers
  `www.keyghost.com/`

Microsoft Indexing Service Query Language Reference
  `msdn.microsoft.com/library/default.asp?url=/library
  /en-us/indexsrv/html/ixqlang_92xx.asp`

Net Optics Fiber Taps
  `www.netoptics.com`

NetCat For Windows
  `www.vulnwatch.org/netcat/`

Network General Network Sniffer
  `www.sniffer.com`

nmap by Fyodor - Windows Binaries
  `www.insecure.org`

PMDump Memory Imager
  `www.ntsecurity.nu/toolbox/pmdump/`

PSGetSID from SysInternals
  `www.sysinternals.com/ntw2k/freeware/psgetsid.shtml`

PSInfo from SysInternals
  `www.sysinternals.com/ntw2k/freeware/psinfo.shtml`

PSList from SysInternals
  `www.sysinternals.com/ntw2k/freeware/pslist.shtml`

PSLoggedOn from SysInternals
  `www.sysinternals.com/ntw2k/freeware/psloggedon.shtml`

PSService from SysInternals
  `www.sysinternals.com/ntw2k/freeware/psservice.shtml`

PuTTY Terminal Emulator
`www.chiark.greenend.org.uk/~sgtatham/putty`
`/download.html`

Sniffer Cable Designs by Diego González Gómez
`www.infosecwriters.com/hhworld/hh9/roc/node3.html`

SpectorPro Keystroke Loggers
`www.spector.com/`

Strider GhostBuster Anti-rootkit Software from Microsoft
`research.microsoft.com/rootkit/`

WinPCap (Required For Ethereal)
`www.polito.it`

Forensic Duplication

Forensic duplication is the copying of the contents of a storage device completely and without alteration. The technique is sometimes known as bitwise duplication, sector copying, or physical imaging. Forensic duplication is the primary method for collecting hard disk, floppy, CD/DVD, and flash-based data for the purpose of evidence gathering.

Copying files from a suspects device using standard techniques (Windows Explorer, cutting and pasting, xcopy) or imaging of logical drives (using Ghost or DriveImage) provides some of the data for an investigation but is usually insufficient for forensic imaging and may violate best evidence rules.

NOTE When applied to a drive as a whole, this imaging is generally not sufficient. Copies of individual files can be made and used as evidence (such as those gathered in a live acquisition or from a shared drive), but it needs to be documented why bitwise imaging was not performed and the examiner needs to understand the limitations.

The failings of standard duplication techniques from a forensic standpoint are as follows:

- **Lack of authenticity.** There is no verification of authenticity in a standard file copy. This can be addressed through the use of external tools such as MD5sum that provide this facility.

- **Loss of non-file data.** Information stored in slack space, un-partitioned space, or free space is not copied. These locations may contain previously deleted content or other information of interest that will not be available with logical imaging.

- **Alteration of metadata.** Depending on the file systems copied To/From, metadata associated with a file may be lost. Rights and permissions stored on a specific file system (for example, NTFS) as well as system attributes (for example, Read Only bit) may be altered or deleted when a file is copied between disparate file systems. This can include the loss of the ability to look up permissions (based on SID) even on copies to similar file systems.

- **Inability to provide context.** A copy of the data in a logical file does not provide the same machine context as an image. Contextual data can include location in a directory tree, or duplication details, and details on other surrounding files.

NOTE Context is very important in investigations. An image of a young child in a bathing suit found in a directory labeled "Relatives - 4th of July 2004" might take on a vastly different meaning than the same image in a directory called Young Kids. Likewise, the surrounding files may be indicators. The same image grouped with 100 other pictures of individuals of varying ages in bathing suits may have a different interpretation than 100 other kids in bathing suits.

- **Failure to copy all data streams.** Alternate Data Streams, a feature of NTFS file systems, are not supported by most other file systems. By copying files to a non-NTFS file system, these streams are lost, as only the primary stream is retained.

Because of these limitations, special tools and techniques exist for forensic duplications. Their usage depends on the specifics of the case. The duplication of a single floppy disk varies greatly from the duplication of a multi-terabyte RAID array.

Hard Disk Duplication

Creating a forensic image of a hard disk is one of the most common forensic techniques used. Images are created as part of investigations for analysis but may be created for other reasons as well:

- Creating hard disk images to fulfill a legal discovery request.

- Imaging the machines of high risk (or all) employees when they leave the company.

- Duplicating an organization's standard or gold-disk build for comparison purposes.

- Transferring damaged or degradable media to an archival-quality format (for example, DVD-R/CD-R).

TIP There are questions regarding the lifespan of DVD-R and CD-R media. Some media created in the 1980s and 1990s had manufacturing defects leading to early degradation, but the optical media is generally expected to last several decades. For best results, use archival-grade optical write-once media such as that available from Mitsui and Delkin.

When a hard disk is imaged, the values of all of the bits in every sector are copied from the suspect's drive to another type of media or an image file. The drive itself can be later recreated exactly by copying the forensic image to another drive of a similar geometry and size (or a larger size in most cases) or analyzed as an image.

NOTE Technically, all of the relevant bits are copied. Drive-specific information such as preambles and CRC data are not generally copied. Likewise, bad sectors on the drive may not be copied (if marked bad by the drive hardware). Since these are not user accessible, there is no inherent data loss by not duplicating them.

While forensic duplication does require all bits be copied in an unaltered fashion, the storage of those bits once copied does not need to be in a bit-by-bit file. Courts have permitted the use of lossless compression to save space. This can be a major factor in imaging times if a disk is mostly empty. They have also allowed reversible encryption to protect the image from prying eyes. Depending on the imaging software used, additional meta-information may be stored with the drive image as well. This information can include hash values, drive geometry information, examiner information, and duplication time/date stamps.

Duplication can be performed locally or remotely, with advantages and disadvantages to each method. Local duplication is faster than remote duplication and provides greater flexibility in acquisition hardware and techniques. There are two methods of local duplication: in-situ duplication (where the drives to be duplicated are kept in their respective machines) and direct duplication (where the drives are removed and directly duplicated using the appropriate hardware). (See the sidebar "Write Blocking.")

WRITE BLOCKING

When performing a forensic duplication, the data being acquired should not be altered in any way. While intentional alteration can be avoided procedurally, accidental alteration is more difficult to achieve. Many programs can inadvertently alter the contents of a disk; Windows itself writes a signature to a drive the first time it is recognized by the system.

To avoid both intentional and accidental alteration when performing a forensic duplication, write blocking software or hardware is used. Both write blocking software and hardware protect the evidence drive from alteration during the duplication process. Software write blockers attempt to catch the system calls generated by any instructions that attempt to write to the disk. Hardware write blockers monitor and block and write commands sent to the disk itself.

Software write blockers, such as PDBlock, allow a user to connect drives directly to the interfaces available on their forensic workstation. This can include FireWire, USB, SCSI, ATA, and SATA-based drives, depending on what adapters are present. For more obscure connection types (for example, some of the older SCSI standards or proprietary RAID-devices), there may not be any hardware blockers available, leaving software blocking as the only alternative. Some software blockers have had problems in the past with older operating system calls that bypass the standard Windows APIs for drive access. When using a software write blocker, make sure it has been court-tested and covers write calls based on both INT 13 and its extensions.

Hardware-based solutions are specific to an interface or set of interfaces. One side of the write blocker is connected to the forensic workstation (generally through a FireWire or USB 2.0 connection), and the other to the drive to be imaged. The Ultrablock and FireFly lines of write blockers from Digital Intelligence support the common SATA, IDE, and SCSI standards for connecting a range of hard disks. Hardware solutions generally allow for the highest speed imaging, as they use the native interface of the drive itself.

A final option for write blocking is to use all-in-one cloning devices. Originally developed for making multiple copies from a single master drive for rapid deployments, hardware-based cloning devices such as the SF-5000 have been adapted for forensic duplication, are ultra-portable and do not require a PC to operate. For high-volume duplications, these devices are must-haves when going on-site.

As an added benefit of write blockers, they can be employed to perform an analysis of a drive without first duplicating its contents. While not the standard technique for analyzing drive information, if a quick analysis is required, the suspect drive can be connected and searched before duplication occurs. This technique is useful when attempting to identify drives requiring additional analysis during a triage operation.

Remote duplication is slower but can be done without the suspect being aware that duplication is occurring. Similarly, remote duplication can be performed when local duplication is not possible because of limited physical access to the suspect machine for whatever reason. Remote duplication always occurs in-situ.

In-Situ Duplication

In-situ duplication is generally slower than direct duplication but provides other advantages. If complex hardware is present (for example, hardware RAID controllers and obscure SCSI cards), the native computer's existing configuration can be used in the duplication. Secondly, there is less risk of damage to the drive itself as it does not need to be removed. Finally, duplication on live systems can be done without powering down for critical systems where downtime is not an option.

There are five primary methods for in-situ duplication:

- **Serial cable.** A null-modem serial cable (used in the past for programs such as LapLink) can be connected between the analysis computer and the suspect computer to perform the duplication. A serial cable is generally the slowest method for connection, and duplication of terabyte-sized drives can take many days depending on the port speed settings, but this may be the only method available on older laptops with proprietary drive hardware (and no parallel or Ethernet ports — they do still exist). Fortunately these laptops tend to have very small hard drives.

- **Parallel cable.** Faster than a serial cable, a parallel cable delivers multiple bits of data simultaneously (in parallel). Products like EnCase rely on parallel port connections as a back method of communicating. While still slow, a parallel port connection can be used when an Ethernet connection is unavailable, or drivers for the Ethernet card in the suspect's machine are difficult to acquire.

- **Ethernet.** Ranging from moderately fast to very fast, Ethernet connections constitute the ideal method for machine-to-machine duplications. Ethernet cards are readily available in most current laptops and desktops at 10 and 100 Mb/s, with 1 Gb/s cards become even more common, and Ethernet drivers (for DOS, which most boot disks use) for the most common chipsets are readily available online. When performing an Ethernet-based duplication, a crossover cable is used to directly connect the machines. The use of a hub or switch will not only slow down the duplication, but will introduce another layer of complexity that is unnecessary.

- **Wireless.** Wireless Ethernet cards are now readily available, though the speeds are generally lower and encryption needs to be used to protect forensic integrity. They are not generally used for forensic purposes, however. Many of the DOS mode drivers that are frequently needed for duplication are non-existent for these chipsets, although bootable Linux drivers generally are.

- **USB.** A fairly recent trend since the introduction of cheap USB 2.0 hard disks, DOS USB drivers are now part of many forensic boot disks and CD's. These drivers enable the examiner to connect a larger USB hard drive to the suspect's machine and perform the duplication directly to that location. The availability of cheap USB hard disks and speed improvements in USB 2.0 has made this one of the preferred choices for local acquisition.

NOTE The times shown in Figure 9-1 are estimated based on the theoretical maximum speeds of each technology commonly in use and do not reflect compression.

In-situ duplications require the use of a boot disk or bootable CD. These media allow the examiner to boot to a memory-only (does not write to the hard disk) version of an operating system which permits duplication. The operating system used is generally DOS or Linux.

The default Windows XP startup disks do not read NTFS partitions and likewise do not have access to CD-ROMs. To remedy this, create a Windows 98SE OEM boot disk and install the NTFS read-only drivers available at www .sysinternals.com/ntw2k/freeware/ntfsdos.shtml.

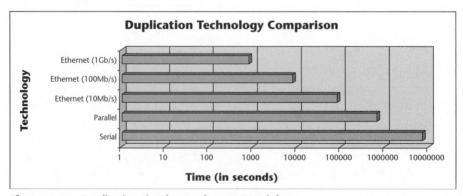

Figure 9-1: Duplication timeframes for 100GB of data

NOTE Images can be created from either the OS itself or from extractable images available at www.bootdisk.com. Technically, one does not need any file system drivers to do a raw drive duplication, but the NTFS driver is read-only and enables the analyst to do a quick check for specific files or their contents on the suspect system as needed.

This floppy can now be used for booting on the suspect's machine. The primary consideration during acquisition is not altering the data on the suspect device. As such, extra caution is needed in booting to ensure the floppy or CD boots first. To boot for the purposes of a duplication:

1. Disconnect the data cable and power cable from the back of any hard disk drives in the suspect's machine.

2. Boot the machine and enter BIOS. This can generally be accomplished by pressing F1, F2, or Del during the initial boot process.

3. Change the BIOS settings to boot first from either the floppy of the CD drive. If possible, disable booting from the hard disk as an option.

4. Reboot the system with the floppy/CD inserted. Confirm the system boots properly.

5. Power off the system and reattach the relevant hard disk cables.

6. Power on the system with the bootable floppy/CD in the drive.

7. Load any necessary drivers to perform the duplication and connect the relevant serial/parallel/Ethernet/USB devices.

8. Begin the duplication.

Because of the size limitations of the floppy disk, a forensic CD used in conjunction with the floppy is extremely useful. A copy of dd.exe and large driver files can be burned to a CD in advance, then accessed or loaded as necessary. Although primarily a Linux distribution, the Helix environment contains several of these files for forensic use. Additionally, both SafeBack and EnCase provide bootable floppy and CD images to enable the imaging of drives with their respective tools. A menu-driven Ethernet/TCP/IP boot disk image created by Teledata from and contains the common Ethernet chipset drivers (both PCI and CardBus) as well as the ability to configure a card with a static or dynamic IP address.

To perform an image using the Ethernet connection, the analyst first needs to boot the suspect's computer using a network boot disk as noted previously. Then do the following:

1. Connect a crossover cable between the suspect machine and the analysis machine.

2. Configure the suspect machine with a static IP address of 192.168.1.1 and a Netmask of 255.255.255.0.

3. Boot the analysis machine and configure it with an IP address of 192.168.1.2 and a Netmask of 255.255.255.0.

4. Start a netcat listener on the evidence machine and pipe the output of that listener to dd:

```
nc -1 -p 23 | dd of=c:\evidence.img
```

5. Use dd to image the drive and send the results to netcat on the evidence machine (www.chadsteel.com on port 23 in the example) by typing the following on the suspect machine:

```
dd if=\\.\PhysicalDrive0 bs=512 conv=noerror | nc www.chadsteel.com
23
```

If a partition needs to be imaged and not the entire drive, the drive letter (for example, c:) can be substituted for PhysicalDrive0.

TIP If multiple partitions are present, PhysicalDrive# can be used with # being the number of the drive to image the entire physical drive. For imaging non–hard disks, using the drive letter will image the whole device assuming one partition is present.

If the drive image files are too large, they can be split using the skip feature of dd. This allows the drive to be broken into manageable chunks to enable easier transmission, compression, and archiving to smaller media. To create 660MB-sized image files (to fit a standard CD), the following commands can be used:

```
dd-gnu if=\\.\PhysicalDrive0 count=660000 of=c:\evidence1.img
dd-gnu if=\\.\PhysicalDrive0 count=660000 skip=660000 of=
c:\evidence2.img
dd-gnu if=\\.\PhysicalDrive0 count=660000 skip=1320000 of=
c:\evidence3.img
    .
    .
    .
```

An additional feature that can be used with the GNU gzip program is compression. Compressing an image will allow it to be transmitted faster and use less bandwidth.

WARNING For most scenarios compressing is faster. However, if the drive is filled (70 percent or more) with MPEG-2 movies or MP3s (or any other pre-compressed file formats), it will actually be slower. Similarly, a drive that has been overwritten with random characters will also be slower.

To perform compression, the image is piped to gzip using the −c option (to send the results to standard output) before piping to netcat. On the listening side, the results are then decompressed before outputting to a file. To enable compression using gzip, on the listening computer type:

```
nc -l -p 23 | gzip -d -c | dd of=c:\evidence.img
```

And on the suspect's computer, type:

```
dd if=\\.\PhysicalDrive0 bs=512 conv=noerror | gzip -c | nc
www.chadsteel.com 23
```

Enabling compression will generally halve the transfer times on a typical machine.

Duplicating an image to a local USB drive is much simpler. Duplication can be performed as follows:

```
dd if=\\.\PhysicalDrive0 of=\\.\f:\evidence.img bs=512 conv=noerror
```

where f: is the drive letter of the USB-attached device.

NOTE All of these examples assume gzip, dd, and nc are in the current path. Include them in the path or explicitly type the directory names where they are located on the particular forensic CD/floppy.

All of the in-situ commands shown previously can be used on a live system as well, though it is not recommended unless other options have been exhausted. If remote duplication of a live system is needed, it is recommended that a specialty tool such as EnCase Enterprise be used.

TIP Social engineering can be used to facilitate an installation of the EnCase Enterprise Servlet or other forensic tools. We once used a "must install this patch immediately" technique to successfully deploy the servlet to a large number of internal machines through a simple email message.

ENCASE ENTERPRISE

EnCase Enterprise, Guidance Software's flagship product, provides comprehensive, court-tested remote acquisition and analysis capabilities. The EnCase tool has an integrated acquisition environment based on servlets, small applications that can be placed on the machine to be duplicated. These are tied together with a central authentication and authorization machine called SAFE, which provides the necessary controls on forensic duplication within an organization. The following figure shows the overall model.

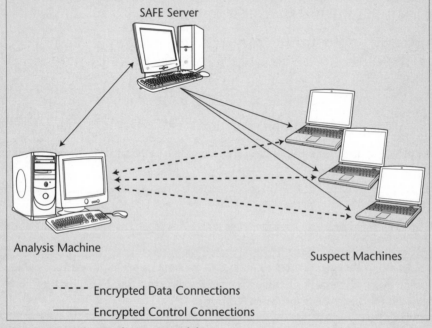

SAFE Server

Analysis Machine

Suspect Machines

- - - - - Encrypted Data Connections

——— Encrypted Control Connections

EnCase Enterprise Deployment Model

When a duplication or analysis of a remote machine is required, the EnCase servlet is installed on the machine to be duplicated. The servlet supports multiple operating systems, and can be installed locally or remotely with administrative rights. Remote installation can be done with SMS or by copying the servlet to the suspect machine and then running it using a remote execution tool such as psexec. The servlet can be installed as memory-only (no copy is made to disk) or as an executable running as service. The service is user-configurable for naming purposes, and can be well-hidden from suspect observation. A listener is opened on port 4445 for instruction connections from the SAFE, and remains present until uninstalled or stopped.

When a duplication is needed, the examiner logs into the analysis machine and connects to the SAFE to be authenticated and authorized to perform the duplication. When the analyst confirms that the user can perform the duplication, he makes a data connection to the remote system to retrieve the meta-contents of the file system (the FAT of the MFT). The contents are cached on the analysis machine for identification of specific files to copy or meta-analysis on the files present.

The duplication can be at a file, partition (logical), or physical level. For a full duplication, the servlet compresses the data on the suspect's machine and then sends it over an AES-encrypted channel to the analysis machine for inclusion as an image file (using a proprietary EnCase image file format). With version 5 of EnCase Enterprise, the connection can be stopped and restarted as necessary with a delta kept at the servlet level of any changes since the last connection — very helpful with laptops, as they disconnect frequently. The image gathered can be automatically hashed when downloaded, allowing for an integrated integrity verification.

Although expensive, the EnCase Enterprise tool does provide a more seamless and streamlined approach to forensic duplication than single, standalone tools. For organizations with multiple sites globally or cost-prohibitive travel requirements for investigations, it can pay for itself in a very short time.

Direct Duplication

Direct duplication is faster than in-situ duplication, as it uses the native drive technology of the disk being imaged. Direct duplication is preferred when there are a large number of drives that need to be imaged, when the drives need to be shipped or carried to a lab for imaging, or when readily available drive formats (for example, SATA or ATA) are being analyzed. Because direct duplication does not require the use of boot disks or CDs, there is no need for a working CD or floppy drive on the target machine. Similarly, as long as the drives are intact, having the ability to use a hardware write blocker increases the integrity of a direct duplication.

A second occasion when direct duplication is warranted is the acquisition of removal media. Devices such as floppy disks, CD-ROMs, DVDs, Digital Cameras, USB Flash Drives, and other removable devices can all be imaged the same way as a hard disk. By imaging these media, they can be analyzed en masse (imaging searching one hundred floppy disk images stored on a fast hard disk versus searching one hundred floppy disks individually) regardless of the original media type.

To duplicate a hard disk directly, the following are the basic steps:

1. Unplug the suspect's machine, following the guidelines for powering down noted previously.

2. Remove any hard drives in the machine.

3. Check any removable media drives and remove any contents.

4. Connect the write blocker to the analysis machine.

5. Connect the disk drive to the write blocker.

6. Power on the analysis machine.

7. After booting is complete, power on the write blocker.

8. Utilize dd (or another duplication utility) to image the drive.

TIP It is possible to remove CD/DVDs even when the machine is powered off. Place a paperclip in the small hole under the drive to eject the media.

Duplicating locally allows for a larger number of possibilities for the storage of the duplicated information. The location to which the initial duplication occurs may or may not become the long-term storage location (for example, multiple disks may be duplicated to a hard disk as a short-term step, burned en masse to a DVD-R for archiving and data integrity, and finally copied back to another hard disk for fast analysis). The primary options for duplication are magnetic tape, hard disks, optical disks, and multi-tiered storage devices.

Magnetic Tape

Magnetic tape is the cheapest per-gigabyte option for the storing of duplicate information. Inexpensive tape media are readily available in a range of sizes and can store images of the largest single drives available on a single tape. Additionally, most magnetic tape cartridges support write protection after the initial writing, making them suitable for evidentiary image storage. Due to the small physical dimensions of tape cartridges, they also qualify as having the greatest storage density per cubic foot (important for large organizations which store hundreds of terabytes or petabytes of data).

Magnetic tape hardware is generally slower than a hard disk for duplicating but fast enough to be viable for the initial storage (although the serial nature of tape-based systems makes them unsuitable media for direct analysis). Like all magnetic media, tapes tend to degrade over time and need to be kept at the manufacturer-specified temperature and humidity to maintain their integrity for an extended period of time. The past ten years have also seen more significant technology changes in the tape backup space that are not backwards compatible than other media types, requiring spares of tape backup units be kept for as long as the evidence tapes themselves are kept.

Despite its limitations, magnetic tape remains an excellent choice for both short- and long-term evidentiary storage of data.

Hard Disks

The fastest mechanism for duplicating a hard disk is to duplicate it to another hard disk. Hard disks are one of the few media that allow direct analysis of the data using a write blocker as well as storage, although in practice they are rarely used as long-term storage options.

Hard disks have a good history of backwards compatibility within the ATA technology chain. An SATA controller can still read an original ATA-1 drive with the proper adapter, but hard disks suffer from the same degradation that affects all magnetic media. The cost per gigabyte of a hard disk is relatively high, and the physical dimensions of hard disks make them less than ideal for high-volume storage.

Hard disks are the best choice when a fast initial duplication is required or a quick analysis is needed and a write blocker is available.

TIP Hard disks used for duplication should be prepared in advance by wiping the disk with a series of zeros and then formatting for the appropriate partition type. NTFS is recommended due to the file size limitations present in FAT drives. Images can grow larger than the 4GB allowed for a single file on a FAT partition. Never assume that an out-of-the-box hard disk is wiped clean for forensic use. Some manufacturers have been known to provide refurbished platters on new disks, and others write-test data to drives as part of their QA procedures.

Optical Disks

Optical disk media, specifically CD and DVD-Rs, are excellent for both portability and evidential integrity. The price per gigabyte on optical media is generally better than that of hard disks, and the longevity of archival quality optical disks purporting to be greater than that of any magnetic media. The inherent write-once capability of the media itself offers built-in protection against intentional or accidental alteration, and optical drives have been made backwards compatible with the first CD-ROMs.

NOTE Although there are rewritable optical media available, they are not suitable for forensic use. Their longevity is less, the inherent advantage of having write-once capability is not present, and their cost per gigabyte is significantly higher.

The speed of optical disks is increasing rapidly but is not as fast as a hard disk for direct duplication. Additionally, the capacity of optical media is fairly small by current standards, although the new high-density DVD standards improve that dramatically, and the need to span multiple disks is a negative.

Optical media are an excellent choice for long-term archiving of evidence, as well as the forensic duplication of smaller-capacity media (for example, flash disks, floppies, or other optical disks).

Multi-tiered Storage

A typical forensic duplication and analysis lab will have multiple storage options available. Here is a typical setup for a complete forensic lab:

- **Multi-terabyte RAID array.** For analysis of multiple disk images at once and short-term storage of working copies for all active cases, a large disk array can be used. This can be a standards RAID array, or a more advanced NAS or SAN solution such as those available from EMC or NetApps.

- **Ultrium tape backup unit (integrated).** To backup the overall array, an Ultrium tape unit can be used with weekly full and daily incremental backups. The tapes are not the copies of record, but backups of the working analysis copies.

- **Ultrium tape backup unit (portable).** For high-capacity, on-site evidentiary copies, a portable Ultrium unit can be used. The unit should be the largest capacity currently available, and be compatible with the integrated server unit mentioned previously.

- **DVD-R drives.** The fastest available (and highest capacity for high-density DVDs) drives should be installed on all analysis machines. Additionally, a portable drive (USB 2.0 and FireWire combo if available) should be purchased. The DVD-R media are used to create and restore the archival, best evidence copies of the disk images as well as perform backups of specific pieces of evidence (for example, log files) and other case information.

- **USB 2.0 hard disks.** Several USB 2.0 hard disks cans be used for quick evidence gathering or as temporary analysis devices. The capacity should be the largest available.

With all acquisition, evidentiary integrity must be maintained and confirmed throughout the duplication process. An MD5 hash of the data can be used to provide this confirmation. To prove alteration has not occurred, an MD5 sum should be taken immediately following every step in the duplication (for example, copying from a local system to DVD-R) and the results compared to the original MD5 hash and recorded as part of the documentation of the duplication.

CASE STUDY: MASS ACQUISITION

Our security team was briefed on an investigation in a secured area that required our expertise. A confidential informant made allegations of fraud, bribery, and embezzlement on the part of a corporate management team. He provided sufficient direct evidence to prove the wrongdoing, but the extent of the corruption was unclear.

Because the investigation spanned an entire management team, we had a minimal amount of time onsite to conduct interviews and collect evidence — only 24 hours for 20 individuals. With the whole group as potential suspects, local support was not an option, and because of the critical nature of the business, we were not permitted to bring the electronic evidence offsite for forensic duplication and analysis.

After our legal department ran a quick contract, the investigation team began preparing for an early morning flight. As a result of the late request, we did not have the ability to pull in additional support or equipment. To make things tougher, half of our duplication laptops were out on other remote investigations. Facing a shortage of duplication equipment (one portable tape backup unit and two duplication laptops with a myriad of interfaces), we were ill-equipped to image and bring back 20 laptops and several local servers.

Relying on our scavenging abilities, we visited our internal desktop support team and commandeered their imaging equipment, which they used for cloning laptops to deploy to the sales force. Another team member was sent to the local CompUSA before closing to purchase 20 of the largest capacity hard disks available. We ended up with a myriad of brands and sizes from what was actually in stock. The remainder of the evening was spent wiping the disks for use and putting a game plan in place. We would focus on interviewing and acquiring while on-site and perform all of the electronic analysis offline. A second trip would be scheduled as necessary if further individuals were implicated as a result of the analysis activities.

When we hit the ground, we split into two teams. The management team was called into a conference room and interviewed one by one regarding the allegations. At the same time, we used the cloning hardware to image their laptop drives directly to similarly sized SATA drives, as well as the drives of four Windows 2000 file servers. Due to its size (15TB total storage space), the mail server was not fully imaged. The mail files of the suspects were copied directly to the tape backup unit for analysis at a later point.

We ultimately identified five other suspects after the interviews. We acquired their machines via the tape backup unit as we had already run out of hard disks. All of the disks and tapes were then packed in anti-static bags and then put into evidence bags and boxed for drop-shipping to the analysis lab.

At the lab, the individual drives were re-imaged and acquired using EnCase Enterprise. The acquired image files were burned to DVD-R for permanent storage, and the individual case files copied to our EMC unit for simultaneous analysis. The mail files were likewise copied to individual DVD-Rs, and copies placed on the analysis array.

(continued)

CASE STUDY: MASS ACQUISITION *(continued)*

Our analysis validated the allegations. A careful reconstruction of several e-mail chains confirmed the bribery allegations, and a series of deleted Excel spreadsheets were recovered from the free space on the drive. They belonged to the vice president of sales and showed two sets of monthly sales figures: one under a worksheet called *Reported* and a second under a worksheet called *Actual*. This was as close to a smoking gun as we could possibly hope for.

The analysis was able to link six of the suspects to wrongdoing. They were immediately dismissed by the company and replaced with a new team. Although the managing partner was not directly implicated, she was likewise replaced because of the magnitude of the corruption that had occurred on her watch.

Log File Duplication

Log file duplication is difficult for many reasons. First, the log files are frequently on a machine not directly involved in an investigation (for example, a DHCP server the suspect obtain and IP address from). Secondly, the log files may reside on a business-critical, shared platform that cannot be taken down (for example, a domain controller). Finally, log files are open and active when in use. Simple copying can lead to errors or corruption of the file contents.

Because duplication of the entire drive is often not feasible or warranted, copying of individual log files may be done. The same applies to other shared storage duplication as well. A 2MB home directory belonging to the suspect on a 100TB Netapps device does not justify imaging the entire drive array, nor does copying all of the drives on an Exchange server to retrieve a single suspect's mailbox file.

NOTE If a suspect had no direct access to the server the logs were stored on, there is little reason to suspect tampering or deletion.

To perform duplication of a single log file or other active file, the following are the steps that should occur:

1. Shut down any services or applications using the active file. This can include disconnecting sessions, temporarily disabling mailboxes, and changing share (but not file) permissions.

2. Connect a forensically wiped, portable DVD-R or hard disk to the server containing the log files.

WARNING For hard disks, always format the disk as NTFS after wiping to enable the preservation of file attributes.

    a. If the server is in a remote location, connect the media that will contain the duplicated image to an analysis machine and allow it to be mapped with a drive letter.

    b. Establish a secure session to the server (Remote Desktop Connection provides this capability on Windows).

NOTE Ensure that Disk Drives is checked under the Local Resources tab within the Remote Desktop Connection options to map the drive.

3. Use xcopy to duplicate the file or files to the destination media. For example, to fully duplicate the directory c:\userdata\asmith to g:\evidence use the following command line:

```
xcopy /E /H /C /K /X c:\userdata\asmith g:\evidence
```

The command line options provide the following:

- /E — Copy all directories and subdirectories including empty ones.
- /H — Include hidden and system files when copying.
- /C — Copy even after errors occur (frequent when open files are present).
- /K — Copy file attributes.
- /X — Copy all file audit settings (and ACL/ownership information).

4. Run an md5sum on each of the files copied and record the results.

5. Restart any services and applications turned off in Step 1.

TIP Xcopy offers several options not available with the standard Windows copy command that support forensically sound acquisition. The ability to copy all files recursively saves time, and the restart ability is useful for poor connections.

When the log files are duplicated, working copies can be made for detailed analysis in the forensic lab.

Additional Resources

Refer to the following list for additional resources:

Bootdisks

  www.bootdisk.com

dd For Windows from George Garner

  users.erols.com/gmgarner/forensics/

Helix Forensic Environment (includes dd-gnu)

  www.e-fense.com/helix/

NetCat for Windows

  www.vulnwatch.org/netcat/

Norton Ghost

  www.symantec.com/home_homeoffice/products/backup_
  recovery/ghost10/

NTFSDOS Drivers from SysInternals

  www.sysinternals.com/ntw2k/freeware/ntfsdos.shtml

PDBlock Software Write Blocker

  www.digitalintelligence.com/software/disoftware
  /pdblock/

PSExec from SysInternals

  www.sysinternals.com/utilities/psexec.html

SF-5000 Disk Duplicator from Logicube

  www.logicube.com/products/hd_duplication/sf5000.asp

Ultrablock and Firefly Hardware Write Blockers

  www.digitalintelligence.com/forensicwriteblockers.php

Universal Network Boot Disk from TeleData

  www.softpedia.com/get/System/Boot-Manager-Disk
  /Universal-Network-Boot-Disk.shtml

CHAPTER 10

File System Analysis

Searching, validating, recovering, and analyzing the contents of an imaged drive are the most common forensic tasks performed by an examiner. Since the largest portion of evidence generally resides on a hard disk, this is where the most effort is spent and the most rewards are found in a large number of forensic scenarios.

File system analysis covers the examination of Windows-compatible file systems (NTFS, FAT, CDFS, and so on), as well as non-file space on a drive (slack space and unallocated space). Many of the listed techniques may also be applied to non-Windows file systems and un-partitioned areas. These are noted where appropriate.

Searching

The most common forensic activity is searching a hard disk for strings of data. The searching can be file-based or slack-space–based, and there are even searches of unallocated space. As in other forensic tasks, the context of the investigation determines the search type used. There are two primary search methods: index-based searching and bitwise searching.

Index-based searching generates a keyword index on the first pass through a series of files. Bitwise searching performs a full, regular expression–based search on the raw data, file-specific or not. An index-based search may be used to provide quick, repeated searches with new terms on files copied from a shared drive. Conversely, a full bitwise search may be more relevant if a hard disk is being searched for deleted files or residual fragments of their contents.

TIP Most of the techniques noted work with re-formatted drives as well. When Windows formats a partition (FAT or NTFS), the actual partition contents are not touched. Only the partition boot sector and file system metafiles are altered.

Index-based Searching

Index-based searches rely on the creation of an index of keywords based on the contents of files. A search tool generally opens all files on a drive/share/image/partition, searches them for repeating strings of printable characters, and creates a table of the repeated strings with pointers to the original content. The initial indexing can take hours or days. However, when completed, searching the index can be done in near-instant time.

Index searching has two primary advantages over bitwise searching. Because it is file-based, index searching can utilize hooks into various file types to index their contents in its native format. This allows the proper searching of contents for applications like Excel (XLS files) and Acrobat (PDF files), which store data in a modified format, and compressed files such as WinZip (ZIP files). Bitwise searches on these file types are ineffective as the data is not stored in a directly readable ASCII formation. Secondly, after the initial indexing, searching is extremely fast. Searching for tangential terms based on initial search results and browsing of indexed words for similar spellings is extremely effective with index searching.

REGULAR EXPRESSIONS

Regular expressions are a symbolic method for representing strings of text for the purposes of pattern matching. A familiar format for individuals familiar with Perl or grep (GNU Regular Expression Parser), regular expressions can perhaps best be described as wildcards on steroids.

Standard wildcard-based text searches are limited in their forensic uses, basic full string and substring matches being the most common. Forensic searches tend to require more complex searches such as looking for IP addresses in log files, finding any credit card numbers on a hard disk, or culling phone numbers from an email file. Regular expressions, when used with supporting programs, enable all of these searches.

A regular expression may look unusual when first encountered. To match a date in the format xx/xx/xxxx for example, a simple regular expression may look like \d+\/\d+\/\d+, which to the untrained eye looks like an obscure form of ASCII art. There are several books written specifically on regular expression construction and use (the O'Reilly books excel in this space), but constructing basic regular expressions can be done with a few simple metacharacters. Any character not specifically listed as a metacharacter will be matched as the character itself. The following table lists basic regular expression rules.

CHARACTER(S)	DESCRIPTION
\	Match the metacharacter immediately following it as if it were an ordinary character. This character is called Escape character.
.	Match any single character.
[]	Match any of the characters in the listed range. [abc] will match a, b, or c. [a-zA-Z0-9] will match any alphabetic or numeric character.
[^n]	Match any character except n. [^0-9] matches any non-digit character.
()	Used for grouping characters together.
{n}	Match exactly n instances of a character.
{n,m}	Match a minimum of n and a maximum of m instances of a character.
|	Or; used to match one or another character. (\/|-) will match a single "/" or a single "-" character.
*	Match zero or more of the preceding character or pattern.
+	Match one or more of the preceding character or pattern.
?	Match zero or one of the preceding character or pattern.
$	Match the end of a line.
^	Match the beginning of a line.
\w	Match any alphanumeric character or "_".
\W	Match any non-alphanumeric character.
\s	Match any whitespace character.
\S	Match any non-whitespace character.
\d	Match any digit character.
\D	Match any non-digit character.

(continued)

REGULAR EXPRESSIONS *(continued)*

A few example regular expressions frequently used in forensics include the following:

- ◆ \s*(\(\d{3}\))?(\s|-)*\d{3}(\s|-)*\d{4}—Matches common U.S. phone number formats, including (xxx)xxx-xxxx, xxx xxxx, xxx-xxxx, and (xxx) xxx xxxx.

- ◆ ftp\:\\\\|http\:\\\\|mailto\:\\\\|telnet\:\\\\—Matches the protocol portion of URL's.

- ◆ [\w\.-]+\@\w+\.\w+—Matches common email addresses.

- ◆ \d{3}-\d{2}-\d{4}—Matches social security numbers.

- ◆ (\d{4}(\s|-)*){3}\d{4}—Matches common Visa or MasterCard credit card numbers.

- ◆ \d{4}(\s|-)*{4}\d{6}(\s|-)*\d{5}—Matches common American Express credit card numbers.

EnCase enterprise supports regular expressions on Windows, as do the ports of Perl and grep. Windows XP also includes an additional text search tool, Findstr, which supports basic regular expressions. To search for a phone number in any files in the current directory, the following would be used:

```
C:\>findstr ([0-9]*)[0-9]*-[0-9]* *
test.txt:Here is a phone number (215)555-1212.
C:\>
```

In the preceding example, Findstr does not support \d, so [0-9] is used. Similarly, parentheses are not supported as a special character, and the + character is not supported, resulting in a weaker but still useful regular expression for phone numbers.

NOTE There are many ways to write the same regular expression and subtle differences between regular expression parsers. This particular regular expression is not all that complete. It will match non-dates that fill a similar format as well, such as 99/999/99999. A better regular expression for dates might be \d{1,2}\/\d{1,2}\/\d{4}. Further refinement can limit the specific numbers entered into each location. How restrictive the expression will determine the number of matches to it.

One of the simplest and most popular tools for index searching is Google Desktop. Utilizing Google search engine technology, Google Desktop installs a spider on the desktop that can index any attached drives and automatically updates based on changes to those drives. This requires images to be mounted as actual drives by restoring them to a hard disk, preferably with a software or hardware write blocker. The Google Desktop search tool will automatically index those drives and after several hours instant searching with a browser interface will be possible. Figure 10-1 shows a search results sample.

Figure 10-1:   Google Desktop search results

TIP In Preferences, exclude any non-evidence drives from Google Search to index faster.

The advantages to Google Desktop are its pricing structure (free), speed, and familiar interface. The same query formats used in the online version of the Google search engine can be used locally, and the results are returned in a familiar, ranked format with highlighted text. The Google Desktop search tool supports web history and AOL Instant Messenger searches also, providing a view into the activities of a suspect not available through standard searching. The major limitation of the Google Desktop tool is format support. Binary files and unrecognized file formats will not be searched and indexed.

For more comprehensive index-based searches, dtSearch Desktop from dtSearch provides a commercial grade toolset for forensic searching. The indexing capabilities in the dtSearch tool are similar to those found in Google, with enhanced support for compressed and non-standard files. The ability to see the index provides for human analysis of similar terms and misspellings, and both fuzzy and phonic search capabilities return words similar to those typed, a helpful feature when dealing with place names or personal names that have alternate spellings. dtSearch uses custom filters for the most common file formats. By removing all files from the Exclude list and enabling the non-filter search, dtSearch can perform searches on binary and other files for text strings. dtSearch offers all of the advantages of Google Desktop with more powerful search and indexing capabilities and at a reasonable price. Sample output from dtSearch Desktop is shown in Figure 10-2.

WARNING It is fairly common to see multiple spellings of the same name in the Western character sets from non-Western languages. Direct translations of names from Kanji, Arabic, and Cyrillic character sets may not have 1-to-1 mappings to Western characters, making alternative spellings common.

Although direct searching of non-file content is not supported by these tools, indirect searching is accomplished through the creative use of dd images. After creating a dd image of a drive's contents, that image file (uncompressed) is placed on the file system indexed by dtSearch (the same technique can be used to search a memory dump). The raw image contents, including slack space and unallocated space included in the image, will be searched for text strings. The inability to easily map the contents found in these locations back to files is a negative, but the ability to search non-file content in real time outweighs this drawback. A slightly better option, the forensic version of WinHex supports the dumping of slack and unallocated space to individual files for searching.

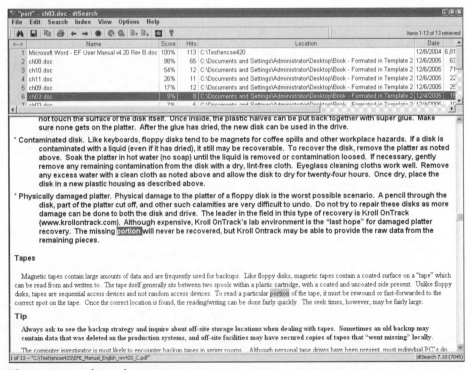

Figure 10-2: dtSearch output

TIP As a general rule, keep the image file sizes to 1GB for indexing purposes. Files larger than that tend to index fairly slowly, and dtSearch does not directly support files over 2GB.

Bitwise Searching

Bitwise searches look for simple text strings or regular expression matches in any sectors on a drive including both sectors that are currently unallocated and those residing in OS slack space. The ability to do regular expression searches enables the examiner to search for complex text terms as well as non-text (binary) values such as file headers. This precludes indexing, and as a result the entire contents of the drive must be searched for each term, making bitwise searches significantly slower than index searches.

WinHex provides basic text and binary (in Hexadecimal) searches of physical drive contents. While not supporting full regular expressions, wildcard searching is supported and all drive contents, including unallocated and slack space, are searched. Figure 10-3 shows a search for GIF87, one of the file headers for the GIF image file format (along with GIF89). This search will reveal not only any standalone or embedded GIF files present on the system but also previously deleted and intentionally renamed GIF files. A standard index-based search would not necessarily return any results with the same search. The headers of files would likely not be searched and the unallocated space where deleted files reside would not be searched at all.

For full regular expression–based searching, EnCase Enterprise supports GREP-based regular expression parsing in addition to ASCII, Unicode, and hex-based searches. As with WinHex noted previously, the hex searches allow the tool to be used to find binary signatures. Unicode permits searching for characters outside of the standard (and extended) ASCII character set. When conducting international investigations, Unicode support is a must.

TIP Search terms can and should be grouped together to minimize the traversals of the drive needed. Although the number of CPU comparisons is not necessarily reduced, the critical path read times from the drive are.

EnCase can search image files that have been acquired with or imported into the software and can perform raw (and remote) searches for keywords. With remote searching, multiple drives can be analyzed simultaneously using their local resources in a forensically sound manner. Instead of the entire drive images, only the search hits can then be acquired. This is a key feature for bandwidth-limited remote investigations. An example of the EnCase search feature is shown in Figure 10-4.

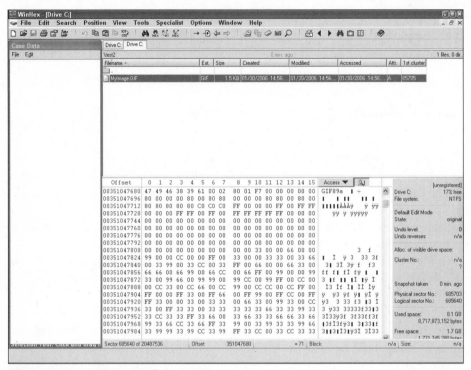

Figure 10-3:   WinHex search for GIF87

As noted previously, the two biggest limitations of bitwise searches are speed and non-standard file formats. A bitwise search can take multiple hours (up to days) depending on the size of the drive(s) or images searched. Consecutive searching (searches based on previous search results) can therefore take weeks to complete successfully and cannot be done on the fly. In addition to the speed concern, file formats such as XLS (Excel) and PDF (Acrobat), compressed files, and encrypted files will not be found by a standard bitwise search. Even simple obfuscation techniques such as ROT-13 will foil a bitwise search.

NOTE The simplest form of a Caesar Cipher, ROT-13 rotates each of the alphabet characters 13 spaces and replaces them with the new character in that location. It is sometimes used to bypass simple mail filters or search tools.

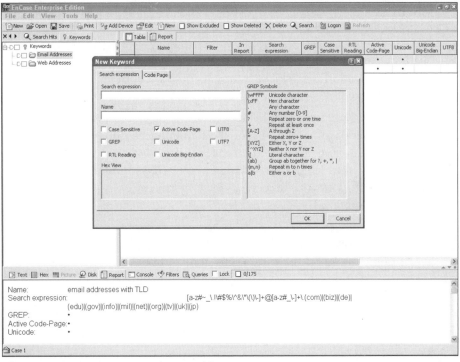

Figure 10-4: EnCase Enterprise searching

A final but less likely way in which bitwise searches can fail is due to file boundaries. On a heavily fragmented disk, many files are stored in non-contiguous sectors. Any text on the boundary of one of these sectors (that is, spanning two sectors) will not be accurately identified by most bitwise tools unless the sectors are contiguous. The odds of missing a keyword based on sector boundaries increase as fragmentation increases and are inversely proportional to cluster size. Since a cluster is the smallest amount of information an OS can address, intact files will have all sectors within a single cluster as contiguous.

Search Methodology

Many investigations call for a combination of searching techniques, and the methodology applied to a particular case needs to be context specific. Factors affecting the choice and order of searching include:

- **Awareness of suspect.** If the suspect is aware that he is under investigation, file-based content may have been deleted, which leans toward bitwise searching. If the content is likely to still be present on the drive intact, index-based searching may be more effective.

- **Likely data format.** If there is a chance that the content resides in PDF, XLS, zipped, gzipped, or Windows-compressed files, index-based searching will be more thorough. A preliminary bitwise search for the header bytes from these file types and subsequent recovery of deleted files before the index-based search will combine both techniques for the maximum effectiveness.

- **Time constraints.** For a single keyword or group of keywords, a bitwise search will be slightly faster in most circumstances due to the overhead created by indexing. If subsequent or real-time searches are expected, which is common when performing an investigation interactively with non-IT investigators or Subject Matter Experts, index-based searches will be faster overall.

- **Search complexity.** When searching for very complex regular expressions (for example, looking for all strings that match a credit card number or phone number), bitwise search tools will have more success. Searches based on synonyms of words, phonetically similar words, and fuzzy spellings of words will be more successful with index-based searches.

TIP On a sparsely populated drive where content is not expected to be present in unallocated space, index-based searching will be significantly faster.

All considerations being equal, for ongoing investigations generating an index for subsequent searching can almost always be performed during downtime. Generating an index overnight immediately following an acquisition allows the investigator to decide what type of search to perform the next day. Since the indexing is complete, an index-based search or searches can be done simultaneously with direct batched, bitwise searches running in parallel.

Hash Analysis

Hashing is the cryptographic term for the generation of a mathematically unique fingerprint from specific contents. In forensic work the specific contents can be a single file or an entire drive. Hashes are used extensively in forensics for both analysis and validation (previously described using the MD5 hash function).

A good hash algorithm has two qualities: it is one way and has a very limited number of collisions. One-way functions have a known algorithm that can be used to produce and reproduce a constant result given constant inputs, but given the result the original inputs cannot accurately be reverse engineered. The most common example of this is the Exclusive Or (XOR) function. The XOR function takes two binary inputs; if one and only one input is a 1, then the result is 1 and otherwise 0. If the output is known (it is 0 or 1), there is no way to know definitively each of the two inputs.

Collisions are a more complex issue in hash functions—and an area in which a lot of research is currently being conducted. A collision is the result of two distinct messages resulting in the same hash value. What this means from a forensic standpoint is that an image can be altered in such a way that it can generate the same hash value, allowing for the alteration of the original data with a valid fingerprint from that alteration. The most commonly used hash algorithm in forensics, MD5, has been shown to have collision issues. At this time they are of minor import in proving integrity (see the sidebar "Hash Algorithm Security" for details).

In addition to generating and validating the forensic integrity of evidence, the two major hash operations performed on a file system are positive comparisons and negative comparisons. Positive comparisons look for files matching a known hash value; negative comparisons look for files that do not match any known hash value.

HASH ALGORITHM SECURITY

The MD5 hash algorithm, based on the earlier MD4 algorithm (which was faster but potentially less cryptographically sound), was developed over a decade ago by esteemed cryptographer Ron Rivest (the "R" of RSA fame). The algorithm generates a 128-bit hash value based on an algorithm using block-based XOR-ing of the source data. The probability of finding two messages with the same hash value was postulated to be one in 2^{64}, which is the subject of a collision attack (based on the birthday paradox from probability theory). The harder preamble attack, which is most relevant to forensic hashing (given a message, find another message that has the same hash value), has a theoretical probability of one in 2^{128}. This results in a computationally infeasible position with current hardware.

From the MD5 algorithms, the government created two additional algorithms, SHA-0, which was found to have fundamental flaws, and SHA-1. Both algorithms as well as the MD5 algorithm are now known to be vulnerable to collisions at a much higher probability than originally thought, one that is computationally feasible. The later and more robust SHA-256 and SHA-512 algorithms have much lower probabilities of collision and have not suffered from the same issue, though they still have a theoretically weakened probability over the expected one in 2^{256} and 2^{512} estimates.

(continued)

HASH ALGORITHM SECURITY *(continued)*

What does this mean for forensic use? First, for signature matching of known files, the probability of a mismatch is extremely unlikely, even at the lowest bounds of the probability scale, now projected to be around 2^{30} for MD5. This means that the odds of two files giving a positive mismatch (one being misidentified as the other) is around one in one billion. While this may seem to be a small number (and many hash sets of known files use MD5), it is not a critical technical issue to investigators for the following reasons:

◆ Any individual trying to match the signature of a known good file to hide content would need to pad it in such a way that it still made logical sense, in essence hiding the good content within specific padding to match that of an expected good file. This would require a preamble attack and is significantly more difficult than the probabilities noted previously, although theoretically possible in the near future.

◆ Accidental matches, the more likely scenario, would be extremely few in number. If one was unlucky enough to get a collision-match, a manual review of the files (which would be done anyway) would show the differences if a positive search was done.

◆ On a negative search to exclude files, there is the possibility, however remote, that a file of interest is excluded. Since negative searches are generally performed from a gold build of one's own making, the analyst can use a more secure hash algorithm (SHA-512 would be the best bet at this time).

◆ The in-practice probability of a collision is significantly less likely than the theoretically obtained probability noted previously.

The other issue is the potential for alteration of evidence by an investigator. Unlike collisions, this type of attack is a preamble attack and has a significantly higher complexity. To do this, the investigator would need to do the following:

1. Obtain a valid evidence image with the hash written down.

2. Alter that image to contain the planted evidence.

3. Alter the remainder of the file in such a way that it results in the same hash value.

Step 3 is where things become quickly infeasible in practice. First, even with MD5 this is computationally impractical. The use of SHA-512 makes it nearly computationally impossible with current hardware and attack methods. Second, the alteration would need to be performed in a way that made the data still logically sound (for example, without changing file headers and directory information). This increases the order of difficulty exponentially for a drive and even for a single file. Because of this, there is no reason to worry in the near future about the reliability of hashing. However, the forensic examiner should do the following:

- ◆ **Use MD5Sum's SHA-512 algorithm for future cases.**
- ◆ **Generate or obtain new hash sets (positive and negative) that use the SHA-512 algorithm.**
- ◆ **Keep an eye on the hash algorithm space for newer algorithms which build on the lessons learned from MD5/SHA, but do not become an early adopter.**

Positive Hash Analysis

Positive hash analysis relies on the examiner having a known hash on which she wants to search. A drive is searched for known content by hashing every file present and comparing it to a list of known hashes. Because a hash value is unique to a specific piece of content, that content can be matched even if the file metadata (for example, name, attributes, dates) has been altered, either intentionally or accidentally.

TIP One way to tackle inappropriate material that propagates through an organization is to add it to an internal database of hashes. Subsequent investigations can then use those hashes to search for the same content (or organization-wide searches for the content can be performed). This can help with discovery motions when you need to identify everyone who has a particular file as well. EnCase Enterprise excels from a distributed standpoint in this area. The same hashes can be used on mail and file gateways also. For software hash libraries, including cracking tools, Mares offers a nice subscription-based product at www.dmares.com/maresware/hash_cd.htm. This incorporates the free NIST hash set from the National Software Reference Library at www.nsrl.nist.gov.

Investigators will frequently search for binary content such as images, movies, cracking tools, and music files. Because there may not be text or easily identified unique characteristics to search these files, positive hash searching is used. A hash is generated of the content from either files in the investigators possession or files from a hash library. For large hash sets, it is generally easier to create a hash of all files on a drive then compare that list to the list of known hashes. For smaller lists, the files can be compared in real-time.

TIP Importing into an Access database is an easy way to maintain a listing of known hashes.

To generate a hash list of all files on a given system, the fsum command line tool comes in handy. It calculates file hashes in all of the major formats and has a built-in comparison capability. To recursively generate a hash list (which would be redirected into a file), fsum can be used as follows:

```
C:\>fsum -r *

SlavaSoft Optimizing Checksum Utility - fsum 2.51
Implemented using SlavaSoft QuickHash Library <www.slavasoft.com>
Copyright (C) SlavaSoft Inc. 1999-2004. All rights reserved.

; SlavaSoft Optimizing Checksum Utility - fsum 2.51 <www.slavasoft.com>
;
; Generated on 03/17/05 at 15:52:22
;
437b9b514e75dcf0b2ef09121230bf0d *anadisk\ADCONFIG.EXE
96484b8ae5acbe0d2d9c924115a91475 *anadisk\ANADISK.DOC
a512353b65fccc078a95fe9564ac4390 *anadisk\ANADISK.EXE
83d1a9bbb0af9f6b3bb251c4977a3641 *anadisk\CRCHECK.EXE
9fa15cfdbc9806f5eac4f1e0ee9cc15b *anadisk\ORDER.FRM
976e33f7df994978ed2e99b0d0a7cd38 *anadisk\READ.ME
6065cce665b3017454792eda15b84bc3 *anadisk\WHATS.NEW
f4d42be7372564cadc89e164f7326b21 *analog 5.91beta1\docs\acknow.html
e3ef9c205a658d16dc5409293d6bae2a *analog 5.91beta1\docs\alias.html
...
```

The MD5 hash values shown previously are the most commonly found in commercial and public domain hash collections. For internal hash collections, SHA-512 is recommended. The fsum command can generate the SHA-512 hashes by using the -SHA512 command line switch.

After comparing the known hash set and the list of files on a given system, any abnormal (unauthorized software, inappropriate material, and so on) content can be quickly uncovered for further analysis.

Negative Hash Analysis

As the name implies, a negative hash analysis looks for files that are not on a known list. This is a common technique for performing quick searches on disk by eliminating all known-good files as well as identifying files which have been modified by a user. The NSRL provides hash values for most common software applications (multiple versions of each) and can be used as a starting point, but a gold-build hash set is more valuable.

A gold-build hash set is generated from the common installation (gold build) in a particular environment. Corporations may have multiple gold builds, and they may be updated frequently to incorporate patches or additions. The latest version of the gold build can be hashed en masse using the fsum tool mentioned previously to generate a database of all installed-by-default files.

NOTE Gold build refers to the original color of CD-R media. The first gold build was created in-house and then sent out to be pressed on commercial equipment.

When applied to a user environment, the hash set generated from the gold build can be used to do a negative hash analysis based on deltas. Only files that are not present on the gold build (or are modified from the gold build) are identified for analysis. The generation of the gold build files is the same as the procedure for generating positive hash search information noted previously.

TIP Many configuration and personalized files change as a normal course of action. These cannot be excluded automatically as someone could rename a file to that of a configuration file to avoid analysis. That said, they can be prioritized appropriately if a manual analysis occurs.

EnCase provides negative hash exclusions as an integrated feature of its search tool. Other utilities can have the list of new files added to their include list (for example dtSearch), or those files can be manually reviewed. They can also be removed from full directory listings when showing what user files were present, significantly reducing the amount of data presented to the critical components.

File Recovery

When a file is deleted in Windows using the del command or from Windows Explorer, it is not actually wiped from the drive. The process of deleting a file in Windows is significantly more complex than in most other file systems. It has the Recycle Bin, which acts as a temporary repository for some deleted files and the exact method of deletion depends on the underlying file system (FAT or NTFS). We will examine the underlying file system deletion and recovery first and then tackle the Recycle Bin itself. One important note on file recovery: always write the recovered file to another drive. Doing otherwise risks overwriting evidence.

Command line deletions, using the del or deltree commands, are used to remove files from a particular partition. FAT-based file systems do not alter file data on deletion. A deletion actually takes the following actions:

1. The first character of the file's directory entry is set to E5h. Searching for E5h in a hex editor can reveal deleted directory entries. This is why undelete programs prompt users for the first letter in the file name.

2. The FAT is updated to mark the clusters previously used by the file as 0 or available.

When the previously used clusters are marked as available, other files written to disk will be able to use them. As soon as an individual cluster is overwritten, the data held there is no longer available, but until that occurs, the data can be recovered. File recovery tools first scan the FAT for entries marked with E5. They then retrieve the cluster specified by that file and any subsequent clusters up to the file size. The user supplies a character for the first letter file name and the file location contents are copied to the hard disk. If long file name FAT entries are used, the character is retrieved from the LFN portion of the entry.

A FAT12 formatted floppy disk has the following initial FAT values, showing used clusters for the directory entry (see Figure 10-5).

The first available cluster for data is likewise shown to have no information.

> **NOTE** Technically, the first available cluster is cluster 33 for file data. Clusters 19–32 are reserved for the root directory entry.

The F6 character is used initially on data sectors for a full format for floppy disks (see Figure 10-6).

Adding a small (<1K) file, test.txt, results in the change to the FAT shown in Figure 10-7. Note the additional cluster now marked as in-use.

Offset	0	1	2	3	4	5	6	7	8	9	A	B	C	D	E	F	Access ▼	☑ 🔍
00000200	F0	FF	FF	00	00	00	00	00	00	00	00	00	00	00	00	00	ðÿÿ...........	
00000210	00	00	00	00	00	00	00	00	00	00	00	00	00	00	00	00	....	
00000220	00	00	00	00	00	00	00	00	00	00	00	00	00	00	00	00	....	
00000230	00	00	00	00	00	00	00	00	00	00	00	00	00	00	00	00	....	

Figure 10-5: Initial FAT values

Offset	0	1	2	3	4	5	6	7	8	9	A	B	C	D	E	F	Access ▼	☑ 🔍
00004200	F6	F6	F6	F6	F6	F6	F6	F6	F6	F6	F6	F6	F6	F6	F6	F6	öööööööööööööööö	
00004210	F6	F6	F6	F6	F6	F6	F6	F6	F6	F6	F6	F6	F6	F6	F6	F6	öööööööööööööööö	
00004220	F6	F6	F6	F6	F6	F6	F6	F6	F6	F6	F6	F6	F6	F6	F6	F6	öööööööööööööööö	
00004230	F6	F6	F6	F6	F6	F6	F6	F6	F6	F6	F6	F6	F6	F6	F6	F6	öööööööööööööööö	

Figure 10-6: First data cluster initial values

Offset	0	1	2	3	4	5	6	7	8	9	A	B	C	D	E	F	Access ▼	☑ 🔍
00000200	F0	FF	FF	FF	0F	00	00	00	00	00	00	00	00	00	00	00	ðÿÿÿ..........	
00000210	00	00	00	00	00	00	00	00	00	00	00	00	00	00	00	00	....	
00000220	00	00	00	00	00	00	00	00	00	00	00	00	00	00	00	00	....	
00000230	00	00	00	00	00	00	00	00	00	00	00	00	00	00	00	00	....	

Figure 10-7: Additional FAT entry for used cluster

The root directory clusters now contain the file name (created under root) as a directory entry (see Figure 10-8).

The data sectors contain the actual file contents (see Figure 10-9).

Deleting the file itself first alters the FAT cluster map to show the used clusters as available (see Figure 10-10).

The directory entry under root is altered to change the first letter of the file name to E5h (see Figure 10-11).

But the file contents are still present (see Figure 10-12).

Offset	0	1	2	3	4	5	6	7	8	9	A	B	C	D	E	F	Access ▼	☑ 🔍
00002600	54	45	53	54	20	20	20	20	54	58	54	20	18	B3	52	57	TEST	TXT ‚'RW
00002610	72	32	72	32	00	00	A9	54	72	32	02	00	0F	00	00	00	r2r2..©Tr2......	
00002620	00	00	00	00	00	00	00	00	00	00	00	00	00	00	00	00	....	
00002630	00	00	00	00	00	00	00	00	00	00	00	00	00	00	00	00	....	

Figure 10-8: File name directory entry

Offset	0	1	2	3	4	5	6	7	8	9	A	B	C	D	E	F	Access ▼	☑ 🔍
00004200	54	68	69	73	20	69	73	20	61	20	54	65	73	74	21	00	This is a Test!.	
00004210	00	00	00	00	00	00	00	00	00	00	00	00	00	00	00	00	....	
00004220	00	00	00	00	00	00	00	00	00	00	00	00	00	00	00	00	....	
00004230	00	00	00	00	00	00	00	00	00	00	00	00	00	00	00	00	....	

Figure 10-9: File contents

Offset	0	1	2	3	4	5	6	7	8	9	A	B	C	D	E	F	Access ▼	☑ 🔍
00000200	F0	FF	FF	00	00	00	00	00	00	00	00	00	00	00	00	00	ðÿÿ.............	
00000210	00	00	00	00	00	00	00	00	00	00	00	00	00	00	00	00	....	
00000220	00	00	00	00	00	00	00	00	00	00	00	00	00	00	00	00	....	
00000230	00	00	00	00	00	00	00	00	00	00	00	00	00	00	00	00	....	

Figure 10-10: FAT cluster map after deletion

Offset	0	1	2	3	4	5	6	7	8	9	A	B	C	D	E	F	Access ▼	☑ 🔍
00002600	E5	45	53	54	20	20	20	20	54	58	54	20	18	B3	52	57	åEST	TXT ‚'RW
00002610	72	32	72	32	00	00	A9	54	72	32	02	00	0F	00	00	00	r2r2..©Tr2......	
00002620	00	00	00	00	00	00	00	00	00	00	00	00	00	00	00	00	....	
00002630	00	00	00	00	00	00	00	00	00	00	00	00	00	00	00	00	....	

Figure 10-11: Directory entry after deletion

Offset	0	1	2	3	4	5	6	7	8	9	A	B	C	D	E	F	Access ▼	☑ 🔍
00004200	54	68	69	73	20	69	73	20	61	20	54	65	73	74	21	00	This is a Test!.	
00004210	00	00	00	00	00	00	00	00	00	00	00	00	00	00	00	00	....	
00004220	00	00	00	00	00	00	00	00	00	00	00	00	00	00	00	00	....	
00004230	00	00	00	00	00	00	00	00	00	00	00	00	00	00	00	00	....	

Figure 10-12: File data after deletion

As the example shows, even after deletion, recovery may be possible.

For NTFS file systems, deletion is slightly different. Instead of altering the MFT record's first character, it is marked as deleted (by changing the IN_USE bit). The cluster chains are left intact as data, and the actual cluster map ($BITMAP) is changed to reflect those same clusters as available. Additionally, the directory pointer to the file is removed so that it will no longer appear as part of the directory listing. To see the results, the file test.txt was added to an NTFS drive. It contains more data than the preceding test.txt file because NTFS allows the storage of smaller files within the MFT record itself, and for this purpose we want to see multiple clusters.

To see this in action, we first view the file's MFT entry (see Figure 10-13).

The actual file data location is as shown in Figure 10-14.

```
Offset      0  1  2  3  4  5  6  7   8  9  A  B  C  D  E  F   Access
0D8E9C3000  46 49 4C 45 30 00 03 00  C0 20 5B 09 00 00 00 00  FILE0...À [.....
0D8E9C3010  06 00 01 00 38 00 01 00  58 01 00 00 00 04 00 00  ....8...X.......
0D8E9C3020  00 00 00 00 00 00 00 00  04 00 00 00 E7 00 00 00  ............ç...
0D8E9C3030  02 00 00 00 00 00 00 00  10 00 00 00 60 00 00 00  ............`...
0D8E9C3040  00 00 00 00 00 00 00 00  48 00 00 00 18 00 00 00  ........H.......
0D8E9C3050  60 32 40 41 F7 2B C5 01  C0 6B AB 4F DB 2B C5 01  `2@A÷+Å.Àk«OÛ+Å.
0D8E9C3060  50 90 08 3E F7 2B C5 01  60 32 40 41 F7 2B C5 01  P▮.>÷+Å.`2@A÷+Å.
0D8E9C3070  20 00 00 00 00 00 00 00  00 00 00 00 00 00 00 00  ................
0D8E9C3080  00 00 00 00 0D 01 00 00  00 00 00 00 00 00 00 00  ................
0D8E9C3090  00 00 00 00 00 00 00 00  30 00 00 00 70 00 00 00  ........0...p...
0D8E9C30A0  00 00 00 00 00 00 02 00  52 00 00 00 18 00 01 00  ........R.......
0D8E9C30B0  05 00 00 00 00 00 05 00  60 32 40 41 F7 2B C5 01  ........`2@A÷+Å.
0D8E9C30C0  60 32 40 41 F7 2B C5 01  60 32 40 41 F7 2B C5 01  `2@A÷+Å.`2@A÷+Å.
0D8E9C30D0  60 32 40 41 F7 2B C5 01  00 00 00 00 00 00 00 00  `2@A÷+Å.........
0D8E9C30E0  00 00 00 00 00 00 00 00  20 00 00 00 00 00 00 00  ................
0D8E9C30F0  08 03 54 00 65 00 73 00  74 00 2E 00 74 00 78 00  ..T.e.s.t...t.x.
0D8E9C3100  74 00 00 00 00 00 00 00  80 00 00 00 48 00 00 00  t.......▮...H...
0D8E9C3110  01 00 00 00 00 00 03 00  00 00 00 00 00 00 00 00  ................
0D8E9C3120  1F 00 00 00 00 00 00 00  40 00 00 00 00 00 00 00  ........@.......
0D8E9C3130  00 40 00 00 00 00 00 00  3D 3E 00 00 00 00 00 00  .@......=>......
0D8E9C3140  3D 3E 00 00 00 00 00 00  31 20 2A D8 72 00 01 00  =>......1 *Ør...
0D8E9C3150  FF FF FF FF 82 79 47 11  00 00 00 00 00 00 00 00  ÿÿÿÿ▮yG.........
```

Figure 10-13: File MFT directory entry

```
Offset      0  1  2  3  4  5  6  7   8  9  A  B  C  D  E  F   Access
00E5B05400  54 68 69 73 20 69 73 20  61 20 54 65 73 74 21 0D  This is a Test!.
00E5B05410  0A 54 68 69 73 20 69 73  20 61 20 54 65 73 74 21  .This is a Test!
00E5B05420  0D 0A 54 68 69 73 20 69  73 20 61 20 54 65 73 74  ..This is a Test
00E5B05430  21 0D 0A 54 68 69 73 20  69 73 20 61 20 54 65 73  !..This is a Tes
00E5B05440  74 21 0D 0A 54 68 69 73  20 69 73 20 61 20 54 65  t!..This is a Te
00E5B05450  73 74 21 0D 0A 54 68 69  73 20 69 73 20 61 20 54  st!..This is a T
00E5B05460  65 73 74 21 0D 0A 54 68  69 73 20 69 73 20 61 20  est!..This is a 
00E5B05470  54 65 73 74 21 0D 0A 54  68 69 73 20 69 73 20 61  Test!..This is a
00E5B05480  20 54 65 73 74 21 0D 0A  54 68 69 73 20 69 73 20   Test!..This is 
00E5B05490  61 20 54 65 73 74 21 0D  0A 54 68 69 73 20 69 73  a Test!..This is
00E5B054A0  20 61 20 54 65 73 74 21  0D 0A 54 68 69 73 20 69   a Test!..This i
00E5B054B0  73 20 61 20 54 65 73 74  21 0D 0A 54 68 69 73 20  s a Test!..This 
00E5B054C0  69 73 20 61 20 54 65 73  74 21 0D 0A 54 68 69 73  is a Test!..This
00E5B054D0  20 69 73 20 61 20 54 65  73 74 21 0D 0A 54 68 69   is a Test!..Thi
00E5B054E0  73 20 69 73 20 61 20 54  65 73 74 21 0D 0A 54 68  s is a Test!..Th
00E5B054F0  69 73 20 69 73 20 61 20  54 65 73 74 21 0D 0A 54  is is a Test!..T
00E5B05500  68 69 73 20 69 73 20 61  20 54 65 73 74 21 0D 0A  his is a Test!..
00E5B05510  54 68 69 73 20 69 73 20  61 20 54 65 73 74 21 0D  This is a Test!.
00E5B05520  0A 54 68 69 73 20 69 73  20 61 20 54 65 73 74 21  .This is a Test!
00E5B05530  0D 0A 54 68 69 73 20 69  73 20 61 20 54 65 73 74  ..This is a Test
00E5B05540  21 0D 0A 54 68 69 73 20  69 73 20 61 20 54 65 73  !..This is a Tes
```

Figure 10-14: File data

After deleting the file and emptying the Recycle Bin, the MFT entry changes as shown in Figure 10-15.

Two things to note: The file name has actually changed to Dj3.txt (performed by Windows when the file is added to the Recycle Bin), and the in-use bit has been set from `1` (active) to `0` (deleted). The in-use bit is at a fixed location in MFT entries (`0D8E9C3016` in the preceding example). This allows programs such as WinHex to scour the MFT for deleted entries.

WARNING **Files deleted from shares or using the command line are not placed in the Recycle Bin. Only files removed using Windows Explorer or its associated API are placed there.**

Showing the data location after deletion reveals the contents of the `$DATA` attribute's location is still intact (see Figure 10-16).

```
Offset      0  1  2  3  4  5  6  7   8  9  A  B  C  D  E  F   Access
0D8E9C3000 46 49 4C 45 30 00 03 00  44 2A 5B 09 00 00 00 00  FILE0...D*[.....
0D8E9C3010 07 00 01 00 38 00 00 00  50 01 00 00 00 04 00 00  ....8...P.......
0D8E9C3020 00 00 00 00 00 00 00 00  05 00 00 00 E7 00 00 00  ............ç...
0D8E9C3030 04 00 00 00 00 00 00 00  10 00 00 00 60 00 00 00  ............`...
0D8E9C3040 00 00 00 00 00 00 00 00  48 00 00 00 18 00 00 00  ........H.......
0D8E9C3050 60 32 40 41 F7 2B C5 01  C0 6B AB 4F DB 2B C5 01  `2@A÷+Å.Àk«OÛ+Å.
0D8E9C3060 E0 CA C8 88 F8 2B C5 01  20 35 77 41 F7 2B C5 01  àÊÈ▌ø+Å. 5wA÷+Å.
0D8E9C3070 20 00 00 00 00 00 00 00  00 00 00 00 00 00 00 00   ...............
0D8E9C3080 00 00 00 00 0D 01 00 00  00 00 00 00 00 00 00 00  ................
0D8E9C3090 00 00 00 00 00 00 00 00  30 00 00 00 68 00 00 00  ........0...h...
0D8E9C30A0 00 00 00 00 00 00 04 00  50 00 00 00 18 00 01 00  ........P.......
0D8E9C30B0 76 00 00 00 00 00 01 00  60 32 40 41 F7 2B C5 01  v.......`2@A÷+Å.
0D8E9C30C0 C0 6B AB 4F DB 2B C5 01  50 90 08 3E F7 2B C5 01  Àk«OÛ+Å.P▌.>÷+Å.
0D8E9C30D0 60 32 40 41 F7 2B C5 01  00 40 00 00 00 00 00 00  `2@A÷+Å..@......
0D8E9C30E0 3D 3E 00 00 00 00 00 00  20 00 00 00 00 00 00 00  =>...... .......
0D8E9C30F0 07 03 44 00 6A 00 33 00  2E 00 74 00 78 00 74 00  ..D.j.3...t.x.t.
0D8E9C3100 80 00 00 00 48 00 00 00  01 00 00 00 00 00 03 00  ▌...H...........
0D8E9C3110 00 00 00 00 00 00 00 00  1F 00 00 00 00 00 00 00  ................
0D8E9C3120 40 00 00 00 00 00 00 00  00 40 00 00 00 00 00 00  @........@......
0D8E9C3130 3D 3E 00 00 00 00 00 00  3D 3E 00 00 00 00 00 00  =>......=>......
0D8E9C3140 31 20 2A D8 72 00 01 00  FF FF FF FF 82 79 47 11  1 *Ør...ÿÿÿÿ▌yG.
0D8E9C3150 FF FF FF FF 82 79 47 11  00 00 00 00 00 00 00 00  ÿÿÿÿ▌yG.........
```

Figure 10-15: MFT entry after deletion

```
Offset      0  1  2  3  4  5  6  7   8  9  A  B  C  D  E  F   Access
00E5B05400 54 68 69 73 20 69 73 20  61 20 54 65 73 74 21 0D  This is a Test!.
00E5B05410 0A 54 68 69 73 20 69 73  20 61 20 54 65 73 74 21  .This is a Test!
00E5B05420 0D 0A 54 68 69 73 20 69  73 20 61 20 54 65 73 74  ..This is a Test
00E5B05430 21 0D 0A 54 68 69 73 20  69 73 20 61 20 54 65 73  !..This is a Tes
00E5B05440 74 21 0D 0A 54 68 69 73  20 69 73 20 61 20 54 65  t!..This is a Te
00E5B05450 73 74 21 0D 0A 54 68 69  73 20 69 73 20 61 20 54  st!..This is a T
00E5B05460 65 73 74 21 0D 0A 54 68  69 73 20 69 73 20 61 20  est!..This is a 
00E5B05470 54 65 73 74 21 0D 0A 54  68 69 73 20 69 73 20 61  Test!..This is a
00E5B05480 20 54 65 73 74 21 0D 0A  54 68 69 73 20 69 73 20   Test!..This is 
00E5B05490 61 20 54 65 73 74 21 0D  0A 54 68 69 73 20 69 73  a Test!..This is
00E5B054A0 20 61 20 54 65 73 74 21  0D 0A 54 68 69 73 20 69   a Test!..This i
00E5B054B0 73 20 61 20 54 65 73 74  21 0D 0A 54 68 69 73 20  s a Test!..This 
00E5B054C0 69 73 20 61 20 54 65 73  74 21 0D 0A 54 68 69 73  is a Test!..This
00E5B054D0 20 69 73 20 61 20 54 65  73 74 21 0D 0A 54 68 69   is a Test!..Thi
00E5B054E0 73 20 69 73 20 61 20 54  65 73 74 21 0D 0A 54 68  s is a Test!..Th
00E5B054F0 69 73 20 69 73 20 61 20  54 65 73 74 21 0D 0A 54  is is a Test!..T
00E5B05500 68 69 73 20 69 73 20 61  20 54 65 73 74 21 0D 0A  his is a Test!..
00E5B05510 54 68 69 73 20 69 73 20  61 20 54 65 73 74 21 0D  This is a Test!.
00E5B05520 0A 54 68 69 73 20 69 73  20 61 20 54 65 73 74 21  .This is a Test!
00E5B05530 0D 0A 54 68 69 73 20 69  73 20 61 20 54 65 73 74  ..This is a Test
00E5B05540 21 0D 0A 54 68 69 73 20  69 73 20 61 20 54 65 73  !..This is a Tes
```

Figure 10-16 File $DATA attribute location after deletion

Recovery using WinHex is automated, and lost cluster entries are added to the Lost and Found folder on NTFS and listed under root on FAT systems. There are several other tools that allow recovery as well. A simple graphical tool, FreeUndelete can recover both FAT and NTFS files and is shown in Figure 10-17. The file Dj3.txt (the renamed version of test.txt) is shown as still being recoverable from the Recycle Bin, even after emptying.

NOTE When a file is deleted from an NTFS drive, all of the attributes actually remain intact, not just the $DATA attribute.

Windows file deletion is further complicated by the Windows Recycle Bin. The Recycle Bin is a special folder that holds the links to previously deleted files for a period of time until it reaches a user-defined capacity. This provides the user of the system an undo capability. Accidentally deleted files can be quickly recovered by simply opening the Recycle Bin and clicking Restore for a given file. If the examiner is lucky (and the user does not think to empty it), deleted files can sometimes be this easy to recover.

The Recycle Bin is partition-specific; there is one bin per partition (per user for NT/2000/XP/2003). The file links for deleted files stored in the bins are located under the Recycler/SID subdirectory in a given partition on a local system to identify which user deleted the file. The files in the Recycle Bin are renamed in the format dx###, where x is the drive letter the partition is mapped under and ### is a sequential number used for indexing. The actual file name and the source directory and deletion time are stored in a file called INFO2. The Foundstone tool Rifuti can display all of the information stored in this file, as shown in the following example:

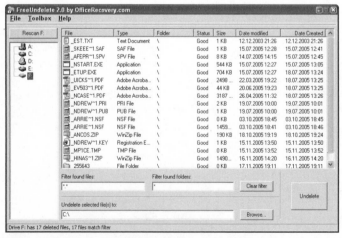

Figure 10-17: FreeUndelete recovery of test.txt

```
C:\RECYCLER\S-1-5-21-448539723-1563985344-1202660629-1003>dir /a
 Volume in drive C has no label.
 Volume Serial Number is 00A8-1CDC

 Directory of C:\RECYCLER\S-1-5-21-448539723-1563985344-1202660629-1003

03/20/2005  11:51 AM    <DIR>          .
03/20/2005  11:51 AM    <DIR>          ..
06/01/2004  08:38 AM            43,279 Dc3.htm
03/18/2005  03:44 PM                65 desktop.ini
03/20/2005  11:51 AM               820 INFO2
              3 File(s)         44,164 bytes
              2 Dir(s)   7,127,973,888 bytes free

C:\RECYCLER\S-1-5-
21-448539723-1563985344-1202660629-1003>c:\tools\rifiuti.exe info2

INFO2 File: info2

INDEX   DELETED TIME           DRIVE NUMBER PATH          SIZE
3       Sun Mar 20 16:51:31 2005   2               C:\report.htm
45056
```

A directory listing in the preceding example shows a single deleted file, Dc3.htm. Displaying the contents of the INFO2 file reveals that the original file was titled report.htm and was present on the root directory of the C: drive (hence the *c* in Dc3.htm) as the third file in the INFO2 index. Of particular interest to examiners is the deleted time. A mass deletion within a short period can indicate a user was tipped off to an investigation.

TIP Wotsit (short for Wotsit's Format) at www.wotsit.org is a treasure trove of useful file format details, including headers.

Several issues can occur with file recovery, making it more difficult than it appears:

- **Deletion of meta-entries.** If the actual MFT record (or directory entry in FAT) is overwritten, the starting cluster and meta-information on the file cannot be found. Some software, such as EnCase, will look through unallocated space for known file headers and attempt to carve old files from subsequent unused clusters, and the same can be done manually using tools like WinHex. For files that do not store length information or have known footers, this is especially difficult.

- **File system fragmentation.** When the starting cluster and file size are known on an unfragmented system, the file can be recovered by simply calculating the number of clusters (file size/cluster size) and reading that many from the starting point. If the file system is fragmented, good recovery programs will skip clusters that are currently in use when recovering a file, but this may result in corrupt files if there are clusters that have been overwritten then unallocated.

- **Overwriting of file data space.** The space that a file previously occupied may now be overwritten by a new file (as shown in the map of used clusters or FAT). If this is known, the remaining portion of the document can be recovered. If a cluster has been overwritten and then subsequently made available again (through a second deletion), this may not be known to the examiner.

STEGANOGRAPHY

Steganography, or covered writing, is the science of hiding information within a carrier medium. Steganography differs from cryptography in that the underlying goal is to prevent the presence of a hidden message from being known. Steganalysis is the science of detecting and extracting messages hidden using steganography.

Non-digital steganography has been used for many years. In the early part of the century, small images or text were hidden in documents by scaling them down and placing them inside of the periods marking the end of sentences. Similarly, various types of invisible ink have been used for centuries to hide the presence of secret messages. One of the earliest proclaimed uses of steganography was documented by Herodotus. In ancient Greece, messages were tattooed on the scalps of slaves. After the hair grew back, the messages could escape detection.

Digital steganography is the use of covert storage channels to store hidden messages. The use of covert transmission channels to transmit hidden information is beyond the scope of this book, but has been well documented with respect to systems based on models such as Bell-Lapadula within innocuous files. The hidden content is frequently stored in image, audio, and video files, frequently by changing the least significant bit (LSB) information within those files. For example, the LSB in a typical high color-depth image may represent the difference between two shades of the same color which is undetectable to the human eye. Likewise, the LSB in an audio frequency (or amplitude) may represent a very slight change that is indistinguishable from the original to human hearing. Other forms of data hiding that could be considered steganography, such as using slack space and streams, were covered earlier in this chapter in the "Bitwise Searching" and "Index-based Searching" sections.

An example of hiding data follows. The program JP Hide 'n Seek was used to hide the message:

```
THIS IS A SECRET DOCUMENT!
THE CONTENTS OF THIS FILE WILL SELF-DESTRUCT IN T-5..4..3..2..1
```

The message was hidden by applying it to the first image to produce the second image. The images are almost visually identical; to an individual without access to the first image, there are no visual clues at first glance that would show the presence of any hidden data.

Note that the Bell-Lapadula model defines subjects that have given rights to a set of objects. It is most frequently associated with classified information systems having data from multiple clearance levels (Top Secret, Secret, and Confidential) on the same system. Covert transmission channels are ways for individuals at a higher level of clearance to covertly transmit information to a lower clearance level using timing and shared resources.

Original image

(continued)

STEGANOGRAPHY *(continued)*

Image with hidden text

In addition to there being a lack of visual cues to detect the hidden text, there are no clues in the basic file details. As a result, a forensic examination of the file system and simple viewing of the images will not show even the presence of the hidden information. How then does a forensic analyst find content that uses steganography?

From a computer science perspective, there are several mechanisms for detecting content that has been altered by steganography programs. Encrypted additions can be detected when the LSB information is too random. There should be some patterns. Likewise, statistical analysis can be performed on the file contents to find anomalies. For images and movies, a palette analysis may show oddities (for example, pairs of colors very close together), and a re-application of the DCT algorithm used for JPEG files may provide unusual results. Fortunately for the computer investigator, there are less sophisticated approaches to finding hidden content.

First, a list of steganography software can be searched for. The presence of steganography products such as JSteg, JP Hide 'n Seek, and Camouflage show a good likelihood of there being hidden content. The easiest way to identify these products is through a hash set analysis. A hash set of steganography tools can be found as part of the National Software Reference Library, available from NIST.

Second, the presence of similar images with different names may indicate the use of a steganography tool. Any thumbnail gallery–generating tools (EnCase and IrfanView are examples) can be used to identify similar-appearing images. If these images have differing hash values, this may indicate the presence of hidden data.

Finally, some of the more sophisticated algorithms mentioned previously have been incorporated into software packages which assist in finding hidden items. Stegdetect and the xsteg front end are freeware tools that can analyze individual files for alteration four of the most common steganography tools. An example of stegdetect is shown in the following figure. Commercial suites which incorporate the NSRL database as well as proprietary hash sets and more advanced algorithmic checks are also available from vendors such as the Stego Suite available from Wetstone.

Stegdetect

Special Files

Windows has several files and file types that can be analyzed using special tools or techniques. These files include the pagefile, shortcuts, printer files, and log files. Other files, such as the index.dat file and registry files, are also of special interest and are covered in Chapter 12, "Internet Usage Analysis."

Print Spool Files

When a file is printed in Windows, it is first spooled to the print spooler directory as a file (or set of files). In Windows 9*x*, this consists of a metadata SPL file with a link to a TMP file with the actual data to be printed. On Windows NT/2000/XP/2003, there are generally two files printed, an SHD file with information about the print job and an SPL file with the actual print job itself and an associated header.

> **NOTE** A final type, the PRN file, contains raw printer instructions and is used when printing explicitly to a file. The type of document can be printed directly by typing copy *filename*.prn LPT1, where *filename* is the PRN file and LPT1 is the port the printer is attached to.

Like other files, SHD and SPL files can be recovered from unallocated space and may still be present on drives after their respective source contents have been eradicated. The files can provide proof on what was printed, who printed it, when it was printed, how many copies were printed, and even the contents of the print job. The spool files reside on the local system under the %SYS-TEMROOT%/System32/Spool/Printers directory, or under the designated spool directory on a print server (in the same directory by default for Windows print servers). The files are specific to a given printer, and cannot be transferred to another, although they can be reprinted by connecting the same model printer.

The first place to find information on the print job is the SHD file (named sequentially and paired with a similarly named SPL file). The meta-data about the print job is stored in this file, but standard string programs will not be able to view it as the data is stored in Unicode and requires a Unicode capable program or hex editor to view accurately. The data of primary importance to a forensic investigation starts with the Windows username of the printer and includes (in order):

- **User name:** Who printed the job.
- **Notification name:** Who is notified when the job is completed.
- **Document name:** The name of the file that was printed.

- **Port name:** Which printer port was used, local or remote.

- **Printer name:** The specific name of the printer (not type, though they may be the same).

The relevant information starts as shown (in reversed bytes) at an offset defined at location 14h within a given SHD file. The type of printer file (EMF for Enhanced Metafile or RAW for RAW) will be present in the file after the basic information given previously as well as driver information and the last non-numeric character string in the printer file which generally contains the name of the computer the file was printed from (on non–Windows 9x systems).

Figure 10-18 shows a sample SHD file from a Windows XP machine. The start of the file is as follows:

The first two bytes, 67 49h, show the file came from a Windows 2000/XP machine. The value (reversed) at location 14h indicates the user name starts at 048C.

TIP The system type the program was generated from can be determined from the first two bytes: 4B49h **for Windows 9x,** 6649h **for Windows NT,** 6749h **for Windows 2000/XP, and** 6849h **for Windows Server 2003.**

Figure 10-19 shows that piece of the file.

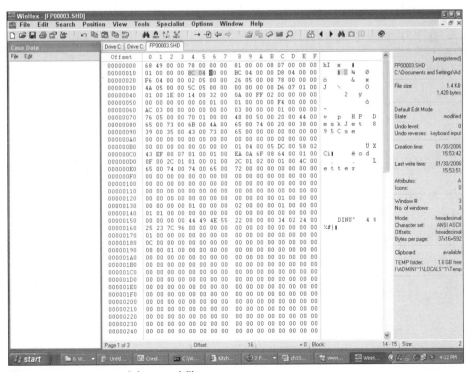

Figure 10-18: Start of the spool file

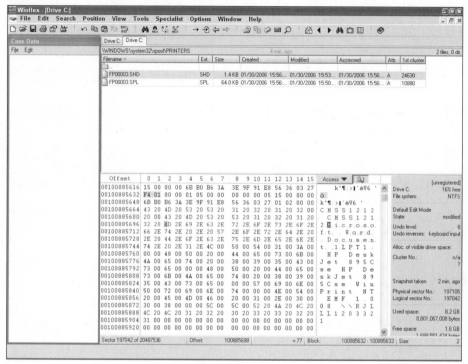

Figure 10-19:   User name in the print file

The user name and notification name are both CMSS1212. The document name was Microsoft Word (printed from Word)—Document1. The printer was attached to LTP1 (the local parallel port) and called HP DeskJet 895 Cse (which was also its type). The job was an EMF job, and the printer was printed from a machine called RJLLL12033121.

The SPL file format depends on the datatype, RAW or EMF. RAW files can be viewed directly using an appropriate viewer (for example, IrFanView works). EMF-formatted SPL files contain a header that needs to be parsed out first. The header contains the document name and its size, and is parsed out when printing. To recover and print an SPL file's contents:

1. Open the file in Winhex and find the word EMF.

2. Select back 41 bytes to find the first valid EMF file byte (usually 01h) and note the location (5Ch in the following example).

3. Select Edit → Define Block and choose the starting location noted previously and an ending location of End of File.

4. Choose Edit → Copy Block and select Into New File. Name the file with an .emf extension.

TIP The Print spooler service needs to be stopped if the file is present in the print queue.

Opening the newly created file in Irfanview shows the actual file sent to the printer from the preceding example (see Figure 10-20).

Windows Shortcuts

Microsoft uses shortcuts to provide links to files in other locations. Microsoft supports two types of file aliasing: symbolic links and LNK files. Windows symbolic links perform similarly to Unix aliases where multiple MFT entries point to the same file data. In practice, symbolic links are rarely used in a Windows environment (although NTFS does support them). Most links are actually file-based shortcuts place in LNK files.

The LNK file format is used for both user and system created shortcuts. Desktop icons and documents listed under My Recent Documents are actually shortcut files within their respective directories (Desktop and Recent under the user profile). Additionally, drives, shared folder and partitions can have LNK-based shortcuts.

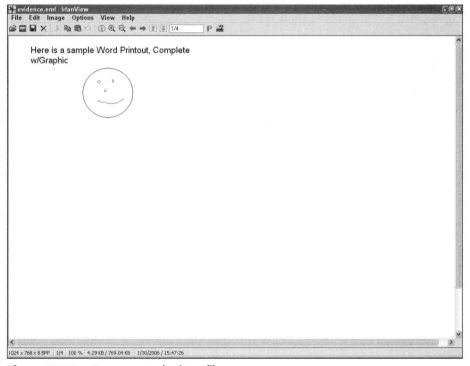

Figure 10-20: Reconstructed printer file

LNK files provide information on files that are (or were) present in a specific location. For investigators, shortcuts to content may exist long after the content itself is deleted. Since shortcuts are not true symbolic links, they can and frequently do point to no-longer-present content. Evidence that an individual accessed a particular file and where they accessed that file can be obtained from shortcuts. Similarly, shortcuts can be used to confirm an individual had a particular drive mapped, connected a specific peripheral (for example, if the shortcut references a USB or DVD-R drive), or accessed a network resource if that resource's name appears somewhere in a local shortcut.

WARNING It is theoretically possible to create a fake shortcut to non-existent content but it would be a willful action and not a likely situation.

The LNK file format is fairly complex, but the primary pieces of use to an investigator are as follows:

- **File location (local or network).** Used to show a file likely existed in a particular location at a particular time.

- **Description.** Can provide details on what the individual used the file for (for example, a shortcut called Interesting Finance Data).

- **Working directory.** Provides a possible location for files related to a particular program such as temporary or configuration files.

- **Command line.** Used for executables, the command line can show the specific options a user ran with a program.

The easiest way to view shortcut information is using the Windows XP explorer interface and viewing file properties. Most programs will not open an LNK file and will open the target of the LNK file instead. For example, the properties of a Google Desktop Search icon are shown in Figure 10-21. This shows the pointer to the Google Desktop Search program, located in C:\Program Files\Google Desktop Search.

Command line utilities can also be used to view the strings present in an LNK file and elucidate information. Using a Windows port of the Unix strings utility on an LNK file called Shortcut to 2005 Purchases.doc.lnk returns the following:

```
C:\temp>strings "Shortcut to 2005 Purchases.doc.lnk"
MYDOCU~1
2005PU~1.DOC
\\ServStore4\cmss
My Documents\2005 Purchases.doc
```

Figure 10-21:   Google Search LNK file properties

The LNK file shows that a file called 2005 Purchases.doc existed on the My Documents directory on the ServStore4 server under the cmss share. This is a good indicator that the individual was aware of the server, share, and file, had permission to the file, accessed the file, and maybe even frequently accessed the file if the shortcut was in a likely user-created location such as the Desktop.

Paging File

The paging file, or swap file, is a file-based supplement to main memory. When programs or data require more memory than is available in traditional RAM, a portion of the RAM (multiple pages) is transferred or swapped temporarily to slower disk-based storage. By doing so, more memory than is available in RAM is provided for program use. In a multitasking environment such as Windows, the operating system may make heavy use of the paging file to allocate the maximum amount of higher-speed RAM for running programs and to abdicate background programs and data to slower disk-based storage.

NOTE The terms paging and swap are used interchangeably here (and many other places), but there is a difference between them. Paging files change out pages of memory, generally 4K in size. Swap files swap out the memory space for a whole process. Paging files are generally more efficient and even allow preemptive exchange of memory pages.

The paging file, pagefile.sys (WIN386.SWP on Windows 9x) is managed automatically by the operating system and can be anywhere from a few megabytes to several gigabytes in size. A common practice is to set the page-file size to be equal to the amount of actual RAM present. Examiners can find copies of information in the pagefile which has been deleted from the disk itself, was never intended to be written to the disk (for example, user names, passwords, credit card numbers), or was though to be transient (a file printed from a website). For long-running systems, the pagefile can contain significant amounts of valuable information. Unfortunately, Windows cleans the pagefile on reboot. This is one of the key reasons not to shutdown a Windows system using the built-in shutdown function.

Analyzing the paging file as well as hiberfile.sys or memory dump files is a matter of string viewing and searching. String viewing can be used for browsing the contents of the file and searching for identifying keywords present. Searching these files is the same as other files and the techniques noted previously work well. Browsing of text is slightly more complex and uses the strings program to dump the contents to a file as there is too much text to directly read from the command line.

NOTE The hiberfile.sys is the same size as RAM and stores what is currently in RAM to disk on a laptop to permit quick restores. It can contain information even older than that of the pagefile, if the computer has not been put into hibernation recently.

Neither the pagefile.sys nor the hiberfil.sys can be directly viewed on a running system. Both are protected by the operating system. The files can only be accurately analyzed on a forensically duplicated drive or a non-booted partition. Using the strings command with a limit option (for example, `strings -n 7` to only show strings of size 7 or greater) on the files can provide a reasonably sized output file that contains possible investigative clues. The strings output from the pagefile can also be directly and quickly searched. As an example, the following is used to generate a text-string output of the pagefile for all strings of seven characters or more then search for hypertext links (truncated listing shown):

```
C:\strings -n 7 g:\pagefile.sys > d:\evidence\pageout.txt

C:\findstr "http://" d:\evidence\pageout.txt


http://www.zug.com/pranks/credit_card/index5.html
http://jgen49.cjt1.net/HTM/712/0/JavaSiteRequest.asp?LV=6000&DC=454&NF=0
&IW=468&IH=60&ORD=1111438276998
http://jgen49.cjt1.net/HTM/712/0/JavaSiteReport.asp?AS=454&PR=221667&SQ=
```

```
5313&IG=0&ORD=1111438277769&PK=0
http://www.yahoo.com/_ylh=X3oDMTEwdnZjMjFhBF9TAzI3MTYxNDkEdGVzdAMwBHRtcG
wDaW5kZXgtY3Nz/s/227051
```

...

FINDING COMPRESSED FILES

Identifying files that have been compressed or encrypted (specifically those with their extensions changed) or that have been created by proprietary programs that do not use standard file headers can be challenging. Ordinary searches and viewing of file contents will not work unless the files are decompressed and unencrypted. However, this cannot be done until the files are identified as compressed or encrypted. There are many file header–based searches that can identify encrypted or compressed files, but a simple test relies on the entropy property of a file.

Entropy, or randomness, can be measured in both binary and text files. All written languages and even binary programs contain repetition and character frequencies that are non-random in nature. The letter e occurs more frequently in text files than q. Similarly, the hex code for the ADD instruction occurs more frequently than a random collection of hexadecimal characters in binary files. Both compression and encryption use these characteristics to their advantage.

Compression algorithms look for repeating patterns in files and replace those patterns. In lossless compression, the most frequent patterns are replaced with smaller, shorthand versions. Because of this, compressed files contain little to no repetition, and a result compressing them a second time actually results in a larger file size than the original file.

Encryption algorithms that are well-written (and there are plenty that are not) should produce ciphertext (the encrypted content) that has no discernible pattern and maximizes the entropy or randomness of characters. This prevents statistical attacks on the output which look for repeating strings or character frequencies which may be useful in cryptanalysis.

Because both encrypted and compressed files contain few or no repetition, they can be identified by trying to compress or recompress them. The easiest method is to use WinZip. Select the files in question to be compressed, add them to a new ZIP file, and sort the list by the Ratio (compression ratio) column. Compressed or encrypted files should compress less than 5%. An example in the following figure shows a suspicious-looking Excel file, Finance.xls, which in fact is a renamed as a ZIP file.

Certain file formats employ compression by default. Most common image formats like JPEG and PNG (shown in the example) are already compressed, as are most movie and music files. Similarly, Acrobat (PDF) files and some executable (EXE) and library (DLL) files are compressed already and may not compress further. Finally, very small files (<5K) may not be compressed depending on the overhead of the algorithm used.

(continued)

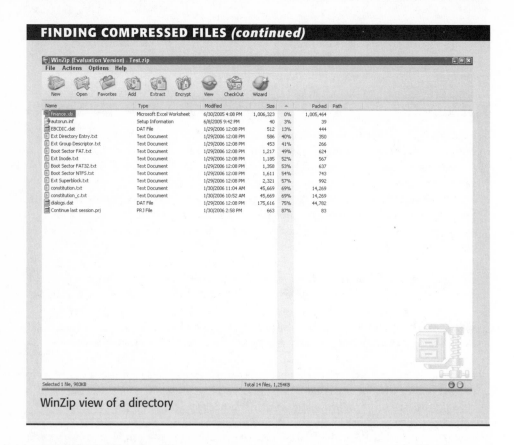

FINDING COMPRESSED FILES *(continued)*

WinZip view of a directory

Additional Resources

Refer to the following list for additional resources:

dtSearch desktop search tool
www.dtsearch.com

File format details (including header information)
www.wotsit.org

FreeUndelete file recovery tool
officerecovery.com/freeundelete/

FSum file integrity checker from Slavasoft
www.slavasoft.com/fsum/index.htm

Gargoyle (and Stego Suite) from WetStone
www.wetstonetech.com/

Google Desktop Search
desktop.google.com

IrfanView image viewer
`www.irfanview.com/`

JP Hide 'n Seek Steg toolkit from Allan Latham
`linux01.gwdg.de/~alatham/stego.html`

LNK file reverse-engineered details from Jesse Hager
`www.wotsit.org/download.asp?f=shortcut`

Maresware Hash Library
`www.dmares.com/maresware/hash_cd.htm`

NSRL National Software Reference Library
`www.nsrl.nist.gov/`

Rifuiti Recycle Bin tool from Foundstone
`www.foundstone.com/index.htm?subnav=resources`
`/navigation.htm&subcontent=/resources/proddesc`
`/rifiuti.htm`

SHD and SPL file format details
`undocprint.printassociates.com/spooler/spoolfiles/`

StegDetect Steganalysis tool by Niels Provos
`www.mirrors.wiretapped.net/security/steganography`
`/stegdetect/`

Unix to Windows ports of common utilities
`tedfelix.com/SupaSoft/wuup.htm`

Log File Analysis

The two areas of Microsoft logging of most interested to the forensic examiner are the standard log repository for system, application, and security events (Event Log), and the key Internet server–based log files (HTTP, FTP, and SMTP). The Event Log details provide insight into what a given user was doing on a machine or what the machine itself was doing. The Internet server log files show what remote activity was attempted or successful on a given system.

Event Logs

Microsoft's answer to Syslog, event logs retain key log event details on Windows systems. The event logs are broken into three areas: application logs, which store information on individual applications; system logs, which maintain operating system event details; and security logs, which hold data on logins/logouts and other security functions.

The standard mechanism for viewing event logs is to use the Microsoft Event Viewer. Event Viewer can be invoked by typing eventvwr from the command prompt on Windows NT/2000/XP/2003 systems. Event Viewer uses the MMC interface to display information on both remote and local logs. By default, the local event logs are viewed. EVT files from other machines can be imported for viewing by selecting Action → Open Log File. The log file format is common amongst Window NT versions and a Windows XP analysis machine will be able to open EVT files generated on another system) or viewed remotely with administrative rights by selecting Action → Connect to Another Computer.

TIP The logs are sortable by clicking the column headings. Note that the Event ID column sorts as a text field, not a number field, so Event ID 21 will appear after Event ID 1000.

Event Viewer has two other capabilities that are useful to an examiner: filtering and exporting. Filtering, available by selecting View → Filter, narrows the displayed contents of a particular log file to only the time period or event types relevant to a particular investigation. The example of the Filter displayed in Figure 11-1 will show only Warning and Error events from January, 2005. Both Success and Failure audits should be logged, indicating whether an action such as a login or installation was successful. A common mistake is to log only failed events.

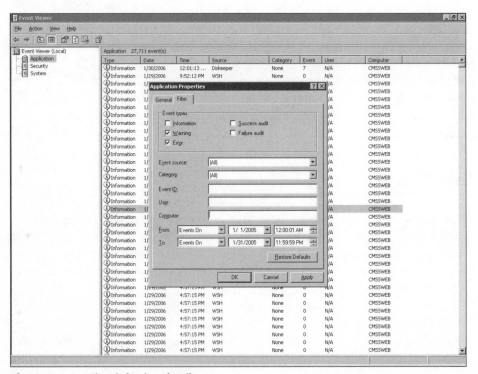

Figure 11-1: Virus infection details

EVENT LOG CORRUPTION

When copying the event logs from a running system, it is often desirable not to stop the event logging services. Stopping to create a forensic copy may involve a reboot and any activities that occur in the interim may go unaccounted for. Because Windows marks the files as open while event logging is running, a direct copy will result in corrupted files that cannot be directly opened on the evidence machine. Fortunately, Windows knows how to self-repair these files when the appropriate steps are taken.

1. Copy the event logs from a system (from %Systemroot\system32\config) and create a read-only, forensically sound copy).

2. Boot a clean analysis machine running Windows XP.

3. Open Services on the analysis machine and change the startup properties of the Event Log service to Disabled.

4. Reboot the machine. The machine needs to be rebooted to actually stop the service in a sound manner. Rebooting also unlocks the analysis machine's log files to allow their renaming in the next step.

5. Rename the AppEvent.evt, SysEvent.evt, and SecEvent.evt files on the analysis machine to include a .fbak extension (for forensic backup).

6. Copy the evidentiary EVT files to the %Systemroot\system32\config directory.

7. Open Services on the analysis machine and change the startup properties of the Event Log service to Automatic.

8. Reboot the analysis machine and run Event Viewer. The logs should be repaired automatically by Windows.

The event logs will now be viewable and not treated as corrupt by the operating system. At this point, the event logs can be analyzed as ordinary event logs, with one exception. There may be additional entries generated by the new system. These should be time-differentiated from the suspect's machine as well as system name delineated. These can and should be filtered (right-click on a log, select properties, and then Filter).

The corrupted copy remains the copy of record. The repaired logs become a working copy. Exports from the repaired copy can be used as evidence in court as long as the actions used to arrive at the final results are appropriately documented.

TIP To help in identifying installed and previously installed applications, use the Event Source drop-down list box on the filter. It will show any application that has generated an application log event. Category is especially useful with security logs in showing only log-on and log-off information.

The second function is Export. Although Event Viewer offers extensive capabilities, the need to export log files does arise. There are two basic types of export: exporting of the log file in the Event Viewer format for viewing on a remote system and exporting to text format. To save the log file itself and prevent the corruption which occurs when the file is copied directly from the open EVT file, choose Action → Save Logfile As and use the default EVT format. For non–Event Viewer analysis, the contents can also be exported as text (comma or tab delimited) by choosing Action → Export List. Text-based logs are useful for raw string searches or importing into programs for more detailed manipulation, such as Excel.

TIP A Windows XP machine should be able to read Windows NT/20002003/XP–generated log files. For even quicker results, run an XP virtual machine under Microsoft Virtual PC.

Application Log

Application logs are used by individual applications. Microsoft permits third parties to write application events through its APIs. In practice, few applications use this capability, but many antivirus and installer programs do.

The application log can be used to assist with the following common tasks from a forensic standpoint:

- **Confirm installation of software.** Installation of a particular software package is indicated by Event ID 11707 for successful and 11708 for unsuccessful installations if Microsoft Installer is used. Event 11724 indicates a product was removed. By viewing these events, the time a piece of software was installed or a user attempted to install it can be noted, as well as the removal time (for example, when a suspect was tipped off).

- **Confirmation/Refutation of virus Infection.** Most of the major antivirus software vendors generate an Event ID 5 event when a virus is detected. If a user is making the "a virus did it" claim, it can be shown that antivirus was running, was up-to-date, and no alerts were generated at the time of the claim by viewing the antivirus software event details. Similarly, a found virus event can prove an infection was present and could have had specific ramifications at a given time. A sample infection notice from Symantec is displayed in Figure 11-2.

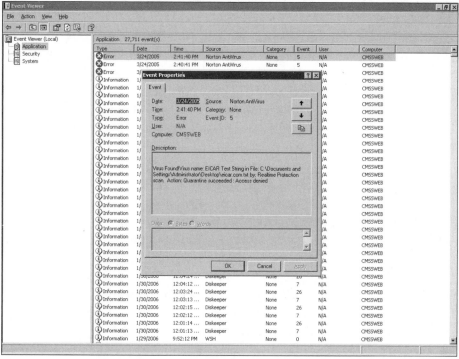

Figure 11-2: Sample application log filtering

- **Startup/Shutdown of firewalls.** On Windows XP, the Windows Security Center service is logged to Event Viewer when a user opens it for the first time in a given session. The service startup can be indicative of a user starting, stopping, or changing firewall settings for the Windows XP SP2 firewall.

- **Detection of hacking attempts.** Many hacking attempts exploit buffer overflows or similar attacks which can cause an application to fail. Applications with Event IDs 1000-1004 show up as errors in the Application log and could indicate exploitation through that application, especially if the application has an associated network listener or interface. Event ID 4097 may indicate similar activity and may indicate the presence of a Dr. Watson debugging log.

Other application log events are highly dependent on the specific applications installed on a particular machine and their independent use of the Event Log service. If an application does not use the Event Log service, it may still have a proprietary local log file. Even if it does use the Event Log, it may supplement that with local logging. Always check program directories for application-specific local logs in addition to those in the application log.

System Log

Events generated by the operating system itself are captured in the system log. Any actions taken automatically or user-driven actions that directly utilize the underlying operating system will be logged, including software and hardware installations, print jobs, and network-level events.

The system events relevant to an investigation are varied and specific to the allegations posed. Some of the more common investigation areas covered by the system log include:

- **Event Log start/stop.** Event ID's 6005 and 6006 represent the Event Log service starting and stopping, respectively. Individuals looking to hide their actions may stop the Event Log service, but the most likely cause of these events is a system shutdown. Look for other 6008/6009 events in the immediate vicinity to verify a legitimate shutdown.

- **System shutdown/restart.** Event ID 6008 indicates an unexpected shutdown, and 6009 the associated restart. Event ID 6009 is generally preceded by a 6006 event to stop the Event Log service. 1074 is used to show the process which initiated a shutdown, and 1076 (on Windows 2003) shows the reason provided for the shutdown.

- **Detection of hacking attempts.** Many hacking attempts exploit buffer overflows or similar attacks that can cause an application to fault. Similar to the events in the application log, Event ID 26 in the system log may indicate a successful buffer overflow attempt. Event ID 1001 indicates a memory dump was performed and will list the location of the dump file.

- **Service Pack update/installation.** Showing a particular patch was installed at a particular time can be useful in refuting claims of infection or exploit by malware. Event ID 19 shows successful installation of an automated patch. Event ID 4377 shows specific package hotfix installations. The initial Windows installation with build number should be one of the first listed events (assuming log recycling has not occurred) with an event ID 60054.

- **Log-on failures.** Network log-on failures, such as those generated by FTP, show up in the system log. Event ID 100 indicates a failure to authenticate against a known account, and a series of these events may indicate password guessing or a brute force tool use.

- **Alteration of machine information.** Event ID 6011 denotes a system name change. Investigations into a particular machine name that does not match with existing information should look for this ID to indicate a potential change of name after an event occurred.

- **Printing.** If the machine in question is acting as a print server, the jobs printed and their source will be listed as Event ID 10. The originating machine for the request is not shown, but the user name of the requestor is. In Figure 11-3, the user Administrator printed out a map from www.mapquest.com on March 24th at 2:34 P.M.

Security Log

The security log is the mother of all logs in forensic terms. Log-ons, log-offs, attempted connections, and policy changes are all reflected in the event contained therein. Unfortunately, security logging is turned off by default. It needs to be enabled by Group or Local Policy to be useful. To support later investigations, the Audit Policy under the Local (or Group) Policy should be enabled for the following actions at a minimum:

Audit account log-on events	Success, Failure
Audit account management	Success, Failure
Audit log-on events	Success, Failure
Audit policy change	Success, Failure
Audit privilege use	Success, Failure

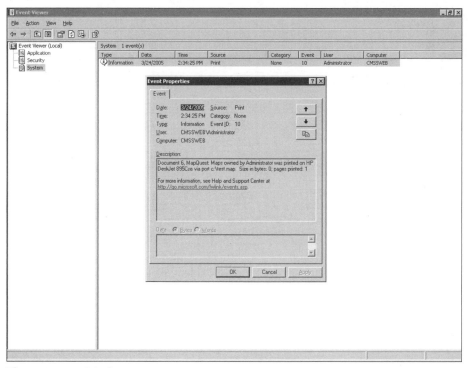

Figure 11-3: Printing event

These major categories will cover 95 percent of the security events analyzed in an investigation. The impact of further auditing needs to be weighed against system performance and disk storage issues. Although it would be useful, from a forensic standpoint, to audit all file access, the practical implications of doing so make it infeasible.

TIP The overhead associated with file access auditing does not mean that no file access should be audited. The company's key intellectual property shares (if they can be isolated) should have auditing enabled and regularly reviewed at a file-level.

Most important to an investigation are log-on and log-off events. These are essential to proving who performed an action on a computer at a particular time. Both failed and successful log-ons are relevant, and other security events support specific investigations. The main event types of use to an investigation are detailed in the next sections.

Successful Log-on/Log-off Events

Successful log-on events are used to show who performed a particular action. Interactive log-on events are characterized by Event ID 528, with a subcategory defining the log-on type. Table 11-1 lists the key log-on types frequently encountered.

Table 11-1   Log-on Types

LOG-ON ID	TYPE	DESCRIPTION
2	Local	Interactive, local log-on to the machine itself.
3	Network	Connecting to a computer across the network.
7	Unlock	Unlocking a computer (which has been locked by pressing Ctrl+Alt+Del or through automatic screen locking).
10	RDC	Connecting using Remote Desktop Connection or Terminal Services.
11	Cached	Logging in locally when a domain controller is unavailable and used the cached user credentials.

Most of the log-ons encountered of interest will be of type 2 indicating a local log-on. Showing an individual used remote access to connect can be done with Type ten log-ons. Connections across a network (for example, via FTP) will appear as type three log-ons, though connecting to or viewing a network share is a different Event ID – 540. Predicting when a user came back from lunch (or reengaged his or her notebook in the morning) can be had with log-ons of type 7.

Log-offs are also of interest. They bound the time an individual was connected. Log-offs are slightly less reliable for time as there can be events that force a log-off that is not recorded such as power outages. Depending on the amount of data logged, the failure event time may be able to be calculated based on the lack of log entries for a specific period. Log-off events are initiated with a 551 Event ID for user-initiated log-offs and completed with a 538 Event ID.

Remote Desktop Connection events can be bounded by connection types other than log-offs as well. Disconnects leave the user logged in but detach the actual terminal machine from the server. Reconnects re-attach and are accompanied by log-on events. The disconnection is an Event ID of 683 and the subsequent reconnection a 682.

NOTE Windows 2003 started recording the source of the log-on/log-off events for network-based connections. Prior versions of Windows recorded only the local workstation name.

Failed Log-on Event

Failures to log on are one of the best indicators of password guessing or brute-force attacks on a system. Failed attempts are logged based on the reason for failure: wrong password or user name (Event ID 529; may be a hacking attempt), account is disabled or expired or locked (Event IDs 531 and 532 and 539, respectively; could be password sharing or disgruntled former employees), or the user tries to log in to a resource to which he or she is not permitted access (Event ID 533; possible unauthorized access).

Unfortunately, failed log-ons also occur in large numbers for legitimate reasons. Users forget passwords, automated tools are misconfigured, and Caps Lock keys are accidentally depressed, making it difficult to separate out malicious log-on failures. In generally, malicious failures will be more numerous in nature, will be closer together (if an automated tool is used), and may show failures to multiple account names (from the same source machine).

Change of Policy

Changing of the audit policy (specifically removing the auditing of certain events) is indicative of a hacking attempt or root kit installation. Event ID 612 is a change of audit policy. Any change from prior 612 Event ID entries that show a removal (minus sign) of policy that was previously present (plus sign) should be questioned.

Successful or Failed Object Access

Auditing for specific NTFS files and folders can be turned on using the Advanced button on the Security tab within the particular object's properties. Enabling auditing on an object can log anything from attempted reads of that object to successful deletion of that object. If this level of auditing is enabled, it can show when a given entity was accessed and by whom and when a file or folder was changed or deleted, or highlight unauthorized access attempts on key objects. The events associated with individual objects are detailed in Table 11-2.

Account Change

Changes to an individuals account settings may be the result of malicious activity. Event ID 642 indicates an account settings change. Event ID 628, the most common follow-up event, indicates that the password and a particular account were changed.

Table 11-2 Object Access Events

EVENT ID	EVENT NAME	DESCRIPTION
560	Object Open	Attempts to open a file or directory (for reading or direct access) generate Event ID 560. Both failed and successful attempts generate the same ID. Attempted deletion may show up as a large number of 560 Failures.
564	Object Deleted	Successful deletions of files or folders show up as Event ID 564. The file or directory deleted will be shown in the most recent Event ID 560 preceding the 564 event which has the same process ID.
567	Object Access Attempt	The attempt to open an object for access shows up as Event ID 567 on Windows 2003 systems. This can indicate opening the file itself or its metadata.

Log Clearing

An Event ID of 517 indicates the security event log was cleared. There is no corresponding event for clearing the application or system logs. Clearing the security log is almost never done without saving the old log to a file for legitimate reasons, but may indicate an intruder covering his or her tracks. A search for EVT files or a text search for common Event ID wording on the drive may turn up old Event Viewer details if the log was saved before deletion.

Internet Logs

Windows servers log access information on individual requests that arrive through their respective services. Connections to and activity on FTP, HTTP, and SMTP (the main Internet Information Server services) are frequently used in forensic examinations of server use or compromise. The logging for these is turned on by default when the service is started and can provide a wealth of information on Internet-based system activity.

WINDOWS XP FIREWALL LOGS

Windows XP firewall, available with Service Pack 2 (SP2), provides logging capabilities that are turned off by default. To enable logging in SP2:

1. From the Run dialog box type firewall.cpl.

2. Open the Advanced tab.

3. Click the Settings button under Security Logging.

4. Select both dropped packets and successful connections.

5. Close the firewall Control Panel.

Logging by default (when enabled) is done to a file under the %SYSTEMROOT% directory called pfirewall.log and can provide details on attacks on or connections to a Windows machine. The log can also provide more detailed information on outbound connections from a particular machine, including HTTP connections that are not deleted when the Temporary Internet Files directory is cleaned. These logging capabilities have actually always been present and are a capability of the underlying Internet Connection Firewall. The SP2 firewall just makes it easier to turn on and log relevant events.

Here is a sample log:

```
#Version: 1.5
#Software: Microsoft Windows Firewall
#Time Format: Local
```

(continued)

WINDOWS XP FIREWALL LOGS *(continued)*

```
#Fields: date time action protocol src-ip dst-ip src-port dst-port
size tcpflags tcpsyn tcpack tcpwin icmptype icmpcode info path

2005-03-22 12:59:55 DROP TCP 10.100.177.123 10.100.177.126 34577 2033
40 S 3955587749 0 2048 - - - RECEIVE
2005-03-22 12:59:55 DROP TCP 10.100.177.123 10.100.177.126 34577 117
40 S 3955587749 0 3072 - - - RECEIVE
2005-03-22 12:59:55 DROP TCP 10.100.177.123 10.100.177.126 34577 624
40 S 3955587749 0 3072 - - - RECEIVE
2005-03-22 12:59:55 DROP TCP 10.100.177.123 10.100.177.126 34577 1516
40 S 3955587749 0 4096 - - - RECEIVE
2005-03-22 12:59:55 DROP TCP 10.100.177.123 10.100.177.126 34577 684
40 S 3955587749 0 1024 - - - RECEIVE
2005-03-22 12:59:55 DROP TCP 10.100.177.123 10.100.177.126 34577 1667
40 S 3955587749 0 3072 - - - RECEIVE
2005-03-22 12:59:55 DROP TCP 10.100.177.123 10.100.177.126 34577 27000
40 S 3955587749 0 4096 - - - RECEIVE
2005-03-22 12:59:55 DROP TCP 10.100.177.123 10.100.177.126 34577 126
40 S 3955587749 0 1024 - - - RECEIVE
2005-03-22 12:59:55 DROP TCP 10.100.177.123 10.100.177.126 34577 392
40 S 3955587749 0 2048 - - - RECEIVE
2005-03-22 12:59:55 DROP TCP 10.100.177.123 10.100.177.126 34577 518
40 S 3955587749 0 4096 - - - RECEIVE
2005-03-22 12:59:55 DROP TCP 10.100.177.123 10.100.177.126 34577 859
40 S 3955587749 0 2048 - - - RECEIVE
2005-03-22 12:59:55 DROP TCP 10.100.177.123 10.100.177.126 34577 227
40 S 3955587749 0 4096 - - - RECEIVE
2005-03-22 12:59:55 DROP TCP 10.100.177.123 10.100.177.126 34577 572
40 S 3955587749 0 4096 - - - RECEIVE
2005-03-23 09:35:41 OPEN TCP 10.100.177.126 209.247.228.201 1422 80 -
- - - - - - - -
2005-03-23 09:35:41 CLOSE TCP 10.100.177.126 209.247.228.201 1421 80 -
- - - - - - - -
2005-03-23 09:36:34 OPEN UDP 10.100.177.126 151.197.0.38 1069 53 - - -
- - - - - -
2005-03-23 09:36:34 OPEN TCP 10.100.177.126 10.24.101.134 1423 3389 -
- - - - - - - -
2005-03-23 09:37:24 OPEN-INBOUND TCP 10.243.100.134 10.100.177.126
2652 3389 - - - - - - - -
```

The preceding log displays both inbound and outbound traffic that is successful in navigating the firewall (that is, it is permitted to go through) as well as unsuccessful (that is, dropped). Several interesting items are ascertainable from the preceding logs. First, there are numerous dropped packets originating from the same machine and trying to connect on random ports, indicative of a port scan. In this case they were generated by an nmap portscan from machine 10.100.177.123. The source of attacks can be identified using this information as it could from any other firewall log. Second, outbound connections are logged. The connection from the local machine to 209.247.228.201 (www.playboy.com) indicates the individual on the local machine may have been viewing inappropriate information. Finally, successful connections on port 3389, both inbound and outbound, show Remote Desktop Connection was used successfully to connect to and from this particular machine.

Automated tools are now being developed to aggregate information from the XP firewall logs. A simple tool, FirelogXP, is shown in the following figure. By aggregating source and destination data, the tool can easily identify port scanning, filter activity to a specific IP, and show only data of interest. In the example that follows, only outbound traffic is shown.

Because of the utility in the XP Firewall logs for forensics and other activities such as identifying spyware, the default client builds should turn on logging by default on SP2 machines.

Firewall traffic originating from the suspect's machine

HTTP Logs

Internet Information Server (IIS), Microsoft's built-in web server, is one of the most commonly used on the Internet (second to Apache) and even more common on intranets.

> **NOTE** Technically, IIS refers to all of Microsoft's Internet Information Services, not just the web server, but common usage equates IIS with the specific HTTP service and associated ASP services.

The web logs for IIS websites are stored by default under %SYSTEM-ROOT%\System32\Logfiles\W3SVC, and each date is provided its own log file (although dates with no accesses will have no log file). Administrators may change the directory for performance and back-up reasons as well as the file cycling frequency.

> **NOTE** If multiple web servers are present, each will have its own W3SVC directory suffixed with a unique number.

The default log file settings contain several key fields that are indicated at the start of the file (shown under the #Fields metadata for the example file that follows). The key fields of interest in an examination are:

- **Date and time (date time).** The date and time, listed in GMT unless an offset is included, is the current time on the server when a request was made. If a website defacement occurs, look at the first request after the defacement. Many times an attacker will use a shell account from a compromised machine to launch an attack, and then view their handi-work from their home machine.
- **Server IP (s-ip).** The IP address of the server that the request was made to. When multiple server IPs are logging to a single file, this will help differentiate where the request (or attack) was directed against.
- **Method (cs-method).** The HTTP method used. For pages disappearing or appearing, PUT or DELETE methods from WebDAV may be present. GET requests to a form will contain the query string sent to the form (but POST requests will not). TRACK and TRACE methods show up with Cross-Site Scripting attacks.
- **URL (cs-uri-stem).** The URL, sans the fully qualified domain name and query string, is shown in this field. The page requested and its associated directory are listed here.
- **Query string (cs-uri-query).** The query string sent to a form is shown in this field. Any query string containing SQL characters should be suspect as a potential SQL Injection attack.

- **Port (s-port).** The port (usually 80 or 443) a web connection was made on.

- **User name (cs-username).** The user name that made the request. Only valid on local Windows domain requests and not generally available outside an Intranet.

- **IP address (c-ip).** The most important piece of information in the log file, the IP address is the location from which a particular request came. The IP address is the single most important piece of information in tracking down an attack source.

- **User agent [cs(User-Agent)].** The browser used to make a request is listed. Attack tools such as Nikto, Nessus, and ISS may show user agents indicating the tool as a source. Similarly, the operating system used to launch an attack may be present in the user agent.

- **Request status (sc-status and sc-substatus and sc-win32-status).** The code returned by the web server is shown in the status field. Table 11-3 lists common status codes.

- **Referer (cs-Referer).** The Referer is not included by default with several log formats but should be added to all web logs for forensic use. The field shows the previous site visited before the server in question, giving a possible homepage location or additional clue to the identity of an attacker. The referring site can include a query string as well, useful if the previous site was a search engine.

Table 11-3   HTTP Response Codes

CODE	DESCRIPTION
100	Client should continue request. Not generally shown in web logs, but may appear on sniffer results.
200	OK. The page was found and returned to the client.
301/302/307	Page moved. The client requested a page that has since been moved. A request to the main directory without a file name will generate a 30x request, as will an old link.
401	Access to a file for which the client is not authorized was requested. Repeated 401 log items may indicate enumeration attempts.
403	Access to a file which is forbidden was made. Requests for common directory names in 403 errors may indicate enumeration tools were used.

(continued)

Table 11-3 *(continued)*

CODE	DESCRIPTION
404	Not found. 404 messages can be indicative of bad links, but also enumeration attempts (if the files are commonly named, from the same IP).
500	Server error. Buffer overflow attacks may generate server error messages.
501	Method not implemented. TRACK/TRACE requests or WebDAV requests may show failed cross-site scripting activity attempts.

HTTP LOG SAMPLE

This sample log shows multiple requests from a client on IP address 192.168.1.113 on the date of 9/4/2003.

```
#Software: Microsoft Internet Information Services 6.0
#Version: 1.0
#Date: 2003-09-04 00:34:01
#Fields: date time s-ip cs-method cs-uri-stem cs-uri-query s-port cs-
username c-ip cs(User-Agent) sc-status sc-substatus sc-win32-status
2003-09-04 00:34:01 192.168.1.113 GET /students/default.aspx - 80 -
146.186.240.68
Mozilla/4.0+(compatible;+MSIE+6.0;+Windows+NT+5.0;+Q312461;+.NET+CLR+1
.1.4322) 302 0 0
2003-09-04 00:34:02 192.168.1.113 GET /login.aspx
ReturnUrl=%2fstudents%2fdefault.aspx 80 - 146.186.240.68
Mozilla/4.0+(compatible;+MSIE+6.0;+Windows+NT+5.0;+Q312461;+.NET+CLR+1
.1.4322) 200 0 0
2003-09-04 00:34:02 192.168.1.113 GET /images/Horizontal.gif - 80 -
146.186.240.68
Mozilla/4.0+(compatible;+MSIE+6.0;+Windows+NT+5.0;+Q312461;+.NET+CLR+1
.1.4322) 200 0 0
```

Detailed analysis may be difficult on large log files, where a quick summary analysis can be used. A summary analysis, using tools like WebTrends or Analog can quickly parse out areas of interest and highlight potential issues. The reports of interest from these include:

- **Browser report.** Scanning tools like Nessus may show up in the Browser report, as shown in Figure 11-4.

- **Directory report.** Requests for non-existent or protected directories will be visible in this report.

- **Failure report.** Failed web page requests are shown, including those which indicate enumeration attempts.

- **Status code report.** The majority of requests should have a status code of 200. Other status codes with large numbers indicate server problems or hacking attempts.

- **Usage reports.** Denial-of-service attacks or attempts and scans may show up as usage spikes in the general usage reports.

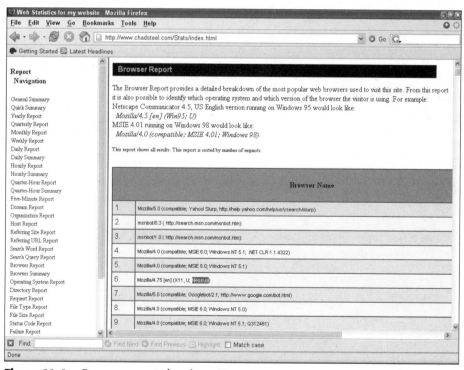

Figure 11-4: Browser report showing a Nessus scan

CROSS SITE SCRIPTING AND SQL INJECTION

Two of the most common exploits of web-based applications are cross-site scripting attacks and SQL Injection attacks. Cross-site scripting gathers information from unsuspecting users by carefully crafted URLs that exploit application issues. SQL Injection attacks attempt to read or delete or alter database information through web application which use poor input validation and detailed error message information.

Cross-site scripting relies on poor parsing of input on a system to steal cookies from a user, execute malicious code on his or her behalf, or launch a denial-of-service attack. A modification of this attack, dubbed cross-site tracing (XST), makes use of the TRACK and TRACE HTTP methods present in IIS to echo malicious code back to a client, done as part of the method itself. URLScan, a Microsoft add-on for IIS, protects against this particular type of cross-site scripting attack by disabling these methods.

The forensic examiner looking for evidence of a website being used for cross-site scripting attacks has two places to look: the method and the query string. If cross-site scripting attacks are used as part of the method, a TRACK or TRACE request will be seen, frequently with an associated HTML tag or tags (the <SCRIPT> tag being the most common). If a GET request is used, the <SCRIPT> tags will be found in the query string itself. Because any legitimate web application should filter out HTML tags (or better yet restrict input to only allowed values), the mere presence of these tags in a web log indicate attempted or actual exploitation of cross-site scripting at the worst or a poorly coded application that is potentially vulnerable to cross-site scripting at the best.

SQL Injection attacks use escape characters, string termination characters, or other SQL commands to interact with an underlying database in unplanned for ways. Like cross-site scripting attacks, SQL Injection relies on poor input validation. Applications that pass values users type into forms directly to database queries are the most vulnerable. A typical SQL injection may show a user entering text such as:

```
' OR '1'='1
```

into a text field meant to capture names, addresses, or other innocuous information. A subsequent query, such as:

```
SELECT * FROM TBL_USERS WHERE NAME=' & fieldvalue & ';
```

becomes:

```
SELECT * FROM TBL_USERS WHERE NAME='' OR '1'='1'
```

Instead of returning a single value, all user values are returned. Different databases are subject to different syntax variations, but common characters include single and double quotes, SQL commands such as SELECT, DROP, UPDATE, DELETE, and INSERT, and other special characters like semicolons, colons, and commas. These values should be disallowed by an application but may not be if it is poorly coded.

(Both client and server-side debugging should be turned off on production servers, as they may reveal information on the sites underlying code. A generic "Server Error" message should be returned instead. While this does not prevent SQL Injection attacks, it makes them significantly more difficult to exploit using techniques such as Blind SQL Injection.)

Searching the HTTP logs for GET requests with any of the previously mentioned terms in a query string is a good indication that a SQL Injection attack was attempted and potentially successful against a website.

To evaluate the likelihood of success of a SQL Injection or cross-site scripting attack, the investigator can reconstruct the attack string by putting the URL stem together with the query string (separated by a question mark) and typing that into a web browser following the site name. The testing should ideally be done on an isolated staging server configured the same as production to prevent damage to the production database or revealing information inadvertently as part of the testing.

To test TRACK- or TRACE-based attacks, the TRACK and TRACE information can be sent using a Telnet client to port 80. A simple test of reflection using Track and Trace should return a 200 status code. A simple OPTIONS request may show a false positive. The PuTTY SSH client in RAW mode is an excellent tool for doing this. An example of the values returned in a successful TRACE is shown in the following listing.

Unfortunately, POST requests will not reveal the information sent in the log files, but they are not undetectable. A large number of POST requests to the same URL from the same IP address which generate 400 or 500 level return codes is a good indicator some type of application-level attack may be occurring. Connecting a sniffer or using an application profiler or detailed application-level logging can reveal more information on these attacks.

```
OPTIONS / HTTP/1.1
HOST: foo.com


HTTP/1.1 200 OK
Server: Microsoft-IIS/5.0
Date: Tue, 29 Mar 2005 18:06:12 GMT
MS-Author-Via: DAV
Content-Length: 0
Accept-Ranges: none
DASL: <DAV:sql>
DAV: 1, 2
Public: OPTIONS, TRACE, GET, HEAD, DELETE, PUT, POST, COPY, MOVE,
MKCOL, PROPFIND, PROPPATCH, LOCK, UNLOCK, SEARCH
Allow: OPTIONS, TRACE, GET, HEAD, COPY, PROPFIND, SEARCH, LOCK, UNLOCK
Cache-Control: private


TRACE / HTTP/1.1
HOST: foo.com
```

In addition to the standard weblogs, a final place to look for web reporting is the HTTPERR directory, under %SYSTEMROOT%\System32 on Windows 2003 machines. IIS 6, included with Windows 2003, runs its application server ASP.Net as a separate process. Errors with the application server are sent to specific logs in the previously mentioned directory. Since only errors are logged, buffer overflow attempts or illegal requests are easier to pinpoint than in a crowded IIS HTTP log file.

TIP When viewing logs and other fixed-format items, use a fixed-width font such as Courier New to line up the columns correctly.

FTP Logs

Similar to HTTP logs, FTP logs record successful and failed File Transfer Protocol interactions. Stored in the %SYSTEMROOT%\System32\MSFTPSVC### subdirectory (where ### is a unique number), the FTP service logs include connections, attempted connections, and commands used when connected. FTP logs are frequently reviewed for two types of attacks: attempts to connect and file creation/deletion for unauthorized users. Additionally, authorized user actions may need to be recorded.

- **Attempted connection.** Attempted connections will appear with a status code (sc-status) of 331 on a USER command followed by 530 on a PASS command. 331 indicates that a user name has been entered and a password is requested. 530 indicates a password authentication failure. Common findings may use password guessing or anonymous account attempts (user name is anonymous; password is email address by convention). The example FTP log here shows an attempt with the account name FTP, then anyone, followed by multiple attempts with the account name root (the name for the administrator account on most Unix systems). The attack shown is likely untargeted and using an automated tool from source IP 10.70.37.249.

```
#Software: Microsoft Internet Information Services 6.0
#Version: 1.0
#Date: 2004-07-26 23:15:03
#Fields: time c-ip cs-method cs-uri-stem sc-status sc-win32-status
23:15:03 10.70.37.249 [40]USER ftp 331 0
23:15:03 10.70.37.249 [40]PASS ftp@ftp.net 530 1326
23:15:03 10.70.37.249 [41]USER anyone 331 0
23:15:03 10.70.37.249 [41]PASS - 530 1326
23:15:12 10.70.37.249 [42]USER root 331 0
23:15:12 10.70.37.249 [42]PASS - 530 1326
23:15:12 10.70.37.249 [43]USER root 331 0
23:15:12 10.70.37.249 [43]PASS - 530 1326
```

```
23:15:14 10.70.37.249 [44]USER root 331 0
23:15:14 10.70.37.249 [44]PASS - 530 1326
23:15:14 10.70.37.249 [45]USER root 331 0
23:15:14 10.70.37.249 [45]PASS - 530 1326
```

■ **Attempted or successful creation of files.** Many scanners attempt to
find open FTP sites to use as repositories for movies, music, pornography, or warez. After connecting successfully (with a 230 status code), an
attempt will be made to create a file (with a code of 226 if successful) or
a directory (with a code of 257 if successful). Failed attempts will show
a 550 error code. Here is an example session of file creation and subsequent deletion:

```
15:37:48 10.221.41.8 [436]USER anonymous 331 0
15:37:56 10.221.41.8 [436]PASS - 230 0
15:38:46 10.221.41.8 [436]created /test.txt 226 0
15:38:52 10.221.41.8 [436]DELE test.txt 250 0
15:39:02 12.221.41.8 [436]MKD test 257 0
```

■ **Authorized user activity.** Authorized users can take unauthorized
actions on an FTP server, or perform authorized actions that need to be
proven at a later date. Authorized users will connect first with a USER
command having status 331 including their user names. Searching the
file for their user names will turn up the start of activity. Next, a PASS
command, with a valid 230 response code will be returned. Following
that will be the valid user activity, and a final log-out QUIT command
and a 550 status code or a Closed message with a 421 status code if the
session was closed by timeout.

CASE STUDY: PHISHING

One of the civil matters that often arise on the Internet is trademark
infringement, frequently as part of another criminal action. Websites claiming
to be something they are not may be used for generating fraudulent
transactions, perpetuating misinformation, or most commonly phishing for
personal information to facilitate identity theft.

A large banking client of ours became fed up with websites impersonating
their online client portal. Phishers would send out spam messages requesting
that users update their passwords or other personal information and embed
links purporting to be at the banking site. In reality, the links used numerous
techniques to bury the real destination and hide the fact that users clicking
them would be redirected to compromised hosts, which were used to serve up
similar-looking web pages to the client's portal. Unlike the portal, individuals
logging into the fake site would have their user name and password stolen,
along with any other personal information (such as social security number)
they entered.

(continued)

CASE STUDY: PHISHING (continued)

Investigations into one of the more sophisticated phishing sites revealed the actual sites were hosted on individual user's machines which had been hacked by the actual identity theft ring. The machines would come up and down frequently, and traces only turned up home machines used as one hop in a chain of machines and became dead ends without a warrant to trace further. Likewise, the e-mail messages directing users to the site were from compromised machines acting as spambots and the DNS entries for the sites made with stolen accounts.

Because the sites needed to maintain the look and feel of the actual website, they needed to visit the real portal site to steal the graphics and underlying HTML. Examining one of the phishing sites revealed a modification date of several weeks earlier on an image from a less-used secondary page, shown only after logging in. The image in question matched almost exactly an image from the actual portal.

To trace the user, we analyzed the IIS HTTP logs from the portal site. The image we were looking for had only been accessed one time within hours of the modification date listed. Because the image was only viewable after authentication, we looked up the IP address in the backend application server log to reveal which specific user session it was identified with. Doing so revealed the account name and personal information of the downloader. It turned out that the individual established a legitimate account with the bank to understand how the site worked.

Through civil means, the bank was able to successfully go after the individual for trademark infringement based on their use of the bank's look and feel. A subsequent criminal investigation for the identity theft was also enacted by law enforcement and is currently ongoing.

SMTP Logs

Microsoft's SMTP server logs details on all messages sent or received, successful or otherwise. Unfortunately, the default log settings capture little information: the commands typed, the IP address the connection was from/to (with no indication of direction), and the status codes. Although somewhat useful in showing a connection was made to a particular server at a particular point in time, the information is still limited.

The example that follows shows a connection to an SMTP server from 192.168.1.1. The connection starts with a HELO command, introducing the connecting server. Following is a MAIL FROM command, indicating the sender of the message, and a RCPT TO command, indicating the recipient of the message. Next, a DATA command starts the message text itself, and finally a QUIT command terminates the connection. As noted previously, little can be determined forensically from the log here except a connection between

192.168.1.1 and the local server was made at a particular time and successfully completed the commands that follow (250 is a success code and 240 a successful termination code):

```
#Software: Microsoft Internet Information Services 6.0
#Version: 1.0
#Date: 2005-03-30 17:20:09
#Fields: time c-ip cs-method cs-uri-stem sc-status
17:20:09 192.168.1.1 HELO - 250
17:20:15 192.168.1.1 MAIL - 250
17:20:21 192.168.1.1 RCPT - 250
17:20:27 192.168.1.1 DATA - 250
17:20:30 192.168.1.1 QUIT - 240
```

To be forensically useful, several additional fields can be added in IIS Administrator to the SMTP logs if the W3C format is chosen, specifically, the date, time, c-ip, cs-username, cs-method, and cs-uri-query fields. The date and time are self-explanatory. The IP represents the address of the machine to which the server is connected. If it is inbound, there will be no OutboundConnection message in the user name field; instead, the domain reported in the HELO message will be shown. The cs-method and cs-uri-query fields show what command was typed and with what detail. Although the data itself cannot be seen in the logs, the source and destination can. The following example that follows shows a successful attempt to exploit an open relay from machine 10.221.41.8 to send a message to a yahoo.com account. The message is successfully received, then relayed to the Yahoo! mail server at 10.28.114.35 10 minutes later:

```
#Software: Microsoft Internet Information Services 6.0
#Version: 1.0
#Date: 2005-03-30 18:27:06
#Fields: date time c-ip cs-username cs-method cs-uri-query
2005-03-30 18:27:06 10.221.41.8 foo.com HELO +foo.com
2005-03-30 18:27:13 10.221.41.8 foo.com MAIL +from:+hacker@foo.com
2005-03-30 18:27:18 10.221.41.8 foo.com RCPT +to:+csteel@yahoo.com
2005-03-30 18:27:34 10.221.41.8 foo.com MAIL +from:+hacker@foo.com
2005-03-30 18:27:34 10.221.41.8 foo.com RCPT +to:+csteel@yahoo.com
2005-03-30 18:27:34 10.221.41.8 foo.com DATA
<CMSSWEByt3cew8k69RK00000015@cmssweb>
2005-03-30 18:27:34 10.221.41.8 foo.com QUIT foo.com
2005-03-30 18:37:00 10.28.114.35 OutboundConnectionResponse -
220+YSmtp+mta151.mail.dcn.yahoo.com+ESMTP+service+ready
2005-03-30 18:37:00 10.28.114.35 OutboundConnectionCommand EHLO cmssweb
2005-03-30 18:37:00 10.28.114.35 OutboundConnectionResponse - 250-
mta151.mail.dcn.yahoo.com
2005-03-30 18:37:00 10.28.114.35 OutboundConnectionCommand MAIL
FROM:<hacker@foo.com>+SIZE=415
```

```
2005-03-30 18:37:00 10.28.114.35 OutboundConnectionResponse -
250+sender+<hacker@foo.com>+ok
2005-03-30 18:37:00 10.28.114.35 OutboundConnectionCommand RCPT
TO:<csteel@yahoo.com>
2005-03-30 18:37:00 10.28.114.35 OutboundConnectionResponse -
250+recipient+<csteel@yahoo.com>+ok
2005-03-30 18:37:00 10.28.114.35 OutboundConnectionCommand DATA -
2005-03-30 18:37:00 10.28.114.35 OutboundConnectionResponse -
354+go+ahead
2005-03-30 18:37:01 10.28.114.35 OutboundConnectionResponse -
250+ok+dirdel
2005-03-30 18:37:01 10.28.114.35 OutboundConnectionCommand QUIT -

2005-03-30 18:37:01 10.28.114.35 OutboundConnectionResponse -
221+mta151.mail.dcn.yahoo.com
```

Additional Resources

Refer to the following list for additional resources:

Analog Web Analyzer
  www.analog.cx

FireLogXP Firewall Log Analyzer from 2BrightSparks
  www.2brightsparks.com/freeware/freeware-hub.html

PuTTY SSH client
  www.chiark.greenend.org.uk/~sgtatham/putty/

Cross-site scripting attack details
  www.cgisecurity.com/articles/xss-faq.shtml

CHAPTER 12

Internet Usage Analysis

The most common investigation in most corporate settings is inappropriate usage, with inappropriate web surfing being the most prevalent form. Depending on policy, inappropriate use may be defined as any usage of computing resources for personal use. Additionally, the viewing of certain types of content may be considered inappropriate. Most corporations frown on employees browsing pornographic materials, hacking websites, or playing on gambling sites using company resources. Finally, storing or exchanging copyrighted material through peer-to-peer services is growing in popularity and is becoming a serious issue in corporations.

In addition to inappropriate usage, an individual's Internet activities may be used to prove or disprove other crimes. Showing that an individual was on the Hotmail website the same time as a harassing email was sent, finding evidence of a POST to a message board of a questionable nature, or noting numerous visits to target website may all be of value to a general investigative response.

Fortunately for the forensic analyst, Microsoft Windows abounds with traces of Internet activity. This chapter reviews the Microsoft-specific activity available locally to investigate these activities.

Web Activity

Most corporate web activity now takes place using Microsoft Internet Explorer, which holds approximately 92 percent of the browser market share. Until recently, Internet Explorer dominated the browser market almost exclusively, but a recent push by Firefox has reignited the Mozilla-based client interest. Capturing almost 6 percent of the market and growing, Firefox is positioned to play a more dominant role in future forensic investigations.

Internet Explorer

Internet Explorer was released in 1995 with the Windows 95 Plus Pack. Since that time, it has undergone numerous revisions. Currently, Internet Explorer 5.*x* and up make up over 90 percent of the market share owned by Internet Explorer. Conveniently for the forensic analyst, the overall structure of Microsoft's storage has not changed drastically since Internet Explorer 4.0.

Internet Explorer stores multiple pieces of information on browsing activities, including a history of pages visited, most recently typed URLs, and form information if AutoComplete is turned on. Additionally, cached versions of previously viewed pages, toolbar search terms, and favorites are all potentially stored on the machine. Finally, the swap file and slack space tend to be excellent places to find URL's of previously visited websites.

Most of the information can be found in folders specific to an individual under his profile. This is generally located under the user name of an individual within the Documents and Settings hierarchy for Windows XP/2000/2003. For Windows 9*x*/NT and single user systems, the relevant locations are under %SYSTEMROOT%. For Windows NT, %SYSTEMROOT%\Profiles\Username is a common location as well.

Users can change the default locations of these folders. To confirm the actual locations of the files, refer to the following registry keys:

- HKCU\Software\Microsoft\Windows\CurrentVersion\Explorer\User Shell Folders\Cache

- HKCU\Software\Microsoft\Windows\CurrentVersion\Explorer\User Shell Folders\Cookies

- HKCU\Software\Microsoft\Windows\CurrentVersion\Explorer\User Shell Folders\History

- HKCU\Software\Microsoft\Windows\CurrentVersion\Explorer\User Shell Folders\Favorites

When conducting an investigation into web activities, the profiles of the current user must be examined as well as other accounts on the system (for example, Administrator) to ensure that all areas are evaluated.

INTERNET-ACCEPTABLE USAGE POLICY

It helps to have a policy clearly defining acceptable usage and defining the company's investigative abilities in a corporate setting. Writing a corporate policy for Internet usage should involve IT, Security, HR, and Legal to be successful. Ideally, the acceptable usage policy is presented to the employee at hiring or orientation, and the employee is made to sign a statement that he has received, read, understood, and agreed to abide by the guidelines. If possible, an annual refresh of the guidelines and re-acknowledgement should be obtained from all employees as well.

Acceptable usage policies cover much more than Internet activity, but they tend to arise frequently in legal matters (for example, lawsuits for wrongful dismissal) based on this particular type of investigation. Specifically to support forensic Internet investigations, an acceptable usage policy should state:

- Internet usage must follow not only the relevant Internet Acceptable Usage policies but also all other corporate policies (for example, the Code of Conduct). Activity violating these policies is expressly forbidden.

- The company has the right to monitor and log all Internet activities conducted using company resources.

- It is the exclusive responsibility of the CSIR team to lead Acceptable Usage investigations. It could also be HR or another body. The point is to ensure that individuals do not investigate their neighbors without approval.

- Failure to follow any piece of the policy may result in disciplinary action, including termination.

If one terminates an employee for violation of an acceptable usage policy, the employee will need to show that:

- The employee had a policy in place prohibiting the actions taken by the employee.

- The employee was aware of the policy.

- The policy is enforced consistently at the organization.

The third area is one of the more difficult to prove. If the policy is overly strict (no non-business use of the Internet), it may be easy for the employee to show that other individuals had violated it as well. If it is overly lenient (limited personal use of the Internet is permitted), it may be difficult to prove excessive usage or inappropriate usage in a particular instance.

Favorites

The first place to start a web investigation is the Favorites folder. The Favorites folder contains URLs of websites saved by the user. Links to frequently visited pages are likely to be stored by the user in this folder, and the explicit storing of these links indicates intent. In addition to the preceding location, perform a search for the Favorites folder and any deleted copies elsewhere on the disk. For users who move between computers, this folder is frequently copied to other locations on the disk. Users looking to cover their tracks will likewise frequently delete this folder.

When examining the Favorites folder, an Internet connection may be required. The folder should be copied to an examination machine with a connection, and all of the URLs viewed independently. As shown in Figure 12-1, the folder contains the name of the link as well as the Date Modified, which reflects the date the link was actually added to the Favorites folder. The Favorites folder may also contain subfolders used to organize links. These should be investigated as well.

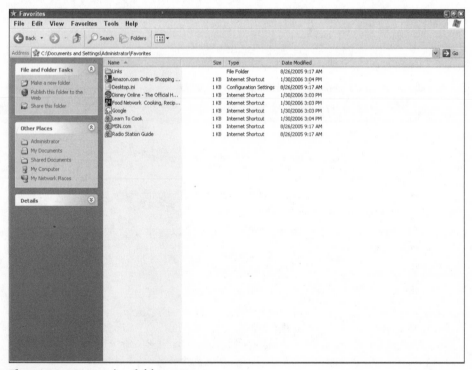

Figure 12-1: Favorites folder contents

NOTE There was a JavaScript bug that could maliciously add an entry to Favorites, but this has been corrected in current versions of Internet Explorer.

The specific link names displayed in the folder default to the contents of the `<title>` tag in the HTML on the page. This may not accurately reflect the contents and is user-alterable. To view the actual link, right-click on the individual document and select Web Document. As shown in Figure 12-2, the link titled Cooking Lessons actually goes to a much different website. As noted previously, any suspicious sites should be viewed from a forensic machine. Sites that sound harmless may contain redirects or content not evident from their URLs (www.whitehouse.com being the canonical example).

TIP To view historical sites the way they appeared at the time, try the Way Back Machine at www.archive.org.

While viewing the properties, also note any sites with "Make this page available offline" checked. These sites may have entire copies of the page content stored on the drive for offline browsing, a definite plus for the forensic analyst.

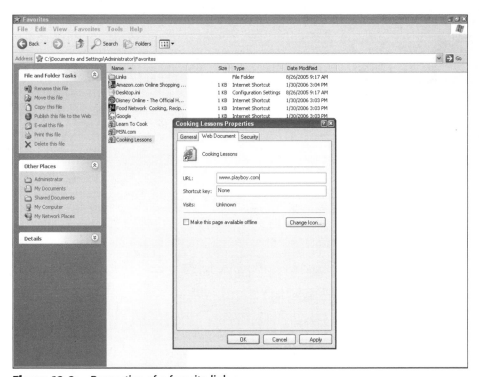

Figure 12-2: Properties of a favorite link

One final note on Favorites: Even if a site sounds innocuous and viewing the site reveals nothing of interest, there is one more location to check. Under %SYSTEMROOT%\System32\Drivers\Etc is a file called Hosts. The Hosts file, shown in Figure 12-3, is used by Windows to resolve web hostnames before checking DNS. Because of this, it is useful for testing and system optimization but can also be used to hide the tracks of potentially incriminating web activity. Note the entry for www.disney.com. Instead of resolving to the Disney website, any URLs with www.disney.com will resolve to the IP address in the Hosts file, which is not the expected location. In one investigation I headed, a user was complaining of pornography appearing when she visited Yahoo!, Google, and other common sites. It turned out that co-workers had redirected the site names in the Hosts file as a practical joke.

Favorites can be exported to a local HTML file as well. By default, the file name exported is Bookmarks.htm. A search for this file on the drive may turn up another copy of the Favorites folder for analysis.

WARNING A recent malicious code trend is to add entries to the Hosts file that redirect popular bank and retail sites to a third party that gathers passwords as part of an identity theft attack.

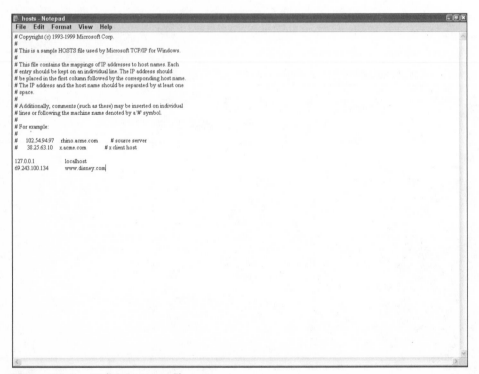

Figure 12-3: Malicious Hosts file entry

History

After checking the Favorites folder, the History folders are the next location of interest. The History folders are best viewed with a tool such as NetAnalysis, shown in Figure 12-4, which will consolidate the results but can be viewed directly as well through the Windows Explorer Interface.

Like NetAnalysis Pasco, a platform-independent freeware tool provides retrieval capabilities, but it lacks some of the more advanced features and GUI of NetAnalysis. Figure 12-5 shows a Pasco sample output.

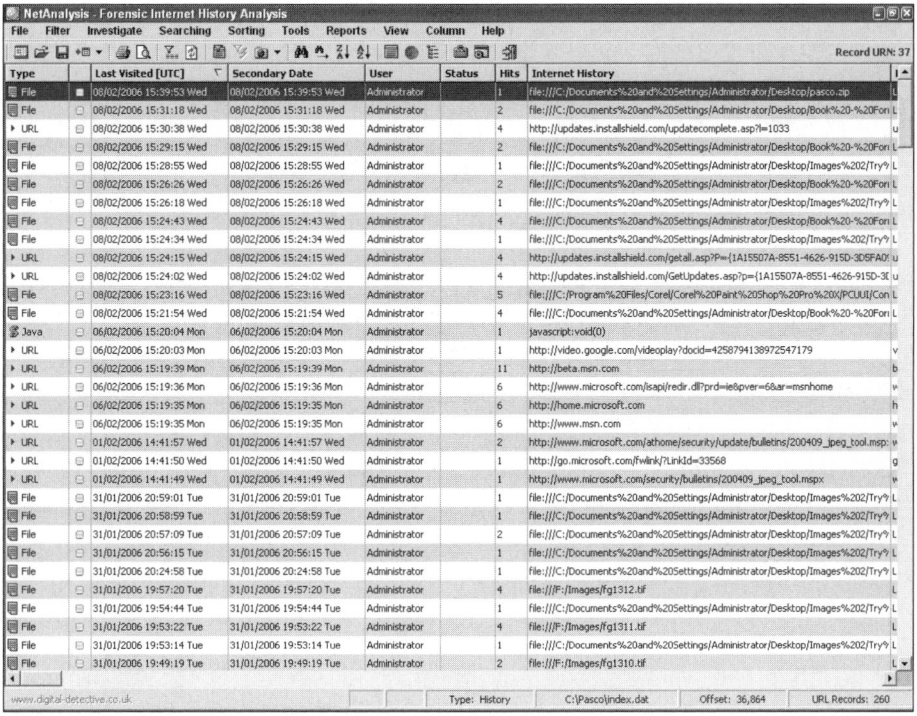

Figure 12-4:   NetAnalysis output

Microsoft Excel - out.txt

	A	B	C	D	E	F	G
1	History File: c:\pasco\pasco\index.dat						
2							
3	TYPE	URL	MODIFIED TIME	ACCESS TIME	FILENAME	DIRECTORY	HTTP H
4	URL	Visited: Administrator@https://accountservices.passport.net/r	Mon Jan 30 16:34:56 2006	Mon Jan 30 16:34:56 2006	URL		
5	URL	Visited: Administrator@http://by16fd.bay16.hotmail.msn.com/	Mon Jan 30 16:38:56 2006	Mon Jan 30 16:38:56 2006	URL		
6	URL	Visited: Administrator@file:///C:/Documents%20and%20Settin	Tue Jan 31 15:11:52 2006	Tue Jan 31 15:11:52 2006	URL		
7	URL	Visited: Administrator@file:///F:/Images/fg1305.tif	Tue Jan 31 18:26:45 2006	Tue Jan 31 18:26:45 2006	URL		
8	URL	Visited: Administrator@file:///C:/Documents%20and%20Settin	Tue Jan 31 19:11:37 2006	Tue Jan 31 19:11:37 2006	URL		
9	URL	Visited: Administrator@file:///C:/Test/constitution_c.txt	Mon Jan 30 15:53:27 2006	Mon Jan 30 15:53:27 2006	URL		
10	URL	Visited: Administrator@file:///C:/Documents%20and%20Settin	Mon Jan 30 16:22:43 2006	Mon Jan 30 16:22:43 2006	URL		
11	URL	Visited: Administrator@http://by16fd.bay16.hotmail.msn.com/	Mon Jan 30 16:33:34 2006	Mon Jan 30 16:33:34 2006	URL		
12	URL	Visited: Administrator@file:///F:/air.tif	Tue Jan 31 15:56:25 2006	Tue Jan 31 15:56:25 2006	URL		
13	URL	Visited: Administrator@file:///C:/Test/Foxxy.jpg	Tue Jan 31 16:44:10 2006	Tue Jan 31 16:44:10 2006	URL		
14	URL	Visited: Administrator@file:///C:/Documents%20and%20Settin	Tue Jan 17 16:16:50 2006	Tue Jan 17 16:16:50 2006	URL		
15	URL	Visited: Administrator@http://www.msn.com	Mon Feb 6 15:19:35 2006	Mon Feb 6 15:19:35 2006	URL		
16	URL	Visited: Administrator@http://login.passport.net/uilogout.srf?lc	Mon Jan 30 16:34:33 2006	Mon Jan 30 16:34:33 2006	URL		
17	URL	Visited: Administrator@file:///C:/Documents%20and%20Settin	Tue Jan 31 13:55:47 2006	Tue Jan 31 13:55:47 2006	URL		
18	URL	Visited: Administrator@file:///C:/Documents%20and%20Settin	Mon Jan 30 18:10:56 2006	Mon Jan 30 18:10:56 2006	URL		
19	URL	Visited: Administrator@file:///C:/Documents%20and%20Settin	Tue Jan 31 18:06:55 2006	Tue Jan 31 18:06:55 2006	URL		
20	URL	Visited: Administrator@--mmc.pagebreak.4	Mon Jan 30 18:02:44 2006	Mon Jan 30 18:02:44 2006	URL		
21	URL	Visited: Administrator@file:///C:/Documents%20and%20Settin	Tue Jan 31 16:38:10 2006	Tue Jan 31 16:38:10 2006	URL		
22	URL	Visited: Administrator@file:///C:/Documents%20and%20Settin	Mon Jan 30 20:41:07 2006	Mon Jan 30 20:41:07 2006	URL		
23	URL	Visited: Administrator@file:///C:/Program%20Files/eMule/New	Tue Jan 31 14:42:59 2006	Tue Jan 31 14:42:59 2006	URL		
24	URL	Visited: Administrator@file:///C:/Documents%20and%20Settin	Tue Jan 31 15:02:04 2006	Tue Jan 31 15:02:04 2006	URL		
25	URL	Visited: Administrator@file:///C:/Documents%20and%20Settin	Tue Jan 31 18:41:59 2006	Tue Jan 31 18:41:59 2006	URL		
26	URL	Visited: Administrator@file:///C:/Documents%20and%20Settin	Mon Jan 30 15:50:32 2006	Mon Jan 30 15:50:32 2006	URL		
27	URL	Visited: Administrator@file:///C:/Documents%20and%20Settin	Tue Jan 31 15:22:15 2006	Tue Jan 31 15:22:15 2006	URL		
28	URL	Visited: Administrator@file:///C:/Documents%20and%20Settin	Mon Jan 30 20:47:44 2006	Mon Jan 30 20:47:44 2006	URL		
29	URL	Visited: Administrator@file:///C:/Program%20Files/eMule/New	Tue Jan 31 14:53:45 2006	Tue Jan 31 14:53:45 2006	URL		
30	URL	Visited: Administrator@file:///C:/Program%20Files/eMule/New	Tue Jan 31 15:06:39 2006	Tue Jan 31 15:06:39 2006	URL		
31	URL	Visited: Administrator@file:///C:/Documents%20and%20Settin	Tue Jan 31 19:54:44 2006	Tue Jan 31 19:54:44 2006	URL		
32	URL	Visited: Administrator@file:///C:/Documents%20and%20Settin	Mon Jan 30 16:16:20 2006	Mon Jan 30 16:16:20 2006	URL		
33	URL	Visited: Administrator@file:///C:/Documents%20and%20Settin	Tue Jan 31 15:59:20 2006	Tue Jan 31 15:59:20 2006	URL		
34	URL	Visited: Administrator@file:///C:/Documents%20and%20Settin	Tue Jan 31 16:54:59 2006	Tue Jan 31 16:54:59 2006	URL		
35	URL	Visited: Administrator@file:///C:/Documents%20and%20Settin	Mon Jan 30 20:32:05 2006	Mon Jan 30 20:32:05 2006	URL		
36	URL	Visited: Administrator@http://media1.break.com/dnet/media/c	Tue Jan 31 13:24:07 2006	Tue Jan 31 13:24:07 2006	URL		

Figure 12-5: Pasco output

The History folder contains a list of sites visited during the previous web browsing sessions, organized by the time of the visit. As with the Cookies and Cache directories, the URLs of these sites and usage details are stored in a file called Index.dat. The Index.dat file is located in the root of the History directory (or under the History.IE# subdirectory for Windows NT/2000/2003/XP), with subdirectories for each day's history. If the History is set to be collected for more than one week, there are additional subdirectories for the previous weeks' histories. These files are labeled MSHistMMYYYYDDMMYYYYD-DMM. The first MMYYYY is the month that the records are relevant for. The second DDMMYYYY is the start period for that directory's records. The third DDMM is the date at which the records stop. Thus, a file with the name MSHist012004011220040119 would contain the URL viewing history for January, 2004. The start date of the history stored in that folder would be January 12, 2004, and the non-inclusive end date January 19, 2004.

The main index.dat file contains a record of all URL's visited during the History period. This is used for AutoComplete on the address bar and for visited link highlighting. When one begins typing "www" and a list of sites starting with "www" appears in the address bar, this is the file used. The sites that appear when the address bar dropdown list box is used are URLs that one explicitly typed in and stored in the registry. The subfolder index.dat files contain basic information on the sites viewed during their respective periods.

Each index.dat file is composed of three parts:

- **Header.** Contains the size of the file, in hex, followed by a NULL (00h) terminated string.

- **Hash table.** These contain pointers to other directories with Internet Explorer stored content. For the Temporary Internet Files directory, these are the hash values that contain the names of the subdirectories.

- **Activity records.** The URL type of activity contains the fields shown in Table 12-1.

TIP If using a hex editor, try scanning for the Type names.

Table 12-1 Activity Records

LOCATION	# OF BYTES	IDENTIFIER	NOTES
00h	4	Type	Key types of interest are URL (for site names) REDR (for redirections), HASH (for Hash table entries) and LEAK (similar to URL). You may also see filler data with a hex value of 0B AD F0 0D. I guess that some Microsoft developers ordered some bad pizza one night while determining the file format for this file.
04h	4	Length	The number of bytes this record uses.
08h	8	Last Modified Time	The time the record was last modified on the web server. REDR records only have the URL after length.
10h	8	Last Accessed Time	The time the URL was last visited on the client machine.
34h	4	URL Offset	The offset to the URL from the beginning of the record.
3Ch	4	Filename Offset	The offset to the file name from the beginning of the record.

(continued)

Table 12-1 *(continued)*

LOCATION	# OF BYTES	IDENTIFIER	NOTES
44h	4	HTTP Header Offset	The offset to the HTTP header from the beginning of the record.
Varies	Varies	URL	The full URL visited by the individual.
Varies	Varies	Filename	The file name downloaded by the individual.
Varies	Varies	HTTP Header Offset	The HTTP header is the full request header sent to the server.

TIP To translate this time in URL activity into the number of seconds since 1 Jan 1970 (Unix time), calculate as follows: Unix Time = 10-7(Last Accessed Time) + 11644473600.

Figure 12-6 shows the actual hexadecimal output of a URL record. Note the Windows user name of the accessing party as well (Chad M.S. Steel) before the URL itself.

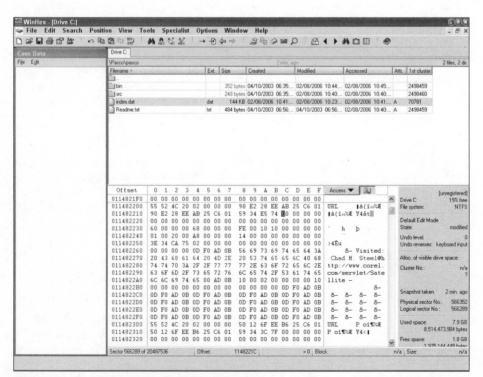

Figure 12-6: WinHex view of URL records

Because of a flaw in how Internet Explorer cleans its History file, deleted records without Hash table entries may still exist. As a result, even if the target cleans out his or her History using the Internet Explorer → Clear History function, there is still potential information in these files for forensic analysis. NetAnalysis recovers these entries, and Pasco will as well with the -d option.

Cache

Internet Explorer stores local copies of recently visited sites for quick retrieval. These are located in the Temporary Internet Files hierarchy. As with the URL History, these directories contain Index.dat files that hold the names and URLs associated with each of the individual files.

> **NOTE** At least one case, *United States v. Sanchez*, 59 M.J. 566 (A.F.Ct.Crim.App. 2003), upheld a conviction for child pornography based primarily on the contents of the Temporary Internet Files directories.

The individual files themselves (including images as well as the actual HTML file) are located under Content.IE5, within individual subfolders (named with eight-character hash names). The Index.dat file under Content.IE5 contains the table linking the cache entries to these subfolders through hash tables. These subfolders are cleared when the user selects Delete Files within Internet Explorer and may need to be recovered using file recovery techniques detailed in Chapter 10.

The Index.dat file may be analyzed using NetAnalysis or Pasco as noted previously in the History section. Some examiners prefer to analyze all Internet activity at one time. I generally separate the analysis of the different entries. The reasoning behind this is as follows. The History folder contains URL's that were visited at a given point in time. While it may be possible to reconstruct what the user viewed using the Way Back Machine, for sites with frequently changing content (for example, news sites) it may be difficult to pin down exactly what the user saw. The Temporary Internet Files, however, have the capability to display the actual content from the cache that the user in question viewed.

To facilitate actual page reconstruction, the analyst can view the Index.dat file and determine what files are associated with a given URL, as well as where they are located in the cache. These files can be copied to a temporary directory and viewed with a browser that is not connected to the Internet. If the computer is connected, the browser may follow absolute URL's which will download the latest version of images from the server—not necessarily the version the suspect viewed at the time. If disconnected, absolute image links will not appear when opening the HTML file in Internet Explorer, although relative image links (IMG tags within the HTML that reference file locations relative to the current HTML page location) will still appear if the images are in the same directory.

> **TIP** Sometimes these images will contain descriptive text that has been added by the web designer through the use of the ALT attribute. Even if the images cannot be recovered, this text may provide clues to their contents.

Images that cannot be found will appear as empty boxes with a red X through them. By right-clicking on the image and selecting properties, the analyst can view the directory structure where the original image was located as well as the image file name. By locating the file name in the Index.dat results and recreating the directory structure locally, the image can be copied to the appropriate location and the web page viewed as it was by the suspect.

Additionally, for cases that rely heavily on visual presentation (the screen-shot of an actual web page can be of greater impact to a jury than a list of file contents) the temporary files can be copied to a local web server (still discon-nected and running on the forensic machine), and the images and HTML files placed in the appropriate directories as noted previously. By putting entries into the HOSTS file for the hostname from the URL (for example, www .illegalimages.com) with an IP address of 127.0.0.1, even absolute links can be viewed locally. While configuring the forensic environment to better simulate the user's environment and allow the display of the page properly is a valid technique, altering the evidence itself (that is, changing the IMG tags in the HTML) to facilitate the viewing of content is not forensically sound.

The techniques noted previously rely on the use of the Index.dat file to iden-tify content of interest. The same techniques can also be used in reverse. If viewing all of the images on a drive, or alternatively doing keyword searches, web pages or files that were downloaded from the Internet may be uncovered. By looking up these file names in the Index.dat file, proof of download can be obtained. From an image standpoint, if an image file that matches the appear-ance of a file in Temporary Internet Files has been saved elsewhere, an MD5 hash can be performed to validate they are the same file. A date comparison between the viewing date and date the file was saved under a different name can provide evidence to this end as well.

The presence of a single image file or even web page does not necessarily indicate that an individual willingly visited the site. If possible, it should be confirmed that the link to an image or webpage was neither part of a FRAME tag nor part of an image from an IMG link on a different site. Additionally, it should be confirmed that the site was not brought up as either a pop-up or redirect. This can be confirmed by a basic temporal analysis. Look at sites viewed immediately prior to the site in question and confirm they have no content which would unintentionally load the content in question.

Cookies

Cookies are stored on a computer when a suspect views an Internet site that uses them for tracking. There are two types of cookies: session and persistent. Session cookies used to tracking individual browsing sessions and are stored in memory. These are lost when the browser is closed, although remnants may remain in memory or the swap file. Persistent cookies are written to disk and stored as text files in the previously mentioned Cookies directory. Persistent cookies are used between browsing sessions to maintain state (for example, when a person visits Amazon.com and her shopping cart still contains the items she placed there a few days earlier, Amazon is identifying the user through a cookie).

Cookies not only identify locations visited, but may indicate activities performed there as well as provide information such as user names and passwords to the analyst. They are restricted to an individual host (for example, you do not want Barnes and Noble to see what is in your Amazon shopping cart) and have set expiration dates. There are no restrictions on what a website may write to a cookie in terms of text. As a result, any number of items useful to the examiner may be present. The general format of a cookie is to include a series of records under a filer called username@sitename.txt. Each record contains the following fields:

- **Key.** The name of the variable stored in the record.
- **Value.** The stored value of the key.
- **Host.** The name of the host from which the record was written.
- **Secure.** True or false depending on whether the cookie was downloaded via SSL.
- **Modified Date.** The date the value was last modified. May indicate the last site visit.
- **Expiration Date.** The date the cookie is no longer valid.

The actual information is encoded by default, so the use of a cookie viewer is required. NetAnalysis has the function built in, and the same company also provides a freeware cookie viewer. The Value itself may be encrypted. This is highly dependent on the server application. Occasionally, user names and passwords can be uncovered from cookies, although a more likely scenario is the uncovering of complementary information to an investigation. The following example shows the contents of a Mapquest cookie:

```
1) COOKIE FILE: cms99999@mapquest[1].txt

Cookie Record    0
Key:             mqs_p
Value:           401e7a61-00046-0014e-cdbcf391
```

```
Host:           mapquest.com/
Secure:         False
Modified Date:  Mon, 02 Feb 2004 16:27:13 GMT
Expiry Date:    Sat, 31 Dec 2005 00:00:00 GMT


Cookie Record   1
Key:            locationhistory
Value:          {419472 -876564 ADDRESS {1060 W Addison St} Chicago IL
60613-4566 {COOK COUNTY} US {}} {388952 -770365 ADDRESS {1600
Pennsylvania Ave} Washington DC {} {} US {}}
Host:           mapquest.com/
Secure:         False
Modified Date:  Mon, 02 Feb 2004 16:33:09 GMT
Expiry Date:    Sat, 31 Dec 2005 00:00:00 GMT
```

As illustrated previously, Mapquest stores the actual addresses entered as saved location, useful in determining if a subject mapped out a given address involved in a crime.

Even if information is encoded in a cookie file, many times that file can be used to perform a masquerade attack. This can be useful for the forensic examiner to see what a suspect had in terms of contents on a given website (for example, whether the Amazon.com shopping cart contained books on lockpicking). To do this:

1. Delete all cookies, history, and temporary Internet files from the forensics examination machine.

2. Identify the cookies of interest on the suspect machine.

3. Copy the cookies to the Cookies directory on the examination machine.

4. Navigate to the websites in question.

For sites that store user names and passwords (even encrypted ones) or session identifiers in the cookie, this will make it appear to the server that the analyst is the suspect. If necessary, use a tool like Cookie Editor to change the expiration date if it has already passed.

In addition to the preceding locations, there may be other information of interest to the examiner in the registry. These locations are detailed as follows:

■ **AutoComplete and Intelliforms.** When a user types information into a form field, Internet Explorer by default offers to remember that information to speed up future typing. This information is stored encrypted in the registry under HKCU\Software\Microsoft\Internet Explorer\Intelliforms. As with many Microsoft encryption implementations, there are weaknesses and the AutoComplete information can be viewed with the appropriate software, such as Windows Secret Explorer from LastBit. Everything from names and addresses to email addresses and passwords can be found here if AutoComplete is being used.

- **TypedURLs.** When a specific URL is typed into the address bar (as opposed to clicking on a link), it is stored in the registry in a separate location from the general History information under HKCU\Software\Microsoft\Internet Explorer\TypedURLs. The TypedURLs key contains a list of the most recently typed URLs, which can not only provide another view into browsing history but also can show intent (it is much harder to accidentally type a full URL in than it is to click a misleading link in an email message or webpage).

WARNING Check with counsel to determine the admissibility and legality of using Intelliforms information in one's individual jurisdiction.

Firefox

Produced as an offshoot of the Mozilla project (itself an offshoot of Netscape), Firefox has grown in popularity at an exponential rate. Although the browser itself is substantially different both architecturally and visually from its Netscape ancestor, the forensic analysis is similar as Firefox uses the same basic file formats. As with Internet Explorer, the analysis can be broken up into Favorites, History, Cache, and Cookie analysis.

Unlike Internet Explorer, Firefox uses file-based configurations in lieu of registry-based configurations, primarily for cross-platform compatibility. Firefox data is stored locally under the Documents and Settings context for a particular user, within the key:

```
\Documents and Settings\profile name\Application
Data\Mozilla\Firefox\Profiles\firefox generated profile name\
```

All of the relevant forensic files will be present in this hierarchy.

Favorites

Favorites in Firefox are called bookmarks and, as with Internet Explorer, indicate web or local locations that an individual has actively chosen to save. The bookmarks are stored in an HTML file called bookmarks.html (a bookmarks.bak file is created when last accessed as well), which contains information on toolbar bookmarks, quick search bookmarks, and menu bookmarks.

Toolbar bookmarks are links actually placed on the toolbar as buttons. The most frequently used sites are likely to be present in this section, titled Bookmarks Toolbar Folder. Quick search bookmarks are links to search engines directly from the address bar. Search engines added to the default list may show a favorite search tool. Menu-based bookmarks are in all other folders (or no folder at all) and indicate locations that are accessible through the Bookmarks dropdown list box. These likewise indicate locations that are likely to be frequently accessed or of enough interest to note.

The bookmarks.html file can be analyzed in three ways: as HTML, as plaintext, or through the Bookmark Manager included in Firefox.

Analyzing the bookmarks.html file as HTML is the simplest but least effective way to view the information contained therein. The file can be opened in any web browser. A copy of a bookmarks.html file opened in Internet Explorer — had to do it for irony — is shown in Figure 12-7; there are links on the Bookmarks toolbar folder to Browser Statistics and Yahoo! in addition to the default Firefox links.

Although it provides reasonable visualization of links, the browser-based analysis does not show the included metadata on link MAC times and does not provide details on where links actually go, only the name given to the links.

Figure 12-7: The Bookmarks.html file viewed as a web page

Viewing the bookmarks.html file in a text viewer such as Wordpad or an HTML editor is likewise possible. Firefox stores bookmarked sites in the following format:

```
<A HREF="http://siteURL.com" ADD_DATE="###" LAST_VISIT="###"
LAST_MODIFIED="###" ID="Firefox generated ">Site Name</A><DD>Site
Description
```

The listed dates are in Unix time (the number of seconds since 1/1/1970). The actual sites are sorted by directory, and if a particular datapoint is not available (for example, the bookmark was never modified), it will not be shown. ADD_DATE is the time the entry was bookmarked, the LAST_VISIT date is the time Firefox was used to visit the bookmark last (by clicking on the bookmark), and LAST_MODIFIED is the time the bookmark was last changed. Site Name is the name given to the bookmark that is displayed in the menu. Site Description is the longer text describing details about the site. Site Name is taken from the TITLE tag by default, and Site Description left blank. Here is a sample entry taken from a visit to IP address 10.60.216.128:

```
<A HREF="http://10.60.216.128" ADD_DATE="1106687067"
LAST_MODIFIED="1106687083" ID="rdf:#$CujRC2">My Homepage</A>
```

TIP Viewing the file in a text editor provides the raw details, but visualization of folder hierarchies and translation of date formats is kludgy. To calculate the time in a more human-readable format, a valuable resource can be found at www.csgnetwork.com/unixds2timecalc.html.

The most effective way to view the bookmarks file is using a clean version of Firefox. Select Manage Bookmarks → File Import and import the bookmarks.html file onto the machine. The bookmarks will be displayed in a hierarchical fashion. Next, select View → Show Columns and add the three date columns. The resultant display, shown in Figure 12-8, has the advantage of both visual representation and completeness of information from both of the preceding options.

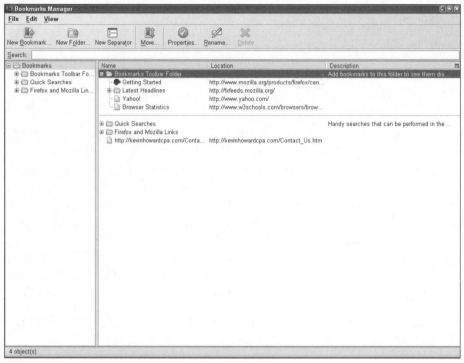

Figure 12-8: Bookmarks.html in Bookmark Manager

History

As with bookmarks, history information from Firefox is stored in a plaintext file titled history.dat. By default, the history.dat file contains the previous nine days history information, including the sites visited, what was typed, and the time visited. Although the file is viewable with an ASCII viewer, it suffers from the same issues as the bookmarks.html file. It is not easily interpretable by direct viewing. Fortunately, NetAnalysis parses these files in a similar fashion to Internet Explorer History files. An example of a history.dat file viewed with NetAnalysis is shown in Figure 12-9.

Unlike Internet Explorer, Firefox indicates whether the URL was typed into the address bar or clicked in the Typed field. Also, the dates noted are not in the local computer format. The date format is DD/MM/YYYY and the time format is UTC.

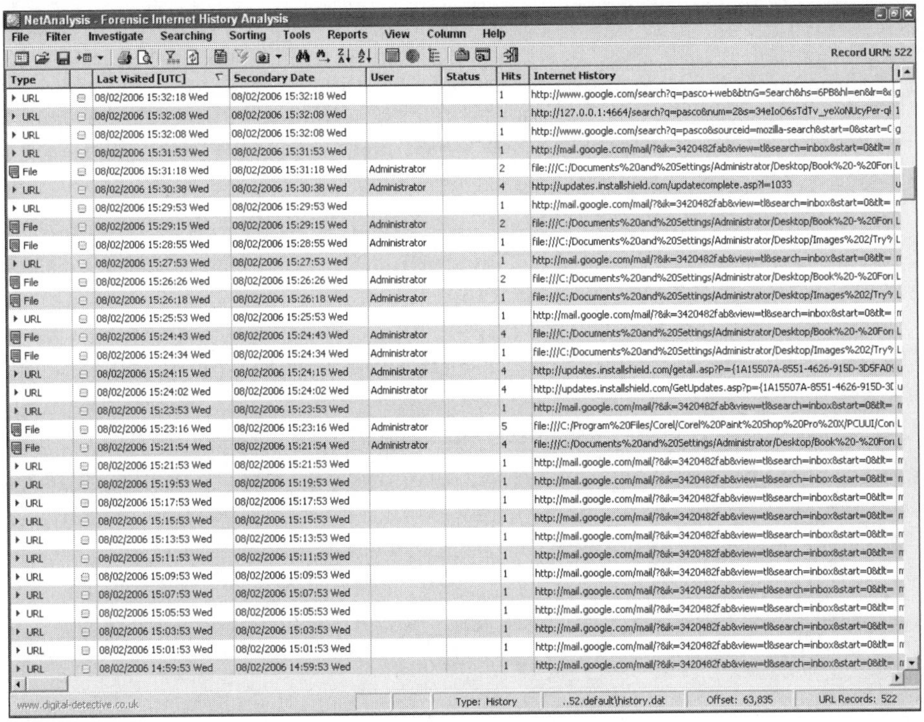

Figure 12-9:   The history.dat file viewed with NetAnalysis

Cache

A local version of all files accessed by Firefox is created to speed up the browsing process. The cache content is located in the Cache subdirectory under the Firefox profile, in a series of binary files. The cache files contain not only the contents of HTML, image, and other files but also the specific HTTP headers that were part of the initial request. As such, the exact time of a particular request can be obtained. An additional field stored the number of fetches to the cache, useful in showing repeated visits.

The cache files are not easily viewable (although text searches and scripts that carve out image files can be run against them), but Firefox includes a built-in viewing capability. To view the scripts in a forensics case:

1. Install Firefox on the analysis machine.

2. Delete the Cache directory.

3. Copy the contents of the Cache directory on the suspect's machine to the analysis machine's Cache directory.

4. Disconnect the analysis machine from the network.

5. Open Firefox on the analysis machine and type about:cache in the address bar.

The built-in viewer will show all of the cache entries, along with their creation time and modified times. Clicking an entry will reveal the HTTP headers associated with it, and a link to the entry itself. Figure 12-10 shows an example of a cache file viewed in Firefox.

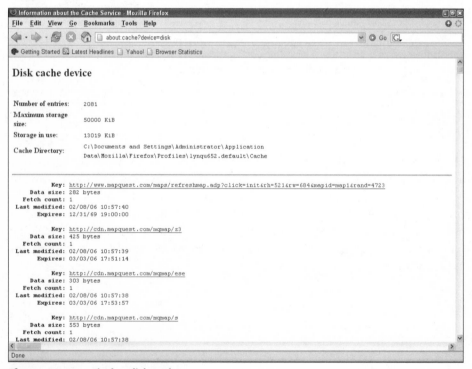

Figure 12-10:   Firefox disk cache

Cookies

Firefox stores persistent cookies in a single file instead of discrete files. This has one primary advantage for the examiner: the consolidation of information. When reviewing cookies, individual files do not need to be accessed or searched, and the cookies file can be copied to another machine.

Cookies in Firefox are stored in the ASCII file cookies.txt. Because the file is ASCII, it can be viewed directly by a standard text editor. Also, like cache files, cookie files can be transported to an analysis machine for viewing in Firefox. To view cookies this way:

1. Install Firefox on the analysis machine.

2. Delete the cookies.txt file.

3. Copy the cookies.txt file from the suspect's machine to the analysis machine's Firefox profile directory.

4. Disconnect the analysis machine from the network.

5. Open Firefox on the analysis machine and select Tools → Options from the menu bar.

6. Select the Privacy icon, and then expand the Cookies section and click View Cookies.

Using the Cookie Manager decodes the appropriate cookie fields and allows the examiner to view individual cookie contents. In the example shown in Figure 12-11, the contents of a MapQuest cookie reveal the location typed by the suspect.

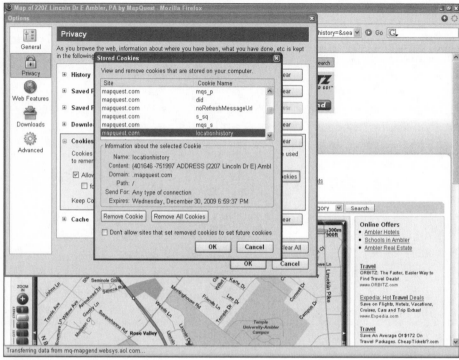

Figure 12-11:   Cookie contents

Passwords

Firefox allows users to store passwords for a given site in an encrypted fashion in a file titled signons.txt. The encryption for signons.txt is by default based on keys included in the file key3.db. By copying both of these files to the Firefox directory on the analysis machine, the investigator will be able to read the user names and passwords from the suspect's system. To read the passwords:

1. Install Firefox on the analysis machine.

2. Delete the signons.txt file (if present) and the key3.db file.

3. Copy the key3.db and signons.txt files from the suspect's machine to the analysis machine's Firefox profile directory.

4. Disconnect the analysis machine from the network.

5. Open Firefox on the analysis machine and select Tools → Options from the menu bar.

6. Select the Privacy icon, and then expand the Saved Passwords section and click View Saved Passwords.

7. Click the Show Passwords button to view the passwords.

The passwords will be automatically decrypted and shown in plaintext.

NOTE Firefox also has a feature that further encrypts the file using a master password supplied every session by the user, creating a vault technology. Keystroke logging or similar techniques may be required to obtain the master password if that feature is used. It generally is not.

Downloads

Downloads in Firefox are managed by the Download Manager. The file prefs.js contains the location of the folder where downloads are saved under the key browser.download.defaultFolder. By default, any programs downloaded will be copied to that directory.

The download data is stored in the downloads.rdf file in plaintext format. Included are the date and time of the download, the download state (one if successful), the location of the saved file, and the original location from which it was downloaded. The downloads.rdf file can be copied to the analysis machine to view download info through the Download Manager (Tools → Downloads), but for this particular scenario viewing the file directly with Wordpad provides easier access to the details. A sample entry for a download of the tool Filemon from Sysinternals is as follows:

```
<RDF:Description
RDF:about="D:\DOCUME~1\CHADMS~1.STE\LOCALS~1\TEMP\NTFILMON.ZIP"
                NC:Name="NTFILMON.ZIP"
                NC:Transferred="92KB of 92KB">
   <NC:URL
RDF:resource="http://www.sysinternals.com/files/NTFILMON.ZIP"/>
   <NC:File
RDF:resource="D:\DOCUME~1\CHADMS~1.STE\LOCALS~1\TEMP\NTFILMON.ZIP"/>
   <NC:DateStarted NC:parseType="Date">Thu Mar 31 12:34:06 Eastern
Standard Time 2005 +482032</NC:DateStarted>
   <NC:DateEnded NC:parseType="Date">Thu Mar 31 12:34:06 Eastern
Standard Time 2005 +502060</NC:DateEnded>
   <NC:DownloadState NC:parseType="Integer">1</NC:DownloadState>
   <NC:ProgressPercent NC:parseType="Integer">100</NC:ProgressPercent>
 </RDF:Description>
```

Toolbar History

Toolbars are growing in popularity for their ability to block pop-ups and enhance searching functionality. These toolbars can store search history, and do so in the registry. The Google toolbar stores the search results history at HKCU\Software\Google\NavClient\1.1\History.

Network, Proxy, and DNS History

Depending on the configuration of the network, log files may not all be stored on the local computer. Many companies use proxying, and relevant logs may be available from the proxy servers. Additionally, Cisco Netflow logs (or their equivalent from other manufacturers) may be available from the network routers. Finally, every web request that has a hostname requires a DNS lookup. If DNS logging is enabled this may provide further sources of information on web activity. The analysis of network activity is a complex topic and beyond the scope of this book. Check out the general forensics books mentioned in the individual chapter resources for further information.

Peer-to-Peer Networking

Peer-to-peer usage is growing steadily in the corporate world, with products like Kazaa, Morpheus, eMule, and Gnutella providing a new challenge for forensic analysis. These clients connect to other clients using an open or proprietary protocol. Each client can be used to share files and to download files shared by other clients. They vary in complexity, and the clients and underlying protocols are in a state of flux, resulting in the need for continuous vigilance on the part of the forensic examiner to understand the latest hot client. Additionally, the presence of peer-to-peer clients may indicate the presence of spyware on the computer (many clients are ad-supported). SpyBot or similar programs should be run on a read-only copy of the imaged drive to validate what been installed. This may be necessary to refute future claims of "spyware downloaded the pictures without my knowledge."

In addition to client-based forensic analysis, the ability to conduct network sniffing when investigating peer-to-peer clients should not be discounted. Network forensics is beyond the scope of this book, but may be useful in cases involving ongoing peer-to-peer activity, especially in target identification. We frequently detect peer-to-peer clients running through basic traffic analysis and firewall rejections.

The two primary goals of peer-to-peer forensics are to identify files that the suspect downloaded and to identify files that the suspect shared with others. The mechanisms for accomplishing this with the most common clients as of the time of writing are as listed here. In general, the following procedures can be used to obtain this information for new clients:

1. Load a clean, base image of the target operating system (Microsoft Virtual PC and VMWare are a tremendous help here with the Snapshot feature).

2. Install and run Filemon and Regmon from Sysinternals.

3. Download and install the peer-to-peer client software.

4. Note any directory creation, file creation, and registry key creation using the preceding tools.

5. Start the client software. View the Options to identify the folder names for default shared folders and download folders.

6. Create a folder with a unique name on the hard drive (for example, c:\FORENSICSHARE215\) and change the shared folder option to reflect that name.

7. Create a second folder with a unique name on the hard drive (for example, c:\FORENSICDL215\) and change the downloaded folders to reflect that.

8. Note any registry key or file changes after clicking Apply or Ok. Close the program and note any changes.

9. View the changed registry key(s) and note the name. This will be the location to search on the suspect machine.

10. Run strings or Find on the files that changed to search for the unique folder name:

    ```
    Find "FORENSICDL215" changedfilename.ext
    ```

11. If the file is ASCII-based, open the file in Quickview or a similar viewer and note the line and any variable name where the previous unique name(s) are located. This is the location to search on the suspect machine.

12. If the file is binary, open the file in WinHex and search for the name. Note any unique hexadecimal values just prior to the start of the unique name. This is the hex value to search for on the suspect machine to identify the location in that file. If there are multiple hex values that can be considered unique, note the ordinal position of the value you are searching as a reference point.

Additionally, the analyst may want to request the download of similar files or place similar files in the newly created shared folder to identify any library or index files or keys that change for targeting on the suspect machine. In the scenario where illegal content has been downloaded or shared, an innocuous file (for example, one filled with all 0s) with the same name and size can be shared and then downloaded again after it has been propagated to infer further details about the client software.

As a final alternative, a copy of the relevant directories and registry key structures can be copied to a virtual machine or the entire drive image restored with the peer-to-peer software installed and the program opened to determine the configuration options and any files that are currently being downloaded or shared.

As a cautionary note to investigators, the files downloaded may not indicate user intent in downloading their associated content. A file with an innocuous name such as Butterfly.jpg may not contain pictures of a butterfly (or pictures at all). A quick search for a file called Hacker Crackdown (purporting to be a copy of the text of the book by the same name) had the following alternative source names (note the same hash values):

```
SimCity 4 crack.exe
urn:sha1:AWVV5MAXXB3I7XSPFZUBJYAPZHAMW723

Unreal Tournament 2003 crack.exe
urn:sha1:AWVV5MAXXB3I7XSPFZUBJYAPZHAMW723

Wolfenstein 3D crack.exe
urn:sha1:AWVV5MAXXB3I7XSPFZUBJYAPZHAMW723

Enemy Territory Aimbot crack.exe
urn:sha1:AWVV5MAXXB3I7XSPFZUBJYAPZHAMW723

Angelina Jolie Sex Game crack.exe
urn:sha1:AWVV5MAXXB3I7XSPFZUBJYAPZHAMW723
```

The actual file content could be any of the preceding, or even none of the preceding. A popular tactic for copyright owners is to upload false content to flood the network as a response to piracy. Despite the differing names, in general most peer-to-peer programs name the actual file downloaded after the filename selected, regardless of other hash values. Just as downloading a file called Butterfly.jpg with questionable content does not necessarily imply intent, downloading a file with the name XXX Nude Girls.jpg, even if it contains pictures of a butterfly, likely does indicate intent.

Gnutella Clients

Gnutella-based clients include the original Gnutella program, Limewire, Gnucleus, Bearshare, and Shareaza. The original Gnutella program was released for a single day by Nullsoft, a division of AOL, and became the first dominant peer-to-peer service. Based on the now reverse-engineered Gnutella protocol, individual Gnutella clients communicated exclusively with peers in a no-servers-involved environment. The protocol was implemented by numerous freeware, adware, and shareware-based clients as noted previously. Unfortunately for the forensic examiner, each of these clients implemented a slightly different structure for file sharing and download management.

Bearshare

Bearshare is installed by default in C:\Program Files\Bearshare. The configuration file, which defines download\temp directories and lists usage times, is named FreePeers.ini and is located in this directory. The following are the key FreePeers.ini entries:

```
[GNetworkLogic]
nSessions = 2 ; Number of times BearShare has run
nUptimeTotal = 4101 ; Seconds BearShare has run (across all sessions)
nLastDailyUptime = 0 ; Last BearShare average daily uptime in seconds
nLastShutdownTime = 1076956236 ; Seconds since Midnight, January 1, 1970
of BearShare last shutdown

[Downloads]
szDownloadsDir = "C:\My Downloads\BS_Download\" ; Directory where
completed downloads are moved
szTempDir = "C:\My Downloads\BS_Temp\" ; Directory where partial
downloads are kept

Downloading. [GNetworkLogic]
nSessions = 0 ; Number of times BearShare has run
nUptimeTotal = 4101 ; Seconds BearShare has run (across all sessions)
nLastDailyUptime = 0 ; Last BearShare average daily uptime in seconds
nLastShutdownTime = 1076956236 ; Seconds since Midnight, January 1, 1970
of BearShare last shutdown

[Downloads]
szDownloadsDir = "C:\My Downloads\BS_Download\" ; Directory where
completed downloads are moved
szTempDir = "C:\My Downloads\BS_Temp\" ; Directory where partial
downloads are kept
```

Downloading

By default, downloads are located at C:\My Downloads\, and temp files at C:\Program Files\Bearshare\Temp. The Temp directory contains two files for each download: the file name and a DAT file with the same name. The file name contains the incomplete download results. The DAT file contains meta-data on the file being downloaded. This includes both download file name and the hash value of the file using SHA1. The hash file is used to uniquely identify the individual file on the Gnutella network. The file name can be changed by individual users locally or remotely and may not indicate the correct content. To identify the actual hash value of the file, use the strings command and grep:

```
C:\Tools\strings Hackers.dat | grep urn:
urn:sha1:AEJBSAW6MRXGX573NWIJQHV73GORP6F3
```

Sharing

Bearshare defaults the shared folder location to C:\My Shared Folder. A listing of all files and directories currently shared is located by default in C:\Program Files\bearshare\db\library.dat, the directory where Bearshare was initially installed. The library.dat file, when located or recovered, can be processed using the strings command to determine which files or folders are being shared.

> **TIP** If too many non-directories are returned, try increasing the *n* value. *n* is the number of characters that need to be found to be considered a string match. Given the standard directory naming convention of drive name, colon, slash (for example, C:\), three characters is the smallest directory name possible and a good starting number for *n*.

```
C:\Tools\strings -n7 library.dat
C:\My Downloads\&
C:\Program Files\BearShare\AUNIQUENAME
C:\My Downloads\
C:\My Downloads\*
How to hack Hotmail or Yahoo Passwords.zip
C:\My Downloads\
Illegal.wav
C:\Program Files\BearShare\AUNIQUENAME\
```

As noted in the previous return, the directories listed are all shared. The first entry with the directory name indicates the specific directory that has been shared. The second occurrence of the name is followed by any individual file names that were indexed and shared. They are located in the directory whose name precedes the file name. In the preceding example, the files How to hack Hotmail or Yahoo Passwords.zip and Illegal.wav were shared from C:\My Downloads\, and there were no files shared from C:\Program Files\Bear-Share\AUNIQUENAME\ the last time the program was run. If files or directories were deleted without running Bearshare again, the names will still appear.

Other Information

Like many peer-to-peer clients, BearShare allows for the integration of chat functionality. Under the [Chat] heading in FreePeers.ini are potential targets for keyword searches or Instant Messenger investigations:

```
szNickname = "" ; chat nickname desired
szEmail = "" ; email address
```

```
szAIM = "" ; AmericaOnline IM screenname
szYIM = "" ; Yahoo IM screenname
szMSN = "" ; MSN IM screenname
szICQ = "" ; ICQ user ID
```

Limewire

Limewire provides a Java-based alternative to Bearshare and also uses the Gnutella network and protocols. It installs the latest Java Runtime Environment on the target machine if not already installed. Limewire installs by default into C:\Program Files\Limewire\version\ where version is the current version number of the client. The install directory can be found in the registry under HKLM\Software\Limewire\InstallDir. Additional configuration information can be found under the .Limewire directory in the limewire.props, including download and temporary directories. Sample items from this file are as follows:

```
DOWNLOAD_SNAPSHOT_BACKUP_FILE=C\:\\Incomplete\\downloads.bak
DIRECTORIES_TO_SEARCH_FOR_FILES=C\:\\My Downloads
SESSIONS=2
DIRECTORY_FOR_SAVING_FILES=C\:\\My Downloads
CLIENT_ID=148A0511222E2E6EFF4CDC50A8A05A00
DOWNLOAD_SNAPSHOT_FILE=C\:\\Incomplete\\downloads.dat
TOTAL_UPTIME=1401
INCOMPLETE_DIRECTORY=C\:\\Incomplete
```

The `CLIENT_ID` is used to uniquely identify the client on the Limewire network. The `SNAPSHOT` and `SNAPSHOT_BACKUP` files contain information on files that are in the process of being downloaded. `DIRECTORIES_TO_SEARCH_FOR_FILES` is a list of all shared directories that will be searched for files to share at startup.

In addition, the installation.props file, located in the same directory as the limewire.props file, contains the timestamp with the exact time of software installation:

```
#LimeWire Properties IO Test
#LimeWire installs file
#Mon Feb 16 14:43:13 EST 2004
```

The createtimes.cache and fileurns.cache files contain the creation times of individual files (download times) and information on downloaded files, respectively. These are a secondary source of information, should the shared or incomplete directories be removed.

Downloading

The default directory for both downloads and sharing with Limewire is the directory C:\Program Files\LimeWire\Shared. Incomplete files are stored by default in C:\Program Files\LimeWire\Incomplete. When a file is selected for download, a placeholder with the same name is stored in the Incomplete directory and the content downloaded directly to that file. When complete, the file is moved to the Shared directory.

Limewire stores download-specific information on files currently being downloaded in the downloads.dat and downloads.bak files. These files are in a binary format, but using the strings command will reveal individual file names in the process of being downloaded and their unique SHA1 hashes:

```
C:\Tools\ strings -n20 downloads.dat | grep -v java | grep -v limegroup
dloaderManagerThreadt
incompleteFileManagert
(EBook) Hackers Handbook.pdft
)urn:sha1:PNGOBTIM67K66XM7MTRX5GZHUN4KH3AGsr
:ebook-pdf-Hacking-Hugo Cornwall-The Hacker's Handbook .pdft
)urn:sha1:PNGOBTIM67K66XM7MTRX5GZHUN4KH3AGq
2C:\Incomplete\T-3845832-(EBook) Hacker's Guide.pdfw
3C:\Incomplete\T-284717-(EBook) Hackers Handbook.pdfw
3C:\Incomplete\T-284717-(EBook) Hackers Handbook.pdfw
)urn:sha1:AGUKGXRNRH6E5R2NZ34I7RGWQBC7FWDZq
2C:\Incomplete\T-3845832-(EBook) Hacker's Guide.pdfw
(EBook) Hacker's Guide.pdfq
+ebook-pdf-Hacking-German-Hacker's Guide.pdfq
)urn:sha1:AGUKGXRNRH6E5R2NZ34I7RGWQBC7FWDZq
```

As shown, the downloads.dat output is less than clean. Postprocessing to remove artifacts can be done, but the basics are shown previously. Individual file names of items to be downloaded are listed, along with their respective hash functions. (Note that the final q in the hash is not part of the hash itself but a termination character.) This data can likewise be viewed with WinHex.

Sharing

Limewire automatically searches for information to share in the limewire.props file under DIRECTORIES_TO_SEARCH_FOR_FILES. Any files in the listed directories will be shared as part of network. By default, the download directory is shared. Others are shared by user action.

FastTrack Clients

FastTrack clients are collectively the most popular clients at the time of this writing. They share a common protocol (the FastTrack protocol, developed by what is now Sharman Networks), and are based on the older Gnutella protocol. FastTrack clients include Kazaa, Kazaa Lite, iMesh, Morpheus, and Grokster. The protocol itself uses HTML to transfer files, and can be detected listening on a number of ports. A favorite trick is to tunnel these clients over another port with outbound/inbound access, such as 80 or 443.

FastTrack clients send files over HTML using standard HTTP headers with a few extensions. The custom HTTP headers added by the protocol generally begin with X-Kazaa-, making this a good search string for drive searches to detect the presence of these clients, even after removal.

Of key importance to investigators is the ContentHash. This is an MD5-based hash of the file's content, and it is how FastTrack uniquely identifies files on its network, even those with different names. By searching for that hash function in another FastTrack client, the true content of a deleted file can be obtained from elsewhere (the forensic examiner's dream: an endless supply of offsite backup copies that are readily accessible and provable to be the same as the shared file).

The FastTrack clients have two areas of interest: the DAT files and the DBB files.

- **DAT files.** These files represent actual content in the process of being downloaded. The files are generally named download-XXXXXXXXXXXXXXXXXX.dat, where the Xs represent a unique local file name. In the case of partial downloads, file repair techniques can be used to view the current portion of the content that has been downloaded. Since FastTrack clients rely on a pull model, these files have been actively selected and downloaded by the user of the machine or an application running locally. Searching for strings within the file will yield the file name and some basic file details. A full analysis can be performed using a tool called KaZALyser. Full details on the DAT format are at http://home.hetnet.nl/mr_6/237/frejon55/ft/KazaaFileFormats.html.

- **DBB files.** These files contain the metadata regarding files that are currently or have previously been shared by the local machine. The content in DBB files is broken up based on record length:
  - data256.dbb holds meta records that fit in 8+256 bytes.
  - data1024.dbb holds meta records that fit in 8+1024 bytes.
  - data2048.dbb holds meta records that fit in 8+2048 bytes.
  - data4096.dbb holds meta records that fit in 8+4096 bytes.

Each record can be viewed with a hex editor, but KaZALyser, noted previously, is highly recommended. Individual file names, last shared times, and other specifics on files made available on the client machine can be obtained from these files. To view them in hex, each record will be the size dictated by the preceding file (for example, a record in data1024.dbb will be 8+1024 or 1032 bytes in size). The layout of the initial fields in each records of interest to the forensic examiner is shown in Table 12-2.

NOTE In the case of Kazaa, the file is shared only if the shared bit is set globally as well in the registry (that is, if HKCU\Software\Kazaa\LocalContent\ DisableSharing is set to 00h sharing is enabled globally; if it is set to 00h it is disabled).

Overnet, eMule, and eDonkey2000 Clients

Overnet and eDonkey2000 are a pair of clients that are part of a competitive network to the FastTrack and Gnutella protocols listed previously. The primary difference between the clients is that the eDonkey client utilizes a server-based infrastructure to connect and perform file searches, while the Overnet client is fully distributed. Both contain the same file structures noted.

Table 12-2 FastTrack Client Fields

FIELD	SIZE (IN BYTES)	DESCRIPTION
Label	4	Record start label to indicate a new record, always "1331" (6C 33 33 6Ch)
Length	4	Byte count of record starting at this location.
Filename	Varies	Local name of the file (terminated with 00h)
Foldername	Varies	Local directory where the file is stored (terminated with 00h)
Filesize	4	Size of the file in bytes
Filetime	4	Last modified time of the file (in Unix time)
Sharetime	4	The time the file was last available for sharing (can indicate deletion time)
Reserved	4	Kazaa reserved bytes
Shared Flag	1	01h indicates file is shared; 00h file is not shared

The default installation directory for Overnet clients is C:\Program Files\Overnet, and the configuration files are located under this directory. Overnet uses individual configuration files for each piece of information stored. The files are ASCII text, and the key items of configuration interest are as follows:

- **Pref.met.** This is the main preferences file. Running strings on the file and searching for temp and incoming will return the temporary download directory and the directory in which files are saved, respectively. The −A1 option returns the next row, which contains the actual directory names. By default, the incoming directory is C:\Program Files\Overnet\Incoming and the temp directory C:\Program Files\Overnet\temp. The commands to obtain this information are as follows:

```
C:\Tools\ strings pref.met | grep -A1 temp
temp
C:\Program Files\Overnet\temp


C:\Tools\ strings pref.met | grep -A1 incoming
incoming
C:\Incomplete
```

- **Share.dat.** Lists the directories and files being shared. The list of directories and files shared can be found by running strings on the file:

```
C:\Tools\ strings share.dat
C:\Program Files\Overnet\incoming
C:\Incomplete
```

- **Known.met.** Stores hashes of all known, shared files. Files that were previously available may be present in this file or its backup. To find names of files that are or were shared, strings can be used:

```
C:\Tools\ strings known.met
Terminator 3.mpg
Speed.mpg
Star Trek 2 - The Wrath of Khan.mpg
Star Wars Episode I - The Phantom Menace.mpg
```

- **Friend.met.** Contains the user names and IDs of individuals placed on the suspect's Friends list. These individuals are likely to be frequent download and chat sources with the suspect. To find the names of individuals, strings can again be used:

```
C:\Tools\ strings friend.met
kbuseme
onetdemon111
movieripperx
```

- **Uploadq.met.** Contains a list of individuals who have recently been queued to upload files from the user. To find the names of individuals, strings can again be used:

```
C:\Tools\ strings uploadq.dat
SJbSC
l'agent
rlnmt
```

- **Log.txt.** Potentially the most useful to investigators, log.txt contains a log of all Overnet download and upload activity. Additionally, start and stop times are noted:

```
C:\Tools\ cat log.txt
[ Tue Feb 17 09:15:27 2004 ]: Start Overnet v0.52
[ Tue Feb 17 09:15:28 2004 ]: Start Old Download: Leaked Star Wars
Episode 3 Foo
tage.avi
[ Tue Feb 17 09:15:28 2004 ]: Start Old Download: Star Wars - Episode
II - Attac
k of the Clones 1 of 2 (DVDRip, XviD, Rus).avi
[ Tue Feb 17 09:15:29 2004 ]: Start Old Download:
Star.Wars.Ep.II.DvD.Ripp.Fr.Ex
Q(Video.EN. .Son.Fr).Shared.by.Bill.Gatez.CD1.avi
[ Tue Feb 17 09:16:53 2004 ]: End Upload:
Star.Wars.Ep.II.DvD.Ripp.Fr.ExQ(Video.
EN. .Son.Fr).Shared.by.Bill.Gatez.CD1.avi
```

Downloading

By default, files are downloaded to the Incomplete directory noted previously. Logs of the download are added to the logs.txt file, and a subdirectory under Temp with the file name is created. Within this subdirectory are a meta file and its backup (for example, 1.part.met, 1.part.met.bak), and individual pieces of the content which are downloaded separately.

Overnet, unlike most of the other peer-to-peer programs, allows for content to be downloaded out-of-order. Additionally, as parts of the content are stored locally, they are shared with other users for download. The files are labeled 1.1.part through 1.x.part, and contain pieces of the actual content. The meta file details which pieces are downloaded and which are still needed, and allows for reassembly. The MET file provides details on the file and times the content was last seen on Overnet within the first several lines:

```
C:\Tools\strings  1.part.met
Leaked Star Wars Episode 3 Footage.avi
Video
codec
```

```
length
0: 0
Last Seen Complete
Tue Feb 17 09:17:22 2004
```

When a download is complete, the pieces are re-assembled and placed in the Incoming directory. The logs.txt file, noted previously, is the best source of previous downloads that have been moved.

Sharing

Files in Overnet are shared while they are being downloaded by default. Individual file parts are shared as soon as they have been stored in the Temp directory, and files are downloaded piecemeal from a number of individual users, any of which may or may not have the complete content themselves.

Additionally, the Incoming directory with complete file names is shared by default. Additional folders may be shared as well by selecting them within the GUI and will be noted in share.dat. Previously shared files may still be listed in logs.txt as well as known.met and known.met.bak. These sources should be searched for evidence of activity.

Instant Messaging

Instant communications today encompasses both traditional chat services such as IRC or Internet Relay Chat and dedicated Instant Messaging clients such as AOL Instant Messenger (AIM) and Microsoft Messenger. Forensic analysis of instant messaging is threefold: identifying the handles/profiles of an individual user, identifying chat partners, and viewing chat logs.

Instant messaging is client-server based; therefore, there is information present on both the clients locally and the server related to chats. Server-based information may not be readily available and may require a subpoena to the host of the service, but client information stored locally is generally available. Additionally, if instant messaging abuse is suspected, network sniffing and/or viewing of IM proxy information (if a proxy is in place) can be fruitful.

Forensic information on the most common instant communication technologies is detailed later in this chapter. Many additional clients for global (for example, Trillian) and intra/inter-company use (for example, Sametime) are available. This is meant to cover the most commonly found clients.

WARNING When conducting an Instant Messenger investigation, be careful not to bring back a restored image while online. If the suspect is logged in to an IM session elsewhere, he will likely receive a notification when the forensic copy tries to log in.

AOL Instant Messenger

AOL Instant Messenger (AIM) was one of the first and is still one of the most popular dedicated instant messaging services. Provided to both AOL users and non-users alike, AIM allows for Internet-based chatting and uses a client-and-server storage mechanism.

AIM works off of screen names, unique identifies specific to an individual. Screen names installed on a given machine can be found in the registry at HKCU\Software\America Online\AOL Instant Messenger (TM)\CurrentVersion\Users\SCREENNAME.

Additionally, each screen name will have a subdirectory under C:\Documents and Settings\USERNAME\Application Data\Aim\.

Associated with each screen name is an individual password under Login\Password below the screen name registry key. Prior to version 5, AIM provided easy-to-decipher passwords, a free utility to decipher them can be found at Digital Detectives. Post 5.x passwords have not been deciphered as of the time of this writing.

Individual identification information (profile) for a screen name can be obtained from a separate AIM client by selecting Buddy Info. This will additionally allow the investigator to search for other info or other screen names associated with an individual. The details for the profile are stored in an HTML file entitled info.htm under the screen name subdirectory.

Individuals with whom the suspect is frequent correspondences are organized into a Buddy List. The Buddy List can have numerous categories and subcategories, and is stored on both the AOL server and locally in the userinfo.bag file for each screen name. Buddies are organized under groups, in the following example Co-Workers and File-Sharing-Friends. By looking up the Buddy Info for the screen names, information on the individuals may be found. Running strings and searching for words returns:

```
C:\Tools\ strings userinfo.bag | grep -e "\w*"
AOL Feedbag 1.1
Buddies
File-Sharing-Friends
CIThief
Istealsecrets
Co-Workers
Bobfromaccounting
maryalice
```

A secondary source of screen names which were looked up on the subject machine or engaged in a conversation are in the registry under the Recent ScreenNames and Recent IM ScreenNames subkeys of the main AOL key noted previously, respectively. The highest listed number is the most recently used.

AIM does not store logs of chats by default; however, main memory and the pagefile may contain this information. A simple grep on the screen names found the Buddy list may turn up more screen names and/or chat session details. The hibernation file and pagefile are both good starting points to search.

Information on visited URLs can be found in the URLcache subdirectory under the screen name. The directory contains TMP files that correspond to other file types, Quickview or other programs which reader file headers can be used to view the images, html, and other content in these files. Additionally, the urlcache.dat file contains meta-information on the contents of the directory. The strings command returns the names of the files, their remote creation times, the last update times (locally, in GMT), and the actual content type. Here is a sample urlcache.dat file:

```
C:\Tools\ strings urlcache.dat
AIM URL Cache {403d93ea-a7f1-11d2-ad33-00104b5f8cd8}
C:\Documents and Settings\Admin\Application
Data\Aim\MyScreenName\urlcache\aim256.tmp:
http://cdn-aimtoday.aol.com/aimtoday_buddyicons/lovedont_1
Wed, 10 Dec 2003 14:10:17 GMT
Tue, 17 Feb 2004 18:57:00 GMT]
image/gif
C:\Documents and Settings\Admin\Application
Data\Aim\MyScreenName\urlcache\aim255.tmp6
http://cdn-aimtoday.aol.com/aimtoday_buddyicons/jayz_1
Wed, 19 Nov 2003 20:14:23 GMT
Tue, 17 Feb 2004 18:57:22 GMT%
image/gif
C:\Documents and Settings\Admin\Application
Data\Aim\MyScreenName\urlcache\aim254.tmp7
```

Finally, AIM enables users to share and receive files over the network. By default, these files are stored locally under C:\Documents and Settings\ USERNAME\My Documents\filelib\SCREENNAME\ and C:\Documents and Settings\USERNAME\My Documents\download\SCREENNAME\. Files in this directory may indicate they were downloaded and/or uploaded by the suspect. These directories can be changed using the Xfer/DirFileLib and Xfer/DirDownload subkeys of the main AOL key.

Microsoft Messenger

Microsoft (MSN) Messenger comes integrated with later version of Windows. It installs by default, but requires a user to provide a valid user name and login. The product performs similar actions to AOL Instant Messenger, and is primarily registry-based from an investigative standpoint. The main registry key is located under HKCU\Software\Microsoft\MessengerService\ ListCache\.Net Messenger Service.

MSN Messenger is based on an individual identity. The identity is the handle or alias the end user presents when logging in, as well as the name shown to others. The last identity to log in is stored under the IdentityName subkey of the main MSN Messenger key. When a new identity logs in, the old identity's information is overwritten with new registry key. As with other IM passwords, the MSN password is able to be decrypted with the appropriate program. The latest version can be decrypted with the Elcomsoft Advanced Instant Messenger Password Recovery program.

IM correspondents are stored in the registry as well, in one of four lists:

- **Contact.** These are the actual contact names of the individuals who the suspect has added to her list of correspondents and can view their online and offline statuses.

- **Allow.** These are the contacts that are explicitly permitted to view the online and /offline status of the suspect's account and send messages to the suspect.

- **Block.** These are the contacts that are explicitly blocked from sending the user messages or viewing her online and offline status.

- **Reverse.** These are individuals that have added the suspect to their own Contacts list.

Correspondent names are stored in keys starting with LISTNAME# (for example, Contact0), where LISTNAME is one of the four preceding lists and # is number starting at zero that is incremented by one for each entry. The value of the key contains the email address of the contact, the alias of the contact, and the number which represents the group that individual belongs to (if any) as the final digit(s) in the entry.

As noted previously, individuals can be placed into user-created groups. The individual groups are listed under keys labeled group#, where # starts at 0 and is incremented by one for each group. This number is used by the preceding contacts' entries to indicate group membership. The value of each group key is the name of the group.

Like AIM, MSN Messenger does not store logs of chats by default. However the main memory and the pagefile may contain this information. A simple grep on the names found the contact lists may turn up more names or chat session details. The hibernation file and pagefile are both good starting points to search. Additionally, a simple grep on Session Start.+Session Close may turn up evidence of full MSN Messenger chat sessions.

As with AIM, Microsoft Messenger permits the sending and receiving of files through the client. By default, downloaded files will be stored in the My Received Files folder in the suspect's My Documents folder. The location of received files is under the registry subkey HKCU\Software\Microsoft\MessengerService\FTReceiveFolder.

Additional Resources

Refer to the following list for additional resources:

Acceptable Use Policy Discussion by Todd Wulffson
www.llrx.com/features/wulffson1.htm

AIM Password Decoder from Digital Detectives
www.digital-detective.co.uk/freetools/aim.asp

Cookie Editor from ProXoft
www.proxoft.com/CookieEditor.asp

CookieView Cookie Viewer from Digital Detectives
www.digital-detective.co.uk/freetools/cookieview.asp

Firefox web browser
www.mozilla.org/products/firefox/

Instant Messaging Password Recovery from ElcomSoft
www.elcomsoft.com/aimpr.html

Internet Explorer Activity File Analysis from Foundstone
secure.foundstone.com/pdf/wp_index_dat.pdf

Kazaa Field Descriptions from the Delaware State Police
128.175.24.251/forensics/dbb2.htm

KaZALyser P2P Analyzer by Paul Sanderson
www.sandersonforensics.co.uk/kazalyser.htm

Market share statistics
www.websidestory.com

NetAnalysis Web Analyzer from Digital Detectives
www.digital-detective.co.uk/intro.asp

Pasco Cache File Analyzer from Foundstone
www.foundstone.com/resources/proddesc/pasco.htm

Unix time calculator
www.csgnetwork.com/unixds2timecalc.html

Windows Secret Explorer
www.lastbit.com/wse/default.asp

CHAPTER 13

Email Investigations

The contents of email messages have incriminated many individuals (and lead to some embarrassing disclosures). When an email is created, the sense of permanence associated with penning a letter is not always at the front of the mind. As such, individuals convey things in emails that they would never put to paper and ink. The medium is treated more like a telephone conversation. Unfortunately for the individuals that treat it as such, this is not the case, and email communications differ greatly from phone communications. Emails are rarely transient. They are stored on the sender and recipient(s) machines as well as any mail servers used, at least until viewed and securely erased. Emails are visible in transit unless explicitly encrypted. They can be routed accidentally to the wrong persons, and they and can be forwarded beyond the intended, original recipients.

Email is a store-and-forward protocol. Copies of messages are actually stored to disk in most cases, on all mail relays between the sender's SMTP server or internal mail server (for example, Exchange), and on the recipient's home POP3, IMAP, or internal mail server.

Email investigations cover the gamut of computer crimes and policy violations. Inappropriate material may be transmitted through email, it can be used as a harassment tool, an impersonation tool (for example, phishing scams), or a communications tool for other activities. Forensic analysis of email can be as simple as performing a pen-register analysis (who sent a message to whom and when) or as complex as analyzing and reconstructing message chains from numerous mail files.

Three primary email products exist in the corporate setting: Outlook, Outlook Express, and Lotus Notes. Web-based mail clients are also encountered frequently (for example, Hotmail, Yahoo! Mail, Gmail), but these do not have a client-side component to analyze unless POP3 or IMAP has been enabled, and other clients on Windows platforms are either less prevalent than before (for example, the excellent Eudora email client) or just burgeoning (for example, the equally excellent Thunderbird from Mozilla). In this chapter, I will cover investigations into the big three and include a brief overview of the Microsoft Exchange Server.

CASE STUDY: INAPPROPRIATE EMAIL USAGE

Policy violations based on the inappropriate usage of IT resources is one of the most common investigation areas plaguing large organizations. With increased controls in place to block web-based inappropriate content, email is becoming a more popular mechanism for distribution of banned material. As one unlucky company found out, investigations into email usage violations can be far reaching and costly.

While working on IT investigations, I received a report from a human resources manager that an employee had seen a co-worker viewing inappropriate material. When questioned about the viewing, the employee reporting the issue noted that a co-worker had "hardcore, pornographic images" on her screen when he walked by her cubicle. The second time he came by, his co-worker immediately turned off her monitor until he passed. He promptly reported the incident as a violation of respectful workplace policies to HR, who recognized it as requiring an IT-lead investigation.

After questioning the complainant, it became apparent that several aspects of the suspect's behavior were suspicious, in addition to the actual viewing of inappropriate material. These included:

◆ Turning off her monitor when others walked by.

◆ Moving her monitor to face away from the common area, despite the ergonomic gymnastics necessary to work with it in that location.

◆ Refusing to let others use her computer. Yet sharing was common in that location, as not all employees were issued machines.

◆ Requesting an anti-glare filter despite being in a low-glare area hours after the initial incident. This filter prevents side-angle viewing of the monitor.

Given the probable cause for investigation noted previously, the protocol for inappropriate usage investigations was enacted. This particular company's protocol called for the viewing of web usage history through proxy log files, the examination of the user's shared drive and local drive for inappropriate images, and the analysis of the employee's mail file.

Analyzing the employee's logfiles and shared drive returned no results. She did not use the network-based shared drive for storage and her web history returned only work-related and appropriate personal browsing. The first sign of trouble came with her local disk. A covert duplication was performed after she left in the evening, and the material was analyzed in the company's forensic lab offline the following day. The analysis was performed using AccessData's Forensic Toolkit and revealed multiple images which were inappropriate for a business environment, mostly deleted files. Further review of the MRU list for Windows Media Player revealed several additional file names of a dubious nature containing words like *Hardcore XXX* and *Young Naked* that triggered further suspicion, although the files noted were no longer present. No inappropriate browsing was found, no network-based file sharing mechanisms (peer-to-peer, IM, IRC, and NNTP) were present, and there was no evidence external devices with inappropriate material were attached.

Based on the inappropriate file names found in the MRU listing, a bitwise text search for those names was done on the entire image. Although the files themselves were still not found, references to the file names were found in slack-space fragments surrounded by what appeared to be email headers. The only email client on the machine was Lotus Notes, and the server name of her corporate mail server obtained from the Notes Addressbook. Read-only access was provided to the forensic account (called Disaster Backup Replicator to reduce the suspicions of anyone reviewing their user logs), and a replication done to the forensic analysis machine. The replica was unusually large for a mail file — around 10GB in size — and was backed up to tape immediately after generating a recording a checksum for the replica.

A working copy of the file was placed on a clean Notes analysis machine, and the All Documents view opened for review. Sorting the files by size (with the largest first) showed numerous large entries with subjects of "Check this out," "Never seen this before," and my favorite, "Don't open when your boss is around." All of the messages were opened individually, and hundreds of movies, images, PowerPoint presentations, Word documents, and even Excel spreadsheets containing XXX-level images were found. We made a list of both senders and recipients of the inappropriate messages, and each message was individually cataloged and stored as evidence. Unfortunately, 20 of the individuals who sent messages were other employees and over 40 internal recipients of the material were implicated in the messages.

Fortunately, this was not the first inappropriate email investigation the company had performed and a scorched-earth SOP was in place to limit the effort required for these investigations. The SOP had two relevant clauses:

1. After 20 individual items of inappropriate material are cataloged for a single individual, the remainder can be viewed for illegal content and stored in a forensically sound manner for later cataloging as necessary.

(continued)

CASE STUDY: INAPPROPRIATE EMAIL USAGE *(continued)*

2. Receipt of inappropriate material was a minor violation of policy (not reporting the violation) but not probable cause to analyze an individual's mail file, thus reducing the potential targets for further analysis in the preceding investigation from more than 60 to 20.

With the SOP already in place, the mail files of the 20 who had been confirmed as sending inappropriate material were acquired and analyzed. (At this point there was no reason to suspect non–mail-related, inappropriate use, and resource constraints limited the investigative scope.) Their drives were imaged in order to provide a forensically sound copy for later analysis if needed. An additional five senders and several dozen recipients were identified from these, and once again the five senders were investigated. In total, 26 individuals were fully investigated and several dozen identified as being recipients of inappropriate material.

Analyzing the email distribution patterns revealed a multiple hub-and-spoke topology. Several individuals acted as *hubs* and received inappropriate messages from others outside of the organization. They would then distribute the messages to small distribution lists of internal and external friends who were the *spokes*. Occasionally, a hub would copy an individual who was also a hub, further propagating the inappropriate material.

The 26 individuals who sent inappropriate material were dismissed from the organization for actively violating the company's Acceptable Use of IT Resources policy. The several dozen recipients were sent a written warning, told to clean up their mail files, and re-enrolled in Acceptable Usage training. Finally, a targeted education effort was made at the two sites where the incident had occurred, focusing on the appropriate and inappropriate use of email.

Outlook/Outlook Express

Microsoft's free email client Outlook Express and its big brother Outlook go beyond basic messaging. Both include contact management features and a newsgroup reader and Outlook adds calendar, note, task management, and journal capabilities. Both products can work with standard SMTP (for outgoing) and POP3/IMAP (for incoming) mail services or with a Microsoft Exchange Server.

Outlook Express

Outlook Express stores all message information in a proprietary DBX format. A separate DBX file is used for each folder a user has created, with Inbox, Outbox, Sent Items, and Deleted Items files created by default.

NOTE Outlook Express version 4 uses two files per folder: an MDX file, which contains the message contents, and an IDX file, which contains message indexing information.

Acquisition

Outlook Express DBX messages can be viewed directly on the analysis machine by copying the DBX files to the local machine's Outlook Express instance or by viewing with a dedicated viewer. To view the DBX files using Outlook Express, follow these steps:

1. Install a clean version of Outlook Express on the analysis machine.

2. Locate the Outlook Express DBX files (generally under Documents and Settings\profilename\Local Settings\Application Data\Identities\ identity name\Microsoft\Outlook Express) on the suspect image.

3. Copy all DBX files from the suspect machine's directory to the analysis machine's Outlook Express directory.

4. Disconnect the analysis computer from the network to prevent accessing any mailboxes inadvertently.

5. Open Outlook Express on the analysis machine.

NOTE The actual identity and profile names will be different on the analysis machine. Copy the DBX files to whatever profile name is present on the analysis machine.

The files and folder present on the suspect's machine will now be visible and searchable on the analysis box. The Outlook Express example in Figure 13-1 shows the standard folders imported and an additional folder titled "Spam."

A second way of viewing DBX files is through a dedicate viewer such as OE Viewer. OE Viewer provides a more forensically sound way of viewing the files. Since it is read only, the messages cannot be inadvertently altered. Using OE Viewer is simple. Just select File → Open and choose the individual DBX folders present. The messages will be viewable in a similar fashion to the way they are in Outlook Express itself. Figure 13-2 shows a sample of messages displayed in OE Viewer. OE Viewer provides an additional tool which is useful in investigations. Selecting File → Gather Email Addresses quickly shows all corresponding email accounts from all messages in a folder, providing a quick-and-easy way to identify associates of a suspect.

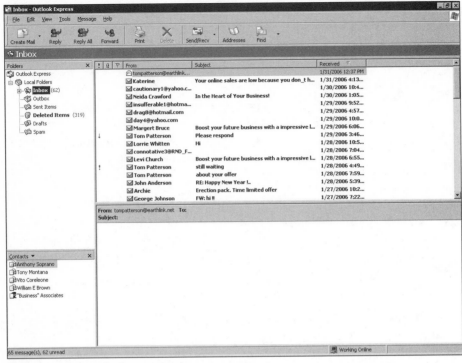

Figure 13-1:   Outlook Express Inbox

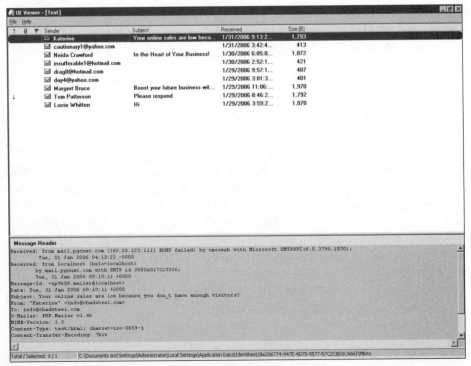

Figure 13-2:   OE Viewer contents of a folder called Test

Analysis

The default folders in which mail is stored are as follows:

- **Inbox.** Contains incoming mail until it is moved to another folder.
- **Drafts.** Contains emails that have been drafted but not sent yet.
- **Outbox.** Stores mail messages for sending when a connection to the server is established.
- **Sent Items.** Contains any files sent (and a copy saved automatically).
- **Deleted Items.** Stores messages that have been deleted from other folders. The Deleted Items folder acts like a mini–recycling bin. Deleted messages are kept until it is emptied either automatically or manually.

Any numbers next to a folder (for example, 272 next to Deleted Items) indicate unread messages. These same messages will be bolded by default to indicate status. In an email investigation, both folder name and unread status are important.

Unread messages indicate it is likely but not certain that the recipient did not read a particular message. First, the recipient may have viewed the message in the preview pane (where the word *Test* is shown in Figure 13-1), which does not change the unread status. Second, the recipient may have changed the status back to Unread after reading the message. This is done be right-clicking and choosing Mark As Unread. Better proof that a suspect reviewed a message is contextual. References to the message content in replies or other documents are a better indication of having read the contents. Similarly, placing the message in a folder based on the contents is a likely indicator of having read the message.

Folder names and structure can be important in determining intent as well. In an inappropriate use investigation, the same message in a folder titled Spam may not be viewed as negatively as one in a folder titled Hot Pics or even Personal Mail. With large mail files, folders can direct an investigation as well. In the preceding inappropriate usage example, Hot Pics is more likely to turn up evidence than a Weekly Project Report folder. An embezzlement investigation, on the other hand, may have more interest in the latter folder name.

Because the views exclude header information by default (and header information may be critical in tracking the source of spam or phishing messages), this information frequently needs to be made available. Header information can be viewed in Outlook Express by right-clicking a message and selecting Properties → Details, and then clicking Message Source (in OE Viewer, it's shown by default in the Preview Pane). The header info and raw message as received by the SMTP server will be shown. Figure 13-3 shows an example of header information which displays both the headers and the encoded attachment. This text can be selected and copied into an evidence file from this screen as well.

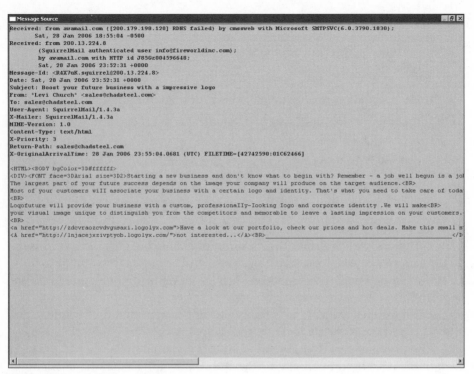

Figure 13-3: Actual message source

Searching messages is possible through the Find option in Outlook Express. Find works similarly to the Search function built into Windows XP and traverses a folder or folders (starting with the folder selected when Find was clicked) looking for messages that meet specified characteristics. Messages can be searched for by sender, receiver, date, or message itself (with wildcards accepted). Another useful option provided is to search for messages with attachments, which can dramatically narrow the number of messages that need to be reviewed in certain cases. The Find panel is shown in Figure 13-4.

WARNING The Find function in Outlook Express will turn up any message text that matches the string but will not search the contents of attachments, attachment names, or header information, including the Subject line.

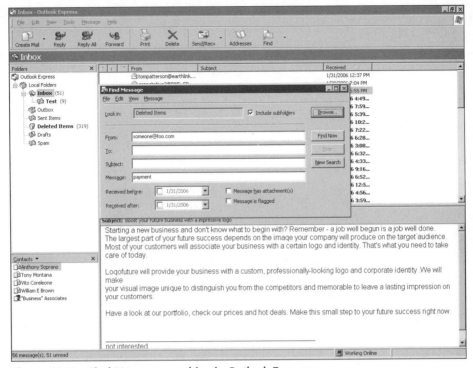

Figure 13-4:   Find Message searching in Outlook Express

Microsoft Outlook Express also includes a Contact Manager. Personal information on individuals is stored in the Addresses section of the program. These can be imported from messages (with vCards) or input directly, and may include names, addresses, email addresses, phone numbers, and personal details about the contact. Contacts can also be grouped into folders, allowing for differentiation between business and personal associates.

The Outlook Express address book information is stored in the Windows Address Book (WAB) format. By default, the address book resides in Documents and Settings\profile\Application Data\Microsoft\Address Book and is named after the individual's profile. The address book can be viewed in Outlook Express by selecting File → Import Address book and choosing the WAB file. Figure 13-5 shows the WAB file as viewed by Outlook Express.

A read-only Address Book viewer, called Address Book Recovery, is as well. This software, shown in Figure 13-6, provides a read-only view of a WAB file, repairs corrupted WAB files, and even recovers deleted contacts that have not been overwritten from these files.

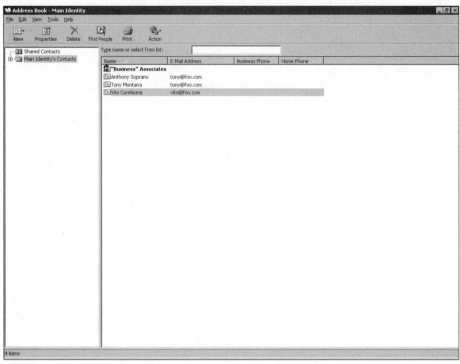

Figure 13-5: Windows Address Book in Outlook Express

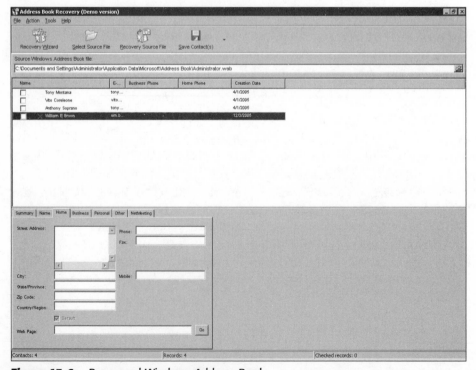

Figure 13-6: Recovered Windows Address Book

Outlook

Microsoft Outlook is an enterprise-class email client. It is generally used in conjunction with Microsoft Exchange for corporate email systems but supports standard SMTP/POP3/IMAP messages also. Outlook adds to the functionality of Outlook Express by providing Calendar, Note, Task Management, and Journaling functions. The basic mail and contact functions are enhanced as well, and the storage formats differ significantly.

> **TIP** A sister format to PST, Exchange also uses an OST Offline Storage format. This can be easily converted to the PST format using tools like Passware ExchangeRecovery, available at www.officerecovery.com/exchange/index.htm.

Outlook data is stored in a consolidated proprietary record format, which within PST files. The PST files for a specific user are located under the user's profile within the Documents and Settings\profile name\Local Settings\ Application Data\Microsoft\Outlook folder by default, and named Personal Folders.pst. Additional PST files can be present for multiple mailboxes or other personal folders such as archive folders. PST files can be password protected and encrypted, making direct viewing of them difficult if these controls are enabled. The files present on the server are in a different, Exchange-specific format in files with EDB extensions. These need to be viewed with specialized software when copied locally.

Because Outlook is a client-server program, the contents stored locally may differ from those on the Exchange server. Depending on the user's setup, some content may reside on only the server (to allow access from the Web Connector–based client or other computers with Outlook), only the client (when server-based mail quotas are enabled), or in both locations. Investigations should look at both the client- and server-based mail locations to ensure complete coverage.

> **NOTE** Looking at both the client and server applies to any mail investigation. IMAP-based mail servers can keep messages on the server, and even POP3 mailboxes may have new mail that hasn't been downloaded stored remotely.

Acquisition

Acquisition of local Outlook mailboxes is a matter of copying the PST file using standard forensic duplication techniques and viewing with Outlook itself or a third-party viewer. To use Outlook to view a PST file:

1. Install a clean version of Outlook on the analysis machine.
2. Locate the Outlook PST files on the suspect image.

3. Copy all PST files from the suspect machine's directory to the analysis machine's evidence directory.

4. Disconnect the analysis computer from the network to prevent accessing any mailboxes inadvertently.

5. Open Outlook on the analysis machine.

6. Select File → Open → Outlook Data File and select the PST file (or files) copied.

Viewing an Exchange database file in the EDB format is more difficult. To view an EDB file, the Exchange server should first be shut down. Next, the relevant EDB file should be copied in a forensically sound manner to the analysis machine and archived appropriately. Finally, a forensic EDB viewer such as PowerControls from Ontrack should be used to view the contents.

Access Control

The Microsoft Outlook PST file format is proprietary and encrypted, and can be further password protected to prevent unauthorized users from browsing it. Because of a weakness in the proprietary encryption algorithm, Outlook passwords can be instantly recovered using Passware's Outlook Key. The tool is run on a PST mail file and actually decrypts the password directly as opposed to using a dictionary or brute-force attack.

Analysis

Outlook stores its mail messages in user-created folders, with several folders created at installation. The standard folders created for mail are as follows:

- **Inbox.** Contains incoming mail until it is moved to another folder.
- **Drafts.** Stores emails that have been drafted but not yet sent.
- **Outbox.** Stores mail messages for sending when reconnection to the server is made.
- **Sent Items.** Contains any files sent (and a copy saved automatically).
- **Deleted Items.** Stores messages that have been deleted from other folders. Deleted Items acts like a mini–recycling bin. Deleted messages are kept until it is emptied either automatically or manually.

Outlook also has user-specific and public folder features. User-specific folders are located on the local system, and each folder may or may not be in a separate PST file. A popular one is an archive folder for older emails, generally in a separate PST file. Shared folders act more like a file share for collaboration. They are set up on the Exchange server itself and are accessible by others across the network.

The Contacts functionality of Outlook provides integrated address book capabilities. Individuals and distribution lists (groups of email addresses) are kept under Contacts, which has similar fields to Windows Address Book and can import Windows Address Book files.

Calendar is an online time management system. Meetings, appointments, and events are all tracked for a user, and in an Exchange-enabled system for groups of users. Knowledge of who was invited to a particular meeting, where an individual likely was at a given time, and known associates (those who have met with the individual) can be garnered from the Calendar view.

Tasks keep track of tasks assigned to or entered by the user. Tasks may be linked to Microsoft Project plans for business activities, and can be a clue as to a suspect's whereabouts at any particular time. Daily, weekly, or longer tasks may indicate a work pattern for a suspect.

The Journal feature provides the most interesting forensic-related feature over Outlook Express by keeping a record of all user activities. If turned on (it is off by default), the Journal feature tracks emails sent and received, Microsoft Office document activity, and Task completion details. If it is present, the Journal provides a daily forensic log of many user activities of interest. A sample Journal is shown in Figure 13-7.

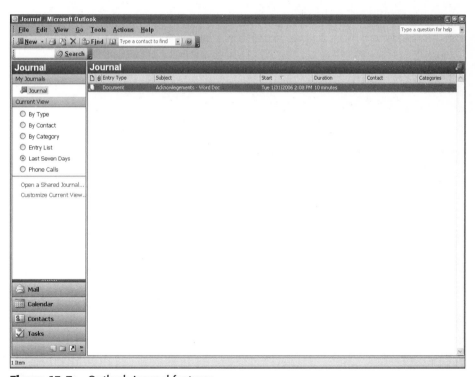

Figure 13-7: Outlook Journal features

The Journal feature does the timeline work for the forensic examiner, showing what was done and when it was done. Everything from document updates to messages sent (even if the message is later deleted) may be present if fully enabled. In general, the Journal feature is used by consulting organizations and others that have client billing obligations (for example, accounting firms and law firms).

Searching a PST file can be done natively in Outlook or using a third-party program, but most third-party packages are limited due to the proprietary and encrypted nature of PST files. Since most third-party programs use the Outlook search capability, or export the data from PST files to another format, first, their forensic value is limited over using Outlook itself for analysis.

Searching a mail file in Outlook is a matter of opening the file on a non-networked analysis machine and selecting Tools → Advanced Find. The search is not indexed and occurs quickly and searches all mail files but not attachments or attachment names. Figure 13-8 shows an advanced search for any messages sent by the suspect to smith@foo.com. Remember to look for cc: and bcc: recipients as well.

By default, the mail headers are not displayed in the Outlook view menu, although add-ins that show them can be purchased. To display the headers for a particular message, right-click the message and select Options. The header info will be displayed in the Message Options dialog box.

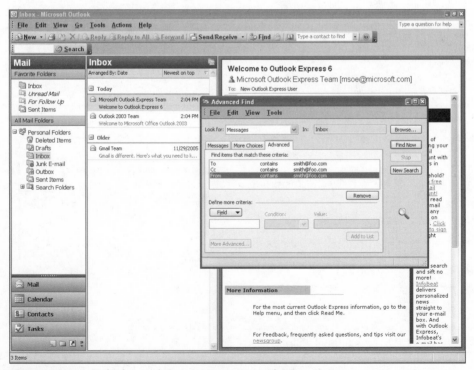

Figure 13-8:   Outlook search for messages to smith@foo.com

USENET AND NNTP

Network News Transfer Protocol (NNTP), the newsgroup-focused sister protocol to SMTP, emerged as the predominant way to exchange Usenet news articles in the mid 1980s. Usenet, developed several years prior, was a collection of communities in specific areas of interest organized into a newsgroup hierarchy. With top-level organizations like alt (for alternative), sci (for scientific), and rec (for recreation), like-minded individuals could connect to their local news server, send and receive messages (articles) organized by group, and have their messages relayed across the Internet. Until it was surpassed by HTTP in the mid 1990s, NNTP-based Usenet traffic represented the highest percentage of traffic on the Internet.

Because NNTP operates in a similar fashion to SMTP, many email clients, including Outlook Express, Outlook, and Notes, include it in their suite of functions. The ability to subscribe to groups of interest, read, and reply to messages in a basic fashion is present in all three products. Specialized newsreaders are available as well.

Newsgroups are historically relevant to forensics because of a few specific hierarchies. These include the alt.binaries hierarchy, whose subsidiary groups contain binaries posted in a translated ASCII format, and the alt.sex hierarchy, whose constituent groups discuss the varied aspects of human reproduction in frequently explicit ways. Although other hierarchies of forensic interest exist, and all alt.binaries and alt.sex groups are not obscene or dangerous, these are the two groups most often frequented by suspects.

Prior to peer-to-peer networking, the easiest way to share inappropriate and sometimes illegal content was through newsgroups. By spoofing an NNTP message (the same way an SMTP message can be spoofed) or using an anonymizing news server, individuals could share pirated software, copyrighted music and movies, and pornography, even child pornography. The contents would be shared globally to anyone subscribing to a particular hierarchy and became a distribution channel for all forms of interesting content. Groups like the alt.binaries.warez have been used to distribute software, alt.binaries .pictures.erotica for pornographic images, and alt.sex.stories for general, inappropriate-for-the-workplace content.

Although losing popularity, Usenet still exists and may still be encountered in an investigation. Any email clients with news readers should be analyzed to determine:

◆ What newsgroups the suspect subscribed to.

◆ What newsgroups the suspect read.

◆ Any attachments that were downloaded by the suspect.

◆ Any postings by the suspect.

(continued)

USENET AND NNTP (continued)

Because binaries are encoded, there may still be messages present which are not found by text searches or hash analyses. Newsreaders should be used to extract and convert any existing encoded messages to their binary form and then analyzed. Any unusual-looking text messages should likewise be reviewed manually. Frequently encodings like ROT-13 are used on Usenet to bypass standard text-based filtering. Finally, the news server used should be noted, even if there are no current subscriptions present. The news server may have a log of past activities for the suspect.

Lotus Notes

Like Outlook, Lotus Notes is targeted at enterprise users. Combining a document database system and standard mail features, Notes relies on a proprietary infrastructure made up of Lotus Notes and Domino servers and Notes clients, generally operating in a hub-and-spoke topology. As is the case with Outlook and Exchange, data can reside on both the client and the server.

NOTE Notes does support POP3/IMAP/SMTP, but in practice most organizations deploy the whole package. Domino is the next generation of Lotus Notes released several years ago. When used here, Notes will refer to both Notes and Domino.

The Lotus Notes client is a free download from IBM, allowing examiners to utilize it for direct examination without the need for pre-existing lab infrastructure. The client opens Notes databases, which are in a proprietary NSF format. Both the client and server store their data in individual NSF files for a specific user. The ID files can be password protected and encrypted, making analysis more challenging.

Notes uses an unusual authentication method that complicates or simplifies forensic examination. Authentication is performed to a Notes client or server through the use of a private key. The key itself is stored in a Notes ID file, and is only viewable through the use of a password, which decrypted the actual private key using symmetrical encryption. When an NSF file is encrypted, only those individuals whose keys were added to the list of valid readers will be able to decrypt its contents, administrators included. To obtain access to these databases, the examiner needs two items:

- A copy of one of the ID files authorized to view the database.
- The password to that ID file.

Obtaining the ID file itself can be done by searching the suspect's computer for files with an .id extension (frequently found under Documents and Settings\profile name\Notesdata\). Failing that, the issuer of the ID can be contacted to see whether she retained a copy, or, if she distributed the file through email, whether the original message still exists.

If the ID file is found (and the key has not changed, which it generally does not due to the administrative difficulties in doing so), the password associated with that individual ID file must be obtained. Since the password decrypts the private key independently from any server or database, any version of the ID file can be used. If the initial passwords are recorded with the initial ID issuance, an original copy of the ID with the initial password can be used to decrypt the mail file. If the original does not exist and the password cannot be obtained through traditional means on the ID file available, dictionary guessing is possible using the Passware Suite.

CASE STUDY: ACCIDENTAL DISCLOSURE

Covert operations rely on secrecy. If a covert investigation is uncovered it may tip off a suspect prematurely and quickly become a salvage operation. This is a potentially difficult situation in computer forensics. A suspect that is aware that she is under investigation may temporarily cease activities of interest, use other systems, or delete evidence. This was the case in a mail investigation gone awry.

Based on the company's procedures, Lotus Notes mail file analysis was a by-the-book operation. Notes mail files would be replicated to the investigators system, the investigators system taken offline (and set to Island as a location), and the analysis performed. After the analysis was complete, any messages present in the mail.box file would be deleted and the system brought back online.

Because of return-receipt functionality, opening messages with a return message header would cause a read confirmation message to be sent to the original sender. In the case of Sent items, the sender could even be the subject themselves. Making matters worse, the message is sent from the investigator's account, an almost immediate tip-off to the subject that he is under investigation.

One such investigation was underway on an individual suspected of collaborating with outside parties to commit fraud through email. The investigation was fairly standard: examine the user's email activity to look for any suspicious messages to or from external parties, or between the suspect and a group of recently terminated individuals. The suspect was placed under video surveillance, and the email analysis needed to occur without the suspect being made aware of it.

The initial acquisition of the mail file from a corporate Lotus Notes was flawless. A Notes account called Server Replicator was used to minimize the risk of the suspect noticing unusual log file activity, the acquisition was done after-hours, and the analysis machine freshly built from the investigation gold-build disk.

(continued)

CASE STUDY: ACCIDENTAL DISCLOSURE *(continued)*

After acquisition, the file was hashed and backed up to DVD, and then analysis was begun on the working copy. The analysis machine was taken offline, and then the Notes client put into Island as a location. Taking the risk of accidentally generating a read receipt, the mail.box file was actually deleted to prevent accidental sending. Therein lay the mistake.

The mail file was indexed then searched, and numerous messages of interest both to and from the suspect were reviewed. No direct evidence of wrongdoing was obvious, but there were several cryptic messages which may have been veiled indication of the alleged abuse. Together with surveillance, a general ledger audit, and interviews with vendors the messages were expected to be of more value. Each message of interest was exported to its own Rich Text Format (RTF) file, saved to CD-R, and printed for inclusion in a hardcopy report.

After analyzing the mail file, a request was made the following day to determine if there were any new messages. The analysis machine was reconnected, and the replication re-enabled from the previous point. To save time transferring the multi-gigabyte file, the analyst simply replicated the changes onto a working copy of the previous mail file. The analysis was performed on the new content the same as it had the previous night.

Early in the morning of the third day, the investigator received an email message from the suspect questioning the presence of return receipts in their mailbox. Why was the investigator reading his mail, and what was going on? Fortunately, the suspect appeared happy with a random audit response, but the investigation had been compromised and the quality of the forensic team called into question.

The analysis that followed revealed an undocumented feature of Lotus Notes had contributed to the compromise. When the investigator deleted the mail.box file, it was believed that the queuing of outgoing mail would not be possible. Instead, Notes assumed that the file deletion was accidental, recreated a new mail.box file, and saved the outgoing messages. When the machine was reconnected for a second replication, all return receipts were sent.

To prevent similar incident in the future, further precautions were built into the procedures. First, the analysis machine for mail was never connected to the corporate network. Working copies were transferred through sneakernet. Second, the ID used for the analysis was the same Server Replicator account used for replication. Third, the analysis machine was re-imaged prior to each replication as opposed to each investigation.

A further restriction was placed on how mail file content was distributed for analysis by legal, Human Resources, and other teams. Mail file content would only be made available in a raw, exported format or hardcopy. Original copies of mail files or the enclosed messages would not be provided. If the message itself was absolutely necessary, a new database containing the same fields as the mail database but not the code to transmit messages was created and messages copied into it for electronic distribution.

> The unfortunate investigator mentioned in the preceding story was the author of this book. After completely revamping the company's incident response procedures and forensic SOPs, a screw-up was changed into a positive, but the lesson was well learned: Make sure that procedures are bulletproof, follow them to the letter, and understand what the consequences of deviating from them will be.

Acquisition

Mail files (.nsf files) found on a local machine can be copied as ordinary files using standard forensic practices. Mail files present on a server provide other difficulties. The server keeps the NSF files open for writing, and a race condition may occur if access to the file is not removed from a server standpoint before duplication. This results in a catch-22 situation, as the suspect may notice that her mail file becomes inaccessible, ruling out assured covert duplication (although at 2:00 A.M. the risk may be fairly low). A second technique is to obtain access to the mail file through an administrative account and using the Notes replication feature to create a new copy on the analysis machine for preservation and analysis. In this event, the examiner's ID file is provided read-only access to the account in question or the suspect's ID file is used (if encrypted), and a forensically sound duplication performed.

TIP The replication will appear in the server logs, so the forensic ID used should be called something innocuous. Help Desk or Backup or Server Replicator are reasonable names.

To replicate a database:

1. Request (or assign) read-only rights to the database for the account that will perform the replication.
2. Open a Notes client and switch User IDs (File → Security → Switch ID) to the examiner ID which will be assigned rights to the suspect's mail file.
3. Select File → Database → Open and navigate to the server and user name of the suspect's mail file.
4. Open the mail file but do not open any messages therein.
5. Close the mail file by pressing the Escape key. An icon should now be present on in the bookmarks for that mail file.
6. Select View → Go To → Databases.
7. Highlight the suspect's mail file and select File → Replication → New replica.

8. Choose a file name on the local machine and ensure that the Encrypt Local Replica and Copy Access Control List check boxes are cleared, and the Create Full Text Index for Searching and Create Immediately check boxes are selected.

9. Click the More Settings button.

10. Clear the Send Documents to Server checkbox.

11. Click OK to create the new replica.

12. After the replication and subsequent indexing have finished, obtain the MD5 hash for the newly replicated file and index (which will be in a subdirectory titled with the name of the replica and an .ft extension) and make a permanent copy (to DVD-R or tape).

13. Create working copies of the replica as needed.

NOTE For court purposes, the replica can be considered an exact, logical copy of the mail file. The physical file may actually be larger and contain fragments of deleted data, a consideration when choosing a duplication method.

Access Control and Logging

Lotus Notes access control lists for a database can be obtained by right-clicking the database and selecting File → Database → Access Control on the file in question. Note that the Server and local copies may have different permissions. Any individuals or groups (including servers) with rights, including delegated rights, will be displayed. A sample Access Control List for a Notes database is shown in Figure 13-9.

When an individual with access uses a Lotus Notes database, an entry is recorded in the User Log. The log can be viewed by selecting File → Database → Properties, clicking the Information tab (the "i") and clicking User Detail. The User Detail entry contains data on when the access occurred and whether Read or Write activities happened (and in what quantity). Unfortunately, it does not specify what documents were modified or how. Deletions will show up as Write actions, and replications as a large number of Read actions. Additionally, the number of read and write activities may not correspond to the number of documents. Design elements, views, and subforms may all register as independent accesses.

WARNING Default logging in Notes is even worse than listed. The log is recorded when a user closes her Notes client. If a user disconnects from the network before closing Notes and never reconnects, her actions are never recorded at all. Use Notes logs with caution.

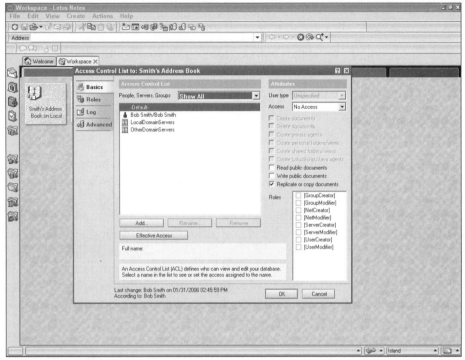

Figure 13-9: Notes Access Control List

Lotus Notes keeps a local log of user activity also on the suspect's worksta-tion if the feature is enabled (it is not by default). A file named Log.nsf contains user-specific activity information, including database connections and times and mail routing activity. Unfortunately, the information is kept at a similar level of detail as that in the preceding User Detail log and is of limited value in most cases.

Analysis

Analyzing a Notes mail file is straightforward and follows the same analysis guidelines as other mail files. The Notes database can be examined on a local machine using a standard Notes client or a tool like Paraben Forensics' Net-work Email Examiner. The primary advantages of the Paraben tool is fourfold: the data is read in a read-only format, the presentation is more suited to foren-sic examination, reporting features are included, and deleted documents pre-sent in the NSF file are automatically recovered. For these reasons, I recommend that organizations that have chosen Notes as their strategic email platform purchase this tool for forensic use.

The mail file itself is made up of several folders, and additional views into those same folders. The default folders of interest are:

- **Inbox.** Contains messages that are received before being filed elsewhere.

- **Drafts.** Stores emails that have been drafted but not sent yet.

- **Sent.** Contains copies of messages that have been sent by the suspect.

- **Trash.** Stores deleted messages until it is emptied.

Unlike Outlook and Outlook Express, Notes does not have an Outbox folder. Outgoing messages are queued in the file mail.box on the local system until a server connection is successfully made.

The other major views of Forensic value are the Calendar, To-Do, and All Documents views. The Calendar view contains scheduling information, including details of meetings, for the suspect. The To-Do view is the To-Do list of the individual user. The All Documents view is the most important view. It is a sortable list of all the documents (including email messages, calendar entries, and to-do items) present in the other views. This is generally the view from which analysis occurs.

Searching in Lotus Notes requires prior indexing to be effective (although slower searches can be performed without indexing). The Notes indexing function is relatively powerful with respect to other email software. Notes indexes the contents of messages, but also their respective attachments (for known, registered file types). To perform indexing in Notes for searching:

- Select View → Search This View.

- Click the More button.

- Click the Create Index button.

- Click the Index attached files check box and select Using conversion filters.

- Select the Index encrypted fields, Index sentence and paragraph breaks, and Enable case-sensitive searches check boxes.

- Click Ok to begin indexing.

When the indexing is completed, the actual contents of the mail file, including Calendar and To-Do items, can be searched for keywords, senders, and receivers. The search allows for fuzzy searching (for close matches and misspellings of names, very useful for an investigator) as well as field-level searching. One caveat on searching: the standard search does not review attachment names. When searching for a particular document, sorting by size is sometimes more effective. In Figure 13-10, a search for any messages sent to users at foo.com is run. The SendTo field has two messages that match.

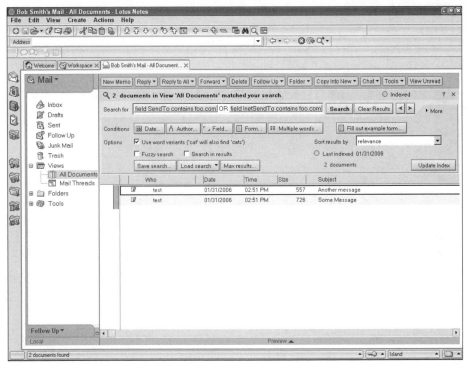

Figure 13-10:   Notes message search

Address Book

Unlike the Outlook/Outlook Express model, Lotus Notes stores addresses in a separate address book database. The Personal Address Book database template, which comes with Notes, contains similar contact management features to those present in other programs. Individual users are likely to have a copy of a personal address book and a company address book present.

The personal address book, like other Notes databases, can be searched by first indexing then using keyword searches as noted previously. The address book itself contains basic contact information (names, addresses, and phone numbers) and details on Lotus Notes certificates and connections. Of particular use to investigators is the Locations tab, which contains all valid locations and will provide potential pointers to servers used by a particular user. Figure 13-11 shows a sample address book.

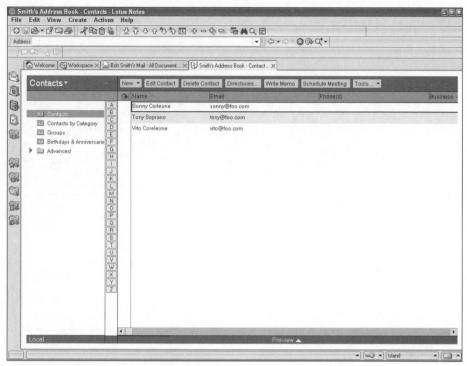

Figure 13-11: Lotus Notes address book

EMAIL HEADERS

To understand how to track an email's source, the analyst must have a basic understanding of how SMTP, the Internet's mail delivery protocol, functions. SMTP is a relay-based protocol for the transmission of email. When a user sends an email, his mail client (that is, Outlook or Notes) connects to an SMTP server that allows that user to send messages. The message is then relayed from the user-configured local SMTP server to the destination server of the recipient. In practice, most organizations do little Internet-based relaying of messages, the exceptions being Internet-based Antivirus and Antispam services which do act as SMTP relays for legitimate reasons to subscribing companies. The MX record of the organization on their DNS server points directly to a corporate mail gateway, which receives mail directly from senders.

The SMTP protocol works fine as long as everyone validates the original sender is authorized to send the message they are requesting transmission of. This can include validating an IP address, machine name, or email address (account name) and password. Poorly configured servers (and servers intentionally configured to do so) do not perform any authentication. They allow anyone to connect without validating identity and then send messages with that invalid identity. To see an example in action, I will spoof a message and examine the results. Note that the following interchange has been edited to change IPs and names:

```
C:\>telnet www.chadsteel.com 25


220 cmssweb Microsoft ESMTP MAIL Service, Version: 6.0.3790.1830 ready
at  Fri, 8 Apr 2005 14:16:27 -0400
helo foo.com
250 cmssweb Hello [12.101.177.126]
mail from: administrator@foo.com
250 2.1.0 administrator@foo.com....Sender OK
rcpt to: csteel@yahoo.com
250 2.1.5 csteel@yahoo.com
data
354 Please start mail input.
To: ceo@foo.com
cc: cfo@foo.com
Subject:  You're fired (not really)!

This is a test of a Spam message.

.

250 Mail queued for delivery.
quit


221 Closing connection. Good bye.
```

Taking the preceding example and analyzing it, five SMTP commands are typed, and the rest is message data.

First, the spoofer telnets to port 25 on any SMTP server on the Internet that accepts connections without authentication as an open relay. The commands typed then are:

◆ **helo foo.com.** The helo statement establishes the connector's domain. I have intimated that I am saying hello from the foo.com domain, when in reality I am connecting from an IP address assigned to a completely different domain name.

◆ **mail from: administrator@foo.com.** With mail from: I have established that this message is coming from the account administrator@foo.com. I could have placed any incoming address in this field.

◆ **rcpt to: csteel@yahoo.com.** The rcpt to: command indicates the recipient of the message. In this case, csteel@yahoo.com. There are two things that the server has done improperly (without violating any SMTP rules at this point): It has accepted a message from foo.com (which it should not act as a sender for) to csteel@yahoo.com (acting as a relay, since it controls only the chadsteel.com domain), and it has not verified that I am from foo.com (which I am not) or that I am from an authorized IP range for chadsteel.com (which I am not).

(continued)

EMAIL HEADERS *(continued)*

- ◆ data. The data command establishes that anything following will be considered the body of the message, until two line breaks and a period are encountered. Note that I type the names of frequently confused headers in here: To, cc, and Subject. These will be displayed as gospel by most mail clients, when in reality they are just part of my text and not validated at all (the To and cc lines likewise do not ensure that the message is sent to the named individuals).

- ◆ quit. When the message is complete, the quit command releases the session and disconnects.

The message as received is shown in the following figure. Without looking at the headers, it appears that the message was sent to ceo@foo.com (which it was not—remember the To: text in the body of the previous message) and cc:'d to the cfo@foo.com (which it also was not—neither of these parties received this email, nor did the foo.com server even see it). The From: field contains the forged administrator@foo.com address.

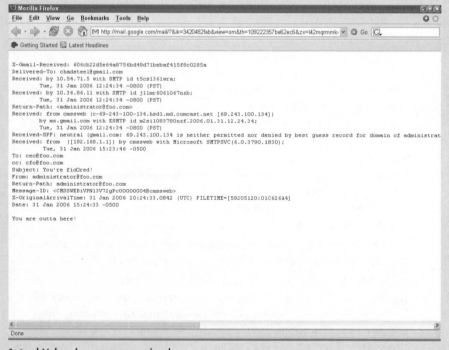

Actual Yahoo! message received

Given the preceding, how can a forensic investigator accurately examine a message? One specific header field cannot be forged as the mail server adds automatically. This is the Received From header, although spammers will frequently add fake Received From headers to the message. At least two Received From headers in any SMTP message will be legitimate: the first and last servers the message goes through. The last server will be one's SMTP server, which should be easy enough to validate. The first server is generally the last line listed unless additional Received From headers have been passed on. In that case, the original sender can still be determined by reviewing Received From headers. All other headers, including X- headers, can be completely ignored.

The relevant pieces of information in the format of a typical Received From header are as follows:

```
Received From IP. Received From Domain Name. Received By Machine Name.
Datestamp.
```

Legitimate, successive Received From headers will have a few things in common:

◆ The dates are generally in order and make sense although datestamps on a particular machine may be awry. Any large jumps in date and time may indicate a header falsification with one or both of the headers.

◆ The Received From/Received By headers agree. In the previous figure, the first server (cmssweb) receives the message, and the next header up shows that it was relayed by the same server (cmssweb), indicating that those headers are internally consistent.

◆ The IP addresses are valid. Although the beginning and end IP addresses may be from private networks, seeing a private, non-routable IP address in the middle of two valid public IP addresses is unusual. Similarly, re-served address space should not appear, nor multicast addresses.

◆ The IP addresses resolve properly. If the domain name of a server is given and resolution is possible, the domain name should resolve to the listed IP address in most cases, although load balancing can affect this. Ideally, there is a reverse DNS entry for the IP address which resolves to the domain name in either case.

◆ There are no unusual, additional headers between Received From head-ers. The presence of additional From or To headers between Received From headers may indicate a cut-and-paste point. There can be valid headers inserted by anti-spam or anti-virus software on the gateways though.

A standard methodology is to start at the known good header (one's server) and work backward until an inconsistency arises. The last good header is likely the sourcing machine, and the IP address that machine received the message from is likely the IP address of the sending machine.

WARNING Because the IP address is associated with a suspect does not always mean that the suspect willingly sent the message. Machines can be compromised by spambot worms. IP addresses can change so the owner at any one time may not be the present owner, and computers can be hacked and used to launch missives. Less frequent but still possible are anonymizing mail relay networks, which will remove the source IP. However, the last anonymous server in the chain will still have its IP listed.

Additional Resources

Refer to the following list for additional resources:

ExchangeRecovery From Passware
  www.officerecovery.com/exchange/index.htm

Network Email Examiner From Paraben For Notes/Exchange Analysis
  www.paraben-forensics.com/catalog/product_info
  .php?cPath=25&products_id=306

Outlook Email Recovery From BVG
  www.oemailrecovery.com/download.html

Outlook Express Viewer By Michal Mutl
  www.snapfiles.com/download/dldbxviewer.html

Outlook Password Recovery From Passware
  www.lostpassword.com/outlook.htm

PowerControls Exchange Recovery From Kroll Ontrack
  www.ontrack.com/powercontrols/

Sample Chain of Custody Form

Chain of Custody		Case #:		
Collected by:				
Signature:				
Date:				
Original Location of the Evidence:				
Evidence #	Quantity	Description		
Custody Log				
Evidence #	Quantity	Received By	Received By	Reason for Release
		Name:	Name:	
		Signature:	Signature:	
		Name:	Name:	
		Signature:	Signature:	
		Name:	Name:	
		Signature:	Signature:	
		Name:	Name:	
		Signature:	Signature:	

Master Boot Record Layout

OFFSET LOCATION	DESCRIPTION	SIZE
000h	Boot code	446 bytes
1BEh	1st partition entry (see Appendix C)	16 bytes
1CEh	2nd partition entry	16 bytes
1DEh	3rd partition entry	16 bytes
1EEh	4th partition entry	16 bytes
1FEh	Boot record signature (55 AAh)	2 bytes

VALUE	TYPE	VALUE	TYPE
00h	Empty	20h	Not used
01h	FAT12	21h	Reserved
02h	XENIX root	22h	Not used
03h	XENIX usr	23h	Reserved
04h	FAT16 (up to 32MB)	24h	NEC DOS
05h	DOS Extended	25h	Not used
06h	FAT16 (more than 32MB)	26h	Reserved
07h	NTFS (or OS/2 HPFS)	27h	Not used
08h	AIX boot	28h	Not used
09h	AIX data	29h	Not used
0Ah	OS/2 Boot Manager	2Ah	Not used
0Bh	FAT32	2Bh	Not used
0Ch	FAT32 (LBA)	2Ch	Not used
0Dh	Not used	2Dh	Not used

(continued)

(continued)

VALUE	TYPE	VALUE	TYPE
0Eh	FAT16 (LBA)	2Eh	Not used
0fh	Extended (LBA)	2Fh	Not used
10h	OPUS	30h	Not used
40h	VENIX	50h	OnTrack
41h	Personal RISC	51h	OnTrack (or Novell)
42h	Windows 2000 Dynamic	52h	CP/M
43h	Linux	53h	Disk Manager
44h	GoBack	54h	Disk Manager
45h	EUMEL/Elan	55h	EZ-Drive
46h	EUMEL/Elan	56h	AT&T DOS
47h	EUMEL/Elan	57h	DrivePro
48h	EUMEL/Elan	58h	Not used
49h	Not used	59h	Not used
4Ah	ADAOS	5Ah	Not used
4Bh	Not used	5Bh	Not used
4Ch	Oberon	5Ch	Priam Edisk
4Dh	QNX	5Dh	Not used
4Eh	QNX	5Eh	Not used
4Fh	QNX	5Fh	Not used
60h	Not used	70h	DiskSecure
61h	SpeedStor	71h	Reserved
62h	Unix System V	72h	Not used
63h	Netware	73h	Reserved
64h	Netware	74h	Reserved
65h	Netware	75h	IBM PC/IX
66h	Netware	76h	Not used
67h	Netware	77h	M2FS
68h	Netware	78h	XOSL FS
69h	Netware	79h	Not used

VALUE	TYPE	VALUE	TYPE
6Ah	Not used	7Ah	Not used
6Bh	Not used	7Bh	Not used
6Ch	Not used	7Ch	Not used
6Dh	Not used	7Dh	Not used
6Eh	Not used	7Eh	Not used
6Fh	Not used	7Fh	Not used
80h	MINIX	90h	FreeDOS FAT16
81h	MINIX	91h	FreeDOS Extended
82h	Linux swap	92h	FreeDOS FAT16
83h	Linux ext2/3	93h	Amoeba (or Linux Hidden)
84h	OS/2 Hidden	94h	Amoeba
85h	Linux Extended	95h	MIT EXO
86h	NTFS Volume Set	96h	Not used
87h	NTFS Volume Set	97h	FreeDOS FAT32
88h	Not used	98h	FreeDOS FAT32 (LBA)
89h	Not used	99h	DCE376
8Ah	Not used	9Ah	FreeDOS FAT16
8Bh	FAT32 Fault Tolerant	9Bh	FreeDOS FAT16 (LBA)
8Ch	FAT32 (LBA) Fault Tolerant	9Ch	Not used
8Dh	FreeDOS FAT12	9Dh	Not used
8Eh	Linux Volume Manager	9Eh	Not used
8Fh	Not used	9Fh	BSD/OS
A0h	Laptop Save-to-Disk	B0h	BootStar
A1h	Laptop Save-to-Disk (or HPVE)	B1h	Reserved
A2h	Not used	B2h	Reserved
A3h	HPVE	B3h	Reserved
A4h	HPVE	B4h	Reserved
A5h	BSD	B5h	Not used

(continued)

(continued)

VALUE	TYPE	VALUE	TYPE
A6h	OpenBSD	B6h	Reserved
A7h	NeXT	B7h	BSD fs
A8h	Mac OS-X	B8h	BSD swap
A9h	NetBSD	B9h	Not used
AAh	FAT12 (Olivetti)	BAh	Not used
ABh	GO!	BBh	Boot Wizard
ACh	Not used	BCh	Not used
ADh	Not used	BDh	Not used
AEh	ShagOS fs	BEh	Solaris 8 boot
AFh	ShagOS swap	BFh	Not used
C0h	DRDOS	D0h	Real/32
C1h	DRDOS	D1h	Multi-user DOS FAT12
C2h	Hidden Linux	D2h	Not used
C3h	Hidden Linux swap	D3h	Not used
C4h	DRDOS	D4h	Multi-user DOS FAT16 (up to 32MB)
C5h	DRDOS	D5h	Multi-user DOS Extended
C6h	Windows NT Corrupted FAT16 Volume Set	D6h	Multi-user DOS FAT16 (more than 32MB)
C7h	Windows NT Corrupted NTFS Volume Set	D7h	Not used
C8h	DRDOS	D8h	CP/M-86
C9h	DRDOS	D9h	Not used
CAh	DRDOS	DAh	Not used
CBh	DRDOS FAT32	DBh	CP/M
CCh	DRDOS FAT32 (LBA)	DCh	Not used
CDh	Not used	DDh	Not used
CEh	DRDOS FAT16 (LBA)	DEh	Dell
CFh	DRDOS Extended	DFh	DG/UX

VALUE	TYPE	VALUE	TYPE
E0h	Not used	F0h	Linux/PA-RISC boot loader
E1h	SpeedStor	F1h	SpeedStor
E2h	Not used	F2h	Unisys DOS
E3h	SpeedStor	F3h	Reserved
E4h	SpeedStor	F4h	Prologue (or SpeedStor)
E5h	Reserved	F5h	Prologue
E6h	Reserved	F6h	Reserved
E7h	Not used	F7h	Not used
E8h	Not used	F8h	Not used
E9h	Not used	F9h	Not used
EAh	Not used	FAh	Bochs
EBh	BeFS	FBh	VMWare fs
ECh	Not used	FCh	VMWare swap
EDh	Sptrytix	FDh	FreeDOS
EEh	Intel EFI	FEh	Windows NT Disk Admin
EFh	Intel EFI	FFh	Xenix Bad Block

FAT32 Boot Sector Layout

OFFSET LOCATION	# OF BYTES	IDENTIFIER	NOTES
00	3	Jumpcode	Contains the jumpshort instruction (1 byte), the offset of the bootstrap code (1 byte), and a NOP.
03	8	OEM name	The name of the OS that formatted the partition. Can be used to determine legacy OS presence.
0B	2	# of bytes per sector	The total number of bytes each sector holds.
0D	1	# of sectors per cluster	The total number of sectors each cluster holds.
0D	2	# of reserved sectors	The number of sectors reserved for the boot record.
10	1	# of FATs	The total number of File Allocation Tables. This is usually 2 (one primary plus one backup).

(continued)

(continued)

OFFSET LOCATION	# OF BYTES	IDENTIFIER	NOTES
11	2	Root entries	The maximum number of entries possible in the root entry. Sets the number of subdirectories off root that are allowed.
13	2	Total sectors	Total number of sectors. Used for partitions smaller than 32MB and floppy drives.
15	1	Media type	F0 for a floppy drive, F8 for a hard drive.
16	2	# of sectors per FAT	Total number of sectors in each FAT. Used for FAT12/16.
18	2	# of sectors per track	Total number of sectors in each track.
1A	2	# of heads per cylinder	Total number of drive heads.
1C	4	# of hidden sectors	The number of sectors in the MBR until the boot record begins.
20	4	Total sectors	The total number of sectors in the partition. Used for partitions larger than 32MB.
24	4	# of sectors per FAT	Total number of sectors in each FAT. Used for FAT32.
28	2	Flags	Reserved for determining FAT mirroring status. Allows for the use of the backup FAT as the primary on FAT32 systems.
2A	2	Version	The file system version number.
2C	4	Root cluster	The cluster number where the root cluster begins.
30	2	Info sector	The sector number of the file system information sector.
32	2	Boot backup location	The sector number of the boot area backup location on the drive (if present).
34	12	Reserved	Reserved for future use.
40	1	Drive Id	00 for a floppy disk, 80 for a hard disk.

OFFSET LOCATION	# OF BYTES	IDENTIFIER	NOTES
41	1	NT reserved	Set to 00 by NT when the drive is formatted.
42	1	Extended boot signature	Set to 29 to indicate the presence of the serial number, partition name, and FAT type are present.
43	4	Volume serial number	A unique number assigned to a partition at format time. Both Quick and Full formats reassign a serial number.
47	11	Volume/partition name	An 11-character name assigned to the volume by the person formatting the drive.
52	8	FAT type	FAT12, FAT16, or FAT32. This is used by some utilities, but not the OS itself.
5A	420	Executable bootstrap	Starts the first file to boot the system itself.
01 FE	2	Executable signature	Added as 55 AA when formatted. Otherwise, the operating system will not be registered by the BIOS as present.

NTFS Boot Sector Layout

LOCATION	# OF BYTES	IDENTIFIER	NOTES
00	3	Jumpcode	Contains the jumpshort instruction (1 byte), the offset of the bootstrap code (1 byte), and a NOP.
03	8	OEM name	The name of the OS that formatted the partition. Can be used to determine legacy OS presence.
0B	2	# of bytes per sector	The total number of bytes each sector holds.
0D	1	# of sectors per cluster	The total number of sectors each cluster holds.
0E	2	# of reserved sectors	The number of sectors reserved for the boot record.
10	3	Always 0	Legacy FAT area not used by NTFS.
13	2	N/A	Not currently used.
15	1	Media type	Always F8 for a hard drive.

(continued)

(continued)

LOCATION	# OF BYTES	IDENTIFIER	NOTES
16	2	Always 0	Legacy FAT area not used by NTFS.
18	2	# of sectors per track	Total number of sectors in each track.
1A	2	# of heads	Total number of drive heads.
1C	4	# of hidden sectors	The number of sectors in the MBR until the boot record begins.
20	4	N/A	Not used.
24	4	N/A	Not used.
28	8	Total sectors	Total number of sectors.
30	8	Logical cluster number for the file $MFT	Starting cluster of the $MFT file.
38	8	Logical cluster number for the file $MFTMirr	Starting cluster of the $MFTMirr file.
40	4	# of clusters per file record segment	Number of clusters in each file record segment.
44	4	# of clusters per index block	Number of clusters in each index block.
48	8	Volume serial number	A unique number assigned to a partition at format time. Both Quick and Full formats reassign a serial number.
50	4	Checksum	Not used.
54	426	Executable bootstrap	Starts the first file to boot the system itself.
01 FE	2	Executable signature	Added as 55 AA when formatted. Otherwise, the operating system will not be registered by the BIOS as present.

INODE #	NAME	DESCRIPTION
0	$MFT	The NTFS master file table. Contains the meta data on all of the NTFS file system entities.
1	$MFTMirr	A duplicate copy of the $MFT file's first four records.
2	$LogFile	Transactional log file used for file system rollback in the event of failure during an atomic operation.
3	$Volume	Contains the serial number and time of initialization for the partition as well as the dirty bit. The dirty bit is set to indicate that the file system may be corrupted due to Windows not shutting down properly. It is set at startup and reset as the last step during shutdown before powering off. If it is set, the OS knows that there was an improper shutdown. The dirty bit set triggers a file system integrity check through a scan of the disk and rolling back of any interrupted transactions.
4	$AttrDef	A file containing the definitions of any file system attributes. The inclusion of this as a file allows for dynamic attribute creation and future extensibility.
5	.	The entry for the main (root) directory of the file system.

(continued)

(continued)

INODE #	NAME	DESCRIPTION
6	$Bitmap	A list (map of bits) of unused and used clusters. Marking a cluster "in use" without a reference in the $MFT can allow data hiding.
7	$Boot	A non-movable file that links to the boot sector of the partition.
8	$BadClus	A list of bad (unusable) clusters. Marking a cluster bad is another way to hide data, although sector-level copies will ignore this file's content and image bad clusters as well.
9	$Secure ($Quota on NT)	Contains the security identifiers for the file system in a single metafile. Earlier versions of NTFS (in earlier NT versions) kept this information with each individual file.
10	$UpCase	A Unicode list of capital letters used for file system sorting.
11	$Extend	A metadirectory contains quota information, reparse point information, and a user-readable copy of the $LogFilec
12–23	Reserved	Reserved for future expandability.
24 and above	Ordinary files and directories	Inodes used by the standard Windows files and directories.

Well-Known SIDs

Full SID details are available online at support.microsoft.com/default.aspx ?scid=kb;EN-US;Q243330.

SID	NAME	DESCRIPTION
S-1-0	Null Authority	An identifier authority.
S-1-0-0	Nobody	No security principal.
S-1-1	World Authority	An identifier authority.
S-1-1-0	Everyone	A group that includes all users, even anonymous users and guests. Membership is controlled by the operating system.
S-1-2	Local Authority	An identifier authority.
S-1-3	Creator Authority	An identifier authority.
S-1-3-0	Creator Owner	A placeholder in an inheritable access control entry (ACE). When the ACE is inherited, the system replaces this SID with the SID for the object's creator.

(continued)

(continued)

SID	NAME	DESCRIPTION
S-1-3-1	Creator Group	A placeholder in an inheritable ACE. When the ACE is inherited, the system replaces this SID with the SID for the primary group of the object's creator. The primary group is used only by the POSIX subsystem.
S-1-3-2	Creator Owner Server	This SID is not used in Windows 2000.
S-1-3-3	Creator Group Server	This SID is not used in Windows 2000.
S-1-4	Non-unique Authority	An identifier authority.
S-1-5	NT Authority	An identifier authority.
S-1-5-1	Dialup	A group that includes all users who have logged on through a dial-up connection. Membership is controlled by the operating system.
S-1-5-2	Network	A group that includes all users that have logged on through a network connection. Membership is controlled by the operating system.
S-1-5-3	Batch	A group that includes all users that have logged on through a batch queue facility. Membership is controlled by the operating system.
S-1-5-4	Interactive	A group that includes all users that have logged on interactively. Membership is controlled by the operating system.
S-1-5-5-X-Y	Logon Session	A logon session. The X and Y values for these SIDs are different for each session.
S-1-5-6	Service	A group that includes all security principals that have logged on as a service. Membership is controlled by the operating system.
S-1-5-7	Anonymous	A group that includes all users that have logged on anonymously. Membership is controlled by the operating system.
S-1-5-8	Proxy	This SID is not used in Windows 2000.
S-1-5-9	Enterprise Controllers	A group that includes all domain controllers in a forest that uses an Active Directory service. Membership is controlled by the operating system.

SID	NAME	DESCRIPTION
S-1-5-10	Principal Self	A placeholder in an inheritable ACE on an account object or group object in Active Directory. When the ACE is inherited, the system replaces this SID with the SID for the security principal who holds the account.
S-1-5-11	Authenticated Users	A group that includes all users whose identities were authenticated when they logged on. Membership is controlled by the operating system.
S-1-5-12	Restricted Code	This SID is reserved for future use.
S-1-5-13	Terminal Server Users	A group that includes all users that have logged on to a Terminal Services server. Membership is controlled by the operating system.
S-1-5-18	Local System	A service account that is used by the operating system.
S-1-5-19	NT Authority	Local service.
S-1-5-20	NT Authority	Network service.
S-1-5-domain-500	Administrator	A user account for the system administrator. By default, it is the only user account given full control over the system.
S-1-5-domain-501	Guest	A user account for people who do not have individual accounts. This user account does not require a password. By default, the Guest account is disabled.
S-1-5-domain-502	KRBTGT	A service account that is used by the Key Distribution Center (KDC) service.
S-1-5-domain-512	Domain Admins	A global group whose members are authorized to administer the domain. By default, the Domain Admins group is a member of the Administrators group on all computers that have joined a domain, including the domain controllers.
S-1-5-domain-513	Domain Users	A global group that, by default, includes all user accounts in a domain. When you create a user account in a domain, it is added to this group by default.

(continued)

(continued)

SID	NAME	DESCRIPTION
S-1-5-domain-514	Domain Guests	A global group that, by default, has only one member, the domain's built-in Guest account.
S-1-5-domain-515	Domain Computers	A global group that includes all clients and servers that have joined the domain.
S-1-5-domain-516	Domain Controllers	A global group that includes all domain controllers in the domain. New domain controllers are added to this group by default.
S-1-5-domain-517	Cert Publishers	A global group that includes all computers that are running an enterprise certification authority. Cert Publishers are authorized to publish certificates for User objects in Active Directory.
S-1-5-root domain-518	Schema Admins	A universal group in a native-mode domain; a global group in a mixed-mode domain. The group is authorized to make schema changes in Active Directory.
S-1-5-root domain-519	Enterprise Admins	A universal group in a native-mode domain; a global group in a mixed-mode domain. The group is authorized to make forest-wide changes in Active Directory, such as adding child domains.
S-1-5-domain-520	Group Policy Creator Owners	A global group that is authorized to create new Group Policy objects in Active Directory. By default, the only member of the group is Administrator.
S-1-5-domain-533	RAS and IAS Servers	A domain local group. By default, this group has no members. Servers in this group have Read Account Restrictions and Read Logon Information access to User objects in the Active Directory domain local group.
S-1-5-32-544	Administrators	A built-in group. After the initial installation of the operating system, the only member of the group is the Administrator account. When a computer joins a domain, the Domain Administrators' group is added to the Administrators group.

SID	NAME	DESCRIPTION
S-1-5-32-545	Users	A built-in group. After the initial installation of the operating system, the only member is the Authenticated Users group. When a computer joins a domain, the Domain Users group is added to the Users group on the computer.
S-1-5-32-546	Guests	A built-in group. By default, the only member is the Guest account. The Guests group allows occasional or one-time users to log on with limited privileges to a computer's built-in Guest account.
S-1-5-32-547	Power Users	A built-in group. By default, the group has no members. Power users can create local users and groups; modify and delete accounts that they have created; and remove users from the Power Users, Users, and Guests groups.
S-1-5-32-548	Account Operators	A built-in group that exists only on domain controllers. By default, the group has no members.
S-1-5-32-549	Server Operators	A built-in group that exists only on domain controllers. By default, the group has no members.
S-1-5-32-550	Print Operators	A built-in group that exists only on domain controllers. By default, the only member is the Domain Users group. Print Operators can manage printers and document queues.
S-1-5-32-551	Backup Operators	A built-in group. By default, the group has no members. Backup Operators can back up and restore all files on a computer, regardless of the permissions that protect those files.
S-1-5-32-552	Replicators	A built-in group that is used by the File Replication service on domain controllers. By default, the group has no members. Do not add users to this group.
S-1-5-32-554	BUILTIN\Pre-Windows 2000 Compatible Access	An alias added by Windows 2000. A backward compatibility group which allows read access on all users and groups in the domain.

(continued)

(continued)

SID	NAME	DESCRIPTION
S-1-5-32-555	BUILTIN\Remote Desktop Users	An alias. Members in this group are granted the right to logon remotely.
S-1-5-32-556	BUILTIN\Network Configuration Operators	An alias. Members in this group can have some administrative privileges to manage configuration of networking features.
S-1-5-32-557	BUILTIN\Incoming Forest Trust Builders	An alias. Members of this group can create incoming, one-way trusts to this forest.
S-1-5-32-557	BUILTIN\Incoming Forest Trust Builders	An alias. Members of this group can create incoming, one-way trusts to this forest.
S-1-5-32-558	BUILTIN\Performance Monitor Users	An alias. Members of this group have remote access to monitor this computer.
S-1-5-32-559	BUILTIN\Performance Log Users	An alias. Members of this group have remote access to schedule logging of performance counters on this computer.
S-1-5-32-560	BUILTIN\Windows Authorization Access Group	An alias. Members of this group have access to the computed `tokenGroupsGlobalAndUniversal` attribute on User objects.
S-1-5-32-561	BUILTIN\Terminal Server License Servers	An alias. A group for Terminal Server License Servers.

Index